THE WHITES OF THEIR EYES

ALSO BY PAUL LOCKHART

The Drillmaster of Valley Forge:
The Baron de Steuben and the Making of the American Army

THE
WHITES
OF
THEIR EYES

*

Bunker Hill,

the First American Army,

and the Emergence of George Washington

*

Paul Lockhart

HARPER

An Imprint of HarperCollins*Publishers*

www.harpercollins.com

HarperCollins books may be purchased for educational, business, or sales promotional use.
For information, please write: Special Markets Department, HarperCollins Publishers,
10 East 53rd Street, New York, NY 10022.

FIRST EDITION

Designed by Jennifer Daddio / Bookmark Design & Media Inc.

Library of Congress Cataloging-in-Publication Data has been applied for.

ISBN: 978-0-06-195886-1

11 12 13 14 15 OV/QGF 10 9 8 7 6 5 4 3 2 1

To my son, Alex
With love, from Daddy

Acknowledgments

* * *

I wrote this book during a particularly difficult time in my life, and hence I owe huge debts of gratitude to more people than I can possibly name here, people who encouraged me, indulged me in long and rambling conversations, and gave me a swift metaphorical kick in the rear when I needed it. Above all I should mention Ms. Sherri Martin, my student and my good friend, who served as my research assistant throughout the process. I have never before made use of a research assistant—though as a single dad with a small child, I *sorely* needed one for this book—and Sherri simultaneously did the work I asked of her and somehow put up with my tentative and uncertain directions. To her, and to her husband, Bill, I am indebted more than I can express here.

At Wright State University, where I have taught for the past two decades, I was helped by Ms. Diana Kaylor, Interlibrary Loan librarian, who as always was gracious and efficient in getting the obscure material I needed. I would also like to thank my interim department chair, Dr. Henry Limouze, and the dean of the College of Liberal Arts, Dr. Charles Taylor, for helping me to arrange a leave from my teaching duties—a break that was as necessary for my health as it was for the completion of this book. My friend, Mr. Daniel Studebaker of West Milton, Ohio, prepared the maps on (as usual) very short notice, and did a very good job of it. The staffs at the Massachusetts Historical Society, Boston, and the Commonwealth of Massachusetts State Archives were especially helpful. In particular, I should acknowledge the assistance of Mr. John Hannigan, formerly an archivist at the State Archives, whose extraordinary expertise in the Revolutionary collections there proved to be nothing short of a godsend.

My agent, Will Lippincott, was—as I have come to expect—a great source of wisdom and encouragement. If I have learned anything about the writing of history for audiences outside of academia, it is because of Will. Elisabeth Kallick Dyssegaard, my earlier editor at Harper, believed in this book enough to take it on with enthusiasm, and her successor—my current editor, Bill Strachan—has been just as vital. Bill has tolerated my many delays with extraordinary grace, and the book is all the better for his advice.

As usual, my family and close friends have been just as instrumental to my writing, even if they were not directly involved in the process. My brother and sister-in-law, Keith and Emiley Lockhart, gave me a second home while I went about my research in Boston. My mother-in-law and brother-in-law, Maria Beach and Ralph C. Beach III, frequently took care of my young son so that I would have more time to work, and they did it without a single complaint or objection. My parents, Newton and Marilyn Lockhart, besides cheering me on when I needed it most, also helped with my son while I was off on research trips. My grown children—Kate, Nicholas, Paige, and Philip—have been no less encouraging to me while I was writing this book than they were with my earlier books, and for that I love them beyond words.

Above all, I must acknowledge the loving patience of my youngest child, my boy Alexander. My writing has taken me away from him more than I care to contemplate, and at a time when he needed his father most. Still, because he's only four years old, it makes me enormously proud when I hear him proclaim to anyone who cares to listen, "My daddy is an author and he's writing a book about Bunker Hill!" To him this book is dedicated. And I dare not neglect to thank Mary Fradin, my partner and my dearest companion, who believed and believes in me, and who lovingly but firmly pushed me to finish this book when I was least convinced that I could.

Kettering, Ohio
September 2010

Contents

✳ ✳ ✳

THE WHITES OF THEIR EYES

Prologue

* * *

Boston, Massachusetts
Friday, June 17, 1825

Forty-two years had passed since the Revolution had drawn to a close, fifty since it had begun, in this very town. During those years, Boston had become something very much different from what it had been in the days of the Massacre and the Tea Party, of Paul Revere's ride and the bloodshed on Lexington Green, a place that would have been unrecognizable to those who had lived through those mythic events. Boston was now everything that America had come to be: big, loud, brash, contentious, exuberant. And growing. Ten thousand souls had called the place home in 1775; now there were nearly sixty thousand, and there was no sign that the burgeoning growth would stop anytime soon. The only thing that could stop it was geography, and modern Bostonians were doing their best to make sure that *that* didn't happen. If the city would no longer fit within the confines of the old Shawmut peninsula, then the geography had to be changed. With spade and pick, the people of Boston altered the very landscape itself, laying low the hills, populating every empty space with homes and warehouses, filling the shallow waters of the harbor nearby to make more room—for more buildings, more commerce, more people.

Beacon Hill had lost its beacon, and was only a mere stub of its former self. The ancient and majestic Trimountain had once towered over the city, but it stood in the way of progress and hence it had to go: the summit of Beacon Hill, the tallest peak in the Trimountain, stood sixty feet below its former height. Laborers carted the earth from the truncated hill to fill the old Mill Pond on the North End. The open green spaces west and south of town rapidly filled in with new neighborhoods until only the Common remained. The physical reminders of the Revolutionary past were dwindling by the year. Within a few decades, most—like the former residence of the royal governors, Province House—would be gone, and only a handful of old churches and government buildings would survive. Boston was a growing city, mindful of its gleaming future, boundlessly confident. Sentimentality was something it couldn't afford.

But today was different. Today, Boston would revel in its past, glory in great deeds of arms, congratulate itself for having done so much to author the new republic. And it would do so in grand style. For fifty years ago this very day—a day that had been just as bright and glorious, a day when the air was just as redolent of the sweetness of late spring in New England—the sons of Massachusetts and New Hampshire and Connecticut fought and died for the cause of American liberty on a grassy, windswept hill that loomed over Charlestown. There, American citizen-soldiers had dared challenge Britain's military might; there the Revolution truly began. Locals called the place Breed's Hill, but in the popular imagination the struggle there was known by another name: the Battle of Bunker Hill.

For several years there had been a humble wooden pillar, lonesome and unprepossessing, placed on the site by the Freemasons to mark the spot where one of their own had fallen in the battle, but to many in Boston it was not tribute enough. In 1823, a group of prominent Bostonians, the great orator and congressman Daniel Webster among them, resolved to erect a more enduring memorial to all those who died in liberty's name atop Breed's Hill in 1775. Two years later they had subscribers, money, a design, and land . . . though ultimately some of that hallowed ground would be sold to raise more funds for the monument. The fiftieth anniversary of the battle seemed a fitting time to lay the cornerstone. The timing was fortuitous, for in that year Boston played host to a distinguished visitor: the Marquis de Lafayette, George Washington's young protégé. He had not fought at Bunker Hill, but at age sixty-seven he was the last surviving general of the Revolutionary War. On the invitation of President James Monroe, Lafayette had come to visit America. He would spend time in all twenty-four states, drawing admiring crowds wherever he went. The old veteran of two revolutions, still boyish in the face, had already visited Boston once during his American tour. He raced back again from Albany in June 1825 just to grace the ceremonies with his magnetic presence.

No one could have asked for a finer morning, sunlit and warm and fragrant, when the solemn procession of celebrants set out through Boston's twisting streets toward the North End, crossing the Charlestown Bridge where the old ferry used to run. Two hundred veterans of the Revolution, some wearing odd items of military gear and uniforms from their service five decades before, led the parade, then a "long array of numerous subscribers to the monument," followed by two thousand Freemasons. They were followed by the Marquis de Lafayette himself, in a "superb calash drawn by six white horses," with the governor of Massachusetts and a flock of dignitaries bringing up the rear. Seven thousand men and women, it was said, marched in the commemoration.[1]

The procession came to a halt just off High Street at the apex of the hill, where the old redoubt had once stood, now surrounded by farmland and marked by a great pit . . . the foundation of the new monument. As thousands of spectators watched and cheered, Lafayette and three other men laid the cornerstone; an artillery salute boomed from the hilltop, and the party walked in stately grace to take their places in a special amphitheater erected for this very purpose. Fifteen thousand people crowded into the amphitheater, while thousands more stood outside, covering the hillside in all directions. The noise of the crowd died gradually, to be replaced by the singing of a choir, and then the speakers. First to ascend the podium was Reverend Joseph Thaxter, an eighty-three-year-old Unitarian preacher who had fought at Concord and Bunker Hill, wearing a massive powdered wig underneath his hopelessly outmoded tricorn, clothing and man alike relics of a bygone age. The audience stilled to listen as Reverend Thaxter prayed aloud in his quavering voice, thanking the Almighty for the blessings He had bestowed on happy free America, pointing out almost apologetically that the object of the dedication ceremony was "not for the purpose of idolatry, but a standing monument to the rising and future generations, that they may be excited to search the history of our country."[2]

The listeners were moved to tears, it was said, by the prayer, but nothing could contain the crowd's excitement when Daniel Webster took the stage. The great orator had given many speeches, and would give many more. His Bunker Hill oration, though, would be considered one of his best, and for decades it found a holy place in schoolbooks, its expressions of patriotic sentiment deemed worthy of memorization. Webster was in fine form, thanking the Revolutionary veterans seated before him, praising the tenacity and the foresight of the Founding Fathers. He spoke of representative government and civil liberties, of tyranny and its malcontents, and every time he praised America for bestowing the gift of freedom on a benighted Europe his audience went wild. Their enthusiasm for the high-flown rhetoric was undampened by the prodigious length of the speech. And in between all his expressions of patriotic reverence, Webster returned again and again to the battle itself. It had been *the* battle of the Revolution; it forced America to break with the Old World and embark on its own enlightened course. And— now that there would be a monument to commemorate it—the battle of Bunker Hill could serve as a reminder that Americans must constantly labor to keep the ideals of their Revolutionary forefathers alive. He took that theme, built upon it, and brought it to a thunderous conclusion: "And let the sacred obligations which have devolved on this generation, and on us, sink deep into our hearts. . . . We can win no laurels in a war for independence. Earlier and worthier hands have gathered them all. . . . But there remains to us a great duty of defence and preservation. . . . Let our object be, our country, our whole country, and nothing but our country. And, by the blessing of God, may that country itself become a vast and splendid monument, not of oppression and terror, but of Wisdom, of Peace, and of Liberty, upon which the world may gaze with admiration forever!"[3]

The thousands sitting in the amphitheater leapt to their feet, as a massive throaty roar of approval rose from the crowd. The procession re-formed, not so solemn this time, and walked a short distance to "an immense wooden building" nearby for a festive banquet. The revelers drank toast after toast to the dignity of the Republic, to liberty and liberation, to the health and honor of the doddering old veterans who were in their midst.

There were among those veterans forty special guests: the last survivors of Bunker Hill. Or at least so they claimed. Historians would interview them later, finding much to their disgust that a fair number of these talkative old men had not been in the battle, or not even in the Revolution, but still there were a few among them who had stood on that day, long ago, with Prescott or Putnam or Stark. They were stooped and gray now, the youngest of them in their late sixties, and all wore ribbons bearing the simple legend "June 17th 1775." As their carriages took them through Charlestown and up Breed's Hill, the real survivors chatted quietly, pointing and gesturing, marveling at how much everything had changed. Where once General Howe's red-coated battalions formed up for the assault, a vast navy yard now sprawled; where once there was only open pastureland flowing into the distance, rolling over and down gentle slopes, new streets and tidy rows of houses greeted their gaze. A long time ago, a lifetime ago, there had been stone walls and broken rail fences, marshes and orchards, and tall grass, stomped down by heavy shoes, dappled with gore. The veterans gazed dreamily at the almost unrecognizable landscape around them, and some of them heard again the song of the musket balls and the screaming solid shot, the haunting cries of men in their death throes and the hoarse animal shouts of men mad with rage and bloodlust, saw the gleam of polished bayonets and the quivering clumps of madder-red bodies, the billowing smoke and fire and death and all the swirling red chaos of battle. And they remembered how, while yet in the blush of early manhood, they had seen the glorious pageantry of war and the dreadful, unspeakable things that they wished they could forget but never would . . . how they—as mere boys—had stared death in the face and done deeds that not one of them would have thought himself capable of doing.

The monument on Breed's Hill did not go up immediately. Another seventeen years would pass before it was completed, and during that time there were many locals who regarded the half-finished monument as an unsightly blot on the pleasant bucolic landscape on the edge of Charlestown. Patriotism and civic pride won out in the end. On June 17, 1843, the sixty-eighth anniversary of the battle, Daniel Webster gave another oration to commemorate the completed obelisk, 221 feet high, that towered over everything in Charlestown.

The battle of Bunker Hill simply would not be forgotten. And that is very curious. Bunker Hill may have been the first honest-to-goodness battle of the Revolution, but beyond that it doesn't enjoy any special tactical or strategic significance. It was not decisive, nor was it an American victory. We often seem to forget that Bunker Hill was, in fact, a British victory and a significant one at that. It was small even when compared to other battles of the Revolutionary War, and laughably puny when compared to lesser-known battles in Europe. Though often portrayed as a day of incomprehensible carnage, the loss of life at Bunker Hill was pretty much typical for comparable European battles of the same time period. As Americans, we tend to associate George Washington—the embodiment of the Revolution itself—with all events of the Revolutionary War, yet that doesn't apply to Bunker Hill: George Washington wasn't there.

There is no earthly reason, no logical reason at least, that Bunker Hill should be so famous, and yet it is. We shame ourselves for our profound ignorance of our history and heritage, but the name Bunker Hill lives on. Few if any battles in American history are remembered so well by name; only Gettysburg and D-Day rival it.

Its longevity in American legend owes to many things, things that transcend its tactical or strategic significance. Bunker Hill was indeed the first pitched battle of the Revolution, a much more equal contest than the rebel ambush of British troops after Lexington, during the retreat from Concord; and while there was still a chance, a real chance, that the grievances of the colonies might have been settled peaceably after Lexington and Concord, there was no chance after Bunker Hill. Once the first volley thundered from a thousand American muskets on the heights above Charlestown, the die was cast, and on both sides men agreed that the contest must now be settled with blood. It was not a "decisive" battle, if indeed it can be said that there are such things: it ended neither the Revolution nor even the siege of Boston, and outside of boosting American confidence—and giving the amateur soldiers a taste of battle that they would not soon forget—it did not further the American cause, nor did it seriously set that cause back. Bunker Hill was, however, the only battle of the Revolution, and one of the very few in American history, that was fought publicly. All of Boston had turned out to watch the drama unfold on that blistering-hot Saturday afternoon. Spectators far outnumbered participants in the battle that day. But there is more behind the battle, more than the details of its place in the story of America's miraculous and violent birth. Bunker Hill captures the essence of American mythology—the stories we tell ourselves about how America came to be, what it means to be American, why it is that America is so very distinctive, so different from the European roots from which it sprang.

Bunker Hill lives on because it is *the* great American battle, more so than Gettysburg, more so than the landings at Normandy. It is the stuff from which classical Fourth of July oratory is wrought, the American spirit writ large in letters of fire and blood. Though the rebellious colonials lost the battle, they emerged triumphant. They proved that American ingenuity, resourcefulness, and pluck trump the staid conventions of the Old World; that free men fighting for liberty, hearth, and home cannot be vanquished by the slaves of despotic regimes. The story of Bunker Hill strikes at the very heart of what it means to be an American, embodies all that Americans believe and have believed about their superior virtue and martial prowess.

Just as the story of Bunker Hill has shaped our national mythology, that mythology in turn has shaped our image of what happened at Bunker Hill. The battle is, and always has been, so central to the grand narrative of our revolutionary beginnings that what the battle stood for has eclipsed the demonstrable facts. We Americans, after all, like our history big and our heroes bigger. We want everything about our nation to be the best, or the worst, or the most original, or the most iconoclastic, or the boldest. The protagonists of our national story must triumph over insurmountable obstacles, but must do so in a uniquely American way; our enemies, conversely, must be formidable, morally inferior, and preferably just a bit ridiculous, too. The danger of this approach is that it confuses history with heritage, it conflates fantasy and patriotic sentiment. The truly wonderful stories from America's past can drown thereby in a sea of false absolutes and hyperbole.

Battles are inherently dramatic events, events that bring out the best and the worst in human nature, and so they easily fall victim to this kind of well-intentioned misinterpretation. Bunker Hill is no exception. It stands out as being among the most misunderstood of battles, even though it is probably the least complex combat of the entire Revolutionary War. Historians—even professional scholars, who strive to be dispassionate—have consistently skewed or ignored a thousand little details, driven by long-standing traditions and stereotypes, and by the desire to highlight the singular courage of the American soldiers who fought and died on Breed's Hill on that hot June afternoon in 1775. Those soldiers, we are told, were not only amateurs but completely bereft of any conventional notion of military discipline. And yet these same neophyte soldiers were products of the frontier; they were skilled marksmen and knew how to fight like Indians—an idea that conveniently overlooks the fact that the average New England soldier in 1775 was not particularly familiar with firearms, had never heard a shot fired in anger, and probably had never seen a Native American, much less fought with or against one. The British, on the other hand, were brave and battle-hardened professionals, the cream of the finest army in the world. They were led by aristocratic dandies who were contemptuously dismissive of American military ability. The Redcoat officers, so the story goes, knew nothing of warfare in the New World, and therefore they pridefully drove their ranks of hapless automatons to the slaughter in unimaginative "parade-ground" assaults in the best European tradition—a tradition that was supposedly irrelevant in the broken wilderness of North America.

In all these regards, the traditional narrative is demonstrably wrong. Bunker Hill was, instead, a clash between two young armies—one indifferently trained and inexperienced, one slightly better trained and equally inexperienced. The American army was not a band of hardy frontiersmen; the British army was not the finest in the world, and the British troops who fought at Bunker Hill were not veterans. The British leadership was neither unimaginative nor unaware of American military abilities.

Recognizing these truths in no way detracts from the valor of the fighting men, both American and British. It does not deny that, at Bunker Hill, the rebels accomplished something quite remarkable. When we throw away the stereotypes of rugged American frontier warriors and imperious, impractical Britons, when we strip away the layers of hyperbole and flag-waving sentimentality, what we find is a much more nuanced, interesting, and ultimately compelling story. It is the story of the first army raised on American soil to defend American interests, made up of men whose sole motivation was the protection of their liberties and their communities, who held together only because they remained steadfastly devoted to a cause that was much bigger than the sum of their individual wants or needs or fears. It is the story of how that army stood its ground in its first real fight, even when pitted against a superior foe, even when led by officers whose courage and sense of duty far outstripped their generalship. It is the story of a new and uncertain George Washington, who came to the army after Bunker Hill and gradually turned it into a force designed to survive the rigors of a prolonged war. And it is also, above all, the story of the heroes of '75, the first leaders of what would soon become an American nation. They were flawed men, some of them proud and sensitive, some not especially talented. Yet their actions ensured that the Revolution would not fail in its tenuous infancy, and when they had done their duty, they withdrew quietly from the limelight. They took the first, unimaginably bold steps toward the creation of the new nation, risking everything, demanding nothing, gaining little, not even the honor of a place in the pantheon of the Founding Fathers. It is, in short, like all great American stories: about ordinary people who, when put to the test, did extraordinary things.

One

* * *

MASSACHUSETTS'S
WAR

"Things at present have a war Like appearance . . ."
JOHN THOMAS TO HANNAH THOMAS, APRIL 22, 1775[1]

*G*od damn it, they are firing ball!"

Timothy Brown gasped, incredulous, as the echoes of the first British volley slowly faded and all around him men crumpled and dropped to the ground. He and his comrades in Colonel James Barrett's regiment of Massachusetts minutemen were advancing on Concord's North Bridge as the Redcoats fell back before them, struggling in their haste to tear up the bridge's planking as they retreated.

The volley had caught the minutemen off-guard. What truly surprised Brown and all of Colonel Barrett's boys was that this was *real*. The Massachusetts men—the "country people," as the British liked to call them—had been genuinely convinced that the Redcoats meant only to frighten them, perhaps with a volley or two of harmless blank charges. Now they knew better. The British meant business. The British meant to kill.

It was not the first blood spilled that day, the nineteenth of April 1775, nor would it be the last. Only a few hours earlier, just before dawn, this same body of Redcoats had marched into nearby Lexington in hopes of finding and arresting the Whig agitators Samuel Adams and John Hancock. The two men were long gone, having been tipped off to the British plan. But the advance elements of the British column, commanded by Major John Pitcairn of the Royal Marines, instead came across Captain John Parker and his company of militia. Neither side wanted a battle, yet in the confusion of the jarring encounter, a firefight broke out, and when the smoke cleared, eight of Parker's men lay dead on Lexington Green.

The entire British column then marched directly on Concord, where the real target of the operation lay. Lieutenant General Thomas Gage, commander of His Majesty's forces in North America and military governor of Massachusetts, had learned that the colony's malcontents—directed by an illicit governing body that called itself the Provincial Congress—had stockpiled munitions, provisions, and even cannon at Concord, deep in the countryside west-northwest of Boston. Even after the unplanned and unanticipated clash at Lexington, the overall commander of the British expedition, Lieutenant Colonel Francis Smith, decided to override the cautions of his nervous subordinates and push on toward Concord. He had his orders, and a handful of country people, armed or not, were not about to deter him. The British column, seven hundred strong, continued down the road to Concord, fifes and drums setting the steady, unrushed cadence, defiantly announcing their presence.

What Colonel Smith—or Gage himself, for that matter—hadn't taken into account was the expanse, the breathtaking breadth and speed, of the provincials' reaction. Gage had sent British columns into the countryside west of Boston before, and on a couple of occasions they had encountered bodies of disloyal militia. In every instance there had been no blood drawn, no gunfire, no exchange of anything more than shouted challenges and sullen glances.

This time things were different. Word of the bloodletting on Lexington Green had spread as fast as the Patriot alarm-riders could carry it by horseback. By the time Smith's men reached Concord that morning, several dozen companies of militia and minutemen were on the road, armed, converging on Concord from all directions and within only a few minutes' march of the town.

At Concord, Smith's Redcoats were admirably well behaved, conducting their search for illicit munitions with a courteous, even gentle, touch. They did indeed find cannon, musket balls, flour, and other vital military supplies, and they did their best to destroy what they found. The people of Concord offered no resistance, and even the local militia companies drew back a respectful distance. But the tension that had radiated from Lexington could not be so easily dispelled. An awkward encounter of Redcoats and minutemen at the town's North Bridge led to the fatal volleys. And then there was no way that further bloodshed could be averted. When the British left Concord, all hell broke loose.

Smith's retreat to Boston began calmly enough, but the Redcoats had put only a mile or so of road behind them when they ran headlong into the first of many ambushes. The militia and the minutemen—not just from Concord, but from a score of nearby towns and even from neighboring counties—were not about to let Smith escape unpunished. To the increasingly frustrated British, who were just trying to get away from the unpleasant business at Concord, it seemed as if the entire countryside had risen against them, armed, gripped by an unquenchable relentless fury. At Meriam's Corner and Brooks Hill, at a sharp wooded bend in the road later dubbed the "Bloody Angle," the citizen-soldiers swarmed upon the retreating British column, front, flanks, and rear. The Americans poured ragged volleys into the Redcoats from behind trees, stone walls, hedgerows, barns—anything that would afford them some cover. Smith judiciously sent out flankers—patrols to sweep the areas immediately adjoining the road—and while they managed to flush out some of the Yankee militia, there were always more coming. The rebels were continually firing, melting away, then reappearing farther down the tree- and brush-lined road. When Smith's men finally found a measure of safety at Lexington, where Lord Percy's relief force stood waiting for them, they were bloody, dazed, enraged, and nearly out of ammunition.

Still the rebels refused their foes a moment's respite. Percy's fresh troops, even his artillery, did little to slow or discourage their tormentors. More roadside ambushes, bitter and bloody house-to-house fighting through the town of Menotomy . . . the casualties mounted on both sides, but there was no question that it was the British who suffered more.

It was approaching nightfall when the British troops halted outside Charlestown. There, on a gentle grass-covered rise called Bunker Hill, they dug in and prepared for an American onslaught that never came. The rebels were thoroughly drained, too. They knew their limits, and conducting an open assault against entrenched British Regulars was clearly beyond them. Some of the militia moved furtively to within a respectful distance of the British position. They gazed in almost innocent curiosity at the soldiers they had just defeated, who stared back in sullen, enervated resentment.

Soon the British would begin their evacuation by boat, across the Charles to Boston. HMS *Somerset*, one of the massive men-of-war keeping watch over the harbor, maneuvered close to the Charles River ferryway to discourage the impudent rebels from attempting any further mischief. But the country people did not interfere further. Neither did they disperse. In the thousands, the sons of Massachusetts had turned out to protect and avenge their neighbors that day, many, many more than the relatively small numbers who had dogged the Redcoats' footsteps all the way from Concord. They clustered at Cambridge to the west and Roxbury to the southwest, and their mass grew visibly through the evening and into the next day.[2]

It had been the Day of Days, the Glorious Nineteenth of April. While there were still those who clung to the hope that there could yet be a peaceful resolution to the impasse that separated the colony from Mother England, the Boston radicals in self-imposed exile were jubilant. Virtue had triumphed over tyranny, liberty over slavery, free men over Gage's madder-clad legions. The leaders of revolutionary Massachusetts, the voices who had counseled resistance on the floor of the Provincial Congress, had been vindicated. And it had been Gage who had struck the first blow, not they.

Massachusetts learned from the experience. The colony, and the Cause, learned of its strength. The armed citizenry had answered the call to arms in numbers almost too great to grasp, risking death and worse without hesitation. It was a deceptive lesson. Few were willing or able to see anything but unqualified triumph in the day's events. It was all too easy to wax overconfident in the martial abilities of citizen-soldiers, to dismiss the failings of the British troops and their leadership with unjustified contempt . . . to fail to realize, in short, that the favorable outcome of the day had been more the result of a unique and unlikely set of circumstances, or unimaginable luck, than anything else.

The rebels felt that they had taught the British a lesson, and indeed they had. General Gage was already familiar with the American character, and he knew something of Americans at war. He had fought alongside the colonists in the last war with the French. Over the past year, he had also learned not to underestimate the influence of rabble-rousers like Adams, Hancock, and the smooth Boston physician Dr. Joseph Warren. It wasn't the fact that the provincials had responded in the way they had that surprised him; it was the scale and ferocity of the response. As he sat in his Boston headquarters, in the stately Province House on Marlborough Street, Gage pieced together the story of the day's events from the reports that nervous orderlies placed diffidently on his desk, looking for answers, racking his brains for a way to explain the defeat to his masters back home. Perhaps these rebels had not—not yet—acquired military discipline in the way that the term was ordinarily understood in Europe. And yet they had organization, some kind of system, some deceptively simple way of mobilizing armed men and bringing them to bear against even his stealthiest moves. He already knew that Americans could be determined, resourceful, clever, and physically and morally brave, but until that day he did not fully comprehend how much. Gage learned quickly. He would not forget the lesson.

More unsettling was what Gage and his lieutenants discovered about their own men. Yes, they were professionals, better drilled than the Americans, capable of moving in large formations with speed and even with grace. Thanks to Gage, the British soldiers had received extensive target practice, something that was all but unknown in most European armies. They were *soldiers* in a way that the Americans definitely were not. They had discipline, organization, and hierarchy. They should have behaved with the utmost calm and professionalism even when caught in the crossfire of hundreds of Yankee muskets. They *should* have, but they did not. For the difficult truth was that the men that Pitcairn, Smith, and Percy led into battle were raw, only slightly less raw than the half-trained farmers who bested them that day. The Redcoats were not ready for combat.

Gage's superiors in London expected the general to quell the local discontent in the Bay Colony before it became a full-blown rebellion. They expected him to do it with the instrument he had at hand. Only now, Gage was beginning to learn just what an imperfect instrument it was.

And that was an especially bitter pill for the ordinarily genial and patient British general to swallow, for the ordeal that lay ahead for him and his humbled army promised to be infinitely more challenging than the one through which it had just passed. Anyone who cared to look—and there were hundreds who did—from the towering summit of Beacon Hill could see the fiery portent: a necklace of glowing orange in the night, ringing the Charles River and the Back Bay as far south as Roxbury . . . the hundreds of campfires tended by the thousands of rebels who had converged on Boston that day. From their posts on Boston Neck, atop Copp's Hill, and along the dark waters lapping rhythmically on the shore of Boston Common, British sentries could hear the drums, the shouts, the occasional random musket-shot from the camps across the water. The ring of fire was there the next night, too, and the next, swelling—shifting perhaps, but never diminishing.

Thomas Gage did not despair. He did not panic. For months he had been expecting this moment, the headlong rush to outright rebellion. Now that it was upon him, he could indulge himself in the luxury of vindication. His masters in London had dismissed his warnings with undisguised contempt, but Gage had been right. The proof was right there in front of him, and for all the world to see. Yet vindication was cold comfort. It could not drive away the uneasy feeling in the pit of his stomach. He was reluctant to accept the unpleasant truth: that his army was trapped in Boston, that there was no easy way out. To Gage, as he gazed sadly and uneasily upon the dancing orange glow on the western horizon, it seemed as if the whole world was afire.

*T*he world had indeed caught fire, and that fire raced as fast as horse and rider could carry the word of the bloodshed at Lexington . . . through Massachusetts to New Hampshire, Rhode

Island, Connecticut, and New York, and eventually across the length and breadth of the Continent, as men called the thirteen contiguous British colonies in those days. The conflagration engulfed nearly all of eastern Massachusetts in a matter of hours. The flames licked at men's hearts, driving them to shoulder their muskets and set out down the roads that led to Boston, to avenge their fallen brethren.

Artemas Ward, the man destined to command the rebels in the fight to come, also sensed the fire. But he was in such gut-wrenching pain that he could scarcely marvel at the flames that burned all around him.

Nor could he pause to consider the danger of the moment, the perils that faced his native Massachusetts, the perils into which his own actions were leading him. Forty-seven-year-old Ward, major general and de facto commander of the colony's military forces, had just ridden into Cambridge to take charge of the men who had congregated there over the past twenty-four hours. And in doing so he had just about signed his own death warrant. For several years he had worked alongside the most ardent Whigs; had in fact become one of them, and was close with Sam Adams and Dr. Warren.

That association was damning enough in and of itself. But so far the rebellion against the ministerial government in London had been fought with words and protests only. True, blood had been spilled once before, five years ago in Boston, but the "massacre" in the snow on King Street was not armed rebellion. What had transpired at Lexington and Concord, and even more so on the road back from Concord, surely was rebellion. And Ward was not just joining the insurrection—he was actually putting himself squarely in the front rank of notorious traitors to the Crown.

But there was much else on Artemas Ward's mind as he rode into Cambridge late in the afternoon of April 20, 1775, exhausted and saddle-sore and all but doubled over with the pain that seared his bowels. Only five days before, he had returned to his stately if plain home in Shrewsbury after nearly four weeks of politicking in the Provincial Congress, which had been meeting in Concord. The long hours, the sleepless nights, the hurried meals had taken their toll on his health. Ward had unwillingly become reacquainted with a malady that had plagued him on-and-off for much of his adult life: what the doctors called "calculus," in his case bladder stones. He had had no more than three days to rest and recuperate at home when he had been called again to duty.[3]

It was just before noon on the Glorious Nineteenth when a man named Israel Bissel tore into Shrewsbury on his frothing and overheated mount. To the gaggle of anxious men, women, and young boys who crowded around him, Bissel breathlessly croaked out the news. Gage's bloodybacks had fired, without provocation, on the militia at Lexington. At least half a dozen innocent men, undoubtedly more, lay dead on the Green there. Now the Committee of Safety—the body of thirteen men appointed by the Provincial Congress to oversee the colony's military affairs—was calling upon all able-bodied men to come to the aid of their oppressed brethren to the east.[4]

Having sounded the alarm, Israel Bissel took a deep breath, dug his spurs into his tired horse's flanks, and in a flash was flying westward again along the Post Road that led to Worcester and points beyond.

Shrewsbury, like nearly every town and crossroads in Massachusetts that day, exploded into action. For weeks, men of military age—especially the so-called minutemen—had been preparing for this day, taking up the habit of carrying their firelocks and their military gear along with them as they worked in the fields, even when they gathered at the meetinghouse for worship on the Sabbath. Now that the time had come, farmers set aside their plows, tradesmen doffed their aprons, wives and mothers and sweethearts hurried to round up whatever provisions they could find or spare.

Within minutes, it seemed, armed men were saying their abrupt and stoic farewells. They took to the road in twos and threes, muskets in hand, lumpy bedrolls slung hurriedly over one shoulder. They did not know what was expected of them, not really, and they had no idea of what they would find once they got to where they were supposed to go.

Artemas Ward, though, did not rush off when the alarm was sounded. Still an invalid, he was in no condition to travel, and despite his prominent position in the community and the colony, no one would have thought ill of him had he declined to make the trip to Boston. But it was not in Ward's nature to make excuses, to shirk his duty, to complain.

There was little heroic about the man. Not quite fat, but by no means trim or athletic, Ward was a man who had enjoyed a sedentary life, with a flat, sallow face surmounted by narrow-set, heavy-lidded eyes that made him appear only half-awake. Though the most prominent citizen of Shrewsbury and possibly in all of Worcester County, Ward did not cut a dashing figure. Yet he had virtues that did not show on the surface, and these virtues suited him to be the man of the hour. Calm, unflappable, and dignified, Artemas Ward knew little of combat, but he knew how to organize, and he had a great deal of native common sense. He knew Massachusetts and its people, their hopes and fears and aspirations, as no one else could. Ward knew how the New England mind worked, and he commanded the respect of his fellow Yankees, men who did not grant respect casually. He was not an especially gifted orator—yet he was the kind of man whose words, even in the most raucous and contentious town meeting, others stilled to hear.

Artemas Ward would not, could not remain an invalid when Massachusetts needed him, and it needed him at that very moment. Rising early the following morning, Thursday, April 20, 1775, he packed his saddlebags and valise with a few personal belongings, donned his militia general's uniform, and climbed awkwardly into the saddle. Then he headed east up the Post Road toward Boston.

Ward made the trip in one day. The weather was in his favor. After an uncharacteristically mild winter, with temperatures rarely dipping below freezing, spring had come early to New England in 1775. The trees were almost fully leafed-out, and since there had been little snowmelt and no recent downpours, the roads were not the impassible expanses of sticky liquid muck that they should have been that time of year. Regardless of the comfort brought by a warm sun and cool air, the journey from Shrewsbury was a nightmare. For a younger, more robust traveler, forty miles on horseback was a demanding ride. For Ward—overweight, sick, and exhausted, his affliction reminding him of its presence with every step his horse took—each moment of the trip was an ordeal.

Ward traveled alone, and yet he did not have the road to himself. The Post Road was alive, crawling with militia companies and small groups of armed men, all headed in the same direction. The groups snowballed in size as they strode along, as individuals coalesced into small bands. Squads became companies, and companies regiments, not only on the Post Road that connected Boston to Worcester and points west but on all of the other roads that converged in the environs of Boston. By afternoon, the thoroughfares were clotted with men.

At long last, toward dusk that same day, Artemas Ward reached Cambridge.

General Ward knew the town well. He was a Harvard man, having graduated from the ancient college nearly three decades before, and he had had occasion to visit the town many times in the years since. But *this* Cambridge was almost unrecognizable. The town of fifteen hundred men, women, and children had burst at the seams, and was now an armed camp of nearly ten thousand souls . . . and all in the space of little more than a day.

The newly arrived men were everywhere: encamped around cook fires on the Common, some in tents, most not; nearly every house, every barn, every sheltered space and pasture in the small town had become a dwelling for the footsore citizen-soldiers. The men had not exactly settled in, though, for rumors continued to fly that the British would mount another, more vigorous, foray into the countryside to seek revenge for the blood and pride they had lost the day before. The men, dressed in the earthen-toned woolen frock coats, breeches, and smocks of ordinary civilian garb, clutched their muskets and fowling-pieces in some apprehension as they milled about the town. Though the formally designated regiments of the colony's militia had begun to cluster together, there was little apparent organization at work here. The militiamen thronged Cambridge's streets, yards, and taverns. Woodsmoke from hundreds of campfires permeated every inch of sky and perfumed every inch of clothing, mixing with the smells of sweat and offal and manure to create an acrid stench that stung the eyes. The usually subdued sounds of a village in mid-spring had been supplanted by an inescapable cacophony of shouts and curses, the ringing of axes, and the squeal of wooden wheels on ungreased axles.

Still on horseback, Artemas Ward somehow threaded his way through the pulsing crowd, stopping to dismount in front of the house of Jonathan Hastings, the steward of Harvard College. The Hastings House, which fronted directly on Cambridge Common, was destined to host personages yet more renowned in the months to come, but already on the twentieth it had become the command post for the Massachusetts "army." Since morning, ruddy-faced General William Heath—the top-ranking officer on the scene before Ward's arrival—had set up his temporary headquarters here, trying as best he could to impose some sort of order on the militia units that had found their way, piecemeal, to Cambridge.

But now General Ward was here, at the very center of things, and the command became his. Ward dismounted, the stabbing pain almost unbearable, and slowly hobbled his way into the Hastings House. Shortly he would call together the ranking officers in town—General Heath and a dozen colonels and lieutenant colonels—for an official Council of War, the first true command act of the American Revolution. The awful responsibility of it all, of the chaos that enveloped him, had fallen on his slumped and weary shoulders.

Ward's burden would be especially onerous because only a few hours before his arrival, a small group of men had settled on a course of action that would drastically raise the stakes in the standoff with the mother country. Without any authority to act, these men had taken it upon themselves to make one of the boldest, most momentous decisions in American history: to make war on Great Britain.

Blood had been spilled, quite a lot of it, but that didn't mean that

Artemas Ward, by Charles Willson Peale, from life, c. 1790–1795. Neither a dashing figure nor a brilliant battlefield commander, Ward nonetheless did what nobody else was ready to do in the spring of 1775: he took a mob of New England farmers and tradesmen and made them act like an army.
(INDEPENDENCE NATIONAL HISTORICAL PARK)

Dr. Joseph Warren. The fashionable young Boston physician—a widower with four children—was without a doubt the most influential Revolutionary leader in Massachusetts until his death at Bunker Hill on June 17, 1775. Portrait by John Singleton Copley.

(MUSEUM OF FINE ARTS, BOSTON)

a full-fledged war had begun. There was no reason to believe, in Boston or Cambridge or Watertown, that a negotiated settlement was entirely out of the question, that the Sons of Liberty and their ilk had already pushed their cause past the point of no return. But there were indeed men who wanted war, who were not sated by Lexington and Concord. And to them, the opportunity presented by the Lexington alarm was just too good to be passed up.

Chief among them was Dr. Joseph Warren, the most influential Whig in Massachusetts. His colleagues Sam Adams, John Adams, and John Hancock would go on to earn undying fame, but in April 1775, Joseph Warren was the very embodiment of the Cause and—in British eyes—the most dangerous man in America. Unlike Sam Adams, the handsome thirty-three-year-old doctor was cultured, polished, refined, and charming; unlike Hancock the merchant, there was nothing venal or self-serving about him; and unlike John Adams, Warren was outgoing and gregarious. He was a born

The Hastings House. This imposing Cambridge house—the residence of Jonathan Hastings, steward of Harvard College—became American military headquarters immediately after Lexington and Concord. It was in the Hastings' dining room that Artemas Ward and his officers entertained the newly arrived George Washington in a loud and informal party on the night of July 2, 1775.

(FROM *THE MEMORIAL HISTORY OF BOSTON, INCLUDING SUFFOLK COUNTY, MASSACHUSETTS, 1630-1880* [4 VOLS., BOSTON, 1880-81], 3:108) leader, and he was tireless. Warren, a Harvard-educated native of Roxbury, was the widowed father of four small children, an actively practicing physician, Grand Master of the St. Andrews Lodge of Freemasons, president of the Massachusetts Provincial Congress, and chairman of the Committee of Safety. He was relatively late to join the ranks of the leading Patriots, but when he did, he put his all into the Cause. His high standing in Boston society and his elegant manners and deportment could not mask his ardor for the cause of Liberty, which bordered on fanaticism.

In talent for bombastic speech and in sheer nerve, Joseph Warren easily equaled his friend Sam Adams. In March 1775, he gave the annual address at Fanueil Hall commemorating the Bostonians who had fallen in the "Massacre" five years earlier. Although there were more than a few British officers in the audience, Warren did not hesitate to make pointed references to the "murders" perpetrated by British soldiers in 1770. His rhetoric was effective in part because he truly believed in it. The Redcoats, he wrote in the Committee of Safety's "official" narratives of the events of April 19, had fired the first shots on Lexington Green, and during the retreat from Concord the British soldiers were guilty of "barbarous murders committed upon our innocent brethren." He absolutely detested Loyalists as "the most abandoned villains on earth." At the same time, he was courtly and genuinely warm, even to his enemies. Immediately after Lexington and Concord he wrote cordially to General Gage, offering to allow British surgeons to treat wounded Redcoats who had fallen into rebel hands. His friendliness, never feigned, gave him a degree of influence in the Provincial Congress that cold, reserved Sam Adams couldn't match. The Committee of Safety was *his* committee, and its recommendations rarely encountered resistance in Watertown where the Congress met. He was the young and charismatic ideologue of the Revolution, a Robespierre with a heart and a human touch. It wouldn't be long before he became the Revolution's first true martyr.[5]

Warren also had the rare ability to shift from being commanded to being in command, and back again; he subordinated his ego and his ambition to his sacred Cause. On the nineteenth, the indefatigable doctor shouldered a musket and fell in with the militia, right in the thick of the fighting around Menotomy. A British musket ball came within an inch of ending his life then and there, neatly removing a pin from his elegantly coiffed hair. With William Heath he rallied the militia and led the withdrawal back to Cambridge that evening, and the very next morning he and Heath rounded up all the senior militia commanders they could find for an impromptu council of war. It was at this moment, as Warren witnessed firsthand the vast scale of Massachusetts's response to the Lexington alarm, that the thought struck him. There were so many men here, armed and ready to fight. If there were to be war with Britain, why wait for the moderates, for the reluctant souls who still hoped for compromise, to be convinced that there was no way but the way of the sword? If there was going to be a war . . . why not *here?* Why not *now?*

Consulting with Heath and the other militia officers, Warren presented a bold proposition. Boston was already under siege, in fact if not in name. The opportunity was right here under their noses. Why not take advantage of the situation and act while Gage was still reeling from yesterday's blow?

It was a big question, pregnant with frightening implications and consequences seen and unseen. All of the men with Warren that morning understood exactly what he was asking them to decide. There was still time—for tempers to cool, for the Provincial Congress to offer Gage some palliative that might stave off a British counterstrike, for something other than out-and-out war. Timothy Pickering, one of the more imaginative military minds in America and fated to be a key administrator for the future Continental Army, was positively terrified by what Warren had suggested. Pickering had just led his militia regiment from Salem to Medford, too late to take part in the fighting, and seeing that the British had already fled back to Boston he was prepared to take his men home again. At Lexington and Concord, Pickering believed, resistance to Gage had been justified . . . but to lay siege to Boston would be an unwarranted act of aggression. The colonel tried to make Warren see reason: "The hostilities of the preceding day," he said, "did not render civil war inevitable."[6]

But Warren had his blood up, and he was the more convincing speaker. Pickering's impassioned plea moved no one. Warren had his way: Massachusetts would go to war.

*D*r. Warren's push for war was rash, optimistic, dangerous, and likely irreversible. Some Patriots had convinced themselves that an army of free Americans was, hands down, morally superior to an army of Redcoat hirelings and jailbirds. But even the most ardent Whig couldn't ignore the vast disparity in weapons, equipment, training, and professionalism between the American militia and Gage's Regulars. For all that, Warren's aggressive stance was not wholly unrealistic in April 1775. Gage's army had retreated to Boston, and it would be a relatively simple task to keep it bottled up there. It didn't take much to besiege Boston, or at least to isolate it, for Boston was little more than an island.

Modern Boston bears little resemblance to its eighteenth-century ancestor. The present-day city, topographically speaking, is the product of land reclamation and regrading on a massive scale. But before the mania for knocking down hills and backfilling salt marshes swept the growing, space-hungry town in the nineteenth century, Boston was a bulbous, oddly shaped protrusion jutting northeast into the harbor. It was technically a peninsula, but only barely: a slender tendril of land, called Boston Neck, tethered the town to the Massachusetts mainland at Roxbury. The Neck—roughly analogous to present-day

Washington Street—was the only means of ingress or egress by land, and at high tide it was commonly awash.

Boston was bounded by the Charles River to the north, and to the west and south by the marshy shallows of the Back Bay, also known as Roxbury Flats. Most of the town's inhabitants crowded into the eastern half of the peninsula, divided almost equally into the North and South Ends. The western half remained, well into the eighteenth century, thoroughly bucolic. On the very far western periphery of the town, the forty-five-acre Boston Common sloped gently down to the waters of the Back Bay. Far from being painstakingly groomed, the Common was a functional pasture for livestock, and hence was as muddy and foul-odored as any heavily used cow pasture. The Common came in handy, too, for mustering militia, or for hanging criminals and troublesome religious dissidents, or for any other public use that Bostonians could dream up.

It was a prosperous town, once the largest city and the busiest port in all of British North America—until Philadelphia and New York usurped its primacy in the 1760s. But even though third in rank, Boston buzzed with life, with commercial vitality. Successful merchants crowded the North End with opulent—opulent by Puritan standards, anyway—grand houses; even in the humbler neighborhoods the houses were plain but well built, with individual yards. Overall the town was tidy, neat, and pleasant. The spare but elegant spires of Boston's many churches dominated the skyline. Wharves studded the waterfront of the North and South Ends, extending as far along the peninsula as the tip of the North End and the giant millpond to the west. The concentration of wharves was thickest around the Town Cove on the eastern shore. Here was Boston's most distinctive maritime feature: the Long Wharf, lined with shops and warehouses, which extended nearly a half-mile into the harbor, allowing even the largest seagoing vessels to unload their cargoes directly into the town.

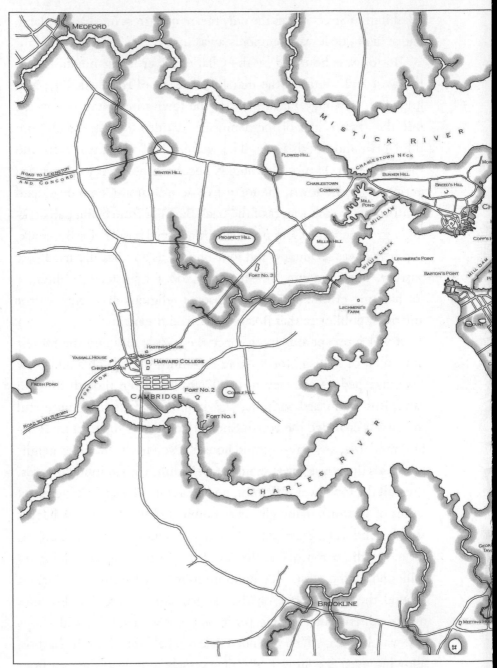

Boston and Environs, June 1775.

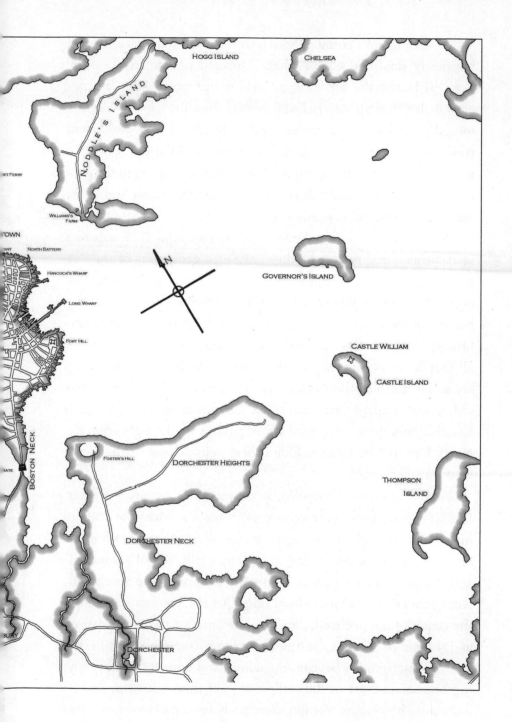

To visitors with cosmopolitan tastes, Boston may have seemed hopelessly staid and quaint when compared to a town like New York. It lacked the kinds of cultural refinements—such as theaters—that Puritan society had found so objectionable. Boston was indeed provincial . . . but it was comfortable. Even after Parliament closed the port in 1774, as punishment for the "Tea Party" of the previous year, Boston had much to offer. British officers in the garrison there feasted on fresh fish and lobster, fresh beef and pork, mutton, and veal, all reasonably priced.

What today are mere suburbs of Boston were, in 1775, separate settlements, made remote by the convoluted geography of the Bay region. Dorchester, Roxbury, and Brookline were all farming villages on the other side of the Back Bay; travel to any of them by horse, via the Neck, could use up the better part of a day. Cambridge, Medford, Chelsea, and even Charlestown were not really all that far away, but they might as well have been, because they lay so far north of the Neck's base at Roxbury. Charlestown was only a few hundred yards across the Charles from Boston's North End, but only those who could afford passage on the ferry from the North End to Charlestown found these neighboring towns to the west truly accessible.

From a strategic viewpoint, what was most significant about Boston—apart from its ready access to the sea—was the scattering of hills throughout the region and even inside the town itself. Near the tip of the North End was Copp's Hill, site of a windmill and an ancient burying ground; Fort Hill dominated the South End. Rising above them all was a high ridge that ran like a spine through the center of the peninsula, known—because of its three separate and distinct peaks—as the Trimountain or Tramount. Pemberton was the easternmost; Beacon, the tallest, was named for the warning beacon set there in the earliest days of the settlement; and finally there was Mount Vernon, commonly known to those with less delicate sensibilities as Mount Whoredom. All offered breathtaking panoramic views of the harbor and the mainland beyond.[7]

Boston was blessed with beautiful, grassy hills . . . but it was cursed with them, too. Immediately to the east-southeast of Boston Neck were the hills overlooking Dorchester and Roxbury, called Dorchester Hill or Dorchester Heights. Northeast of town were the hills of the Charlestown peninsula. If a besieging army were to take possession of these two groups of hills, fortify them, and mount heavy guns there, then it could pound Boston into submission at its leisure. Gun emplacements on Dorchester Heights could sweep Boston Neck with artillery fire, effectively negating any possibility of escape from the town. Charlestown Heights, by virtue of its proximity to Boston, commanded the northern extremity of the peninsula. Artillery sited there could harrass shipping in the harbor and make life a living hell for any unfortunates trapped in Boston. "The country near Boston," noted one British general, " . . . is all fortification."[8]

The rebel militia under Artemas Ward's tentative command did not occupy either Dorchester or Charlestown Heights. Lord Percy occupied the highest point outside Charlestown, a windswept rise then known as Bunker Hill,* on the evening of the retreat from Concord, but the British abandoned the position almost as soon as the Redcoats had all found safety in Boston. British fortifications on Boston Neck, at least for the time being, guarded Dorchester Heights. Anyone, British or American, could easily see the overwhelming strategic importance of both positions. If the rebels got hold of good artillery and set it up on either or both, then General Gage would be in a very bad spot indeed.

First things first. The rebels were not in a position to go on the offensive, to undertake any operation that involved something more

---

* At the time of the siege, locals invariably referred to this larger prominence near Charlestown as "Bunker's Hill," but since the Revolution it's become far better known as "Bunker Hill."

active than sitting tight in their camps and waiting for Gage to re-taliate. Making a war meant making an army. There were thousands of armed men at Cambridge and Roxbury, from the Mystic River to Boston Neck and a dozen points in between, but the force that had been summoned on the Glorious Nineteenth of April was most as-suredly *not* an army. Nor was it ever intended to be one.

*I*t was not that no one in Massachusetts had foreseen that an or-ganized, trained, paid, professional army might be necessary at some point down the road. The Provincial Congress had raised the issue when it first convened in the fall of 1774. Since then the Congress had taken solid steps in that direction. The Committee of Safety had made the creation of an "Army of Observation" its top priority for the first months of 1775. The Committee had nominated generals, investigated sources for gunpowder and other vital muni-tions, proposed a pay scale for all ranks, composed a set of official regulations, and even written out the oaths that prospective recruits would have to swear upon enlistment . . . all for an army that ex-isted only on paper. Nothing of substance had been accomplished when the Congress adjourned on April 15. The clash at Lexington had interrupted the process before it could be carried through to completion.[9]

The events of April 19 did not require an army. Massachusetts al-ready had a time-honored and time-tested mechanism for confront-ing immediate threats quickly and in strength. It worked. It worked, in fact, far better than anyone had expected . . . almost *too* well.

The massive, spontaneous outpouring of patriotic ardor on April 19 was no accident. Nor was it, despite appearances, all that spontaneous. The provincial militia had been the mainstay for local defense since the colony's founding more than a century before. Like the institution upon which it was patterned—the "trained bands" of Elizabethan England—it required all men of military age, from sixteen years to sixty, to serve when called to duty, to attend regular militia musters, and to furnish their own weapons. Field officers were appointed by the colonial government; company commanders and other junior officers were elected by the men themselves. Because of the frequent clashes with Native Americans, the militia was vital to the survival of the English settlements in Massachusetts. Over time, the militia evolved into a permanent organization with a formal structure. The Provincial Congress and the Committee of Safety, understanding how valuable the militia might be in the event of an armed confrontation with Mother England, gave it special attention, encouraging the militia companies to train and drill more frequently than had been the custom, and gradually weeding out officers with Tory sympathies. By the time of the Lexington alarm, Massachusetts had raised a secret army, tens of thousands strong, ready and willing to fight when called upon.

Bitter experience on the frontier, though, showed the colonists that the militia was too unwieldy, too slow, to be of much use in situations where speed counted more than anything—an Indian raid on a frontier settlement, for example. Hence there developed, parallel to the militia, an informal "first-responder" force of volunteers from the militia regiments. These were younger, more agile, men, usually men without families, who pledged themselves to be ready for action "on a minute's notice." Troops like these had played an important role in the colonial wars prior to 1763. The concept was revived in 1774, but for a wholly different purpose: to frustrate the British. In response to a successful British raid on the powder magazine near Winter Hill (modern-day Somerset, Massachusetts) in September 1774, Patriot leaders at Worcester called for the creation of minuteman companies. The example took hold, and soon the newly fashioned Committee of Safety authorized the recruitment of minutemen from the standing militia.[10]

Lexington and Concord proved the awesome potential of Massachusetts's illicit military institutions, the deceptively simple nexus of regional "committees of correspondence," alarm-riders, militia, and minutemen. Relatively few of the men mobilized by the Lexington alarm—only those within a few hours' march of Concord—would take an active part in the battles of April 19. But many, many more men were well on their way toward the sound of the guns as daylight faded, arriving on the scene just after the fighting sputtered to an end.

And they kept coming. Some of the militia didn't quite make it to Boston. One company set out from Hatfield at the double-quick and went as far as Ware, twenty-three miles away from home and nearly seventy miles west of Boston, only to hear that the immediate crisis at Boston was over. The men did an immediate about-face and went straight home. Some towns kept their militia units nearby, fearing British incursions closer to home: militia from Bristol and Plymouth counties, north of Boston, marched instead to confront a small British detachment then stationed at Marshfield. But most of those who took up arms completed the trek to Cambridge and Roxbury.[11]

So, too, did men from the other New England colonies. The alarm-riders had ranged far beyond the borders of Massachusetts, and most of New England knew about Lexington and Concord within a couple of days. A week or more would pass before government authorities and leading Patriots in New Hampshire, Connecticut, and Rhode Island—Vermont and Maine did not yet exist as such—could formulate measured and appropriate responses to the Committee of Safety's pleas for aid. But in the meantime Dr. Warren's carefully phrased tocsin worked its intended effect. Their minds filled with lurid images of an unfeeling soldiery murdering innocent civilians, men from southern New Hampshire and eastern Connecticut leapt to arms without waiting for official sanction. In companies and as individuals, they sped toward the scene of the fighting as if Gage's men had invaded *their* soil.

Cautious militia officers and local officials tried to rein in the outpouring of warlike sympathy, hoping to achieve better results with time and organization, but to no avail. An enthusiastic militia captain in New Haven mustered his company and prepared to set out for Boston; when the city fathers refused to grant him access to New Haven's powder magazine so that his men could equip themselves, the impetuous captain—a patriotic young merchant named Benedict Arnold—threatened to take the keys to the magazine at bayonet-point if need be. One militia colonel in Farmington, Connecticut, complained that he had to physically restrain his regiment from marching to Boston before receiving orders from the government in Hartford. And a fifty-seven-year-old veteran Indian fighter turned gentleman-farmer, one Israel Putnam, literally set aside his plow, mounted his plow-horse, and rode furiously for Boston the very minute he found out about the alarm. "The ardour of our people is such, that they can't be kept back," the Connecticut Committee of Correspondence boasted to John Hancock.[12]

In a little over a week, about twenty thousand militia and minutemen had descended upon the makeshift camps outside Boston. To British officers still shaken by the battles of the nineteenth, it seemed as if the entire countryside had risen against them. Even the rebels themselves were taken aback by their own accomplishment. No one in Massachusetts, in fact no one in British North America, had ever seen the like before. Most of the men had never seen that many people in one place at one time.

But the militia had not come to Boston to fight a war. They had come because they had been called to protect their colony, their counties, their friends, relatives, and neighbors from the depredations of Gage's soldiers. They had done that, and more. They had not planned on a prolonged stay. Few of them had brought much food with them. Most of the militiamen had left vital work unfinished at home. They were farmers, not soldiers, and it was planting season. There were fields to be tilled, crops to be sown. Neither the militia nor the minutemen had signed on for an indefinite term of service. Once the immediate danger had passed, once their duty had been done, the men intended to go home.

Go home they did.

It wasn't a mass exodus, nor was there anything organized about it. But by the afternoon of the twentieth it was obvious that Gage had no intention of retaliating anytime soon. And even if he were so brazen as to send his lobsterbacks into the countryside again, the process would simply repeat itself. The alarm would sound, the riders would carry the word, and the minutemen and the militia would heed the call. If Gage hadn't learned this by now, then the Yankees were more than willing to teach him again. Until then, there was no earthly reason why they had to sit, uncomfortable, dirty, and hungry, in the camps, no reason why they had to play soldier.

As the men began to leave the camps and head for home—some in full companies, led by their officers, some in small groups or as individuals—others came to take their places. The men from the central counties were just arriving on the twentieth, and it took a week or more for the militia companies from the hill country in the west to reach the Boston area. The net result of all this coming and going was that the rebel force was in perpetual flux. Neither Artemas Ward, who had just assumed command in Cambridge, nor John Thomas, the ranking general in Roxbury, had even the foggiest idea of the number of individuals, or companies, or regiments in their commands. Even if they could have ascertained such a thing, the statistic would have been meaningless, for the numbers would have changed within minutes. And there was no telling how long the influx of fresh militia would continue . . . or how long it would be before the camps at Cambridge and Roxbury would finally empty out.

Joseph Warren and the other rebel leaders did not want to find out how long it would take. The Committee of Safety was already in session on the twentieth; it presented its first recommendations to the Provincial Congress the very next day. The two governing bodies worked well together, and with surprising efficiency. The thirteen-man Committee had taken it upon itself to serve as the colony's directorate of military affairs, and though the Congress had the final say in all matters, it generally deferred to the Committee's opinions. It helped, of course, that Joseph Warren stood in such high stead in both institutions, and that the physical distance between the two bodies was minimal. The Congress met at Watertown, the Committee at the Hastings House in Cambridge, only three miles away by road. Artemas Ward, therefore, had direct access to the Committee, and questions referred to the Congress by the Committee were usually taken under consideration—and answered—the very same day.

Building an army in such pressing haste, however, was beyond the experience of anyone in the Committee or the Congress. On the twenty-first, the Committee recommended the creation of an army of eight thousand Massachusetts men, sworn to serve until the end of the year. The Congress promptly accepted the proposal, though it deemed the number insufficient, and called instead for an army of thirty thousand men: 13,600 from Massachusetts, the remainder to be supplied by Rhode Island, New Hampshire, and Connecticut, each of which had already voiced their support for their rebellious neighbor. Each man who enlisted would receive a uniform from the Congress and a blanket from the town in which he resided. Plus, of course, pay: forty shillings a month. It wasn't much, and it would be paid—when it was eventually paid—in depreciated provincial scrip, but pay was pay . . . and no Yankee was about to sign away his freedom for the next eight months without it.[13]

The method of recruitment was simple: colonels—regimental

commanders—were nominated by the Congress, and they in turn each distributed what were called "beating orders" to their designated captains—"beating" referring to the beating of a drum to announce the recruiting captain's presence. Once a captain had filled out his company with the requisite number of privates, noncommissioned officers, musicians, and junior officers, he would submit his muster-roll to the Congress and receive his official commission.

It all seemed so very easy, so uncomplicated, and in practice it should have been. The system of "beating orders" had been used during the French and Indian War to raise provincial regiments, with great success. Many members of Congress, not to mention the senior militia officers, had served in that conflict, and therefore it was the system with which they were most familiar and comfortable. Indeed, it should have been easier this time around. The appointed colonels already held rank in the militia, the designated captains were already in camp, and the bulk of the men likely to enlist were right there, within easy reach, at Cambridge and Roxbury. The recruiters would not have to range far to find recruits. It *should* have been a simple matter . . . but it wasn't.

The first signs of trouble came during the very first days that the Congress discussed the issue, and over a seemingly trivial matter: the number of men in an infantry company. The Committee had first recommended that a company should include seventy men "rank and file," and only hours later changed its recommendation to fifty men. The Congress likewise dithered over the number of men, first stipulating a larger number and then reducing it. The reason behind the debate was not trivial: larger companies meant proportionately fewer officers per regiment, which meant in turn that many of the militia officers currently in service would lose their rank in the new volunteer army. Nor would the enlisted men be happy. Most of the militia and minuteman companies numbered no more than fifty, and usually much less. If they had to be consolidated with other units to make larger companies, many of them would not be serving under the officers they had elected. And to New Englanders, serving under an unknown officer from a distant town was unthinkable.[14]

Important issues, to be sure, but they wasted valuable time. Recruiting could not begin until the Provincial Congress finished debating the relative merits of larger or smaller companies. And those militiamen and minutemen who felt that they had already done their part did not wait around for the Congress to come to a decision. They departed in growing numbers, leaving Artemas Ward to worry about what he would do if Gage decided to launch a counterstrike. When a group of five hundred Hampshiremen packed up and left—one of their captains told them, falsely, that Ward no longer needed their services—the general practically exploded. "My situation is such," Ward wrote angrily to the Congress on April 24, "that if I have not enlisting orders immediately I shall be left all alone. It is impossible to keep the men here, excepting something be done."[15]

Congress took Ward's admonition seriously, and that very day it printed and distributed the beating orders. The first independent American army was born. It would take the better part of two months before most of the twenty regiments were filled and officially commissioned, but on that same day, April 24, the prospective new captains were already stomping through the camps, orders in hand, cajoling their men to become full-time soldiers.

Even then it was hardly a smooth process. There were plenty of volunteers, and most of them were already armed and at least partially equipped and trained. Most were enthusiastic, propelled by a common hatred for the British, by a sense of adventure, and by all the things that make young men eager to go to war. But localism, pride, and ambition all got in the way. Prospective captains feuded viciously over potential recruits in their hometowns, tried to poach soldiers from each other's minutemen and militia companies, and jockeyed for appointments as staff officers in the newly constituted regiments. There was a "strugling with the offisers which shold be hiest in offist," noted Amos Farnsworth of Groton, a minuteman in Colonel William Prescott's regiment.[16]

Nor were the enlisted men all that cooperative. The newly raised companies did not always conform neatly to the previous militia and minuteman companies from which they were recruited. Sometimes incomplete companies had to be consolidated to bring them up to full strength; sometimes entire companies had to be shifted from one regiment to another for the same reason. It all made good administrative sense, but that did not satisfy men who were taken from familiar surroundings and thrust into unfamiliar ones. The provincial Yankees recoiled in horror at the notion that their officers might be appointed for them by Congress, without their say, or that they might have to fight alongside men from another village or—God forbid—another county. Many petitioned the Provincial Congress about the selection of their commanders. Some of the new recruits outright refused to serve under unfamiliar officers. How could they possibly trust the integrity, let alone the skill, of a man they didn't know from civilian life, a man who was not accountable to them for his rank?

The result was absolute chaos, in the camps and at Watertown. One company from Colonel John Nixon's regiment protested to Congress after it had been transferred to Colonel Thomas Gardner's regiment, "contrary to our inclination, and repugnant to the promise made us at our enlisting."[17] Recruits from Newbury demanded that Congress not attach them to Colonel Samuel Gerrish's regiment, "or any other where it would be disagreeable to them." The men felt that they had every right to make such demands. The Provincial Congress, after all, had promised them that "they shall have liberty to be under the command of such officers as may be appointed by the Committee of Safety . . . and the utmost care will be taken to make every soldier happy in being under good officers."[18] Rather than fighting the closed-minded clannishness of its constituents, the Congress tried to accommodate them. They understood the men's concerns and sympathized with them, and feared the dissolution of the army if those concerns were not addressed.

It might have been much easier to start fresh, to disband the militia organizations and create new regiments in their stead, but instead Massachusetts was stuck with having to transition from one institution to the other. "We are embarrassed in officering our Army by the Establishment of Minute Men," James Warren of the Provincial Congress groused to his good friend John Adams. "I wish it had never taken place."[19]

Regardless of their common antipathy for British rule, the men of Massachusetts did not see themselves as Americans, or even as citizens of Massachusetts, but as men of Salem, or Worcester, or Roxbury, or whatever hamlet they hailed from. Strangers—anyone who lived somewhere else, even if only a few miles away—were only slightly less suspect than the Redcoats themselves. It was a mindset that no one could break down, not Ward, not Warren, not the Provincial Congress. Only the experience of war and victory and hardship would eventually build the kinds of bonds that hold an army together.

* * *

Two

YOUNG SOLDIERS WHO HAD NEVER BEEN IN ACTION

*"Courage is a good thing; another ingredient, obedience,
is also absolutely necessary for your soldiers."*

ADJUTANT GENERAL EDWARD HARVEY TO

ROBERT PIGOT, JUNE 26, 1775[1]

*T*hree miles and a world away from Cambridge stood Province House, the largest public building in Boston. For nearly three generations, the narrow brick building fronting on Marlborough Street had dominated the skyline of the South End. Only church steeples, like that of the Old South Meetinghouse immediately opposite, outreached its height. Plain and spare but dignified, as most of Boston's public structures were, it stood out not only on account of its considerable size but also because of its muted ornamentation. Atop its cupola was a weathervane, a tall and gaunt Indian archer, squealing on its post whenever the winds spun it about. Above the main door hung a device carved in wood, brightly painted in blue and red and gleaming gold: the coat of arms of the King of England. For in

Province House the royal governor of Massachusetts Bay, the king's clear voice and strong right arm, tended to the colony's affairs.

And it was in Province House that Thomas Gage now stewed and fussed and fumed over the ugly turn—ugly but not unanticipated—that affairs had taken since he had given Colonel Smith his marching orders on the night of April 18. Gage, once welcome, now reviled . . . royal governor and military commander, charged with the daunting task of restoring Massachusetts to obedience to king and Parliament. Province House served as Gage's military headquarters, but the atmosphere in and around the place was nothing like the chaos and uncertainty that thickened the air at the Hastings House in Cambridge, where Ward and Warren and the Committee of Safety labored to cobble together some semblance of order. There were no swarms of armed men wandering to and fro before the windows of Province House. Gage could gaze through the windows into the street below and see nothing out of the ordinary—guard details marching in perfect order, sentries standing stiffly at attention, nattily dressed staff officers flitting officiously in and out of headquarters, all the comforting routine of a day in garrison. No chaos. Not among the soldiers, at any rate.

But there was still much to cloud General Gage's mind and torture his dreams: the failure of Smith's expedition, the troubling loss of British lives, the fearlessness of the "country people," the persistent and growing presence of rebel militia to the west. And the civilian population was in absolute turmoil. Colonists loyal to the king had been seeking refuge under the guns of the British garrison in Boston for some months now, propelled by the taunts and catcalls of their malcontent neighbors, intimidated by threats of physical harrassment, of tarring and feathering, fears that were entirely legitimate. In the immediate wake of Lexington and Concord the number of Tory refugees swelled. Entire families of them trudged dejectedly

General Thomas Gage. American colonials complained of his alleged cruelty; American historians like to think that he was weak, vacillating, and oblivious to American military strength. Yet the truth was that Gage treated the Bostonians with tact and restraint. General Gage fully understood how difficult it would be to make war on the Americans...but his superiors in Britain wouldn't listen until it was too late. Portrait by John Singleton Copley.

(YALE CENTER FOR BRITISH ART)

through the town gates, their pathetic few personal belongings piled up in oxcarts, having suffered the humiliation of being searched by the dirty grasping hands of the bands of militia who watched the roads. Some, those with means but little hope, were already finding berths on ships bound for England. And while the prominent Whigs, the true firebrands, had long since fled town for the relative safety offered by the countryside, there were still would-be rebels in Boston. Hundreds of them. Many of them wanted to leave town for the very same reasons that the Tories wanted to come in.

The rebel sympathizers remaining in Boston were a genuine danger, and Gage knew it. Long before the fatal day of Lexington, men and women in town brazenly smuggled weapons and other contraband through the gates to the mainland. One man—one unimaginably brave or foolish man—had attempted to sneak off with musket cartridges . . . 19,000 of them. When alert British sentries discovered the ammunition and confiscated it, the incensed smuggler had the temerity to demand that the cartridges be returned to him, as his personal property.[2]

For months, Gage had suspected it, but the events of April 19 and the days that followed brought it home to him with blinding intensity: although he commanded the king's troops in Boston, indeed in all of His Majesty's American possessions, in reality he controlled very, very little. Massachusetts was aflame with rebellion, and Boston, Gage's unruly charge, was teetering on the brink

Province House. This stately edifice, the residence of the royal governors of Massachusetts Bay, served as Gage's military headquarters before and during the Siege of Boston. Allowed to fall into decay during the nineteenth century, it was finally leveled in 1922.

(FROM *THE MEMORIAL HISTORY OF BOSTON, INCLUDING SUFFOLK COUNTY, MASSA-CHUSETTS, 1630-1880* [4 VOLS., BOSTON, 1880-81], 2:88)

of despondent anarchy. Everything Gage had worked so hard to preserve over the past few months was coming undone right before his eyes. And unless things changed, unless reinforcements arrived from Mother England and soon, Gage was all but powerless to stop the rebellion and uphold the law.

*A*t age fifty-five, Lieutenant General Thomas Gage could count himself a success. A veteran soldier and a conscientious administrator with a track record of proven competence, Gage was part of the power elite of Britain's vast colonial empire. He had been royal governor of Massachusetts for the better part of a year and commander-in-chief of His Majesty's forces in North America since the end of the French war more than a decade before. The second son of Thomas, Viscount Gage, scion of a prominent East Sussex family, young Thomas was born to privilege. He began his military career as an ensign in the British army in his late teens and gained extensive combat experience in Europe during the War of the Austrian Succession. Because of his family's high standing and his own knack for making valuable political connections, Gage rose quickly in rank: captain at age twenty-three, major at twenty-eight, lieutenant colonel at thirty-one. Clearly he was destined to figure prominently in the British high command.

In 1755, Gage's regiment—the 44th Foot—shipped out for America to fight the French and their Indian allies. The young colonel's experience in the French and Indian War was similar to that of his later friend George Washington: his battle record was not especially distinguished, but it gave him invaluable preparation for high command. He commanded the vanguard when General Edward Braddock led his ill-fated expedition into the Ohio country in the summer of 1755, an expedition that met with sheer disaster when it was ambushed at the Forks of the Monongahela by

French and Indian forces. Gage was wounded, and his regiment severely bloodied; worse yet, unfounded accusations of cowardice in the battle temporarily damaged his reputation. He accompanied General James Abercrombie in his equally disastrous frontal assault on the French at Fort Carillon three years later; he led an expeditionary force, attached to General Jeffrey Amherst's command, in Amherst's successful campaign down the St. Lawrence River in 1759. At the end of the war Gage held the post of military governor of Montréal, and shortly thereafter succeeded General Amherst as commander in North America.

Gage's time in America made him a mature and thoughtful commander. Serving alongside provincial troops, he came to understand and appreciate the American character, and developed a healthy respect for the American "way of war." He was a strong proponent of training British troops in "irregular" tactics. And he grew to like Americans. Indeed, he married one: in 1758 he tied the knot with Margaret Kemble Gage, the beautiful and cultured daughter of a well-to-do New Jersey family.

It would be wrong to argue that Gage was a brilliant military leader. But neither was he the unimaginative, passive, do-nothing general that historians like to portray, a man who never transcended bland mediocrity and was stymied by his inability to comprehend American resourcefulness and courage. And there is no denying that Gage was a well-intentioned, popular, and overall happy man. Of medium height and with a slightly pudgy build that hinted at the comfortable life he enjoyed in America, Gage had a pleasant oval face and kindly eyes. He did not have any visible personal failings: he rarely drank, rarely gambled, and was fiercely devoted to his American wife and their bevy of children. Few generals—few men—could boast of as many friends as Thomas Gage. "I have had a real affection for very few men," wrote Charles Lee, fellow officer and future enemy, in 1774. "You, sir, amongst these few . . . have ever held one of the foremost places. I respected your understanding, lik'd your manners and perfectly ador'd the qualities of your heart."[3] Generous, loyal, affable, honest to a fault . . . everyone who knew him loved him.

Yet in 1775, Thomas Gage was probably the most hated man in Massachusetts. He may have been the most hated man in America.

That wasn't his fault, for the most part. In 1774, with the ouster of Governor Thomas Hutchinson, the king made Gage royal governor of Massachusetts and charged him with the responsibility of upholding the Coercive Acts, including the closure of the port of Boston. Even the most ardent Whigs couldn't have asked for a more indulgent, more fair-minded governor. Not that he was a weakling; not that he sympathized with the disaffected colonials. But he had nothing against Americans. He was absolutely in love with New York City, where he had spent most of his tenure as military commander since 1763. New York, in turn, liked him well enough, and his pretty, gracious bride as well.

Everything changed when Gage moved to Boston in 1774. He had done so only when he had to, when he was picked to take the place of the hated Thomas Hutchinson as royal governor of the colony. Gage was in no way responsible for Parliament's decision to close the port of Boston, nor for any of the punitive measures collectively called the Coercive Acts, but he made a convenient target. He quickly became the object of Patriot wrath and indignation over British "tyranny." The general did his best to placate the unruly Bostonians. He kept his soldiers on a tight leash, swiftly punishing officers and men who gave any offense to citizens of the town, sometimes looking the other way when insolent colonials harassed or badgered or threatened his men.

The kid-gloves treatment did not appease the rebels. If anything, it only encouraged them to step up their rhetoric, to act more openly disrespectful of British authority. Patriot newspapers continued to rail against the hapless governor as if he were tyranny and oppression incarnate. Worse yet, Gage's own men felt as if their commander had abandoned them, sacrificing them so that he could ingratiate himself with the mob and keep the peace. Many of them resented him for it. "*Tommy* feels no affection for his Army," spat John Barker, a lieutenant in the 4th Regiment of Foot.[4]

Gage practiced appeasement not because he harbored any goodwill toward the colonials, as some of his soldiers thought. Nor—contra the arguments of historians over the years—was it because he was weak or passive or indecisive. Gage handled the discourteous Bostonians with tender care because he had no choice.

Overriding Gage's affection for Americans was his sense of duty to king and country. The law of Parliament was *the* law, and it was his duty to enforce it. Disobedience and lawlessness could not be tolerated, and in Gage's estimation the problems he saw in Massachusetts in 1774 were only going to get worse. By the time the Provincial Congress first convened in October 1774, Gage knew that a violent outburst was just around the corner. The only way to head it off, he repeatedly opined to his masters in London—the Earl of Dartmouth, the colonial secretary, and Viscount Barrington, secretary at war—would be through the swift and unsparing application of brute force. "I hope you will be firm, and send me a sufficient force to command the country . . . sending off large detachments to secure obedience thro' every part of it," he prodded Barrington in December 1774. "Affairs are at a crisis, and if you give way it is for ever."[5]

Gage knew that Americans could be daring, resourceful, and obdurate. But he was also painfully aware that the force he had at hand in Boston was not up to the task of coercion. He would need many, many more troops to force the rebellious Yankees to kneel: at least twenty thousand, plus perhaps some mercenaries hired from the German states. Only a massive show of force would do. "A large force will terrify, and engage many to join you," he wrote. "A middling one will encourage resistance, and gain no friends."[6]

His warnings appear eerily prophetic. But in London, the general's gloomy jeremiads elicited nothing but scorn. Surely the protests did not reflect the majority opinion, but only the tantrums of a few loudmouth troublemakers. Round them up and the crisis would be over. Gage had made few enemies in his long career, but in 1775 he had plenty of critics in England. It wasn't that Gage was incapable of silencing the Boston incendiaries, they argued; he was unwilling to. What America needed wasn't more troops but a hard hand and a cold nerve. Privately, influential men in the government back home doubted Gage's competence, dismissing him as timid and calling for his immediate recall and replacement.[7]

Gage did what he could with the resources that were available. He shifted individual companies and entire regiments from Canada and New York to Boston. By the time Colonel Smith's contingent marched on Lexington in April, there were around 3,500 men and officers stationed in Boston, armed and fit for duty. Such a force was too small to do what it was expected to do *before* the outbreak of hostilities. Gage could scarcely throw his weight around, hoping to frighten the rebels into quiet submission; he had no weight to throw. On occasion, he sent small expeditions out of Boston on brief marches through the countryside. It was a clever tactic: it kept the troops alert and fit, reminded the rebels of Britain's military might, and accustomed the locals to the sight of British troops on the march. Actual confrontation with armed militia, though, was a different matter altogether. If Gage didn't understand this before the nineteenth of April, he most assuredly did afterward.

Once shots had been fired, once blood had been shed, once the ring of campfires engulfed the western horizon at night . . . then it was clear that Gage's army could do nothing in its present state. It could not leave Boston unguarded. It could not go on the offensive.

The rebels, disciplined or not, outnumbered Gage's tiny army by a wide margin. And if Lexington and Concord had proven anything, it was that the entire population would rise up if the British dared to attempt another foray into the countryside.

But it was not numerical weakness alone that stayed Gage's hand, that restrained him from sending his army marching out of Boston, colors proudly snapping in the cool April breeze, to crush the rebels and put a quick end to the rebellion. Something else weighed heavily on the general's mind and on the minds of his lieutenants. There was no question that, man for man, the Redcoats were superior to their ill-equipped enemies. Yet Lexington and Concord revealed a disturbing truth: for all their training and organization and discipline, Gage's regulars were not battle-hardened veterans. They were, in fact, little more than raw troops.

*B*ritain had, in 1775, a middling sort of army. It was neither the best nor the worst, neither the largest nor the smallest, that Europe had to offer. Russia, Austria, Prussia, and France all maintained larger land forces. The British army could not rival the French for intellectual vitality, nor the Prussian for tactical proficiency. During the Seven Years' War, the British army—though it performed quite well—could not escape the long shadow cast by its Prussian allies and their legendary warrior-king, Frederick the Great.[8]

In the quality of its officers and enlisted men, the British army was typical of the period. Officers were drawn, as elsewhere, from the political and social elite, from the nobility and the landed gentry. Since the military life was a hard one—the prospects for advancement or wealth or even financial security were remote at best—it attracted only those who were unswervably bent on a military career. Pay was poor, especially so for junior officers, who were also expected to cover most of their expenses from their own pockets. Promotion was based less on ability than on political connections and cash. Officers purchased their commissions and their commands; sadly, the costs of attaining and holding rank were so high that talented but indigent officers were often compelled to quit the service just to avoid bankruptcy. And promotion was slow, doubly so in peacetime, for without battle deaths to create vacancies there were few opportunities for advancement. Many a good officer was stuck for life at the lowly rank of captain.

For all that, for all the frustration and insecurity that made up the daily life of an officer, British officers were by and large a competent lot, dedicated to their profession, their king, and the men they led. They knew their craft and practiced it dutifully. They were hardly the bumbling, condescending, effete buffoons that American myth has made them out to be.

The enlisted men were, likewise, pretty much the same as soldiers anywhere. If life was unpleasant and trying for the officers, it was positively hellish for the men. Service in the king's army was voluntary, and for life, but that didn't mean that recruits were eager to serve. The possibilities of death in battle or by disease were very real; the primitive state of military medicine practically guaranteed a shockingly high mortality rate. Rations were meager by modern standards, and not calculated to promote good health in the long term. And the pay was negligible—eight pence a day, a rate set by Parliament back in 1660. No soldier ever received that daily wage; innumerable deductions—for rations, for the baking of bread, for clothing, for equipment lost or damaged, even for time spent in the hospital—whittled down the ungenerous allotment to virtually nothing.[9] If there was anything left, most soldiers would quickly throw it away on strong drink if they could. Then there was the discipline, one of the true terrors of a soldier's life in the eighteenth century. Military justice prescribed liberal floggings for virtually all offenses. In all fairness, though, the typical Redcoat suffered no more—and probably less—than his counterparts in other European armies. Some British commanders made a point of curbing the excesses of brutal discipline practiced by their junior officers and NCOs. One of them was Thomas Gage: while at Boston, he routinely commuted death sentences for convicted deserters and urged his subordinates to show greater leniency.

Still, the life of a British soldier was a parade of horrors, and so it was a life that attracted no one. A soldier's life, it was said, was no better than a dog's, in comfort or in social prestige. Even common sailors in the fleet were accorded a much higher social status. Only the drunk, the desperate, or the gullible enlisted, men escaping the gallows or debtors' prison, men dimwitted or inebriated enough to accept a drink from a recruiter, paid for with the "king's shilling." Most soldiers came to regret the decision once made. Some of them did their best to escape service through desertion, even if thousands of miles away from home. Gage's army was plagued by desertion. Others sought to flee the army in a more desperate and final way. It was not uncommon for new recruits, shortly after boarding the miserable, tightly packed transports that would take them to America, to throw themselves overboard, preferring a lonely death by drowning to life in the ranks.

The British army was a decent little army despite its shortcomings, despite the fact that its men came from the lowest elements of society or that its officers had little incentive to excel. Above all, it had an inestimable advantage over its American enemies: it had a *system*. As a professional army, the Redcoats had a structure, an established procedure, a pace for doing just about everything. While Ward's army outside Boston still struggled to collect and distribute food, ammunition, and medical care, or to carry out such vital tasks as guard duty, the British already had these things settled. British soldiers, moreover, were accustomed by habit to obedience and deference. Not until it passed through the crucible of Valley Forge nearly three years later would the rebel army be able to boast of such essentials. The American fighting man was just beginning to make the transition from *fighter* to *soldier*; the Redcoat was a soldier, or very nearly one, before he set foot on American soil.

*T*homas Gage's force at Boston was nothing more and nothing less than the British army in microcosm. In April 1775, it consisted of ten infantry battalions, grouped informally into three brigades: the 4th, 23rd, and 47th Regiments of Foot in the First Brigade; the 5th, 38th, and 52nd Foot in the Second Brigade; and the 10th, 43rd, and 59th Foot, plus a few companies from the 18th and 65th Foot, in the Third Brigade. Another battalion, the 64th Foot, garrisoned the harbor fort of Castle William. Five companies of the 4th Battalion of the Royal Artillery rounded out the force. The Admiralty contributed to the land forces, too: a battalion of Marines landed at Boston at the end of 1774, commanded by Major John Pitcairn, the very same man who would confront Captain Parker's militia at Lexington in April. Technically, the Marines were part of the navy, but Gage grabbed them as soon as they debarked. Additional reinforcements were already on their way from England or Ireland to Boston, including more Marines and a regiment of light dragoons. They would arrive piecemeal in May and June, some of them debarking—seasick and thoroughly useless—only days before the battle of Bunker Hill.

The infantry was the backbone of Gage's army, and the basic tactical and administrative unit in the infantry was the regiment. A British infantry regiment contained one or two subunits called "battalions." Typically only one battalion of any given regiment served in America during the Revolution, and hence the terms "regiment" and "battalion" were used interchangeably. The regiments in Gage's command were nearly identical in structure: each contained eight companies of regular (or "line") infantry, plus two elite "flank" companies—one each of light infantry and grenadiers. The light infantry companies recruited smaller, more agile, more intelligent and enterprising soldiers, who were trained to fight both as conventional line infantry and as "irregular" troops maneuvering in open order. The grenadiers no longer carried the primitive hand grenades that had given them their name, but were usually the largest, most physically imposing soldiers in the regiment, employed frequently as shock or assault troops. Each company was supposed to include three commissioned officers, five sergeants and corporals, one drummer, and thirty-eight privates, but in active service companies were invariably smaller. A ten-company battalion at full strength numbered 477 officers and men.[10]

The typical Redcoat, we are told, was an experienced soldier, the veteran of many battles. Strict discipline had reduced him to slavish obedience to his unimaginative officers. He was thoroughly trained, at least in the tactics of "conventional" warfare, where European armies slugged it out in long, tightly packed lines on flat, featureless terrain, unloosing poorly aimed volleys at an enemy less than half a football field's distance away. Indeed, British officers actively discouraged their men from aiming their muskets—just the opposite of American citizen-soldiers, who were accomplished marksmen almost to a man. If the typical Redcoat was not an automaton, he was at the very least a stalwart for fighting in the conventional fashion, though the tactics of European linear warfare had no place in the rough terrain of North America. He was part of the "finest infantry in the world," and if he was unable to vanquish his American foes it was due to the ignorance and contemptuous indolence of his officers. For British commanders, it is said, knew nothing of fighting a war in the American wilderness, and consistently underestimated the military skills of the maverick Americans they fought.

It is a portrait that is hideously flawed on almost all counts. The British army was more familiar with wilderness warfare than any army in Europe. It had to be. The army had had to subdue the wild-eyed Jacobites in the glens and hills of the Scottish Highlands, and to struggle with the French and their native allies in the forests of North America. Through bitter and bloody experience, the British learned how to adapt their tactics to broken terrain and unconventional enemies who refused to fight in the way that European armies usually did. After decades of failure, British troops finally squelched the Highlanders under Bonnie Prince Charlie in their last great rising, the '45, all but massacring them on the field of Culloden in 1746. But it was in America, especially in the French and Indian War, that the British army showed its newfound flexibility to best advantage. The British succeeded not by completely doing away with conventional linear tactics, but by carefully and judiciously melding those tactics with more open formations, by training their soldiers to fight both in line-of-battle and as individuals.[11]

To be sure, there were mediocre generals who suffered crushing defeats because they stubbornly refused to tailor their tactics to the terrain or the enemy. The massacre of Braddock's command in 1755 stood as an object lesson to British commanders in North America. Even then, the wholesale slaughter of Braddock's mixed force of Regulars and provincial troops—a force that included the British officers Charles Lee and Horatio Gates, a rough-spoken uneducated Virginia frontiersman named Daniel Morgan, and an ambitious young George Washington, in addition to Thomas Gage—owed more to plain carelessness than to arrogance or hidebound tactics. Braddock had failed to take the appropriate precautions when marching through heavily forested country; French and Native American forces caught him wholly unawares, and Braddock fell—along with a frightfully high proportion of his command—in the bloody battle that followed.[12]

But for every Braddock, there were more capable British officers who understood that there was something to be learned, and taken to heart, from their time in North America. During the campaigns of the late 1750s and early '60s, the British would make heavy use of "ranger" units—American woodsmen who knew the backcountry and knew how to fight Indians. The ranger unit led by the famous Indian-fighter Robert Rogers was by far the best-known. Intelligent British commanders did not hesitate to make heavy use of the rangers for raids and for reconnaissance work; younger, more enterprising British officers eagerly volunteered to fight with Rogers despite the obvious hazards of ranger duty and the humbling prospect of serving under provincial officers. Pretty soon, the British army began to incorporate specialized light infantry units within the regular establishment. One of these units owed its origins to none other than Major Thomas Gage. Braddock's defeat made a great impression on Gage; conventional linear tactics, he believed, still had their place, but the British had to learn to fight in more open and flexible formations. The result was his proposal to create a specially trained light regiment. The men would be given shorter, lighter muskets and more practical uniforms, and would be trained in marksmanship and individual fighting skills. The army and the king readily agreed, and Gage spent part of 1757–58 raising this new regiment, the 80th Foot, known colloquially as "Gage's Chausseurs." The concept caught on quickly. By 1771, each British infantry regiment was directed to maintain one full company of hand-picked and intensively trained light infantry.[13]

By the time of the American Revolution, then, there were more than a few British commanders who understood Americans and were experienced in American warfare. Thomas Gage was one; William Howe, who would come to join Gage at Boston in May and would ultimately replace him as commander in North America, was another. The high command of the British army was anything but narrow-minded when it came to tactics. As much as it could be, it was prepared for war in America.

The rank-and-file of the army, though, was a different story.

Gage's army was a young army. There was a smattering of men who had seen long service, sergeants who had been in the line for a decade or more, but these were the exceptions. Most of the men in the ranks had been soldiers for no more than three or four years at the time of the Lexington fight. Britain had been at peace since 1763, and the British army had not fought a significant engagement since 1762. Some of the regiments in Gage's command had long histories and distinguished battle records—but that didn't mean that the soldiers of '75 had shared in that glory. The 23rd Foot (Royal Welch Fusiliers), for example, was famous for its role in the victory over the French at Minden in August 1759 . . . but that was nearly sixteen years before Lexington, and the men of the 23rd at Boston were not the same ones who had advanced against the French lines, bayonets leveled, at Minden. Few of Gage's junior officers, and very, very few of his enlisted men, had heard a shot fired in anger before April 19, 1775. They had not seen combat. They were not veterans. They were most assuredly *not* battle-hardened.[14]

But while they weren't veterans, they were reasonably well trained. Drill was an inescapable part of a British soldier's life. It had to be. Drill broke down individuality and suppressed independent thinking; it converted men into unthinking cogs in a military machine, obedient, responding instinctually to the commands of their officers. The movements taught in drill made it possible for armies to execute the complex maneuvers and changes of formation that were vital to success in battle. Drill was also necessary to inculcate what was known as "fire discipline." Infantrymen had to be trained to load and fire their muskets in unison, but—most important— they had to be taught to restrain themselves. Untrained soldiers, in the heat of battle, were likely to fire off their muskets when they first caught sight of the enemy, or when the musket balls whistled about their heads . . . and not when their officers ordered them to open fire. Well-trained troops, who had obedience beaten into them, would wait for their officers' commands.

The soldiers in Gage's army practiced small-unit drills and the "manual exercise"—the postures of the musket and the time-consuming procedure for loading and firing—almost daily. At Gage's urging, colonels were also supposed to drill their regiments each and every "fine day."[15] The duties of garrison life undoubtedly cut into the time allocated for drill, and drill for larger units—like brigades—was rare. Even so, Gage's Redcoats were infinitely better trained than Ward's troops laying siege to Boston.

One aspect of that training was truly remarkable, because it contradicts common assumptions about the British way of war. British soldiers were trained in marksmanship. In Europe, the idea was that aimed fire was a waste of time, and target practice a waste of both time and valuable ammunition. The smoothbore musket was simply too inaccurate beyond fifty yards to merit such attention; it was held, and massed volley fire directed against dense, slow-moving targets hardly required great skill with a firearm. Speed of fire, not accuracy, was the main objective of drill; aiming a musket, rather than merely pointing it in the general direction of the enemy, ate up valuable seconds. It was not a fallacious argument in the context of European linear warfare. But British officers serving during the French and Indian War came to the conclusion that the kind of open-formation battles that they experienced in North America required steady aim and the ability to hit individual human targets. Disciplined volley fire was still important, and nothing destroyed enemy morale faster than a crisp, well-timed volley delivered at point-blank range, a blast of lead and smoke and thunderous noise that felled entire ranks of men at one blow. Yet even here, training in marksmanship was a great asset, for it discouraged battle-nervous men from firing wildly into the air.

During the French and Indian War, savvy and progressive leaders like General James Wolfe encouraged their regimental commanders to subject their men to regular training in marksmanship, firing at targets with live ammunition. And Thomas Gage, as one of the leading proponents of light infantry tactics, required it of his army in Boston. As early as the fall of 1774, Gage ordered that all men practice "firing at marks," and that the new recruits receive especially intensive training. "The men [should] be taught to take good aim," Gage wrote in November 1774. The general became more insistent after the outbreak of hostilities in the spring of 1775. Target practice would now be a part of the soldiers' daily routine. "The Regiments will drill their Recruits and Drafts without a Days delay after receiving them," read his orders from June 14, " . . . and, teach them to fire Ball, proper Marksmen to teach them in taking Aim, and the position in which they ought to stand in firing, and to do this man by man before they are suffer'd to fire together."[16] Lieutenant Frederick Mackenzie of the Royal Welch Fusiliers described the usual method of marksmanship training in Gage's command:

> The regiments are frequently practiced at firing with ball at marks. Six rounds per man at each time is usually allotted for this practice. As our regiment is quartered on a wharf which projects into part of the harbor, and there is a very considerable range without any obstruction, we have fixed figures of men as large as life, made of thin boards, on small stages, which are anchored at a proper distance from the end of the wharf, at which the men fire. Objects afloat, which move up and down with the tide, are frequently pointed out for them to fire at, and premiums are sometimes given for the best shots, by which means some of our men have become excellent marksmen.

Target practice was nearly as important as learning the basic maneuvers of the platoon and the company. British officers did not discourage aimed fire in combat any more than they discouraged obedience to orders. Whether Americans wanted to accept it or not, the truth was that the typical enlisted man in Gage's army was probably as familiar, comfortable, and skilled with firearms as the average Massachusetts farmer was. Perhaps even more so.[17]

The advantages given by regular drill were not trifling ones. Still, as veteran officers recognized, nothing instilled discipline and self-confidence like combat experience. "It requires one campaign, at least, to make a good soldier," observed a lieutenant in the 23rd Foot.[18] And that was precisely what Gage's men lacked. General Gage himself was all too conscious of the fact. All of the officers were too, especially those who had been with Pitcairn, Smith, or Percy on the nineteenth of April. The battles that day left many officers in shock—not so much because of the intensity and ferocity of the American reaction, but because of the behavior of their own troops. Discipline had come undone; men refused to heed their officers' commands; soldiers became overexcited and panicky. After the exchange of musketry on Lexington Green, the Redcoats had lunged after Parker's retreating rebels despite their officers' attempts to restrain them. "The men were so wild," noted one lieutenant, "they could hear no orders." On the retreat from Concord the men were equally "wild and irregular." The men failed to show any of the "coolness and steadiness" of veteran troops because they were "young soldiers who had never been in action." There was no reason to doubt the Redcoats' courage.[19] There was every reason to doubt their worth in battle.

Gage chided his command shortly after the battles. They showed "much courage and spirit," he conceded, but also "great inattention and neglect to the commands of their officers (which, if they had observed, fewer of them would have been hurt)." He expected that "on any further occasion . . . they will behave with more discipline and in a more soldierlike manner." But secretly he—and his officers—were worried, and with good reason. How would the soldiers do in a stand-up fight?[20]

*T*he British had one resource at hand that the rebels couldn't even hope to match: sea power. Britain may not have had the largest or most effective army in the world, but it could definitely claim a superior navy, even if it had fallen victim to more than a decade of peacetime neglect. The admiralty had stepped up its naval presence in New England waters when Parliament closed the port of Boston in 1774. That summer, Samuel Graves, Vice Admiral of the Blue, arrived in Boston to take over his new appointment as naval commander on the North American station.

Graves was sixty-one years old when he came to Boston, a veteran naval officer with a solid if not especially stellar career behind him. He had captained two different ships-of-the-line during the late war with France, and though advancement was as slow for naval officers in peacetime as it was for their comrades in the army, Graves moved ahead to a vice admiral's rank in 1770. Political influence, more than talent, propelled him forward: the Earl of Sandwich, First Lord of the Admiralty, was a close friend.

Samuel Graves was not well liked when he was alive. Modern historians almost revile him, and his poor reputation is largely deserved. Graves was corrupt, openly giving preferment to his four nephews in the service—but then nepotism was a common feature of life in the fleet, and in this regard Graves was merely a creature of his time and place. He was an unpleasant man, peevish and prickly, given to choleric fits of sputtering, foul-mouthed wrath. Officers who served under Graves found little to admire in the man. When General Gage made it clear to him that Pitcairn's Marines would serve on land under army command, the admiral was incensed, and took out his anger on his subordinate Pitcairn. In March 1775, Graves ordered the crusty major to embark fifty Marines aboard the ship-of-the-line *Asia*; when Pitcairn coolly refused, pointing out that he was "absolutely" under Gage's command, Graves exploded. "The Admiral distresses me much," Pitcairn reported to Lord Sandwich. "It is needless for me to tell your Lordship how he talked to me and what he said."[21]

There is little positive to say about Samuel Graves. He was competent, though barely so, and by no means an inspiring or imaginative leader. But if he failed to contribute in a meaningful way to British military operations at Boston, it had little to do with his faults and flaws. It had everything to do with the nearly impossible task that he had been handed, and with the inadequate resources at his disposal.

When Graves arrived in Boston in late June 1774 aboard the fifty-gun fourth-rater HMS *Preston*, he found waiting for him there four sloops-of-war—*Mercury, Tartar, Savage,* and *Lively*—lightly armed, with between eight and twenty-four guns on board each. There were also three small schooners and a handful of smaller craft. Boston was the headquarters, or "rendezvous," for the North American squadron, and because of the port closure it was the focus of Graves's attention. But Graves also had to patrol the entire Atlantic seaboard, from Halifax to the tip of Florida. He had only the vessels stationed at Boston, plus three more sloops and a dozen or so smaller vessels. It wasn't much to work with. And since Boston was not the only port where disloyal activities threatened British interests, there was simply no way that Graves could do what he was supposed to do with such a thin cordon of sail.

Boston was a navigator's nightmare, a complicated maze of shoals, islands, and twisting channels. The labyrinth reconfigured itself daily with each ebb tide, which revealed new islands and more treacherous shallows, and reduced deep-water channels into waist-deep creeks. A moment's negligence could—as Graves would shortly discover—result in disaster. It was difficult enough to conduct routine patrols around Boston; keeping an eye on the entire expanse of the harbor, monitoring all maritime traffic, apprehending smugglers . . . such things were well nigh impossible.

The Admiralty finally got around to reinforcing Graves's sorry little squadron toward the end of 1774, after a great deal of nagging from Graves. Three ships-of-the-line—*Asia* (64 guns), *Boyne* (70 guns), and *Somerset* (64 guns)—sailed into Boston Harbor in the very last days of December. More than just a welcome addition to the squadron, the ships were meant to overawe the colonials. At this they were successful. Well into the siege, long after the rebels had figured out that the Redcoats were not invincible, the big warships still inspired respect. Their long, sleek black sides and their three decks' worth of heavy iron cannon hinted at the unfathomable power of the British Empire. Yet the massive third-raters like *Asia* and *Boyne* were of limited practical use. The big ships drew too much water to move freely through the harbor. They were too big and slow to pursue smugglers or privateers, and to use them as waterborne artillery emplacements against rebel positions on land required painfully careful maneuvering. In the end, sea power counted very little for the British in Boston. It guaranteed only that the garrison would not starve.

What the British needed more than hulking men-of-war was small craft—whaleboats, skiffs, cutters—that could carry men and cannon through the shallows and up the rivers. Since Boston Neck provided the only land route to the mainland, it would have been of immense advantage to the British if they could conduct amphibious operations. Thomas Gage understood this, and he repeatedly pestered the government back home to send him boats. To no avail. As in everything else, the armchair strategists in London hobbled

Gage. They were too contemptuous of Americans to hear his entreaties, and too cheap to give Gage the tools he needed.[22]

*I*t is easy to fault Thomas Gage as a strategist. He quailed indecisively before the bugbear of American resistance, keeping his troops inactive in Boston while he—in the words of one recent historian—"twiddled his thumbs." Gage inexplicably rejected any plan to attack the rebel lairs at Cambridge and Roxbury, refused to seize Dorchester Heights or Bunker Hill . . . studiously avoided any course of action, in fact, that might have secured a quick victory or at the very least a better chance of rendering Boston impregnable. We are told that Gage fundamentally misunderstood Americans and simply couldn't comprehend American pluck or resourcefulness or courage. We are also told, ironically, that Gage so feared Ward's pathetic army—and the possibility of another rising like the one at Concord—that he was paralyzed into sitting tight in Boston and waiting passively for something to happen.

But the plain truth is that Gage had an army that was too small to defend Boston and attack the rebel camps simultaneously, too raw to be trusted in an open battle against superior numbers. He had, under Graves's command, warships that were imposing but of limited use in the close confines of Boston Harbor. And without small boats, Gage did not even have the means to fight an amphibious or riverine war, something that would come to haunt him in the scorching-hot days of mid-June. He did not have the ability to achieve surprise: rebel spies lurked everywhere, and everything that happened in Boston was known in Cambridge within hours. Some even falsely suspected Margaret Kemble Gage, the general's American wife, of passing secrets to the Americans via Joseph Warren. Gage had spies of his own—one of them was very high-placed, the first true American traitor—but their secret dispatches to the general only reinforced what he already knew: that the rebels were disorganized but strong in numbers.

Gage's strategic options were limited. He could, perhaps, have launched a massive strike against either Roxbury or Cambridge or both simultaneously, destroying half or all of the rebel army in one crushing blow. But with fewer than four thousand men at his command—roughly equal to the aggregate rebel strength at either of the two points at any given time—he could hardly afford to send a very large force on the offensive, not if he kept back enough men to defend Boston and The Neck. And if the minutemen and the militia came out—for there was no reason to believe that they would not materialize again—then the result was likely to be the same as before: they would swarm all over his troops, fighting for every hedgerow and barn and fence and copse, melting away, then reforming, driving his flustered troops into a fatal mixture of fury and confusion. No, Gage knew better than to tempt fate again. Far from not comprehending Americans, he was instead so well acquainted with the rebels that he knew how easily they could turn a spirited offensive into a bloody and humiliating defeat.

More intriguing is the possibility that Gage might have done something to forestall a true siege, to render ineffectual all of Massachusetts's bumbling if earnest efforts to catch the British in a trap. And the keys to a truly successful siege were those heights, the hills by Dorchester and Charlestown. The rebels had no heavy artillery yet, hardly any artillery at all. But it would only be a matter of time before they did, and if they held onto Dorchester and Charlestown . . . the combination of big guns and those hills would likely be fatal for Gage. He would have to surrender or evacuate, and though Gage would have preferred to have removed his force to more-defensible New York City, he was not going to be bullied about by these ruffians. He had to stay put—but if he could keep the rebels away from Dorchester and Charlestown, then they wouldn't have a prayer of being able to intimidate the British. The Americans would be vulnerable, the siege effectively lifted. Gage could take his time, waiting leisurely for reinforcements, and *then* go after the rebels—if they hadn't melted back into the countryside again.

Gage *could* have done this. On the evening of April 19, as the battered soldiers of Smith's and Percy's commands dug in on Bunker Hill, Gage's army commanded the entire Charlestown peninsula. The rebels wouldn't dare attack them there, and in a day or two Gage could have moved artillery to the summit and the position would have been just about impregnable. Admiral Graves thought it a worthy stratagem. Graves, like Gage a man with faults but overall more enterprising and clever than historians like to admit, proposed a tantalizing plan to Gage on the night of the nineteenth. Gage should burn Charlestown and Roxbury, denying them to the rebels, strengthen the presence on Bunker Hill, and send another force down Boston Neck to take possession of Dorchester Heights. It would have been a sensible plan—if it weren't for the inconvenient fact that Gage had only 3,500 or so men. Even if he completely denuded Boston of soldiers and marines, dividing his forces evenly between Dorchester and Charlestown, the long-term prospects were disturbing. The rebels could mass on either strongpoint. They could swarm the Redcoats if Gage ventured to seize Dorchester. Gage could not maintain much more than a thousand men at each point. The rebels could muster far more.[23]

So Gage nixed Graves's plan, and justly so. He could not take the offensive without risking a humiliating and perhaps catastrophic defeat; he could not take possession of the heights at Dorchester and Charlestown and be confident that his positions there would hold; he could not risk further enraging the locals by setting Charlestown and Roxbury ablaze. So on April 20, Gage ordered his troops withdrawn from Charlestown. The men retreated by boat, rowing under the vigilant guns of HMS *Somerset*, scurrying for the safety of Boston itself. And there they would stay, not venturing outside of town for eight long weeks.

The Americans were in no condition to storm the town, and they never would be, even at the end of the siege in the spring of 1776. They had the numbers, perhaps, but lacked the ammunition for any kind of prolonged engagement, though Gage was not fully aware of that. For days after Lexington and Concord, rumors flew through Boston that a rebel assault was in the offing. The rumors were preposterous but convincing, so Gage made ready. By his order, all officers were to move out of their billets in private homes and into the barracks with their men, so that each regiment could respond quickly to an alarm. The general began to move the troops out of their barracks by the end of April. The canvas cities reappeared, on Boston Common, atop Beacon Hill and Mount Whoredom, on the Common and on Fort Hill.[24] Being outside was considered to be healthier for the men than remaining in the stuffy, smoke-filled barracks. And as old soldiers agreed, life in the barracks made soldiers shiftless and ill-behaved. A tented army was more responsive when it counted: "it is impossible to have troops altogether so alert in quarters as in tents."[25]

In the meantime the British dug in. The seaward edge of town was already adequately protected by the North and South Batteries. But Gage had no reason to fear an attack from that quarter; the landward defenses were the concern, and before 1775 those defenses were sparse. Since the beginning of the century, brick-and-stone walls with cannon embrasures flanked the town gates on Boston Neck. Gage began to beef these up in the autumn of 1774. The old fortifications at the gates received a mantle of timber and earth, built up until the walls were twelve feet thick, and armed with twelve cannon. A wooden blockhouse was transported with great care from the old fort on Governor's Island and reassembled forty rods—220 yards—in front of the rebuilt breastworks, in the direction of Roxbury.* Another fifty rods toward Roxbury, Gage and his engineer, John Montresor, laid out two forbidding earthen breastworks, eight feet high and twelve thick, surmounted by ten iron cannon. In front of these last works, toiling Redcoats dug a deep fosse, or moat, which filled up at high tide and effectively severed Boston Neck, temporarily isolating the town from the mainland.[26]

The pace of construction picked up dramatically after Lexington and Concord. More guns, and more forbidding walls, appeared on the Neck. *Abatis*—sharpened wooden stakes protruding diagonally from the ground, their points facing toward the enemy—and *chevaux de frise* (sharpened stakes held together in rows) fronted the earthworks and blocked the road leading to them. The works on the Neck continued to grow over the succeeding months, but even in May they presented an all-but-impenetrable barrier to an American attack by land, and the town of Roxbury was now well within range of the heavy cannon in the forts. British soldiers, who thought of these fortifications as the focal point of the siege, referred to them casually as "the Lines." Gun batteries and small arrowhead-shaped forts called *flèches* popped up almost overnight alongside the wharves and on the vulnerable landward side of town, where the Charles flowed past the swampy western perimeter of the Common. More substantial forts arose atop Beacon Hill and at Barton's Point northwest of town. The digging went on day after day, and it was backbreaking work. George Harris, captain of the grenadier company of the 5th Foot, was "as often taking the spade as telling others where to employ it" while he coaxed his sweating grenadiers to keep up the exhausting pace.[27]

The fort that attracted the most attention was Admiral Graves's doing. Fearing that *Somerset*, almost immobile at its watch post in the Charlestown ferryway, might be easy prey for enterprising

---

* One rod equals 5.5 yards, or 16.5 feet.

saboteurs, the admiral obtained General Gage's permission to construct a special battery on the summit of Copp's Hill in northeastern Boston, directly across from Charlestown. Within a couple of days, Graves's marines and brawny sailors had dug a formidable earthwork, and a well-armed one at that: at Graves's command, sailors aboard *Boyne* and *Preston* had dismounted two huge twenty-four pounder cannon from each of the two ships. The four huge cannon tubes were manhandled from the decks of the two men-of-war into waiting barges, then rowed to town, dragged up Copp's, put on carriages, and mounted in battery again. It was a herculean effort, and soldiers in the British garrison for some reason found it endlessly amusing, laughing at what they dubbed in mock reverence "The Admiral's Battery."[28]

Impeding the military preparations around town were the civilians. For Gage, dealing with Bostonians before April 19 had been tricky enough; now that hostilities had erupted, much more was at stake. Patriots still in Boston wanted to get out, and to take their families and belongings with them; Loyalists outside wanted to get in, and those already in Boston hoped to be able to fetch some of their possessions from their former homes. It promised to be a long standoff, and there was no telling when—or *if*—they would be able to get to their homes again. But without some sort of control there was no telling what the Patriots in town would try, or how the Patriots outside hoped to manipulate the confusion. Overall, Gage and his enemies in the Provincial Congress, Joseph Warren in particular, behaved like gentlemen, seeing no reason to make things difficult for noncombatants regardless of their political sympathies. Warren offered safe conduct to British surgeons so that they could treat wounded Redcoats in rebel captivity; Gage allowed wagons and teamsters into Boston so that they could move Patriots out, though he tried to set limits on the traffic. Mostly, Gage worried about the prospect of an insurrection inside the town, so he entered into negotiations with the selectmen of Boston: they wanted freer movement in or out of town; the general wanted the citizens disarmed and made harmless. A week after Lexington and Concord, the two parties came to a compromise. All who wanted to leave Boston could do so, with all their personal effects, and those who stayed behind promised to behave if the American army were to attack the town. Most important, Gage got the people of Boston to surrender their weapons—1,778 muskets, 634 pistols, 973 bayonets, and 38 blunderbusses—to the selectmen of the town; they were deposited securely under lock and key at Faneuil Hall in one day.[29]

Even disarmed, Boston civilians frightened their British occupiers. The prospect of a rebel attack—by boat at the thinly defended western shore along the Common, or from Roxbury toward the Lines—kept the Redcoats on their toes, no matter how improbable it would have appeared from Ward's headquarters. "The panic of our chiefs," wrote Gage's adjutant, "has got amongst the troops. . . . Every idle report . . . is magnified to such a degree that the rebels are seen in the air carrying cannon and mortars on their shoulders."[30] But the febrile rumors of an attack from within were the stuff of nightmares. Patriot operatives in Boston, it was said, intended to sound a false alarm in the dark of night; as the officers scrambled from their private billets to join the men in their barracks, rebels would pounce from the shadows and quietly slit the throats of the unsuspecting officers. It was a truly insidious plan, to render the British leaderless and therefore harmless. Insidious, and ridiculous, too, but after Lexington and Concord the Redcoat officers were not about to take American resourcefulness for granted.[31]

So there wasn't much that Thomas Gage could do. Boston was his stronghold, but it had also become his trap. He didn't have the strength to break out. The town was surrounded by water, and the harbor was full of powerful British warships, but command of the sea meant little at the moment. The larger men-of-war could not work in close to the shore. Without many boats or smaller watercraft an amphibious assault would be problematic, and a quick killing lunge up the Mystic toward Cambridge was out of the question. Admiral Graves did have an aggressive side, as his plans for Charlestown and Roxbury demonstrated, but given the circumstances he resigned himself to playing an almost passive role in the defense of Boston.

Gage would pay for his inactivity, whether it was justified or not. It would sour his reputation in England, bring his career to an abrupt and ignominious halt, and ruin his legacy. And the confinement in Boston acted like a poison on the garrison. Officers and men who had arrived in Boston the previous year found it pleasant enough, a pretty town where the houses had generous yards and gardens. Boston was provincial and not very exciting—Lieutenant Barker of the 4th Foot pronounced it "amazingly dull"—but there was something very charming about it, about the tidy port surrounded by pristine, unspoiled natural beauty. "I have now before me one of the finest prospects your warm imagination can picture," glowed Captain Harris of the 5th Foot, waxing poetic as he gazed toward Roxbury from his camp on Boston Common. "My tent-door, about twenty yards from a piece of water, nearly a mile broad, with the country beyond most beautifully tumbled about in hills and valleys, rocks and woods, interspersed with straggling villages, with here and there a spire peeping over the trees, and the country of the most charming green that delighted eye ever gazed on."[32] Cultural refinements were lacking, but for the not so high-minded more earthly diversions abounded. "No such thing as a play house, they were too puritanical a set to admit of such lewd Diversions," noted Lieutenant Williams of the 23rd Foot, adding slyly, "Tho' ther's perhaps no town of its size cou'd turn out more whores than this cou'd. They have left us an ample sample of them."[33]

The siege changed much of that. The supply of produce and meat from the countryside dried up as trade between town and hinterland shut down. A few enterprising soldiers tended private vegetable gardens in their encampments; Captain Harris beamed proudly about the spinach, radishes, turnips, and cucumbers he grew in his little plot in the Common. "Such salads!" he exclaimed in a letter only a few days before Bunker Hill.[34] But for the most part the men, and the officers, too, were reduced to eating ordinary rations: salt beef and pork, hard bread, and dried peas. As rebel privateers preyed on shipping entering New England waters, there was some concern that even these sorry provisions might become scarce before too long. Gage kept a close watch on the army's larder, and strictly enforced the rationing of food to the hundreds of soldiers' wives and other women who accompanied the army as laundresses or cooks. Though the British army in Boston was never really in any danger of starving, officers complained bitterly about the reduced quantities and poorer fare.

Gage's men also found that they didn't much like the locals. Technically, Bostonians were Englishmen, but to the Britons and Irishmen in the garrison, the character of the colonials left much to be desired. "A Bostonian," griped young Lord Rawdon, a lieutenant in the 5th Foot, "is perhaps the only man who could ever do all manner of mischief before your face and then deny it to you; they are the only people, probably, who from a habit of falsehood will lie though they are sure not to do themselves any good by it."[35]

The Redcoats were, however, starved for action, any kind of action, as they suffered the claustrophobia of a city under siege. Gage could not march the troops out into the countryside as he had done before the siege began. There was no lack of work to be done in town—there was constant drilling, constant digging of fortifications, a never-ending cycle of routine camp duties. Being forever confined to town, though, with no chance of getting out anytime soon . . . that was a grim prospect, more so because of the humiliation of Lexington and Concord. The men itched for action, for a chance to redeem their tainted reputation, to show themselves and their officers and their enemies that they were indeed soldiers. And at the same time the Redcoats were unsure of themselves, as their officers were of them.

Low morale was the predictable result. It showed in all sorts of ways. Fights broke out more than usual, even between gentleman officers. And drinking—a bane of all eighteenth-century armies—got worse. Gage's army was an unhappy army, eager to fight and skittish at the same time. Yet there was a glimmer of hope. By the end of April, every soldier in Boston, from the lowliest private to the officers who flitted in and out of Province House, knew that help was on the way. More troops, even some cavalry, were en route from home and were expected daily. And with them sailed three generals, sent by Parliament to goad Gage into action.

*A*cross the Charles, largely out of Thomas Gage's sight but never far from his mind, a very different sort of army was being born. General Gage fretted over an army that was frustrated, bored, and lacking in self-confidence. General Ward was drowning in problems that made Gage's troubles look like minor inconveniences by comparison.

Three

* * *

THE GRAND
AMERICAN ARMY

As April came to an end, so, too, did the long stretch of unseasonably clear skies and warm days in eastern Massachusetts. In the first week of May the storm clouds began to roll in. The skies opened, and several days of steady downpours turned the dusty roads in and around Cambridge into thick, clingy muck. The Common and the other campsites in town, already befouled by the presence of so many men and the almost complete absence of well-dug latrines, became so fetid that the stench was unbearable. The rain drove down the dust, which had risen in great choking clouds every time a horse or an ox-drawn wagon passed through the camps, but that was a mixed blessing. The sour reek of sweat on filthy bodies mingled with the odors of sodden wool, decaying offal from butchered livestock, horse manure, human waste, and woodsmoke—the thick, acrid kind that comes from burning green wood—and the heavy damp air served only to hold the offensive smells close to the ground, to concentrate them.

Thanks to the dedicated if clumsy labors of the Provincial Congress and the Committee of Safety, the army at Cambridge and Roxbury had come a long way since the Glorious Nineteenth. Recruitment for the eight-months' army was well underway; men in the thousands responded to the beating drums of the recruiting officers and "listed" in the newly formed regiments. Nearly all of those who decided to enlist would do so by the second week of May. But on the surface, it appeared as if nothing had changed since the day after Lexington and Concord. If anything, the chaos in the camps only worsened in the last days of April. Some of the militia and minutemen had balked at the notion of a long-term enlistment, yet felt it was their duty to stay on as long as they might be needed. They were the exceptions. Most of the men who opted not to enlist left the camps wholesale and without ceremony, drifting home to tend to tasks left undone since the Lexington alarm. Often they did not even take the trouble to inform their commanding officers what they were about. The Provincial Congress did what it could to fix the problem, pleading with the towns to send substitutes to fill the gaps in the ranks, begging the militia to hang on until the substitutes arrived. Many men complied, but not enough. More than 3,700 Connecticut men marched for Boston before April 26; fully two-thirds of them returned home within ten days.[1] At Roxbury, General Thomas had approximately six thousand men under his command on the morning of April 24—but nine days later, on May 3, he could account for 2,500 at most. General Ward understood the absolute necessity of keeping Roxbury safe—since it lay closest to the British lines, it stood to reason that it was the target most likely to be attacked first—and he sent Thomas all the reinforcements he could spare. By the second week of May he could not transfer any more troops from Cambridge to Roxbury. His own force, he noted sadly, was dangerously thin.[2]

Artemas Ward's army was hemorrhaging men.

The constant and casual departure of militia and minutemen took its toll on discipline. "The army . . . is in such a shifting, fluctuating state," wrote congressional delegate James Warren (no relation to the good doctor) in early May, "as not to be capable of a perfect regulation. They are continually coming and going."[3] Regiments drilled or sat idle, depending on the whim of their officers, who had little incentive to be dutiful. The process of the beating orders ensured this. Potential recruits, naturally, wanted to serve under officers they knew and liked, and nothing killed an officer's popularity faster than a reputation as a martinet. Hence company commanders hesitated to enforce the rules, to act like real officers, for fear of alienating the men under their command. Men did not respect, much less fear, their officers; unguided and unwatched, they meandered about the camps as they pleased, not feeling obligated to remain with their units if there was no fighting to be done at the moment.

There was nothing to be done, in fact, but sit and wait for Gage to act, and so the men fell victim to all the ills that usually beset an untrained and unsupervised army. Rum flowed freely from the very first day—"we had as much Liquor as we wanted," a private in Colonel Greaton's minuteman regiment recorded, laconically, of his unit's arrival in Roxbury on April 20.[4] Brawls and vandalism were the predictable results. No one made a concerted effort to build fortifications, at least not at first. Guard details were deployed haphazardly or not at all. Little if anything was done to make the camps secure against a British attack. Gage, it was commonly believed, could attack anytime he pleased . . . and most of the men believed that such an attack was bound to happen sooner or later, probably sooner.

In the camps, the prevailing order was disorder, and if any one thing reflected that condition it was the disturbing sound of gunfire. Audible above the raucous thrumming of the camps, individual musket shots rang out at all hours, day or night. Not from any skirmish, not from target practice, not from exchanges of potshots between nervous sentries. The shots came instead from within the camps. Men cleaned their muskets without checking first to see if they were loaded. Some used the flintlock firing mechanisms as convenient (if potentially lethal) fire-starters. Others simply fired their muskets into the air for the pure sophomoric thrill of it. It was an unconscionable waste of powder and ball in an army that could spare very little of either, and of course it was dangerous. Men died from gunshot wounds inflicted by accident or through carelessness. On April 28, when Greaton's regiment paraded and drilled on Roxbury Common, eighteen-year-old Abiel Petty of Walpole accidentally discharged his musket. The ball hit his twenty-two-year-old neighbor, Asa Cheney, wounding him in the left side and the right wrist. The wound was mortal; Cheney died two days later. If the colonials were familiar and comfortable with firearms, they didn't show it. Military life had transformed farmers and family men into irresponsible children.[5]

The army—"if that mass of confusion may be called an Army," Gage's American informant Benjamin Thompson dryly observed—had no structure. Nor did it have a support system. If the army were to be kept in the field indefinitely, then it would have to be fed, housed, and cared for indefinitely, too. Food, clothing, shelter, weapons, ammunition . . . all were needed, needed *now*, and all required some organized means of distribution. There would have to be medical care, too, for contagion stalked the camps. The men had little notion of public sanitation, and their habits of personal hygiene were highly impeachable. Days passed after the Lexington alarm before anyone took it in their head to build "necessary houses" or dig "sinks"—pit latrines. In the interim—and even afterward—men urinated and defecated wherever the mood struck them, sometimes right outside their tents, sometimes in close proximity to supplies of fresh water. Garbage and stinking offal from slaughtered animals piled up all around the camps, but especially at Cambridge. It would be only a matter of time before various and sundry "camp fevers" and smallpox—the bane of eighteenth-century armies—showed themselves in such pestilent conditions. Yet there were no arrangements to house or quarantine the sick, no protocol to force the men to keep their encampments, or themselves, clean.

Everyone recognized these problems. They were inescapable. The clamor of the camps was perpetually deafening, and the noisome stench arising from the army's shantytown hung like a poisonous curtain over Cambridge, wafting through the open windows of the Hastings House, where the Committee of Safety met daily. But recognizing the symptoms of a critically disorganized army and doing something to correct them were two different things altogether. None of those in charge had ever tackled anything remotely like this before.

That was precisely what made the achievement of Ward, Warren, and the others so remarkable. The creation of the New England army in the spring of 1775—the first truly independent army in American history—ranks among the most important events of the Revolution, unsung but equal in significance to the miracle of the Valley Forge winter nearly three years later. At Valley Forge, George Washington and the Baron de Steuben transformed battle-hardened but demoralized veterans into professional soldiers, capable of facing the British on equal terms. At Cambridge and Roxbury in 1775, though, the revolutionary leadership of Massachusetts took a mob of willful individuals with no military experience, no notion of hierarchy, and made them into a reasonable facsimile of an army. A prosaic achievement, perhaps, but more fundamental than that of Valley Forge. The end result, the army that gave George Washington a lukewarm greeting when he took command at Cambridge that July, was far from perfect. In all candor, it was still a pathetic little army in most regards. But that army, which formed the heart of the newborn Continental Army, had weathered two months of duty in the lines, had fought a major pitched battle, and had remained intact through it all. Were it not for the combined efforts of Ward, Warren, and company, General Washington would have found no army to command, and the Cause would have died at Boston that summer.

*C*hanging the attitude and the demeanor of the soldiery was by far the most challenging task. But the rebel leaders were exceptionally well suited to working with the raw material at hand: the stubborn and fiercely independent Yankee farmer or tradesman. And here Artemas Ward made his greatest contribution to the Cause. No one, except perhaps for his devoted descendents who tried to make him an American hero, would ever accuse General Ward of great military talent or charismatic leadership. He did not have the flamboyance of a born soldier, or even the kind of personal eccentricities that might endear him to those who followed him. Ward was about as plain a leader as the Revolution would produce.

Forty-seven years old at the time of Lexington and Concord, Artemas Ward was a solid, honest man who had dedicated his life to public service. He matriculated at Harvard College, graduating there in 1748, and went on to a brief career as a schoolteacher in the town of Groton. In Groton he met Sarah Trowbridge, the daughter of a local preacher. It was a perfect match; Sarah, like her husband, was grave and serious, with nothing frivolous about her. The two married, and then moved to Artemas's hometown of Shrewsbury in Worcester County to raise a family. Artemas opened a general store in Shrewsbury, and the family flourished: Sarah gave birth to five sons and three daughters in the course of twelve years.

The Ward general store had not been open for very long when Artemas was first drawn into public service. His honesty and unquestionable integrity drew favorable attention, even at a relatively tender age. In 1751, not yet twenty-four, Ward received an appointment as tax assessor for Worcester County. The following year he became justice of the peace, and in very short order he was elected to the General Court, the legislature of colonial Massachusetts. He was briefly sidetracked by an uneventful military career. Like his father before him, he held a commission in the Massachusetts militia; with the outbreak of the French and Indian War, he found himself saddled with big responsibilities—first, as major of the 3rd Militia Regiment, then as colonel commanding the very same regiment. He saw combat once: in 1758, his regiment took part in General Abercrombie's disastrous frontal assault on the French lines at Fort Carillon. His combat experience was trivial, but his time in the provincial ranks taught Ward a great deal about military organization and administration.

It was during the Carillon campaign that Ward's health first began to deteriorate—namely, his first experience with bladder stones, which forced his retirement from the 3rd Regiment. But his health problems did not deter him from returning to public life. Along with Sam Adams and James Otis, Ward was one of the most vocal opponents of British commercial policies in the late 1760s, so much so that he was stripped of his militia rank by the royal governor. He was in the thick of things during the meetings of the Provincial Congress, too. Though in great pain from his affliction, he served without complaint on innumerable committees and subcommittees. In the Provincial Congress he was almost revered. When the Congress first nominated three generals to lead the militia, Ward's name was second on the list. His superior, sixty-seven-year-old Jedediah Preble, ultimately declined to serve on account of his advanced age, so Ward had command by default. He assumed the mantle of leadership at Cambridge on April 20 not because of ambition or a drive for power; he did so because it was his duty. A full month would pass before the Provincial Congress granted Ward the official title of commander-in-chief, but as soon as Ward set foot in Cambridge, the Provincial Congress—and everyone connected with the army, for that matter—tacitly assumed that the general would perform that role.

And Ward—pale, portly, quiet, ill—was perfect for the job. By modern standards he appears almost comically straight-laced. As an undergraduate at Harvard, he had once led a crusade to eliminate cursing on campus; as a justice of the peace, he was notorious for his intolerance of foul language. In his twilight years, he could always be seen patrolling the streets of Shrewsbury on Sunday afternoons, walking stick in hand, intent upon apprehending any soul brazen enough to profane the Sabbath with unnecessary travel. Charles Lee, who would first meet Ward when Washington took over the new Continental Army at Cambridge, would refer contemptuously to Ward as a mere "church warden," and it's not hard to see why. But in Massachusetts, Artemas Ward was the beau ideal of virtuous Puritan manhood, dedicated to his colony and his community, and was respected as few men were.[6]

Ward was the right man because he was serious, imperturbable, patient, and conservative. And because he knew the routine of army life. Until the army was ready for combat, it needed an administrator, an organizer, not a warrior. For the remainder of his days, Ward would be hounded by criticisms of his command style—that he was not aggressive, that he did not try to take the war to the British, that he failed to take any kind of action at all. The points were true . . . but specious. What the rebel army most certainly did not need in the spring of 1775 was a gambler, a general who might be tempted to risk it all in one grandiose but futile assault on Boston. The army needed time to grow, to prepare, to survive. Ward—with Gage's involuntary help—gave it that time.

Ward knew the army and its problems intimately. Each and every day he convened his Council of War at the Hastings House, conferring with his ranking officers; he rode out on frequent inspection tours of the camps clustered around Cambridge, and went to Roxbury to see General Thomas when his other duties permitted it. Ward was constantly on the move, tireless, silent but fiercely dedicated to his men, biting back on the pain that tormented him every time he mounted a horse. Few military commanders in American history were as well informed about their men as Artemas Ward was.

There was nothing particularly innovative or imaginative, or even clever, about General Ward's method. He understood that Yankee civilians were unaccustomed to being told what to do and when to do it, much less to being told so day after day after day. Yet that was exactly what the men had to accept, and so Ward simply bashed at the problems he found with bullheaded obstinacy. At the very beginning he set a basic schedule for the military day, specifying times for reveille, meals, and lights out; he insisted upon regular and accurate returns from all units. Each and every regimental commander was expected to parade his regiment on Cambridge Common twice daily, and to exercise it in drill at least as often. And once these things had been established, he moved on to address specific but vital concerns—to make the camps cleaner, to make the army safer, to make the soldiers busier and keep them out of trouble. On May 2, Ward ordered the digging of latrines and garbage "vaults," and the daily cleaning of each camp and of the parade ground on Cambridge Common. A guard was posted around the water pump at the Common, the primary source of potable water, with strict instructions to "take particular care that no person *put anything into* said pump." Sometimes the general had to threaten, even when it came to something as obvious as personal hygiene: each commanding officer, for example, was to "daily visit his Soldiers whether in Barracks or Tents & oblige them to keep themselves clean. The Officers who do not strictly adhere to this order are to be reported at Head Quarters. And the Soldiers that disobey the Officers Orders in this Respect are to be confin'd, at the main Guard till they shall receive some punishment adequate to a crime so heinous."[7]

General Ward was equally concerned about the spiritual well-being of his army. He was not alone: the Provincial Congress, which had its own chaplains and began every session with prayers, felt the same. There were chaplains for the army, too, and Ward didn't even have to go looking for them, for less than a week after Lexington and Concord the Congress was practically flooded with offers from patriotic preachers who wanted to serve. The soldiers were, by and large, God-fearing, church-going types, who wanted and expected religious guidance. Ward was more than happy to oblige. Even in an army as avowedly Christian as this one, men were prone to exhibit their baser natures when divorced from the comfortable restrictions of home, family, and community. Theft and drunkenness were the most common ills, topped only by cursing. "I see no kind of seriousness," wrote one visitor to the camps, "but on the contrary my ears are filled with the most shocking oaths, and imprications; and the tremendous name of the great God is taken on the most trifling occasions."[8]

This would not do, not for Artemas Ward, not when the Cause was a holy one and the men and women of Massachusetts were God's chosen people. The daily orders coming from the Hastings House contained as many proscriptions on moral failings as they did regulations on cleanliness and guard duty. "Every officer and Soldier [must] Strickly Attend Prayers"—and that meant daily—and "Profane Cusing or Swearing" would not be tolerated. Severe punishments would be meted out to civilians who sold liquor to the soldiers without prior authorization. Regular courts-martial in Cambridge served swift justice to thieves and other troublemakers, with whippings as the most common penalties. Prostitutes ordinarily mobbed armies in camp, for encampments presented lucrative opportunities for "lewd women" to ply their trade. But few such women—"fire ships," as one soldier called them—got very far in Ward's army. They were banned from the camps. Indeed, *all* women were made distinctly unwelcome. Artemas Ward was a God-fearing and pious man; he would have a God-fearing and pious army. There was too much at stake to risk losing God's favor through the frivolous or lascivious behavior of His servants.

Ward couldn't fix everything that was wrong with the army. He could tell the men to obey their officers, and he could tell the officers to see to it that orders were followed, but he couldn't change the Yankees' deeply engrained democratic habits. They were free men; they saw no reason why they should subordinate themselves to a man who was no better than they were. A visitor to the Roxbury camp overheard a captain order one of his privates to get a pail of water for his company. The private showed no inclination to so much as stir on the captain's account. "I sha'n't," he responded blankly. "It's your turn now, captain, I got the last." Junior officers were put in the ridiculous position of having to work to please their men rather than the other way around. One day in early May, right after the morning parade on Cambridge Common, Captain Thomas Poor of Frye's Massachusetts regiment "spok very rash" to his company, scolding them for choosing their own sergeant—something that Poor felt, rightly, was his province and not theirs. Captain Poor was well within his rights to lecture his men, but they didn't take kindly to the tongue-lashing. The captain "displesd the soldiers very much," and in revenge the men "went [off] & did no duty that day." Facing the resentment of his own men, Poor had no choice but to cave in. "Capt Poor come & said that he was mis under stod & the [company] setld with him by his making som recantation."[9]

Slowly, painfully, Ward managed to retrieve order from chaos. He had taken care of the basic survival needs of the army: the men were being fed, well and regularly, and according to a fixed schedule; rudimentary medical care was available, and the army was as prepared as it could be for the worst ravages of the smallpox. The men were digging new fortifications every day. Guard details became part of the daily routine. Every task, every chore, had its appointed time and place. Most important, the men themselves noticed the change and responded to it. In the week following Lexington and Concord, they did as they pleased and went where they pleased, behaving more like armed tourists than soldiers with a job to do. They didn't exactly resent dress parades, or drill, or guard duty, but neither did they see such things as part of the rhythm of their lives as soldiers. Ward's orders changed all that. The men were usually too busy to wander off, and they were becoming accustomed to following orders, at least most of the time. Drill and dress parades and all of the once-novel duties of soldiering had become routine to them. The men began to see themselves not as a group of individuals from different towns, counties, and even colonies, but as members of a single community, a living organism . . . an *army*.

*T*he material needs of the army were simpler to address. Either supplies could be acquired or they couldn't, and if they couldn't, then there was precious little that Ward or the Congress could do about it. But the Massachusetts leadership did very well in providing for the army, considering their collective lack of experience. Pure dedication and enthusiasm went far toward making up for inexperience.

First the essentials: food, housing, medical care, weapons, and equipment . . . these were the pressing needs of the army, the ones that required immediate attention. An army without discipline was not likely to survive a campaign or even a single major battle; an army without food or shelter wouldn't survive a week. The militia and the minutemen had grabbed what they could from their larders at home before setting out in response to the Lexington alarm, but some had arrived on the scene with no food at all. A number of towns sent out the old men of the alarm companies to ferry provisions to the active militia—a workable stopgap, perhaps, but hardly a long-term solution. The decision to lay siege to Boston required a more permanent arrangement.

Fortunately there was one at hand: a special Committee of Supplies, set up by the Provincial Congress and the Committee of Safety back in the fall of 1774. The Committee of Supplies had already started to gather ammunition and provisions before the outbreak of hostilities, including those that would later be destroyed by the Redcoats at Concord on April 19. Now it faced a much more intimidating task—to supply an entire army, a *real* army, not just a paper one that existed solely in the Patriot imagination. And it did a remarkable job.

The Committee of Supplies set up its headquarters and its central storehouse in Watertown, seat of the Provincial Congress. Two satellite depots—one at Cambridge, the other at Roxbury—catered to the immediate daily needs of the army. The day after Lexington and Concord, patriotic—or possibly opportunistic—farmers delivered food to the depots by the wagonload; two days later, the depots were making regular issues to all the units of the growing army.

The supply of food was never a problem. Foodstuffs poured into the depots, brought in by farmers, by provisioners working on contract for the Congress, or by army foraging parties who eagerly confiscated livestock from known Tory landowners unfortunate enough to live near the camps. One Boston Loyalist warned his sister in Cambridge to guard her cattle from the rebels: "As soon as any attempt is perceived [by the rebels] to save your stock by putting it out of the way of your Army or its Friends, so soon will it be driven off or destroyed."[10] However acquired, the army's storehouses were brimming with provisions in a matter of days . . . vast mountains of food, and in such quantities and variety as to make an old campaigner's mouth water: tons—literally—of fresh-baked bread; beef and pork, both salt and fresh; fresh veal and salt fish; rice, peas, beans, potatoes, butter, even asparagus and raisins![11]

The real trick lay in fair and efficient distribution. Early on, Ward had cautioned the new commissary-general, a Committee of Safety member named John Pigeon, not to obsess over precision— "supply the troops with provisions in the best manner he can, without spending time for exactness"—but even here the system worked astonishingly well.[12] The Provincial Congress would later set the daily ration at a pound to a pound and a quarter of beef or pork, one pound of fish one day per week instead of meat, and a pound of bread, supplemented with smaller quantities of milk, rice, peas, beans, beer, vinegar, butter, and soap. It was a generous ration by the standards of the age. In most armies, official regulations about food were optimistic fictions, rarely adhered to except in good intentions. But in the Massachusetts army the stipulated ration was very close to actual practice in the field, and often the reality was more opulent than the regulation. Of course there were problems and occasional shortages. Soap was a rarity. Milk was supposed to be an item of regular issue but was difficult to distribute very far beyond the depots—long treks in hot weather from the storehouses to the far-flung outposts rendered fresh milk "unfit for any person in camp to eat." But every day the depots at Cambridge and Roxbury doled out gargantuan quantities of food. And every day—thanks to General Ward's careful attention to detail—wagons brought the food to the individual regiments on a strict and regular schedule.[13]

For as long as men have fought wars, common soldiers have rarely griped about anything more than food, or lack thereof, but the rebels outside Boston never complained about the rations. Some of the poorer men had never had it so good. Tempting as it is to think of our Revolutionary forefathers as perpetually starving, the daily reality was just the opposite for the rebels at Roxbury and Cambridge. While Gage's Redcoats got by on skimpy issues of salt meat and hard bread, their American enemies were growing fat on liberal helpings of fresh veal, pork, beef, and vegetables.

Food was just the beginning of the Committee's responsibilities. It accumulated tremendous stocks of all sorts of necessary items: wooden mess bowls, canteens, iron cookpots, spades and axes and all manner of tools. It contracted with sailmakers to make tents, and with local harness shops to fashion crude cartridge boxes from leather and wood. But the Committee of Supplies could not meet every need. It could not transcend the stark reality that Massachusetts—indeed all of America—had little if any industry to speak of. All of the things that were available to the British in profusion remained out of reach for the rebels. Small ironworks could not be transformed into cannon foundries overnight, nor local gunsmiths into major arms contractors, nor village weavers into textile manufactories.

And so the army suffered from major shortages of everything but food. Shelter was the army's most obvious and most urgent need. In and around Cambridge, the American commanders billeted their troops in barns, in private houses, in the Anglican (and mostly Tory) Christ Church, and in the mansions abandoned by Tories who had fled for safety to Boston. Harvard College was pressed into duty as a vast barracks. The academic year was supposed to resume on May 1, but the army needed the space, and the Committee of Safety bluntly informed the college authorities that summer break would begin early. That month, upwards of 1,600 soldiers crowded into Massachusetts, Stoughton, and Harvard Halls, plus the college chapel; the college retained only a tiny space in Harvard Hall for storing books and scientific equipment.

Everyone agreed that the crowded, fetid barracks were slowly killing the army. "The Houses are all full," wrote Joseph Trumbull to his father, Connecticut governor Jonathan Trumbull, in early May. "They have been so nasty, that [the men] are growing Sickly and daily dying out of the Barracks." The men needed tents and open air as summer approached. Massachusetts owned only 1,100 tents—and at roughly six men per tent, this was clearly inadequate. Commissary agents scoured the seacoast for sailcloth, but the results were discouraging. Roxbury Store could account for only 245 tents of all kinds, in all conditions, as late as June.[14] The supply could not meet the demand. Soldiers without tents cobbled together what shelter they could with the materials at hand, guided by necessity and Yankee ingenuity. Strange patchwork hovels, built from odd weather-beaten boards, scrap iron, sod, and brush, clumped promiscuously together in the shantytowns in Cambridge and the outlying villages.

And the men lacked blankets, despite the Congress's promise of a blanket for each man who "listed" in the eight-months' army. Appeals to the towns yielded little. John Stark, colonel of a New Hampshire regiment at Medford, noted that "a great part of the Regiment or Army here, are destitute of blankets." A veteran of the siege, who had served as a fifer in Paterson's Massachusetts regiment, later recalled the miserable discomfort of his quarters in a private home in Cambridge that May: "to call it living is out of the question, for we had to sleep in our clothes upon the bare floor."[15]

The Congress had also promised a fine wool uniform coat for its soldiers—but this was a pipe dream and everyone knew it. Neither the Committee of Safety nor the Committee of Supplies made much effort to get clothing for the soldiers. The men were reduced to wearing what they had on their backs, and since most of them were far from home it meant that clothing wore out quickly and wasn't replaced. The absence of women in camp amplified the problem, for few of the men were accustomed to mending, tailoring, or laundering. Letters home were full of abject pleas for garments, for linen shirts and stockings and drawers. The Committee of Supplies tried to keep a few hundred pairs of shoes on hand at all times, but it was never enough. The soldiers were already dirty and bedraggled by the end of April; by the time of Bunker Hill in mid-June, the army was clothed in tattered filthy rags and worn-out shoes.

In one area, at least, the Massachusetts leadership was highly experienced: medicine. Physicians abounded in the high command: two members of the Committee of Safety—Joseph Warren and Benjamin Church—were medical doctors, and General Thomas had been both a practicing physician in civilian life and an army surgeon. Not until after Bunker Hill would the Committee of Safety take measures to create a structured medical department, with a surgeon and a surgeon's mate in every regiment, but right after Lexington and Concord it established a general military hospital in Cambridge. The chief concern was lack of medical supplies and instruments. There was not enough of either to go around, and the Committee grabbed greedily at every well-stocked medical chest it could scrounge.[16]

The dearth of munitions was just as bad, if not worse. Not all of the men had brought their own firearms from home when they responded to the Lexington alarm, and the Committee of Safety scrambled to make up the difference. They urged civilians to turn in their household weapons, and with their tacit sanction, Ward's troops went house-to-house in search of muskets and fowling-pieces, paying for some, confiscating those belonging to known Tories. Much to the consternation of Harvard's students, the army borrowed the fifty muskets stored on campus for the use of the student militia.

Patriot newspapers, like the *Massachusetts Spy*, advertised for qualified gunsmiths to repair worn-out or broken muskets for the colony.
Muskets surrendered by British deserters helped to fill the gap, but it
was still not enough. Only four days before the battle of Bunker Hill,
the regiment of Colonel Ruggles Woodbridge, with 305 enlisted
men, could account for only 266 serviceable firearms.[17]

The colony's stock of artillery was almost laughable . . . *almost*,
because in a siege the absence of effective artillery was no laughing matter. Through the Congress, the Committee of Safety had
established an artillery regiment under the command of a seasoned
veteran, Colonel Richard Gridley. It was an act of profound optimism. At one point the Committee of Safety thought that there
were twenty-four cannon of various calibers in the possession of
the colony, but for most of the spring no one seems to have known
precisely how many guns there were, or where they were, or what
condition they were in. The majority of the cannon were small-to-
medium field pieces—two-, three-, and six-pounders, referring
to the weight of the cast-iron round-shot they fired. They didn't
have the range or the power necessary for a successful siege. If the
inventory of cannon at Roxbury in early May is any indication, the
Massachusetts artillery was truly pathetic: "One 3 pound[er] Bad
Constructed Carriage, not fit for Service/ one Dutch 2–1/2 pdr,
Bad Carrage/ one 3 pdr . . . in good order/ one 2 pdr compleat in
a Barn . . . two 3 pdrs Bad . . . wanting Ladels, Rammers, Spunges,
worm Linstocks aprons, Drag Roap, Ordinary Carridge one unfit
for Service . . . One 2–1/2 pdr, Carridge unfit for Service/ One 3
pdr & 4 pdr Carriages Bad . . ."—to which the clerk added, " . . .
and many things wanting," as if that really needed to be said. This
was at Roxbury—and if cannon were needed anywhere, it was
there.[18]

And gunpowder. No more would be coming from England, the
principal source of supply for the colonies, and there were very few

powder mills in North America. All that the Committees of Safety and Supplies could do was to round up such stores of powder as could be found in towns and villages throughout the colony, and these were often loath to give up the precious substance when some-day it might be necessary to defend *their* homes against marauding Redcoats. There would never be enough powder, no matter how much Artemas Ward fretted.

But at least the army was fed, and fed well, thanks to the efforts of the Committee of Supplies and the commissary-general, John Pigeon. Without reliable funding from the Provincial Congress, the officials at the Cambridge and Roxbury depots often paid for delivered goods from their own pockets. "He has greatly exposed himself by making Contracts for the Army," Joseph Warren saluted John Pigeon, "which if not complied with He says must ruin him . . . without his aid the Army would certainly have been dismissed."[19]

*T*hat army did not yet have a name. One newspaper referred to it as the "Grand American Army," which was not en-tirely accurate. The Provincial Congress and the Committee of Safety simply called it "the army" or "the new army." Some officers had already taken to calling it the "Army of the United Colonies." That wasn't precisely correct, either, for the colonies were not yet fully united in spirit or purpose, and most of them had contributed nothing but good intentions to the army outside Boston. One thing was certain: it was no longer an exclusively Massachusetts army. All of New England had gone to war.

The Massachusetts leadership had anticipated that—it had, in fact, hoped and prayed for this very thing. The Boston Whigs clearly thought of their struggle as America's struggle, fought out on a Mas-sachusetts stage; sooner or later, they reasoned, the other colonies would wake up and come to their aid, for if Massachusetts were to be defeated then all of the colonies would suffer for it. But the involvement of the other New England colonies was never taken as a given. There were no real ties—formal or otherwise—that obliged Rhode Island, New Hampshire, or Connecticut to come to the aid of the Bay Colony. There was no history of regional cooperation, in wartime or in peace, save for the sharing of information between the radical Whigs in the various Committees of Correspondence. And there was every reason for the other colonies to resent Massachusetts for casting the die in the spring of 1775. Patriots abounded throughout the region, to be sure, men who sympathized with Boston's plight after Parliament closed the port in 1774. But open resistance, as at Lexington and Concord, threatened to bring the firestorm down on all of New England. The farther Massachusetts strayed from obedience to Mother England, the more difficult it would be for any of the colonies to find a peaceable solution with Britain.

New England sprang to the call anyway. Hampshiremen and Connecticut Yankees streamed across the border toward Boston in the hundreds as soon as the Lexington alarm spread into their villages and hamlets. Just as with the Massachusetts men, though, their presence was impermanent and tentative, fueled only by the desire to help their neighbors fend off the hated Redcoats. Once the immediate danger was past, these volunteers had no more reason to stay than their comrades from Massachusetts.

Yet while Artemas Ward struggled to bend the Yankee character to military discipline, the other three colonies did their level best to regroup, to muster legitimate, organized armies, and contribute something substantial to the Cause, which they saw increasingly as their own. For Connecticut the process was relatively clear-cut. Alone among the New England colonies, Connecticut had a governor who was an avowed Whig. Dour-faced Jonathan Trumbull, sixty-five years old, had every intention of helping Massachusetts in its hour of need. The vast majority of his citizens concurred—

forty-six of the colony's seventy-two towns dispatched troops to Boston, while others raised militia to protect New York City and Connecticut's coastal towns. But there were still voices, powerful and influential, who counseled negotiation with Gage and the king. Trumbull dealt with these moderates with consummate skill. When the Connecticut Assembly convened exactly one week after Lexington and Concord, Trumbull placated the moderates by writing directly to Thomas Gage, asking the British general to explain his conduct and pleading for peace. It wasn't long before virtually everyone knew of Trumbull's letter. The Connecticut forces outside Boston were mortified by what they saw as their trustworthy governor's bald-faced treachery. The Massachusetts Committee of Safety was equally aghast, reminding Governor Trumbull—needlessly—of British perfidy. Since Massachusetts was determined to drive Gage and his men "out of the country" or "meet an honorable death in the field" rather than allow themselves "to be butchered in our own houses, . . . to be reduced to an ignominious slavery," Connecticut must side with Massachusetts or suffer the same fate. But crafty old Trumbull had a trick up his sleeve: he deliberately picked the two fiercest proponents of reconciliation to deliver the letter to General Gage.

With these two men out of the way, Trumbull and the Assembly rolled up their sleeves and went straight to work. They authorized the recruitment of six thousand men in six regiments, under the overall command of Major General David Wooster, a sixty-four-year-old veteran of two wars. Recruitment for the regiments proceeded with astonishing speed. During the first week of May, two regiments—under brigadier generals Israel Putnam and Joseph Spencer—received their marching orders. Spencer's regiment split, one part joining Thomas at Roxbury, the other encamping near Cambridge. Israel Putnam's boys took over the Inman farm outside Cambridge. The farm's owner, Ralph Inman, was a prosperous

Tory merchant who had taken refuge in Boston. Inman's wife and daughters, though, remained behind, and despite the differences in their political views they got along famously with Old Put and his officers.

The reaction in New Hampshire was no less enthusiastic. About two thousand Hampshiremen rushed toward Boston in the first day or two after Lexington and Concord; and just like their Connecticut and Massachusetts brethren, many of them went home after a few days of inactivity. The colony was slow to act officially because it had no real government. John Wentworth, a man steadfastly loyal to the king, still occupied the governor's office, and several weeks would pass before the colony's Congress could meet. But a rump Congress of patriots, calling themselves the Convention, met anyway, and— without any authority to act—called for the recruitment of two regiments. Their colonels, John Stark and James Reed, had nearly filled their quotas when the colony's new Revolutionary government gave its formal approval to what the Convention had done. The Hampshiremen, unofficially under the overall command of Colonel Stark, encamped at Medford, just northeast of Cambridge.[20]

Rhode Island was the slowest to act. Some volunteers hurried to Boston in those first frantic days, but it was not until the beginning of May that the colony's Assembly took definite steps to create an "Army of Observation," fifteen hundred strong organized in three regiments, with a company of field artillery. They began to show up in late May, handfuls of men at a time, at Jamaica Plain near Roxbury, where they joined General Thomas's command. There was something hesitant in Rhode Island's commitment to the Cause: the army was officially intended to come "to the assistance of any neighboring colony in distress," and the soldiers themselves were enlisted in "His Majesty's Service . . . for the preservation of the Liberties of America." Curious, perhaps, yet a reflection of what many Patriots truly believed—that their fight was not with the king himself, but with Parliament and the wicked ministers who unduly influenced poor George III.

But there was nothing half-hearted about Rhode Island's commitment once the army was in the field. Its three regiments were markedly better disciplined and better trained than any of the units from Connecticut, Massachusetts, or New Hampshire. They were well supplied, too, and to one observer the neat and regular rows of "proper tents and marquees" in the Rhode Island encampment "look[ed] like ye regular camp of the enemy."[21] That owed almost entirely to the personal influence of the odd man inexplicably chosen to lead the Rhode Island troops: Nathanael Greene, a thirty-three-year-old Quaker with a gimpy leg, who knew nothing of war except what he had learned in books.

The tiny colony contributed something else of inestimable value: twelve large cannon, a mix of eighteen- and twenty-four-pounders, the first real siege artillery in the army that claimed to be conducting a siege.

These were four separate armies, technically speaking. The government of each colony had named them as such. The remarkable—and fortunate—thing is that these individual identities disappeared once the armies joined with Ward's. In mid-May, New Hampshire would formally place its army under the command of the Massachusetts generals, but long before that the various New England armies had already made their obeisances to the Bay Colony. The Connecticut and New Hampshire troops around Cambridge reported to Artemas Ward; the Connecticut and Rhode Island troops who gathered at Roxbury reported to John Thomas. There was no attempt to segregate these four forces, no pretense that a general from Connecticut or Rhode Island was independent of Artemas Ward's authority. Massachusetts was generous in turn. It supplied the other New England regiments with food and ammunition just as it did its own troops. The Committee of Safety enlisted—and promised to pay—New Hampshire soldiers who enlisted before their own colony formed regiments of its own, and then turned them back graciously to New Hampshire. Ward and Warren and all of the Massachusetts leaders acknowledged the ranks given to the other New England leaders by their respective assemblies without hesitation or complaint. General Putnam and General Greene were as welcome at Ward's council table as if they had been commissioned by Massachusetts.

*I*t was a solidly New England army, then, that taunted Gage's Redcoats from across the Charles and the Back Bay in May 1775. And it was a young army. The typical enlisted man was in his early twenties. In Moses Little's Massachusetts regiment, for example, the age of the average private or noncommissioned officer was twenty-four; fully two-thirds ranged between the ages of seventeen and twenty-two. These were not the "raw lads and old men" that veterans liked to recall, years later, when they looked back with patriotic sentimentality on their soldiering days and the part they played in the birth of a nation. Only a handful of the men were in their forties and fifties, and there were very few genuine youngsters in the bunch. The first American army was little different from any army in any age: young men in their late teens and early twenties, usually men without families of their own, would do most of the fighting and dying.[22]

It was young in experience, too. A good number of the officers had served during one or more of the wars against the French. Nearly all of the generals had: Ward and Thomas of Massachusetts, and Israel Putnam of Connecticut, were commissioned officers in provincial units during the French and Indian War; Joseph Spencer of Connecticut had fought in King George's War as well. Only William Heath and Nathanael Greene were new to war. Most of the regimental colonels were likewise veterans, and a fair proportion of the captains, too. What that meant in terms of actual combat experience, though, was a different matter. There was a world of difference between commanding a militia company in a battle or two, or serving with a regiment guarding supplies at Crown Point, and commanding an entire army. None of the generals—neither Ward nor Thomas nor even the famed warrior Putnam—had ever been called upon to create an army and lead it into battle.

The enlisted men were, by contrast, mere innocents. There was a sprinkling of older men, men who had served in provincial regiments during the French and Indian War, but by and large the men who marched off to fight the Redcoats in April and May 1775 had never heard a shot fired in anger. Only a handful of them had joined the "fracas" of April 19, and even that action was hardly the same thing as facing a determined and disciplined professional army on equal terms. The Americans outside Boston were just as raw as the equally young British army under Gage. But while the British had the advantage of regular practice in drill, the Americans did not. Not the kind that counted, anyway. For while the minuteman companies had been practicing drill on a fairly regular basis since the fall of 1774, they rarely went beyond the manual exercises with their muskets—the postures for carrying, loading, and firing. Rarely did they work on the more essential elements of drill—marching in unison, changing face, wheeling, moving from column of march to line of battle; never did they engage in large-unit drill at the level of the regiment or brigade. The manual exercise was important, for it taught men to act as a unit, but it was the more mundane things like marching and changing formation that were absolutely necessary for the correct execution of linear tactics. As late as 1778, the Prussian drillmaster Steuben would find the veteran Continental troops utterly lacking in these all-important skills. The militiamen of '75 were decidedly less expert than the men Steuben found so awkward three years later.[23]

To someone who had seen New England men muster to fight the French and the Indians in 1756, the army of 1775 would have looked very familiar, though larger. It wasn't much different, truth be told, than these earlier provincial armies, at least not on the surface. The difference—and it was a big one—was that this army was an entirely home-grown institution. It had been raised, organized, equipped, and fed without any help whatsoever from the British. It had its shortcomings, needless to say, but Massachusetts had nonetheless accomplished something remarkable, something that neither the British nor the Americans themselves truly expected.

More remarkable still: the army was not entirely white. In late May, the Committee of Safety considered the possibility of enlisting slaves, but the notion was bluntly scotched with little ceremony. The reasons—at least the publicly stated reasons—were ideological rather than racial: this was a fight for liberty, freedom from British "slavery," hence the recruitment of slaves would be "inconsistent with the principles that are to be supported, and reflect dishonor on this colony."[24] Free black men, though, were a different matter. The Provincial Congress neither rejected nor explicitly espoused the recruitment of African-Americans other than slaves. They appear in the historical record, unheralded and almost invisible, and if their white comrades found anything unusual about their presence, they didn't bother to mention it. Yet African-Americans served as common soldiers in the ranks, motivated by the same things that drove white New Englanders to enlist. The total number of black men in the army outside Boston is yet unknown, but it is certain that at least twenty-one black men fought at Lexington or Concord, and at least eighty-eight—and likely more—would fight at Bunker Hill. These men were not placed in specially designated units, but were mixed in among the regular regiments in the provincial service. Most of the black soldiers hailed from Massachusetts, but New Hampshire and Connecticut each contributed a few also.[25]

Massachusetts, though, went out of its way to bring Native Americans into the army. Gage had been actively courting the Six Nations and others, and among the rebels there lurked a strong fear that Britain's Indian allies would sweep in from Canada and New York, laying waste to the settlements of New England's western frontier in an orgy of scalpings and burnings. Warren and the Committee of Safety were not about to give up without a fight. "Brothers, the great wickedness of such as should be our friends but are our enemies, we mean the ministry of Great Brittian," the Provincial Congress addressed the Abenaki and Penobscot Indians along the coast, "have laid deep plots to take away our liberty & your liberty, they want to get all our money, make us pay it to them when they never earnt it, to make you & us their servants . . . and prevent us from having guns & powder to use." The Congress offered powerful incentives to potential Indian enlistees: "a Blankit & a Ribbon." They could even expect to be paid![26]

There were plenty of Native Americans who wanted to join the fight outside Boston without waiting to be remunerated so generously. The Mahican of western Massachusetts—commonly known to the colonials as the Stockbridge Indians, named after their main settlement at Stockbridge, in the Berkshires—had been converted to Christianity quite some time earlier, and lived on comparatively good terms with their white neighbors. Already on May 1, General Thomas excitedly told his wife about the "Number of Stockbridge & Sum Mohegan Indians Painted for war" who had arrived in Roxbury. A full company of Colonel John Paterson's Massachusetts regiment, stationed at Cambridge, consisted exclusively of Stockbridge

Indians. Many of the younger men, especially those from the eastern counties, had never seen a red man before, but—as with the free blacks in the ranks—their existence didn't seem the least bit controversial or even newsworthy.[27]

As the army settled down into the routine that General Ward had so laboriously hammered into them, the numbers of men began to stabilize, too. Most of the Rhode Island, New Hampshire, and Connecticut regiments had made their way to their camps at Medford, Cambridge, and Jamaica Plain. There were a few predictable hitches, stemming from the clumsy recruiting process in Massachusetts. Most of the beating orders had been filled in the first two weeks of May; most of the men who wanted to enlist had already done so. The Provincial Congress, however, balked at the final step: "commissioning" the individual regiments raised for eight months' duty, which meant officially accepting the regiments, commissioning the officers, and paying the men. Not even the general officers, not even Ward himself, had as yet been commissioned into the new army. A minor administrative matter, perhaps, but it drove Ward to distraction—the prospect that nothing but patriotism kept the soldiers from packing up and leaving on their own. "It appears to me absolutely necessary," Ward chided the Committee of Safety, "that the Regiments be immediately filled, the Officers commissioned, the Soldiers mustered and paid agreeable to what has been proposed by the Congress—*if we would save our Country.*"[28] Congress responded. The commissioning of regiments and their officers began on May 19. The following day, Artemas Ward finally received his formal commission as major general and commander-in-chief of the Massachusetts forces.[29]

Still, the army was undersized. It never achieved the numbers that Congress had stipulated and that Ward expected. As the Committee of Safety noted sourly, there were a number of minuteman companies hanging uncomfortably around headquarters, fully manned and equipped, and ready to enlist—*eager* to enlist. But because the Congress had already distributed all of the beating orders, there were no vacancies left and the men could not be lawfully recruited. None of the other colonies had completely fulfilled the quotas assigned to them by Massachusetts . . . but Massachusetts needed the men, not only for the siege but also to guard other potential targets along the seacoast.[30] The Committee petitioned the Provincial Congress, begging that these men be permitted to enlist, but their plea fell on deaf ears. The Provincial Congress was growing visibly uneasy about the potential monster it had created in the army and had no intention of making that monster any bigger.

Actually, the Congress worried a great deal about the army, and with good reason. It needed to pay the army and pay for supplies for that army, but had no money with which to pay for anything. Even with the support coming in from Connecticut, New Hampshire, and Rhode Island, the Bay Colony was carrying most of the war effort alone. Most of all, though, the Congress worried about the attitude of the army. It found itself caught on the horns of the same dilemma that has tortured nearly every representative government that has ever gone to war since the days of the Roman Republic: the civil government needed the army, was in fact utterly dependent on the army . . . but did the army need the Congress? Did the army even *respect* the Congress? What was to keep the army from dictating policy to Congress rather than the other way around?

It wasn't that the Provincial Congress had any reason to distrust the army's leaders. But just to be safe, the Committee of Safety took the very wise step of recommending that army officers be barred from serving as congressional delegates. "The Sword should be subservient to, and under the Control of the Civil powers of Government," the Committee declared. Artemas Ward, who was in his heart not a soldier but a politician, and a selfless and unambitious one at that, they trusted almost implicitly. Only once would the Massachusetts leadership find any reason to scold him. Late in June, the Provincial Congress directed the Committee of Safety to distribute any remaining muskets to officers who applied for them; Ward hastily scribbled a note to the Committee, ordering it to hand over the weapons. Ward meant nothing by the gesture—he was merely trying to save time and red tape—but the Committee was appropriately shocked. The army, it lectured Ward haughtily, received orders from the Committee, and not the other way around.[31]

A minor issue, perhaps, but one that belied a deeper distrust of those who served General Ward. Overall the army was well behaved, considering how new and how amateur it was, and how easy it was to get rum. The army was dedicated to the Cause; desertion was all but unknown in the Grand American Army. Still, there were enough cases of individual soldiers misbehaving to give even tolerant Joseph Warren pause. Civilians living near the camps complained to the Congress about how soldiers browbeat them into surrendering their livestock and personal weapons to the army. Hannah Jones, a resident of Roxbury, begged General Thomas for protection: late one Saturday night, "a Number of Armd men" forced their way into her house, and "under Pretence of Want of Armes" they confiscated a couple of muskets, two pairs of pistols, and a silver-mounted sword, without so much as offering to pay for the weapons. The next night—the Sabbath, no less—they returned in greater numbers. They "gairded my House & Kept Help of the nabors from aproching to my ascestance," the aggrieved Jones told Thomas, "While they Entred the House Broke open Dores & aproch'd my Rum." "The Tretment," Jones concluded, as if it weren't obvious, "Was Beyound Conception."[32]

Sometimes the army's officers voiced their opinions about the Congress a little too freely. Abijah Brown of Waltham, lieutenant colonel of Woodbridge's Massachusetts regiment, compared the Congress to "a poor unhappy man, that is *non compos mentis*," and publicly declared that "all the power was and would be in the army; and if the Congress behaved as they did, within forty-eight hours the Army would turn upon the Congress, and they would settle matters as they pleased." These were the unthinking words, no doubt, of a drunken loudmouth, but episodes such as this weighed heavily on Dr. Warren's mind. "It is with our countrymen as with all other men, when they are in arms, they think the military should be uppermost," Warren intimated to Sam Adams.[33]

What it all boiled down to was this: Massachusetts could not carry the war on its own any longer. The colony was fighting America's war. The delegates of the Provincial Congress knew it; the disheveled men in the camps around Cambridge and Roxbury lived it. They had taken an oath to fight "for the defence and security of the rights and liberties of this and our sister Colonies in *America*."[34] It was high time that the other colonies learned it, too.

* * *

Four

THE FIERCEST MAN
AMONG THE
SAVAGE TRIBES

*I*n the spring of 1775, America fell in love with war.

The infatuation had been building for some months. The First Continental Congress, meeting in Philadelphia in the autumn of 1774, had foreseen the possibility of an armed contest with the mother country, and the delegates urged the individual colonies to make preparations for self-defense. Massachusetts, of course, responded in full measure, but it was not the only colony to heed the call. Even where colonial governments held no truck with disloyal sentiments—as in Virginia—militia companies turned out to drill and parade in growing numbers on every town square and village green.

Once the news of Lexington and Concord spread south—it took only a matter of days—that infatuation became a full-blown obsession. A *rage militaire*, a mania for all things military, gripped the colonies. It was no longer a matter of citizen-soldiers preparing clumsily for war, stumbling through the postures and steps of the Manual Exercise in eager earnest. Now, Americans, from New Hampshire to Georgia, reveled in the worship of battle, gloried in their own obvious warlike virtues, and congratulated themselves that they possessed some intangible quality that made them superior to all possible foes. Their enthusiasm and their boastful self-confidence blinded them to their shortcomings, which anyone could see. Militia companies—some of them nattily uniformed, most of them not—drilled even more frequently, now to the hearty cheers of onlookers, now followed by wide-eyed young lads who did their best to emulate their elders. Henry Melchior Muhlenberg, the prominent Lutheran preacher, saw the same scene enacted again and again in the towns around Philadelphia that spring: "One sees boys, who are still quite small, marching in companies with little drums and wooden muskets."[1]

If America's amateur soldiers were maladroit in executing the complicated maneuvers outlined in the printed drill manuals, it was because the colonists were not terribly concerned about precision. Americans, they told themselves, didn't need the kind of discipline used by European armies. Unlike European soldiers, they weren't the slaves of tyrannical regimes; their native intelligence and love of freedom would see them through. Timothy Pickering, the Salem militia colonel who tried to dissuade Joseph Warren from making war on Gage, reflected the views of most Patriots. "Away, then, with the trappings . . . of the parade," he wrote in his *Easy Plan of Discipline for a Militia*, a drill manual he composed for Massachusetts soldiers. "*Americans* need them not: *their* eyes are not to be dazzled, nor their hearts awed into servility, by the splendour of equipage and dress: *their* minds are too much enlightened to be duped by a glittering outside." There was a huge chasm separating spirit and intention from skill and accomplishment, but few Patriots were level-headed enough to recognize it. "Simple people who have never experienced the bitter fruits of an internal or domestic war expect that an all but universal military spirit will spread," Pastor Muhlenberg commented in his journal, shaking his head in disbelief at the naïveté of these innocents. "[It] will seize upon all adult males and youths and even children in their cradles so that practically everyone . . . will begin to drum and fife and shoot, albeit without powder or lead."[2] God had imbued Americans with righteous courage and an innate talent to perform great deeds of arms. In no time at all, their soldiers would be superior to the Redcoats. At least that was what they wanted to believe.

It was a dangerous mindset, to be sure, for it set Americans up for disappointment and dashed hopes, but in that wonderful, hopeful spring of '75 it acted like a tonic for the Cause. No one saw that with greater clarity than the heroes of the hour at the beginning of May 1775: the delegates to the Second Continental Congress.

When the First Continental Congress had adjourned in late October 1774, it had resolved to meet again the following May. The first congress had been fruitful but contentious, but the second—coming as it did right on the heels of Lexington and Concord—promised much better things. The delegates, regardless of their origins or their politics, found themselves honored in nearly every town or hamlet through which they passed as they made their way to Philadelphia. The Massachusetts delegation, though, stood head-and-shoulders above the rest. John Adams, Sam Adams, John Hancock, Thomas Cushing . . . none of them had shouldered a musket on the Glorious Nineteenth, none of them—except maybe the "great incendiary" Sam Adams—was known by name to most people outside New England, but it mattered little. They represented the colony that had actually taken up arms against British tyranny. Joseph Warren's propaganda had worked its intended effect: Gage's Redcoats had butchered innocent civilians, the men of Massachusetts had made the murderers pay, and now the heroes of the Bay Colony had come to Philadelphia to share their triumph.

From Stamford, where they rendezvoused with the Connecticut delegation, a large military escort accompanied the Massachusetts men all the way to New York City. New Yorkers, by the score, rode out to meet them; militia and a "tollerable band of music" marched with them through the city itself, as throngs of spectators pressed together to catch a glimpse. Two days later, on May 8, the delegates of Massachusetts and Connecticut joined with those of New York and set off on the final leg of the journey, again accompanied all the way by yet another well-dressed military guard. They reached Philadelphia precisely on the day appointed, May 10, 1775, and their stately triumphal progress ended with a flourish. Hundreds of well-wishers, and hundreds more of militia, came out to greet the delegates. Crowds cheered them all the way into town, all the way to the door of the City Tavern, where the exhausted but elated men finally halted for a rest. "The public entry of the Bostonian delegates into this city," observed Delaware representative Caesar Rodney, "was very grand."[3]

Philadelphia's hospitality—indeed, America's hospitality— to the delegates set the tone for the opening of the Congress. Those delegates were well aware of the gravity of the tasks that lay before them—"I tremble when I think of their vast importance," wrote Silas Deane of Connecticut—but the wild acclaim to which they had been treated, the constant parades and militia-musters held every day in Philadelphia, could not help but infect them with a great measure of enthusiasm. Solidarity, too. From the very first day that the Congress convened in the Pennsylvania State House, the delegates displayed a unity of purpose and intent that was simply remarkable, given the differences that existed between them and between their colonies. There was as yet little or no talk of independence, and many ardent Patriots still held that a reconciliation with Mother England was possible . . . but nearly everyone agreed that, first, the British would have to be shown that Americans were willing to fight for their liberties as Englishmen. "There never appeared more perfect unanimity," Virginian Richard Henry Lee claimed proudly, "among any set of men than among the Delegates, and indeed all the old Provinces, not one excepted, are directed by the same firmnes of union and determination to resist by all ways and to every extremity."[4]

Everything moved smoothly at first. Under the direction of their president, Peyton Randolph of Virginia, the delegates settled upon the procedure they would follow in their deliberations and heard the latest news from each of the colonies, without making any significant decisions. Detailed, lurid accounts of the bloodshed at Lexington and Concord held them spellbound, as did Joseph Warren's letter to the Congress, explaining the reasons behind Massachusetts's decision to raise an army and go to war. Only a week after the opening session, the delegates were treated to tidings so wondrous that they were almost beyond belief. On the very morning that the Continental Congress first met, a Connecticut roughneck named Ethan Allen—accompanied, reluctantly, by a touchy but ambitious and capable militia officer named Benedict Arnold—had captured Fort Ticonderoga, a British-held outpost guarding New York's Lake Champlain. With about eighty poorly armed frontiersmen, Allen and Arnold had captured the minuscule British garrison there without firing a shot, without a single casualty on either side. Ticonderoga was a moldering ruin, neglected by the British since the end of the French and Indian War, but it guarded the vital land route from New York City to Montréal via lakes George and Champlain. Possession of the fort denied that route to the British. There were some men, especially in New England, who hoped that Canada might be induced to join the Americans in their resistance to Britain; the capture of Ticonderoga, to them, seemed to put that goal within reach. Most important: Ticonderoga housed dozens of heavy cannon and tremendous stockpiles of gunpowder, cannon-balls, and musket ammunition—one of the reasons that both Ethan Allen and Benedict Arnold had been so keen on taking the place.[5]

The news of Ticonderoga electrified the Congress. In April, the vaunted British army had been forced to retreat outside Boston, and now, in May, a British garrison had been captured intact by a small band of disorganized but enterprising American woodsmen. If these two events were any indication of American military prowess, then maybe, just maybe, the colonies had a fighting chance of bring-ing the king and Parliament to the negotiating table. There were no voices of caution or of dissent heard in the State House. Why should there be? If anything, the taking of Ticonderoga became a source of levity in the Congress. Shortly after Ethan Allen's dis-patches were read in Congress, a New York Loyalist—one Major Phillip Skene—was apprehended in Philadelphia. Hauled before the Congress for questioning, it was revealed that Skene owned a great parcel of land right next to Fort Ticonderoga, and that before Allen attacked the fort, his men stole two large boats from Skene's property. What made Skene's appearance in Philadelphia so timely was that the hapless man—who had just returned from a visit to England—carried royal documents proclaiming him to be "gover-nor of Ticonderoga." The entire Congress convulsed with raucous laughter when Skene's commission was read to them. John Adams observed that poor Skene would have to take up the matter with Allen and Arnold. Eliphalet Dyer of Connecticut was less kind: "The dunce Imagined he should have easy work to settle the whole Controversy."[6]

But levity and celebration could not stave off the more serious business for very long. There was a great deal that had to be done. The fraternal solidarity of the first days soon gave way to a gentle but perceptible split. Some, like John Dickinson of Pennsylvania, clung tightly to the hope for reconciliation with Britain . . . reconciliation, that is, with explicit constitutional guarantees protecting American liberties, something that was about as likely as a voluntary grant of independence from George III. Others, like John Adams, believed that the gulf separating America from Mother England was too wide to be bridged by compromise. That split made all the difference when it came to giving out military advice. Compromise would involve making peaceful overtures to king and Parliament; rejecting compromise would mean preparing for all-out war.

Each of the colonies forwarded to the Congress its petitions and suggestions, its requests for advice or for aid. Many if not all of the petitions and requests were urgent, and the delegates felt beholden to respond to them promptly. It was an overwhelming burden, almost too much for the delegates to bear. None of them had expected *this*. "Our business has run away with us," lamented Silas Deane. John Adams quailed before the awful gravity of the issues confronting him and his colleagues: "Provinces, nations, empires are small things before us. I wish we were good architects."[7]

And it wasn't entirely clear what the Continental Congress was supposed to do. Like the first congress, it was intended to facilitate the exchange of ideas and concerns between the colonies, to coordinate individual actions rather than to take united action. It was not meant to act as the governing body of a union of colonies. There was no such union, not really, and the Congress had neither the expectation nor the mandate to do the things that a government does. Congress had neither power nor authority.

Yet it was obvious from the tone of the sessions that the colonies did indeed want something more from Congress, some degree of leadership in very uncertain and perilous times. New York wanted to know what it should do if British troops landed in force on its shores. New Hampshire wanted to know "the united plan of the colonies." Massachusetts, Connecticut, New Hampshire, and New

York all wanted to know who should be responsible for safeguarding Ticonderoga.

The disturbing question, the one that got right to the heart of the American cause, came from Massachusetts: since Massachusetts was fighting for America, would America fight for Massachusetts?

*A*ctually, Massachusetts had two questions for the Continental Congress, and both of them were urgent. The Provincial Congress in Watertown wanted, needed, to form a permanent and legitimate government for the colony. Its delegates—tradesmen and farmers mostly—were painfully aware of its origins: it had formed itself in the midst of the dramatic political scuffles of 1774, in opposition to Parliament for revoking the colony's sacrosanct charter, and in opposition to General Gage for executing the will of Parliament. The Provincial Congress had no place in that charter, no official justification for its very existence. It had been acting as a governing body because—for the Whigs—there were no convenient alternatives.

The Provincial Congress had no legitimacy as a government, and in the eighteenth century "legitimacy" meant as much to a legislature as it did to a king. The Second Provincial Congress would soon be coming to an end, to be supplanted by a Third if Gage did not reinstate the charter. The delegates wanted a government that all of "the Continent"—meaning the other twelve colonies—would recognize and acknowledge. They wanted a government that could, with right on its side, trumpet its supremacy over its army, which was just beginning to reanimate the specter of Oliver Cromwell and bloody struggles between military and civilian authority. They wanted a government that had the legal right to raise taxes and print money, to do all of the things that a government would normally do in support of an army and a war effort.

So the delegates in Watertown tossed the matter to the delegates at Philadelphia. They carefully drafted a letter—the process took four full days—and entrusted it to the safekeeping of a member of the Committee of Safety, a man whose attachment to the Cause was beyond reproach: Dr. Benjamin Church, to whom they gave a fast horse and sulky to speed the important missive to its destination. "We are now compelled to raise an Army, which, with the assistance of the other Colonies . . . will be able to defend us and all *America* from the further butcheries and devastations of our implacable enemies," read the Provincial Congress's appeal to the Continental Congress. "But as the sword should, in all free States, be subservient to the civil powers . . . we tremble, at having an Army (although consisting of our own countrymen) established here, without a civil power to provide for and control them." So how, the Watertown delegates asked, should Massachusetts go about the process of making a new government?[8]

It was indeed a strange predicament, as one historian noted, "an illegal legislature seeking legality from another more illegal still."[9] But the Provincial Congress was asking for advice, not support or action, and the Continental Congress could answer without too much fuss or wringing of hands. The Provincial Congress should call for a convention charged with electing a new legislature, and worry no longer about observing the niceties of the old charter if Gage had already trashed that charter. But the other question—*the* question—was a different matter. "As the Army now collecting from the different Colonies is for the general defence of the rights of *America*, we would beg leave to suggest to your consideration the propriety of your taking the regulation and general direction of it. . . ."[10]

Massachusetts had good reason to ask. Its leaders, especially Dr. Warren, had been careful from the start to enlist the sympathies and aid of the other New England colonies. Boston had been a troublemaker, to be sure, but in the eyes of Massachusetts Whigs the battle it was fighting against Gage was not a battle fought solely for Massachusetts's benefit, nor for New England, but for *all* the American colonies. If Patriots in the colonies to the south hadn't shared that opinion, most of them did so now, thanks to Warren's effective and blood-soaked propaganda. Throughout the colonies, the general impression was that the Lexington and Concord fights were not caused in any way by the Boston incendiaries—Gage had attacked and butchered American civilians without provocation and the stalwart minutemen had driven the Redcoats ignominiously into hiding. Britain had started the war, but Americans were fully capable of finishing it.

But Massachusetts needed help fighting America's battle. Miraculously, there was still an army outside Boston, and it was growing stronger and better with each passing day. It was generously fed, adequately clothed, but barely sheltered and armed. Basic equipment was lacking, and gunpowder in particular was in dangerously short supply. Nearly every day Artemas Ward bewailed the dearth of gunpowder, yet it made little difference, for there was only so much that the hard-pressed Committee of Supplies could scrounge. So far, with little actual fighting after April 19, the army needed very little powder on a day-to-day basis. Yet as everyone in Massachusetts knew and knew well, Gage was not going to stay passively in Boston forever. More Redcoats were on their way across the Atlantic. If the Provincials could not procure more powder, and if Gage were to push his troops from the Lines on Boston Neck toward Roxbury . . . then the results were not likely to be happy ones. It was entirely possible that the fate of America rested on the army's supply of ammunition.

The Continental Congress didn't know quite what to do with Massachusetts's plea for help. The Provincial Congress was, in essence, asking the Continental Congress to *act* like a government: to convince the other colonies to help, to coordinate the efforts of the individual colonies, and to take over direction of the war at Boston. Those were actions that required both authority and money. Those were the actions of a sovereign power.

It was a disturbing prospect, to be sure, and the delegates in Philadelphia dragged their feet, hoping that the problem would somehow solve itself. The Provincial Congress had sent its original request on May 16. Dr. Church arrived in Philadelphia, letter in hand, a week later; it wasn't read to the Congress until June 2, and even then it was immediately sent to committee for review. John Adams and Sam Adams were cautiously optimistic—*very* cautiously—that "the Continent" would rally to save their colony. The silence emanating from Philadelphia caused much worry in Watertown. Joseph Warren, still fearful that the army would slip the restraints placed upon it by the Provincial Congress, fretted to Sam Adams: "I see more & more the Necessity of establishing a civil Government here and such a Government as shall be sufficient to control the military Forces. . . . The Continent must Strengthen & support us with all its Weight the civil Authority here, otherwise our Soldiery will lose the Ideas of right & wrong, and will plunder instead of protecting, the Inhabitants. . . . I hope Care will be taken by the Continental Congress to apply an immediate Remedy, as the Infection is caught by every new Core [corps] that arrives. . . . For the Honor of my Country, I wish the Disease may be cured before it is known to exist."[11]

Not having heard a word in response, the Provincial Congress sent another letter on June 11. By that point, the Continental Congress had already taken the plunge. In late May the delegates began to discuss raising money, a clear indication that they did not entirely rule out the possibility of acting on behalf of all the colonies. On June 10, having had the Massachusetts request in hand for more than two weeks, the Congress took definite steps toward taking control of military operations in Boston. That day, the delegates "recommended" that all towns and villages throughout New England send all the gunpowder they could spare, without delay, straightaway to Ward's army at Boston. The other colonies were likewise asked to hand over all available stocks of saltpeter and sulfur, so that powder mills in New York, Philadelphia, and elsewhere could begin full-scale production. All was to be paid for "by the Continent." All was for the "use of the Continent." For the first time, Congress had taken it upon itself to act, to govern, and on behalf of all the colonies together as one. There was still no talk of a United States, of an independent nation, nor indeed of any nation at all . . . but Congress was going about its business as if an American nation did indeed exist.

The delegates in Philadelphia didn't stop there. Ardor for the Cause, and a feeling of solidarity with beleaguered Massachusetts, overcame caution . . . and the *rage militaire* helped, too. Philadelphia was as taken by war fever as anyplace in the colonies, and the delegates thrilled to the constant parades and drill exercises that occupied their host city. "Oh that I were a soldier!" John Adams wrote wistfully to his wife, Abigail. "I will be. I am reading military books. Everybody must, and will, and shall be a soldier."[12] Four days after passing the resolutions on gunpowder—on Wednesday, June 14, 1775—Congress made a decision whose mild wording belies its boldness. It authorized the recruitment of ten companies of "expert riflemen"—six from Pennsylvania, two each from Virginia and Maryland—to serve for one year, as light infantry in the army at Boston. American frontier riflemen were the subject of great and stirring tales, often highly exaggerated: these woodsmen, armed with highly accurate long rifles rather than muskets, were so skilled as marksmen that "they can kill with great Exactness at 200 yards Distance," marveled John Adams. "They have Sworn certain death to the ministerial officers."[13] So it was said, at least, and at the State House in Philadelphia the delegates—few of whom had ever handled a firearm of any sort—were inclined to believe these tales. Nothing would be so disheartening to the British than to lose officer after officer to the deadly aim of invisible foes.

It really didn't matter what kind of soldiers Congress settled on contributing to the forces outside Boston. What *did* matter was that Congress was authorizing the formation of troops, contributed by individual colonies but paid for and dispatched by *all* the colonies through Congress. And this new army had a new name. It was never formally christened—Congress denied posterity any dramatic moment or instance of pomp to commemorate—but the name appeared subtly, in the wording that Congress approved for enlistment forms to be signed by the new recruits: "The American continental army."

Some time would pass before the name—*Continental Army*—would catch on. It did not actually exist; the riflemen had yet to be recruited, there was no commander or command structure, and Ward's army outside Boston remained a New England army under mostly Massachusetts leadership. Even when the new army took form in the siege lines outside Boston, later in 1775, the name was not in common use. Titles like "the Army of the United Colonies" or—as its own commander called it—"the Army of the United Provinces of North America" were heard just as frequently. Everyone understood the significance of the name, and of what the Continental Congress had done. Massachusetts's war would soon be America's war, and the Continental Congress was in charge.

*I*f the Continental Army were to be recruited in all the colonies, paid for by all the colonies, then it would have to be truly representative of all the colonies. That much was obvious to all the delegates at Philadelphia. The burden would be distributed equally. It followed, then, that the rewards must be distributed equally, too.

And therein lay a potentially thorny problem. No one in the Continental Congress wanted the creation and maintenance of the army to become a political issue. All understood, as good Englishmen, the necessity of subordinating military authority to civil authority, and the possible dangers of an independent army that was answerable to its commanders and not to the politicians. That was not the difficulty. Rather, the difficulty was that the Congress would have to create a military command structure, and it would have to appoint commanders. It would have to find experienced military men who were enterprising but not politically ambitious, who could build and lead an army without succumbing to the temptation to use that army for their personal gain. It went without saying that the commanders would also have to share the ideals of the revolutionaries. Such men would be hard to find. It would be difficult enough just to round up a few experienced commanders.

Experience was, sadly, not the only consideration. Regional politics mattered, too, no matter how much the delegates intended otherwise. If the colonies outside New England were to sacrifice blood and treasure for the army, should it not follow that they should also be rewarded with generalships? Did it not follow that the leadership of the army ought to be as diverse as the rank-and-file?

These questions had been silently nagging each of the delegates long before they officially concurred in the raising of a national army. They all recognized that war was likely in the offing, whether they wanted it or not, so privately and individually they could not help pondering who could rise as the American Cincinnatus, what unheralded military genius might put aside his plow to take up the sword, lead the army to victory, and then willingly fade into obscurity as soon as his services were no longer needed.

All of Philadelphia was abuzz with talk about potential candidates for supreme command. In private moments in the State House, and when gathering informally in City Tavern at the end of each day, the delegates could talk of nothing else. By June 14, when the Congress voted to create the Continental Army, the choices had boiled down to a relatively small pool of qualified or hopeful applicants.

Artemas Ward was, naturally, one of them. He had been in command from the beginning, and certainly in the eyes of the New England delegates his appointment would have much merit. Ward had built the army, he knew the men, and the men knew him. Even before Lexington he had possessed some experience in military administration, and in the weeks following the battle he had accumulated much more. There was no doubting Ward's courage or his devotion to the Cause, but his poor health was a matter of common knowledge and a cause for concern.

Another serious contender was Charles Lee. The forty-three-year-old Lee was undoubtedly the most experienced soldier in the colonies. He was a Briton by birth and had been a professional soldier nearly all his life. As a company officer in the British 44th Foot, he had served in America during the French and Indian War. Along with Thomas Gage, Artemas Ward, and Israel Putnam, he was with General Abercrombie in the disastrous assault on Fort Carillon (later Ticonderoga) in 1758, and he had in fact been seriously wounded there. He grew to love America and Americans. After a brief sojourn in the Polish army, in which he held a general's rank, he moved to Virginia in 1773 and purchased a large estate near present-day Leetown, West Virginia. He thought of himself as an American and considered himself an ardent Patriot. No one in America could match his knowledge, theoretical and practical, of the art of war. Unfortunately for Lee and for those who would later run afoul of him, he was quite conscious of his superior background and did not hesitate to flaunt it. Certainly he knew the British high command better than anyone else. Gage, William Howe, and Henry Clinton were among his closest friends.

Lee had a lot to offer. But he was British-born, and—worse—he was thoroughly unattractive. Short and thin, stooped in posture, with a pinched, unfriendly face and a sharp beak of a nose, Charles Lee looked distinctly unsoldierly, an impression that his inattention to personal grooming only exaggerated. His character matched his appearance. He was loud, opinionated, long-winded, and tactless . . . faults that might have been forgiven him if he were not also uncouth, with an undisguised taste for strong drink and low-born whores. "A queer Creature," John Adams politely called him; "a good scholar and soldier . . . full of fire and passion, but little good manners," was how one of his friends described him. "A great sloven, wretchedly profane, and a great admirer of dogs."[14] Indeed he often remarked that he far preferred dogs to people. Such qualities were not likely to endear Lee to New Englanders. There was no doubting his military talents, though, and in 1775 there was no foreseeing the problems he would cause the Continental Army and the Cause. And Lee had a strong advocate in his friend and fellow Virginian George Washington.

Perhaps the strangest candidate was John Hancock. Hancock had been, along with his mentor Sam Adams, at the forefront of the Whig movement in Boston, and enjoyed a popularity and a notoriety equal to those of Adams and Joseph Warren. At age thirty-eight, he was probably the wealthiest man in Massachusetts and one of the wealthiest in all America, having inherited a mercantile empire from his uncle. Worldly, extravagant, and a touch vain—not exactly the characteristics that one associated with New Englanders at the time—Hancock was almost as popular and influential in the Second Continental Congress as he was in Boston. He was unanimously elected President of Congress in late May. Apart from his former post as commandant of the Boston Cadets—a post that was taken away from him by Thomas Gage in 1774—Hancock had no military experience whatsoever. But he fancied himself a soldier, and although he made no public expression of his desire to command, he could not hide his martial ambitions from those closest to him, like John Adams.

The final candidate was also present in the State House that spring, and he was the least self-promoting of the bunch. He was a loyal, if cautious and moderate, Patriot, with less military experience than Charles Lee but more than virtually any native-born American in 1775. During the First Continental Congress, and in the first sessions of the Second, he had quietly made himself known as a man with sound military sense, while maintaining tact, reserve, and even humility. Best of all, he refrained from advertising himself. His quiet authority spoke for itself, and his imposing physical presence was the very embodiment of military leadership.

Without even trying, George Washington of Virginia had become the talk of Congress.

There was a time, and not so long ago, when to speak ill of George Washington—or even to admit that he had any faults beyond an excess of patriotism—would be tantamount to blasphemy. We know now that Washington did indeed have flaws, actually quite a few of them, and that he was not the greatest general in the history of warfare . . . that he was a man, not a marble icon, and that as a man he was fallible. During his military career he committed many mistakes, some of them quite grave and potentially catastrophic in their consequences. Wide-eyed reverence for the man has jaded over the intervening centuries. It is easy to make jabs at Washington's qualities as a commander, as a politician, as a husband, as a man, and therefore it's not at all difficult to be cynical about his rapid and easy rise to command of the Continental Army in 1775. Where his contemporaries saw selflessness and humility in his motives and demeanor, we are tempted instead to see false

"George Washington as Colonel in the Virginia Regiment," *Charles Willson Peale, 1772. Peale painted him, three years before the Revolution, in the militia uniform he probably wore in the French and Indian War, but at the Second Continental Congress in 1775 the imposing Virginian showed up in a brand-new uniform of blue trimmed with buff.*
(WASHINGTON-CUSTIS-LEE COLLECTION, WASHINGTON AND LEE UNIVERSITY)

Charles Lee. As the most experienced soldier in America in 1775, Lee was George Washington's only real rival for the position of commander-in-chief of the rebel army. But his rough manners and eccentric habits—he kept dogs with him everywhere, even at the dinner table—diminished his popularity. Ultimately Lee's growing contempt for Washington would prove his undoing.
(THE LIBRARY OF CONGRESS)

modesty and calculated self-promotion. But in truth there is little or nothing to suggest that George Washington wanted, let alone sought, the responsibility of leading a nonexistent army against a powerful and relentless foe.

Next to his friend Charles Lee, George Washington was the most experienced soldier in British North America in 1775, but that was not saying very much. Born in 1732 to a wealthy Virginia tobacco planter, Washington enjoyed all the advantages of high birth and a privileged life—all the advantages except formal schooling, a shortcoming of which he was painfully self-conscious. He did not, however, settle down to a life of ease. Even at a tender age, ambition drove him on. Washington was only seventeen when the governor of Virginia appointed him as surveyor of Culpeper County, the first step in his rise to prominence in his native colony. Though he craved money, power, and high social standing, young Washington yearned for the life of a soldier. His older half-brother and mentor, Lawrence, had held a commission as a captain in the British army. George wanted the same for himself, but luck was not with him and he was unable to secure a royal commission. But he enjoyed the friendship and patronage of men in high places, including Governor Robert Dinwiddie, and this helped to slake Washington's thirst for action, honor, and promotion.

Washington's military career before the Revolution was a patchy one. At age twenty he applied for, and got, a commission as a district adjutant in the Virginia militia. Less than two years later he had his first command. It was a disaster. In April 1754, on Governor Dinwiddie's orders, Lieutenant Colonel Washington led an expedition into the Ohio country to drive out the French troops then operating near the Forks of the Ohio (present-day Pittsburgh, Pennsylvania). His mixed force of Virginia militia, volunteers, and Indians overwhelmed and ambushed a small body of French troops and their Indian allies; in revenge, a larger French-led band caught Washington in his lair, a poorly sited stockade that the colonel dubbed Fort Necessity, compelling the Virginians to surrender.

The battle at the Great Meadows, as it came to be known, humbled Washington. It was his first real combat and his first defeat, and the only time that he would ever surrender in his entire life. It taught him something of the qualities and faults of militia forces. And he was fortunate in escaping not only with his life but also with his reputation intact. His officers defended him, his colony and his governor stood by him, and though the defeat could easily have wrecked his career it did not. So when General Edward Braddock showed up in Virginia at the head of a British army, bent on accomplishing what the militia colonel had not been able to, Washington was almost immediately suggested as a local guide for the expedition. Acting as personal aide-de-camp, without rank, to General Braddock, Washington was with the British column when it fell victim to an ambush by French and Indian forces at the Forks of the Monongahela in July 1755. But if the Virginian had lost face at Fort Necessity, he regained his honor with interest under Braddock's command. Braddock fell, mortally wounded, early in the fight, but the twenty-three-year-old Washington rose to the occasion—first getting Braddock's bleeding body hoisted onto a cart and shunted to safety, then riding all along the column trying to rally the panicked Redcoats and provincials into some semblance of order as the French and their Indian allies massacred them.

Colonel Washington's gallant conduct, his flagrant disregard for his personal safety as he endeavored to save Braddock's shattered command, made him the hero of a truly dismal defeat. It was during his time with Braddock, too, that Washington became friends with a young British officer in the 44th Foot who led the vanguard at the time of the disastrous battle, one Captain Thomas Gage.

Washington continued to rise in rank, ultimately becoming brigadier general and the commander of Virginia's entire militia, but he saw little further action. After accompanying British General John Forbes on his successful but uneventful attempt to force the French from Fort Duquesne, Washington resigned his commission and returned to civilian life.

George Washington's military career before 1775 had by no means been a stellar one. His tactical abilities, if measured by the example of the Great Meadows, were mediocre at best. Throughout the war, his dealings with government officials and fellow officers showed him to be overly sensitive to criticism and inclined to look for personal enemies where none existed. Washington read a great deal, and steeped himself in books on military theory, but he was a man who learned on the job, and he learned quickly and profitably from his mistakes. He discovered, from Braddock's massacre, that the Redcoats were not invincible, and that lack of discipline was the bane of armies. He had an utter disregard for colonial militia, and the forces he commanded at Fort Necessity only diminished his opinion of such troops. Yet from his experiences in reforming the Virginia militia during the first years of the war, he also came to believe that Americans—if properly trained, disciplined, and led—could be made the equal of professional European soldiers.

The George Washington who retired from military service at the end of 1758 was a much wiser, more subdued, more mature man than the one who had surrendered Fort Necessity only four years before. And he was through with soldiering. He dreamed no longer of martial glory, had no further desire to lead men in battle. He withdrew instead to the life of domestic ease that a man of his station could expect. Marriage to the wealthy widow Martha Custis, guardianship over Martha's young children, and the responsibilities of running their estate at Mount Vernon worked their change on the man. He would now be a planter, a gentleman, involved in public life but focused mainly on his family and his crops. His ambition did not leave him, but merely metamorphosed into something a tad more prosaic: a progressive, even scientific, farmer, and an astute businessman. Washington became enormously wealthy during the years between the wars.[15]

His business concerns and his domestic bliss absorbed his attentions to the point that he took only a passing interest in the rumblings of colonial discontent in Massachusetts . . . at first. Washington's political views, though, were framed early on, and remained remarkably consistent in the years leading up to the outbreak of rebellion.

In 1769, he confided to a close friend that, in his view, the colonies should not "hesitate a moment to use arms in defence of so valuable a blessing" as their liberties. By the time the Coercive Acts went into effect in 1774, Washington had become quite outspoken, even brazen. He was no "great incendiary," no demagogue, but his patriotism was just as plain and as heartfelt as Sam Adams's or Joseph Warren's. He publicly blasted the Coercive Acts as a "Tyrannical System . . . to overthrow our Constitutional Rights & liberties." Such expressions won him more attention than he anticipated, probably more than he was comfortable with, and soon he ranked among the most prominent Patriots in Virginia. He helped to draft the Fairfax Resolves, Virginia's unofficial, bitter indictment of British colonial administration; he was chosen to represent Virginia at the First Continental Congress. In the spring of 1775, he returned to Philadelphia for the second congress.[16]

*T*he Second Continental Congress was Washington's moment in the light. It was the point at which he allowed himself to be drawn back into public life. This time he assumed a much greater responsibility than ever before, though not from ambition, not from thirst for glory, not from a boyish attraction to the military life and great deeds of arms. If anything, Washington—the happy family man with an active but comfortable life—wanted to escape responsibility. He found no pleasure being in the spotlight.

Hence Washington had no interest in seeking command of the new Continental Army, not even after Congress decided to create that army. He was done with being a soldier. Virginia, though, had called him to represent the colony in this time of crisis, and he answered the call. In no time at all he became one of the stars of the Congress. His expertise on military affairs put him in great demand as the delegates talked more and more about war. Near the end of

May he was made chairman of a special committee to "consider ways and means to supply these Colonies with ammunition and military stores," where Washington worked alongside such luminaries as Philip Schuyler of New York and Sam Adams of Massachusetts.

In his quiet hours alone, when he wasn't in the State House or dining with colleagues at City Tavern, Washington pondered, studied, reflected . . . and in his thoughts he kept returning to military matters. He pored over the written accounts of Lexington and Concord. What he read bolstered his long-cherished conviction that Americans *could* beat the British if properly trained and handled. He felt the soldier within him stir at the prospect. The Virginia militia colonel sensed that he would take the field again; late in May, he hired his friend Edmund Pendleton to compose his will. But there was a world of difference between contemplating war and craving supreme command, between knowing that Americans would fight and actually preparing them to do so.

Washington was not about to advertise himself or promote his services. He did not seem to want command, and even if he did, he was hardly the kind of person to covet it openly. But that didn't restrain his fellow delegates from promoting him of their own volition. Whether he liked it or not, he was noticed. His grave and self-effacing manner, his gentility and friendliness, had won him many admirers. "He is Clever, and if any thing too modest," wrote Eliphalet Dyer. "He seems discreet and Virtuous, no harum Starum ranting Swearing fellow but Sober, steady, and Calm."[17] His physical presence also put him well above his competitors. Ward was ill, pale, and overweight; Hancock handsome but effete; Lee scrawny and bent. George Washington, at the relatively advanced age of forty-three, was tall—six feet two inches—broad-shouldered, muscular, and athletic. Despite his height, which was quite remarkable in that age, there was nothing ill-proportioned or freakish about him. He was preternaturally graceful, a skilled dancer and an exceptional equestrian. He *looked* like a soldier, or how a civilian might imagine a great leader of men would appear. Washington exuded authority, strength, calm, and common sense—and, barely suppressed just beneath the surface, a fire and a passion that could make him just a little bit dangerous. "All of his features," observed the painter Gilbert Stuart, "were indications of the strongest and most ungovernable passions, and had he been born in the forest, he would have been the fiercest man among the savage tribes." An imposing personal aura may not be one of the most important traits a commander-in-chief can possess, but it didn't hurt Washington.

The Virginian inadvertently helped further his candidacy. Washington had been in Congress for less than a month when John Adams—soon to be his most devoted ally and advocate—noticed something different about him. "Colonel Washington," Adams wrote approvingly, "appears at Congress in his uniform." And what a uniform! Not the faded blue-and-red coat he had worn as a young man in the French and Indian War, but a brilliant ensemble: a regimental coat of dark blue, trimmed in the yellowish cream color known as "buff," with buff-colored breeches and waistcoat—the "antient Whig Colours of England." He had ordered the suit in November—specially tailored just for him, loose in the seat and the legs, since Washington didn't much care for the tight fit of fashionable men's breeches. The garments were still new and crisp and unstained, guaranteed to turn heads.[18]

Neither vanity nor ambition compelled Washington to don military garb in Congress. It was not a signal to his colleagues that he wanted command, or even that he was available. He did it to make a simple political statement: the time for compromise, for words, was over. The contest would have to be settled with blood.

His fellow delegates read a different message. Washington's choice of clothing elevated his candidacy to the point where it was difficult to imagine anyone else in command of the yet-to-be-raised army. Still, some of the New England delegates would have preferred one of their own as general, and scoffed at the notion that the middle and southern colonies would not fully trust a New Englander in command. Others thought that Charles Lee's broader experience made him better suited. But a growing number of delegates had come to understand John Adams's preference for the Virginian: " . . . by his great experience and abilities in military matters, [Washington] is of much service to us."[19] Even Elbridge Gerry and Joseph Warren, who put great store in Artemas Ward, saw that Washington might be the ideal choice.

Indeed he was. And that was not just because of his military experience and his personality. Appointing Washington to supreme command made good political sense, too. A New England general might be more to the tastes of the troops laying siege to Boston, but if Congress was going to take over the war effort, if the other colonies were going to send their troops and their resources, then it would be a good idea to appoint a general who was not a New Englander. The Continental Army should be commanded by a Continental general, a man who represented American unity and solidarity. Ward could not do that, nor Hancock, and Charles Lee was—for all his suspiciously loud expressions of patriotism—an Englishman born and bred.

No one saw that better, or earlier, than John Adams of Massachusetts. Adams wielded no small amount of influence, and of all the New England delegates he was the least bound to the narrow interests of his home region. For weeks he had worked tirelessly, behind the scenes, on behalf of Washington's candidacy, and on June 14—after airing his ideas to Sam Adams—he made his case. As the delegates discussed the military situation, Adams rose to his feet and made an impassioned—and wonderfully engineered—plea. Massachusetts needed the support of the other colonies, and needed it now. If Ward's army were to fall apart, the results would be catastrophic.

An army recruited from all of British North America must come to Boston, led by a general who represented Congress and all the colonies. An *American* general.

The time might not be right, Adams admitted, to go so far as to name a general, not yet, but having said that, he declared that he had only one person in mind. Two men in the meeting chamber responded visibly. One of them was John Hancock, president of Congress, who flashed a confident smile. Surely, he thought, his friend Adams was just about to nominate *him*. Washington felt precisely the same thing, and flushed with embarrassment. Then, Adams ended the suspense abruptly: the man he thought most suited to be commanding general, he continued, came from Virginia. George Washington was the man, he argued, and Adams went on to trumpet his virtues.

It was an awkward moment in the meeting chamber. As soon as John Adams uttered the word "Virginia," Washington knew what was coming. Mortified with fear and simply overwhelmed, he jumped up from his seat and escaped into the State House library, where he could be alone for a while. At precisely the same instant, proud Hancock—who, as president of the body, could not make himself invisible as Washington had—reacted in shock, obviously crestfallen, especially since so low a blow could come from a friend and fellow Yankee. Hancock's face fell, his eyes blazed, and much as he tried to compose himself he could not hide his disappointment. "I never remarked a more sudden and striking change of countenance," Adams noted gleefully. "Mortification and resentment were expressed as forcibly as his face could exhibit them."[20] Sam Adams, Hancock's idol and mentor, immediately seconded his cousin's nomination of Washington. John Adams found the whole thing marvelous. He didn't expect Sam to agree with him, at least not so quickly, and he truly enjoyed watching proud, stiff Hancock all but writhe in jealousy.

$\mathcal{G}$eorge Washington was, if anything, even more disappointed than John Hancock. In fact, he was devastated. He had already resigned himself to the near certainty that he would be called upon to soldier in some capacity, and he was well aware that his name was being tossed around in Congress. But until that moment, when John Adams spoke his name aloud in front of the entire Congress, he did not fully comprehend that he was a mere vote away from being given the worst job in America.

Once he had fled to the library, Washington could not bring himself to face his friends and colleagues. He stayed out until the very end of the day. It was just as well, for in his absence the delegates could discuss Washington and the other hopefuls freely, frankly, without fear of hurting the Virginian's feelings. The debate was lively but in no way mean-spirited or acerbic, and no one raised any personal objection to Washington as commander. There was only one argument against his appointment, and it was a weighty one: didn't the men in the army—the real army, that is, the one at Boston—deserve a general they knew and respected?

The day ended without a vote. The deliberations resumed the next day, after Washington's proponents—headed by John Adams—did their best to win over the opposition. By the time Congress resumed the discussion, on Thursday, June 15, the delegates were in agreement. Most southerners had already embraced Washington. Not all New Englanders would go so far as to concede that the Virginia planter was most qualified to command. "He is a gentleman highly esteemed . . . ," wrote Eliphalet Dyer of Connecticut, "though I don't believe, as to his military and real service, he knows more than some of ours."[21] But no one could argue with the political wisdom behind the choice: Washington's appointment would virtually guarantee that all the colonies would stand by

Massachusetts's side. Thomas Johnson, a delegate from Maryland, nominated Washington on the floor. The vote was immediate and unanimous, with no opposition, no other candidates suggested or discussed. George Washington was chosen to serve as general "to command all the continental forces, raised, or to be raised, for the defence of American liberty."

Washington had absented himself from Congress that day, June 15, 1775, far too uncomfortable with the discussions—and fearful of their outcome—to stomach the ordeal. He got the news that evening, for his friends could not resist the temptation to address him as "general." The following day, in Congress, he responded. His address was not exactly what his fellow delegates expected to hear. "I am truly sensible of the high Honour done me in this Appointment," Washington said, " . . . yet I feel great distress, from a consciousness that my abilities & Military experience may not be equal to the extensive & important Trust." Washington was not merely being modest—he was genuinely terrified, of failure, of dishonor, of doing harm to the Cause. He tried hard to cover himself: "I beg it may be remembered . . . that I this day declare with the utmost sincerity, I do not think myself equal to the Command . . ."[22] Nonetheless he accepted the post. Like many men of his high position in society, he clung to the belief that a man of virtue and honor was obliged to serve when called; family and the comforts of domestic life had to take a backseat to duty. It was the same motive that drove him to turn down the $500 monthly pay that Congress had allocated for his position.

There was so much to do and so little time, for if the Massachusetts Provincial Congress were to be believed, the army at Boston was hanging on by a slender thread. Both Washington and Congress got down to business. A special committee composed the general's commission and drew up basic orders for him. Washington took one evening to celebrate—though he didn't much feel like celebrating—at a party held in his honor at the Vauxhall Tavern, outside Philadelphia, on the evening of the eighteenth. He spent as much time alone as he could, having had precious little time to himself for the better part of a week, and as he contemplated the tasks awaiting him he felt no more confident of success than he had when first nominated. To his friend and fellow Virginian Patrick Henry, he talked morosely, as if he had already been defeated: "Remember, Mr. Henry, what I now tell you: from the day I enter upon the command of the American armies, I date my fall, and the ruin of my reputation."[23]

Over the next few days, the Congress completed the army's command structure, appointing major generals and brigadier generals to serve under Washington. In comparison to the smooth and untrammeled process of selecting a commander-in-chief, the debate over the subordinate generals was messy and even acrimonious. Washington himself had little say in the choices, which had more to do with politics than with military talent or experience. Every colony wanted to claim a general, and not all could be accommodated.

The selection of major generals and brigadiers would return to haunt Washington and Congress, and nearly destroy the army, all within a few short weeks. But for now, George Washington was the unwilling hero of the hour. On June 22, 1775, he bid adieu to Congress and left Philadelphia. After penning one last sad letter to Martha, the tall, gravely serious man in the blue-and-buff uniform pushed his way through the dense crowd of cheering, adoring Philadelphians, each of them pushing in on him to grasp his hand, touch his shoulder. Once in the street, he mounted his horse and joined with his four traveling companions. They made an odd group: the scrawny, unkempt Charles Lee, beaming at all the attention lavished upon him, and Philip Schuyler, cool and confident and almost arrogant on the surface, Washington's northern counterpart. The first two members of Washington's newly adopted "military family" were there, too—Thomas Mifflin and Joseph Reed, both of Pennsylvania, young sophisticates in their early thirties, both articulate and cultured.

The five men rode from the city in pomp and splendor. Cavalry escorted them; innumerable politicians and well-wishers, military bands, and youths with toy guns followed along for a few miles before tiring of the procession and heading home. Three days later they were in New York City. The Patriots there greeted them wildly, without dignity, in the view of New York's many Tories.

That evening, as Washington tried to rest his aching bones and sore legs in his temporary lodgings on Broadway, an express rider arrived with letters from Watertown to the Congress at Philadelphia. Without thinking, Washington opened one of them, and what he read made him forget all about the glamour of his triumphal entry into New York City, the admiring crowds, the shrill and buoyant music of fife and drum.

The letter was from the Massachusetts Provincial Congress, and the news was both bad and good. There had been a battle outside Boston, eight days ago, on the hills overlooking Charlestown and the Charles River. The British had suffered heavily but had taken the ground from the American army. Washington's heart both raced and sank as he scanned the letter, but nothing hammered home the awful weight of his new responsibilities like its last sentence, a desperate appeal from one colony to all the others:

"We beg leave humbly to suggest, that, if a commander in chief over the army of the United Colonies should be appointed, it must be plain to your honors, that no part of this continent can so much require his immediate presence and exertions, as this colony."[24]

Five

ELBOW ROOM

*T*he buoyant optimism that filled the chamber of the State House in Philadelphia in the last sparkling weeks of spring was not mirrored in Boston—not on either side of the Charles. Little had changed since the beginning of May, for the British or for their American tormentors. No grand plans unfolded; no grand plans were even made, and it seemed as if nothing had so much as moved in those days. As far as the members of the Committee of Safety and the Provincial Congress were concerned, the Continental Congress had yet to justify the hopes that had been invested in it. The only tangible advantage that Massachusetts had derived from the meeting in Philadelphia was the removal of Benjamin Church from Cambridge. And since Dr. Church's unspeakable after-hours activities were yet undiscovered, unknown to all save General Gage and the doctor's own conscience, the revolutionary leadership had no reason to take comfort from his absence.

Still, change was in the air—everyone could feel it—and it filled the British in Boston with something very much like confidence. While the rebels clung desperately to the ephemeral hope that the Continent just might come to their aid, and in time, the British in Boston were certain that things were going to get better. Help really was on the way: a few more regiments were making their way across the North Atlantic toward Boston. Redcoat officers and men all knew it; all cast their eyes seaward from time to time, scanning the horizon for the telltale signs of the transports that could appear any day. "We are anxiously wishing for the arrival of the Genl. Officers and Troops that are expected," Lieutenant Barker of the King's Own confided to his diary. "We want to get out of this coop'd up situation. We cou'd now do that I suppose but the G[eneral Gage] does not seem to want it."[1]

Gage, too, looked anxiously for their arrival, but with mixed anticipation, vindication, and dull dread. He had been pleading with London for reinforcements for months and finally he would have them, yet the fact that the reinforcements had been sent was itself a signal, if a subtle one, that the ministry had found him wanting. For aboard one of the government vessels speeding toward the New England coast were three major generals, the best England had to send. Gage outranked them, but it mattered little. The king felt that the crisis in America required new blood. It did not bode well for Thomas Gage's career.

But even Gage had to admit that the reinforcements couldn't arrive fast enough. Finally, he hoped, the stalemate would end, the siege would be lifted, and the rebellion could be crushed.

The Americans were also well aware that more red-clad legions were on their way. Boston was crawling with rebel spies, and nearly everything that Gage did—and nearly everything he knew, for that matter—was common knowledge in Cambridge within hours. Obviously the rebels didn't find much to celebrate in the knowledge that their numerical superiority, their foremost advantage, might be slipping away, but neither did the imminent arrivals cause much panic. They knew it would happen, sooner or later, and in their minds the bombast of patriotric rhetoric lingered on . . . that there should be "no apprehensions from General *Gage's* ever being able to penetrate into the country thus far, if he was even reinforced with fifty thousand men."[2] And there was more pressing business requiring attention closer to home.

*W*hen conducted properly, sieges were drudging affairs, stultifyingly boring, at least for the foot soldiers and their commanders. Engineers supervised the process with scientific precision: parallel lines of fortifications were gradually moved closer and closer to the town or strongpoint under siege, until—hopefully—the besieger's lines were so close that his guns could pound the defending works into rubble . . . or into submission. The American army outside Boston had so little artillery that it couldn't even contemplate conducting a siege in the conventional way. Instead, the rebels sat passively in their positions at Cambridge and Roxbury—not because of an unimaginative or lethargic commander, but because they really had no other option.

Artemas Ward's efforts to mold the men into a functioning army had paid off, but not enough. When Nathanael Greene arrived in camp with his Rhode Island boys on May 27, he was dismayed by what he saw. "The want of government, and of a certainty of supplies, had thrown everything into disorder. . . . it is very difficult to limit people who have had so much latitude, without throwing them into disorder." Several companies were on the verge of marching home, Greene noted, and the commissaries bringing supplies into camp had been so badly abused by his men that they, too, intended to quit their jobs and go home the very next day. "A few days longer in th[is] state of excitement . . . would have proved fatal to our campaign," he added dolefully.[3]

Generally, though, the army had settled into a routine of regular guard mounts, digging fortifications, and going through drill. Individual companies drew issues of vinegar and precious soap for cleansing the hospitals and the smallpox quarantines. Men in camp, with no other duties, made musket cartridges for the army. It didn't take much skill to make cartridges—they were nothing more than a powder charge and a musket ball rolled up in a small piece of paper—but it was necessary work; for as most military experts agreed, it was much faster to load a musket using one of these self-contained rounds than it was with loose musket balls from a pouch and loose powder from a powder horn.

And there was church. When General Ward ordered his men to attend prayer services regularly, he probably could have spared himself the effort. He was preaching to the choir, for the army was a religious one. Even without the constant ministrations of the chaplains who tended to their spiritual needs, the men were already convinced that their cause was a holy one, that the Lord of Hosts fought by their side and guided their steps. Attending worship service was a comforting connection to their former lives as civilians, a reminder of more peaceful, more certain times. Many of the men attended prayers twice daily if they could, noting in their diaries the details of the sermons they heard. A good sermon was the highlight of the week: "o this was fine Preaching," wrote young Amos Farnsworth of Groton after listening to a sermon by Reverend Thaxter, chaplain of Prescott's regiment.[4] It was the way that rural New Englanders were raised; it was the way that men who faced death, who worried about their salvation, made things right with their Creator.

The prospect of death was not all that remote, at least not in

Roxbury. In Cambridge, a soldier stood a much greater chance of being killed by the accidental discharge of a comrade's musket than he did at the hands of his adversaries across the water. But in Roxbury, the true focal point of the siege, where the American defensive works lay within easy cannon range of the British lines on Boston Neck, things were quite different.

At Roxbury, John Thomas led an army that was practically independent of Cambridge. Ward kept tabs on Roxbury, but he had his hands full with the army at Cambridge and his dealings with the civil government, and so he allowed Thomas almost unfettered command. Thomas was perhaps the most experienced soldier in all of New England. A physician by training—the Cause, it seems, was steered by medical doctors in the first year of the rebellion—Thomas had started his own medical practice in Kingston, Massachusetts. Soon thereafter, the young doctor accepted an appointment as a surgeon in a provincial regiment during King George's War. He found that military life agreed with him, preferring leading men in combat to treating them for wounds and fevers and venereal diseases. A lieutenancy followed a year later. In the French and Indian War, he rose to the rank of colonel of provincial troops. Soldiering was his true calling: none other than Sir Jeffrey Amherst, the most successful British commander in North America during the French war, so trusted Thomas that he gave the provincial officer command over an entire division in the attack on Montréal in 1760.[5]

Thomas was a soldier's soldier, six feet tall and athletic, soft-spoken and gentle but still a strict disciplinarian. His men loved him, and even his enemies found much to like and respect in the man. One local Tory, grateful to Thomas for his even-handed dealings with all civilians, presented the general with three barrels of cider. The officers at Roxbury marveled at his dedication and his stamina; Thomas, it was said, went for nine consecutive days without any sleep following the Lexington alarm, as he tried

John Thomas. Second-in-command to Artemas Ward and de facto commander of the rebel forces at Roxbury, Thomas was undoubtedly the most gifted of the Massachusetts military leaders. Though he pined for his wife and children, his remarkable sense of duty compelled him to stay with the army. Thomas died a lonely death in the closing phases of the Quebec campaign in 1776. Portrait by Benjamin Blyth, 1775.
(COURTESY OF THE MASSACHUSETTS HISTORICAL SOCIETY)

Sketch of General Israel Putnam, by John Trumbull. "Old Put" was a living legend of the American frontier, immensely popular, dedicated to the Cause, indefatigable, honest to a fault… though not, perhaps, a highly talented general.
(WADSWORTH ATHENEUM MUSEUM OF ART, HARTFORD, CT/ART RESOURCE, NY.)

to secure his improvised command against a retaliatory strike. If Thomas had a weakness—if it can indeed be called a weakness—it was his profound devotion to his family. His sense of duty to Massachusetts won out by only the barest of margins over his love for his wife, Hannah, and their three children. He wrote Hannah, his "Best Friend," nearly every day, asking her for sugar loaves, snuff, and clean linen shirts, hoping that she could come to Roxbury and visit him. He told his son Natte, in charmingly misspelled prose, of skirmishes and cannonades, while counseling the boy "to Lern your Book & Every other thing you Shall be directed to so when you Grow up you may be Capable of being a Good man which is the Greatest wishes of your Papa."[6] Thomas loved being a soldier, but he was homesick and yearned for the domestic comforts of home and family.

Thomas's headaches were very different from Artemas Ward's. Ward worried about recruitment and supply and administration; Thomas worried about British cannonfire destroying Roxbury or British troops overrunning his lines. Such fears weren't far-fetched. Thomas watched with mounting unease as the British fortifications on the Neck, only a few hundred yards from his own positions, multiplied and thickened and fairly bristled with heavy cannon and mortars, as Admiral Graves's patrol boats menaced the shallows of the Back Bay. Thomas hoped and prayed that the cannon captured at Ticonderoga might somehow make their way to Boston. In the meantime he had to make do with what he had. When the Roxbury lines were thinnest, in early May, a rumor spread throughout the camps that Gage was preparing an attack via Boston Neck; Thomas paraded his entire force—probably just over two thousand men—in a long, drawn-out column following a circular route . . . a ruse, meant to give the British the impression that Thomas's little force was many times larger than it actually was. But General Thomas knew just how vulnerable he was. His informants in Boston passed along the word that the British were "Determined to Drive that Damned Thomas / as they call me / from the Hills in Roxbury. . . ."[7]

Thomas kept a few hundred men stationed as pickets on the base of Boston Neck to give advance warning of any British movement in the area. But what he would do if Gage really did try something, Thomas hadn't a clue. Except for a few light fieldpieces, he had no artillery. He had nothing that could stave off a determined attack for very long. "Anyone may Judge," he wrote in a rare moment of candor to Artemas Ward in May, "what Defence Can be made with small arms. Had I Even so many men on the Spot in Case they are Determind I have thorewly Reconuterd the Ground Sence I have bin here & much Dispare of Deffending of it unless we had . . . sum Regular Intrenchment & Placeing Sum Canon There & Person to Take the Proper Direction of Them." In the meantime, all Thomas and his men could do was to endure the occasional (and usually short) bombardments from the British cannon on the Neck . . . and collect the spent cannonballs to hoard in case any of the Ticonderoga guns ever did make it to Roxbury. But "I should be Sorey that our Troops must be obliged to Retreat in Case of being attacked which I am under sum apprehention must be the Case."[8]

Fear of a British attack was not limited to Roxbury. The Americans, soldier and civilian alike, had a hard time believing that the British were so weak that Gage didn't dare launch a thrust into the countryside . . . that Gage was just as concerned with getting his army into fighting trim as they were with theirs. Rumors of invasions spread, and often, and no matter how febrile they may have appeared, the generals and the Committee of Safety couldn't take any chances. On May 9, reports of an imminent British strike against Roxbury worked their way to headquarters; the Committee, fearing the worst, called upon the towns nearest Roxbury to send two thousand minutemen to come to General Thomas's support. It was the swan song of the minutemen; never again would they be sum-moned for duty.[9]

Ward, and Thomas as well, saw no alternative to sitting still and husbanding their forces as long as they possibly could. Warren felt the same way, even if only a few weeks earlier he had been eager to send the half-formed army headlong against the British lines in a wild, bloody rush. But not everyone shared their view, especially not the Connecticut brigadier Israel Putnam. Old Put, as he was almost universally called, was already a legend in the army, and not just among his Connecticut boys. Everyone knew about his frantic ride from his farm in Mortlake (present-day Pomfret) to Cambridge on the day after Lexington and Concord—a hundred miles in eight hours—and everyone believed it, too, because everything about Putnam was beyond belief. As a young man, it was said, he had killed the last wolf in Connecticut, crawling alone into her den with nothing but a musket and a torch. His exploits in the French and Indian War were the stuff of adventure stories: serving as an of-ficer in Rogers' Rangers, and ultimately rising to the rank of major; being captured by Indians near Crown Point in the summer of 1758, and being saved from being burned alive by the intercession of a sympathetic French officer; getting shipwrecked while en route to Cuba to participate in the British attack on Havana in 1762. After the war, he became both a devout Congregationalist and a devout Patriot. Old Put was a living frontier hero, almost as famous among the British officers as he was throughout the colonies.[10]

Israel Putnam was a fearless bull of a man, with a stocky pu-gilist's body surmounted by a great cube of a head and a face that was comically akin to a bulldog's. He was loud and brash and bel-lowing, but not a bully in any way. All who knew him loved him, and most who didn't know him loved him, too. Putnam didn't have an enemy worth mentioning. He exuded action; those who served under him would follow him anywhere. There was no pretense, nothing frivolous, about the man. "He does not wear a large wig, nor screw his countenance into a form that belies the sentiments of his generous soul," Silas Deane lauded him. "He is no adept either at politics or religious canting and cozening; he is no shake-hand body: he therefore is totally unfit for everything but fighting."[11]

Putnam *was* a fighter, nothing more, nothing less. He was born for the brawl, and was happiest when the smoke of battle stung his eyes and the musket balls sang around his massive head. And that was both his chief quality and his chief shortcoming. Old Put did not dwell too much on the consequences of his actions, and hence he was no strategist. He was a leader, but no general, regardless of his rank. At Bunker Hill he would see his finest hour, and whatever good came from the battle there owes much to Putnam's stolid and reassuring presence; but had he been in Ward's place, the Cause might well have been in very serious straits.

There was one thing, though, that Old Put had right: something had to be done with the men to keep them busy, to keep their spirits up. In this way he was the perfect counterpoint to Ward. After attending Ward's Council of War on April 21, he returned to Connecticut to report what he had seen at Cambridge and to drum up support for Massachusetts, and then rode straight back to Cambridge. Once he had returned, he found plenty of work for his boys to do. He carefully laid out three small fortifications—known only as Forts One, Two, and Three—to guard the approaches to Cambridge, and every day sent out work details to build the forts in accordance with General Ward's orders. But to make the men feel like soldiers and not day laborers, he reasoned, there must be some kind of action, even if it didn't actually result in battle.

On May 13, Putnam acted, and apparently on no one's orders but his own. With a mixed force of Massachusetts and Connecticut troops, two thousand strong, Putnam marched onto the Charlestown peninsula with no other object than to demonstrate to the

British that the Americans weren't afraid of the Redcoats—"to Shoe themselves to the Regulars," as Amos Farnsworth expressed it in his diary. Marching in an irregular column—for the Americans were not yet very accomplished at maintaining tight formations or marching in cadence—Putnam's improvised brigade paraded over Bunker Hill, then over Breed's Hill, not making any attempt to hide themselves from British eyes. The column descended Breed's Hill into Charlestown itself, practically strutting along the waterfront in full view of the massive HMS *Somerset* and her sixty-four big guns. They didn't fire on the imposing British man-of-war, but shouted a defiant "War-hoop," turned around, and retraced their steps up the peninsula and to Cambridge. The British did nothing to impede their progress. Even the guns of the *Somerset* remained silent throughout the strange procession.[12]

It was an impressive display of courage, and it made the New Englanders' hearts soar. They had challenged the British, and the British did not respond. The pointless expedition made Putnam even more of a hero, if that were possible, but Putnam's little march revealed something troubling about the nature of the army. Putnam had acted without orders, and had acted in a fashion that could very well have provoked a bloody confrontation with the British, a confrontation for which the army was ill prepared. The chain of command in the rebel army was nowhere near as solid as it should have been. There was only the most tenuous connection between Artemas Ward in Cambridge and John Thomas in Roxbury. That an officer of Putnam's rank and caliber, who met with his superior Ward on an almost daily basis, should take it upon himself to engage in such conduct did not bode well for the rebel army.

The British were not impressed by Putnam's daring march. If anything, the Redcoats who watched the spectacle of two thousand unsoldierlike "country people" found it depressing . . . not Putnam's action, but the reaction of their own commanders. Lieutenant Barker, who never bothered to disguise his contempt for General Gage and Admiral Graves, saw in the day's events a missed opportunity. "It was expected [they] wou'd have fired on the Somerset, at least it was wished for, as she had everything ready for Action," the eager young lieutenant lamented, "and must have destroyed great numbers of them, besides putting the Town in Ashes."[13]

Putnam did nothing to damage British morale. But the fact that he *could* do it was symptomatic of the demoralizing situation in which the British found themselves in May 1775. The army was cooped up in Boston, without the chance to redeem its disappointing performance of April 19, and officers and men alike practically ached for another go at the rebels who had humiliated them, and who taunted them still in actions like Putnam's. The army was not starving, for there was yet plenty of salt provisions, and there were even rare moments of feasting: at the end of May, Gage's commissaries managed to get their hands on a small number of cattle, and over the following couple of days all the regiments were marched to Bryan's slaughterhouse near the Common to receive their dole of two days' worth of fresh beef.[14] But the transition from the abundance of fresh meat and vegetables only a few months before to "the coarsest food" once the siege had begun was chipping away at the army's spirits. "On our landing," wrote an officer whose regiment debarked at Boston at the end of May, "we found everything in the utmost confusion, partly arising from the murmurs of the soldiery . . . the want of fresh provisions, the great unhealthiness of the troops, and above all, the misery of the wretched inhabitants."[15]

Disciplinary problems were the predictable result. The officers noted, with mixed alarm and distaste, that drunkenness—a constant problem in all armies, and one that scarcely deserved a mention unless it had really gotten out of control—had become prevalent among the men. Gage tried to cap off the flow of rum into the camps, repeatedly threatening dire punishments to women caught in the act of bringing these "pernicious spirits" to the soldiers, but to no effect.[16]

When the British *did* try to do something about their less-than-satisfactory condition, it backfired. Although General Gage could rest assured that his men were being adequately fed, there was not enough fodder for the horses and other livestock in the garrison . . . but there was plenty of it to be found outside of Boston. Gage set his sights on Grape Island, off Weymouth far to the south, where a Tory named Elisha Leavitt had once farmed. On May 21, Gage sent a couple of the admiral's smaller vessels out to seize any hay to be found on Grape, and with the aid of a kidnapped pilot the flotilla reached the island and debarked a few dozen Redcoats. As the soldiers swiftly covered the island, carrying all the hay they could find to the waiting boats, all hell broke loose on the mainland.

Before the Regulars had even landed on Grape Island, couriers brought the news to General Thomas—whose troops were closest to the island—that the British were attacking Weymouth itself. Thomas didn't wait for confirmation; three companies of his Roxbury command were soon hurrying south to see what they could do. Even Joseph Warren, who despite his political duties longed to be in the thick of the action, mounted his horse and rode to Weymouth at breakneck speed. At Weymouth and in the surrounding towns the alarm sounded, just as it had on the day of Lexington. Frightened women and children fled inland; the militia turned out in force. In nearby Braintree "the alarm flew like lightning," Abigail Adams wrote to her husband, John, then in Philadelphia attending the Congress. "Men from all parts came flocking down, till two thousand were collected."[17] The masses of militia and curious onlookers watched from the shore in helpless anger as the Redcoats proceeded to ship the hay. Low tide had beached all the small craft along the coast, but once the tide lifted, floating a few lighters, Thomas's boys and the militia crowded onto the boats and took to the water. Beaching their boats on the near end of the island, the colonials sprinted ashore, and the surprised Redcoats retreated precipitously to their boats after firing a couple of ragged volleys. "Thay was mad," reported Amos Farnsworth.[18]

The Grape Island affair meant little in strategic or material terms. The British got quite a bit of hay; the Americans burned the rest. Both sides claimed to have killed enemies but to have suffered no losses themselves. But it was another black eye for Gage and his army, and for Graves, too. The Americans had forced the British to run away with their tails between their legs. Lieutenant Barker of the 4th Foot could find nothing redeeming about the event at all: "It was surely the most ridiculous expedition that ever was plan'd."[19]

The Americans were appropriately elated with their little victory. Not once, but twice, armed citizens had driven off the king's soldiers, with few if any lives lost. Maybe it was time for *them* to try something a little more daring.

*I*n the midst of such humiliations, the British in Boston could at least reassure themselves that it would not always be thus. Help was on the way, as fresh regiments piled onto transports in Ireland and in England, bound for America. Gradually they began to arrive in Boston: another battalion of Marines, seven hundred strong, landed in mid-May. On the very day of the episode on Grape Island, the new infantry regiments made their appearance in Boston, but it would be several days before any of these new additions could be considered effective. Landsmen who had just completed a transatlantic crossing were hardly in good physical condition. It took a

William Howe. The seniormost of the three major generals sent from Britain to Boston in the spring of 1775, Howe was a skilled and innovative commander. But his heart was not in the war, and he would take much of the blame—unfairly, as it turned out—for the high British casualties at Bunker Hill.

(EMMET COLLECTION, MIRIAM AND IRA D. WALLACH DIVISION OF ART, PRINTS AND PHOTOGRAPHS, THE NEW YORK PUBLIC LIBRARY, ASTOR, LENOX AND TILDEN FOUNDATIONS)

Sir Henry Clinton. Contentious, shy, and difficult, Clinton was the most learned of the three newly sent British major generals. He would play an important part in the closing phases of the Battle of Bunker Hill. In later life, Sir Henry obsessed over his role in the battle, and was firmly convinced that the battle would have gone better for the British if Thomas Gage had listened to his advice. Portrait by Andrea Soldi.

(PRODUCED COURTESY OF THE AMERICAN MUSEUM IN BRITAIN, BATH, UK)

Sir John Burgoyne. Burgoyne was by no means the equal of leaders like Howe and Clinton, but his boisterous presence in Boston after May 1775 helped to bolster sagging British morale. Portrait by Sir Joshua Reynolds.

(COPYRIGHT THE FRICK COLLECTION)

while just for the seasickness and disorientation to wear off, and for more wholesome food to restore constitutions weakened by rotten pork and putrid water.

The most anticipated arrival, though, came on Thursday, May 25. HMS *Cerberus*, a sixth-rater of twenty-eight guns, threaded its way into Boston harbor late that afternoon. As the crew brought the warship alongside the Long Wharf and secured it there, a crowd gathered to greet its distinguished guests. The first was a courier, bearing the welcome news—welcome to Admiral Graves, at least— that Graves had been promoted to Vice Admiral of the White, a considerable distinction, given his unimpressive performance thus far. Then came the real attraction: the three major generals. William Howe, Sir Henry Clinton, and Sir John Burgoyne stumbled clumsily down the gangplank and onto the wharf, where they were quickly whisked away to Gage's headquarters at Province House.

They made a curious and unlikely trio. Not one of them had been eager to come to America, and in fact each of them had protested against his orders. But no one else was suitable. Jeffrey Amherst, the highest-ranking general in the service and a hero of the French and Indian War, had steadfastly refused to go; he knew, probably better than anyone save Gage, how quickly a tour of duty in America could wreck a career. Gage's second-in-command, Major General Sir Frederick Haldimand, was an experienced soldier and had been a capable administrator in Canada. He had been in Boston since the previous fall—Gage had called him in after the Powder Alarm— and Gage had given him very little to do while he was there, but still Sir Frederick knew the situation on the ground intimately. Haldimand's main failing, though, was that he was Swiss-born, and the feeling in London was that a foreigner couldn't be fully trusted in a domestic squabble such as the American rebellion.

As major generals, Howe, Clinton, and Burgoyne each ranked below Gage. They had not been sent to replace him—not explicitly, and not yet—but their presence had a meaning that poor, frustrated Gage could not mistake: they were there to remind him that the king and Parliament expected action, immediate action, and that the rebellion must be crushed *now*.

William Howe was the senior of the three in rank. He was well acquainted both with Gage and with America. He and his two older brothers had made their careers in the king's service. Their mother was half-sister to King George I, which assured them of rich opportunities and a good life, but all three proved themselves to be exceptional leaders. George Howe, one of the most capable British commanders in the French and Indian War, would almost certainly have risen to the very highest ranks had his life not been tragically cut short by a French musket ball during Abercrombie's botched assault on Fort Carillon in 1758, gasping out his last breaths in the arms of his friend Israel Putnam. The provincials loved him—loved him so much that Massachusetts honored him with a memorial in Westminster Abbey. The third brother, Admiral Richard Howe, was already well on his way to a distinguished naval career.

And William shared their qualities. He had been an officer since the age of seventeen and had fought in Europe during the War of the Austrian Succession. It was in America, though, that Howe made his name. He was one of the younger, progressive officers— like Gage—who embraced the new tactics and the concept of specially trained light troops. In General Wolfe's improbable assault on the fortress of Quebec, it was thirty-year-old Lieutenant Colonel Howe who led his light infantry up the Heights of Abraham, clambering up the sheer rock face as if he were a boy. After the war he was widely regarded in military circles as the foremost expert on light infantry and irregular warfare, and he spent much of 1774 training light troops on Salisbury Plain.

Like Tommy Gage, William Howe knew Americans, understood the American character, and though he found them wanting in some respects, he had a healthy regard for their abilities. Howe liked Americans and disliked the prospect of making war on them. One year earlier, as a solid Whig, he had been elected to Parliament from Nottingham on the solemn promise that he would never take up arms against the king's subjects in America. He meant it. But the king had other ideas, appointing Howe to command under Gage. Howe had no choice; he obeyed his king. Many of his constituents, many of his fellow Whigs who sympathized with the colonials, were very disappointed in the general.

Despite his distaste for the assignment that had fallen into his lap, Howe was a good choice. There was probably no one in the entire army who so thoroughly fit the mold of an ideal soldier than Howe. He had an obvious physical presence, much like his later adversary Washington: he was six feet tall, broad-shouldered, and full-lipped, with a dark complexion and a stormy demeanor. Introspective and thoughtful, an excellent tactician and a passable strategist, Howe was nonetheless possessed of a common touch that made him invariably popular with the men who served under him. Physical courage accounted for part of that popularity; he was one of those rare commanders who would not ask his boys to do anything he wouldn't do himself. On the other hand, his considerable charm was partly his undoing: Howe loved the high life and although married was very much a ladies' man. His soft life showed in his noticeably ample midriff, and his love for women would eventually distract him from his duties.

In nearly every way, Howe was a very different man from the next general of the trio, Sir Henry Clinton. Clinton was only a few months younger than Howe but little like him in experience or character. He was actually born in America, where his father, Admiral George Clinton, served as a naval commander, governor of Newfoundland, and then governor of New York. After a brief and uneventful tour of duty as a junior officer during King George's War,

Henry left the colonies for Britain at the age of twenty-one. Family influence advanced him rapidly. By age twenty-six he found an appointment as aide-de-camp to Sir John Ligonier, soon to be commander-in-chief of the army in Britain; by twenty-eight he was a lieutenant colonel. He never returned to America—not until now, that is—and his extensive service in the Seven Years' War was entirely on European battlefields. That was no minor issue. There was a divide, subtle but wide and tangible, between high-ranking British officers who made their careers in America and those whose experience was primarily European. Officers trained in the "German school" held themselves to be more erudite, more experienced in the kind of warfare that truly mattered, than their comrades who had wasted their lives fighting against irregular Canadian militia and wild savages. Little surprise, then, that Clinton was as unwilling as Howe to risk his fortune in America. "I was not a volunteer in that war," he noted plainly in his memoirs. "I was ordered by my Sovereign and I obeyed."[20]

To his credit, Clinton was as well read and thoughtful as Howe, but he was not a particularly likeable man. Short, stooped, and introverted—"a shy bitch," he once described himself—he was ready to perceive slights where there were none, ready to bristle at any kind of criticism. He was outspoken, which was not in itself a bad trait . . . but he had great difficulty finding merit in the views of others when they conflicted with his own. He felt smugly superior in being a product of the "German school," and since Howe and Gage were pupils of the "American school" Clinton would, from the very moment he crossed the threshold of Province House, feel that his two superiors dismissed his opinions out of hand. Brilliant but suspicious, brave but difficult, Clinton's personality would hamper his command effectiveness for the remainder of his career.

And John Burgoyne—"Gentleman Johnny," as he was often called, for his aristocratic air and his sartorial tastes—shared almost nothing in common with either Howe or Clinton other than rank and nationality. At fifty-three, he was the oldest of the bunch, though it was hard to tell from appearances. John Burgoyne had a dashing but unserious manner and a handsome face, and although soldiering was his career it was hardly his life. Like most general officers, he had purchased his commission while yet in his late teens; he unintentionally put his career on hold early on, though, eloping with a daughter of the influential Lord Derby and taking up a voluntary exile abroad. He returned to the good graces of his father-in-law, and to his vocation, at the beginning of the Seven Years' War, rising to the rank of lieutenant colonel in 1758. He proved valuable in promoting the concept of light cavalry in the British service, and justly earned a reputation for his progressive notions of military discipline—notions that included such revolutionary ideas as that officers should refrain from verbally abusing their men, and that even enlisted men should be treated as thinking individuals. In this sense, at least, Burgoyne was truly ahead of his time. Otherwise—except in his own estimation—he never distinguished himself as a soldier, and never would. What he prided himself on most, though, was his literary ability. Burgoyne fancied himself a playwright, penning two plays before called to duty in America. One of them, a maudlin little piece titled *Maid of the Oaks*, was produced just before Burgoyne's departure for Boston in 1775.

In politics, Gentleman Johnny was just as flamboyant, though not without substance. As a member of Parliament he led the crusade against corruption in the East India Company, never shrinking from ruffling feathers when he felt it necessary. His attitude toward America was ambivalent. He had no connection to the colonies or the colonials; he counseled against the use of force, yet thought of America as a "spoiled child." Plainly, Burgoyne had the least to contribute of the three generals aboard the *Cerberus*, and he knew it. He suspected that, as junior to Gage, Howe, and Clinton, he would be little more than a useless cipher. Burgoyne hoped that, perhaps, his connections back home might be able to wangle him another appointment—maybe in New York?—one in which he would have at least a chance to shine on his own.

Though the three generals were indeed very different men, close quarters aboard the *Cerberus* forced them to spend a great deal of time together. Howe and Burgoyne were naturally extroverted and outgoing; not so Clinton. Yet even the "shy bitch" had to be sociable—he was tortured by seasickness for the duration of the voyage, made worse by the cramped quarters that he shared with six other men, and only above deck in the open air could he find a small measure of relief from his illness. Here he, Howe, and Burgoyne fell into easy and familiar conversation, leading to mutual admiration and even something approaching friendship. "I could not have named two people," Clinton wrote in his memoirs, "I should sooner wish to serve with in every respect."[21] The three men found, too, that their ideas on strategy were not all that dissimilar. "We do not differ in a single sentiment upon the military conduct now to be pursued," wrote Burgoyne. Undoubtedly they did agree on one central principle: Gage had been needlessly passive. Yet even with Howe's extensive knowledge of America, they had very little idea of what lay ahead in Boston's gilded cage.

They were optimistic and boisterous nonetheless, and none more so than the perpetual actor Burgoyne. As the *Cerberus* approached Boston harbor on May 25, she hailed another vessel, and their captains exchanged news. Boston, as the crew and passengers on the *Cerberus* found out, was surrounded by warlike, armed, insolent Yankees who by their very numbers were able to keep Gage's army immobilized. Burgoyne couldn't suppress his theatrical nature or his wont to brag. Like an overconfident adolescent, he shouted to the captain of the other ship, "Well, let us in, and we shall soon make elbow-room!"[22]

*I*t would take some days before Howe, Clinton, and Burgoyne could settle in and regain their land legs, and for Clinton to calm his sore and heaving stomach. It would take some time for them to gain the lay of the land as well. Everything they knew about the situation in Boston came from news that was dated by several months. Even the events at Lexington and Concord, nearly five weeks old now, were unknown to them until their arrival. While they consulted with Gage and Haldimand, they were treated to a spectacle that was utterly unlike anything they had expected. For the first time, the rebels went on the offensive.

So far the Americans had been content to sit tight and let Gage sit tight as well. There wasn't much else they could do, anyway, as Ward, Warren, and Thomas knew all too well. The anxiety in the rebel camps meant that rumors of British forays outside Boston became frequent and very, very convincing. The alarm of May 9 lasted for well over a week. It didn't take much to stir up fear of a British counteroffensive. On the night of May 17, flames lit up the night sky over Boston when a fire broke out in the barracks of the 65th Foot, on Treat's Wharf in the North End. British soldiers were hard pressed to douse the flames—on Gage's orders, they had earlier confiscated all the civilian firefighting equipment, so the job of extinguishing the blaze fell into their inexperienced hands—and the conflagration burned well into the morning, consuming storehouses and barracks on Dock Square. The 65th Foot lost all of its clothing, weapons, and equipment, and the 47th Foot lost most of theirs. The flames leapt so high as to be easily visible in Charlestown and Cambridge. The Americans instantly suspected that Gage was up to something, and that soon Redcoats by the score would be rowing their way across the Charles ferryway to attack. The British were equally suspicious that rebel sympathizers had started the fire as a diversion to mask an American assault on the town.[23]

The strange little venture at Grape Island earlier that week had changed things. It revived the colonials' faith in their militia system. It also reminded those in command that all around the harbor, even on the many islands that populated it, there were valuable commodities to be had, like hay and livestock, that were there for the taking—by the British or by the Americans.

Northeast of Boston's North End, just off the sleepy little bayside towns of Chelsea and Lynn, lay two large islands, then named Hog Island and Noddle's Island. Typical of the harbor islands, both were open country, grassy, and devoid of trees, with gently rolling hills. On Noddle's, a devout and prosperous Whig, one Henry Howell Williams, made his home and kept a substantial farm, with hundreds of sheep, hogs, and horses. On Hog Island lived sheep and cattle and nothing more. Farmer Williams, "a Man of strict Integrity & a warm Friend to his suffering Country," had tried his best to keep his head down during the siege. He knew his farm was a tempting target, and he wanted very much to get his livestock to safety on the mainland, but Admiral Graves had confiscated all his boats. Several times Williams had appealed to Israel Putnam for help in removing his animals. So far nothing had been done.[24]

After Grape Island, there was much concern in Cambridge that Gage or Graves would try their luck with the two northern islands. The garrison needed fresh meat, and there was none closer or more easily taken than that on the hoof on Noddle's and Hog islands. On May 26, the day after William Howe and his companions came to Boston, Artemas Ward gave the order: it was time to take the animals—or at least destroy them—before the British could make use of them. Colonel John Nixon and his regiment would see to it.

Nixon's regiment, accompanied by John Stark's Hampshiremen, marched toward Chelsea under the cover of darkness that night.

The enterprise had more the character of a schoolboy prank than of a regular military operation. Men from other regiments—Gerrish's, Prescott's, and Doolittle's—eagerly took up their muskets and followed Nixon as soon as they knew that the colonel was up to some interesting mischief. The procession escaped Gage's notice, and on the morning of the twenty-seventh the men went to work.

From Lynn the men forded a tiny channel, only waist deep at low tide, and crossed to Hog Island. They rounded up all the horses, sheep, and cattle they could find; some soldiers drove them back to the mainland, while the rest of Nixon's men proceeded on to Noddle's.

By now British patrol boats had spotted the activity on Hog Island. Word soon got back to Admiral Graves, who took immediate action. In Williams's warehouses on Noddle's, Graves had secreted away tons of vital naval stores, and while he was hardly eager to confront the rebels, he wasn't about to let them get their hands on *his* property. The schooner *Diana*, commanded by the admiral's nephew Lieutenant Thomas Graves, sailed into Chelsea Creek, the tidal estuary that separated Noddle's from the mainland at Chelsea, while a party of Marines—Graves had managed to keep a few from Gage's clutches—landed on Noddle's.

Nixon's boys on Noddle's had been very busy, rounding up sheep, hogs, and horses, burning Williams's supply of hay, destroying what they could of Graves's precious naval stores. But they couldn't restrain themselves from committing acts of outright vandalism. They raided Williams's house and several other dwellings nearby, then put the torch to several buildings on the farmer's estate. Loot in hand, they got to the mainland as best they could. Some of the men had to swim for it, losing their clothing, muskets, and equipment in the process; most managed to get ashore with the livestock and the plunder . . . rum, household furniture, women's clothing, bed linens, anything and everything that they could tuck under an arm or sling over their backs. A lieutenant in Gerrish's regiment somehow convinced his men to help him drag off a couple of heavy ship's anchors, which he then claimed as his personal property.[25]

But the British had not yet given up. *Diana*'s crew worked the schooner's four four-pounder guns, lobbing solid shot at the retreating rebels, while Marines let several volleys fly from the shore of Noddle's. Some of the Americans, having gotten to the mainland, fought back. Amos Farnsworth and his comrades "Squated Down in a Ditch on the mash and Stood our ground. . . . And we had a hot fiar untill the Regulars retreeted." Miraculously, no one on either side was killed, though "the Bauls Sung like Bees Round our heds."[26] A party of Stark's New Hampshire boys made their appearance, covering the retreat of the raiding party, and it was all over.

Or so it seemed. The day had just begun for Lieutenant Graves and the crew of the *Diana*. The schooner had yet to extricate herself from the narrow, shallow channel of Chelsea Creek, and at sunset, when Lieutenant Graves started his journey back to the harbor, the tide was going out. Just as the *Diana* got under way, the wind died. Lieutenant Graves ordered his crew to kedge the vessel down the creek, letting go an anchor and using it to drag the ship forward. The admiral sent barges to help tow his nephew's ship, and also the sloop *Britannia* to cover the operation with her guns.

What the British hadn't counted on was the sudden appearance of a fresh American force. Israel Putnam, drawn to action as if by instinct, popped up at Chelsea with a thousand men and two small fieldpieces . . . and with Joseph Warren, who was perhaps more like Putnam than anyone would have recognized. They waited for the *Diana* to approach the shallows at Winnisimet Ferry. Graves countered, landing a few cannon of his own on Noddle's, while General Gage came to his aid with yet more cannon and a detachment of Marines. Old Put shouted to the *Diana*, demanding the ship's surrender; Lieutenant Graves opened fire on the rebels, and the rebels responded in like measure.

Putnam had his blood up; he was in his element, and nothing could hold him back now. As the gun crews worked their pieces from the bluff overlooking the rapidly emptying channel, the old Indian-fighter jumped into Chelsea Creek, dampened white locks bobbing atop his bare head, bellowing to his men to follow him. He charged into the water, hip deep, to get as close to the schooner as possible, while his men sloshed through the creek to catch up. They fired on the schooner as fast as they could, priming, loading, pulling the triggers of their muskets, roaring like demons. The *Britannia* tried to help the *Diana* with her guns, but darkness had fallen and the shots had little effect. The barges that had just started to tow the *Diana*, however, abandoned her as soon as they came under the fire of Putnam's men. And the *Diana*, with no wind to fill her sails, immediately ran hard aground at Winnisimet.

Lieutenant Graves still fought back gallantly, as long as he could, until the *Diana*—now resting on dry ground—began to roll onto her side, her sails hanging crazily downward from tilting masts, the crew grasping for handholds on the sloping deck until they couldn't help but slide across it. Graves saw no way out. Reluctantly he ordered the men to abandon ship. And immediately Putnam's men swarmed over the beached vessel, stuffing hay around and beneath her, and finally setting her afire while stripping from the ship everything that wasn't lashed down. Graves made one last valiant effort to return to his dying command, but Putnam's men opened fire and drove the sailors back toward Noddle's. By now the ship had caught fire, the flames lighting up the black sky. Around three o'clock in the morning the fire reached the powder magazine, and the *Diana* finally, mercifully, exploded.[27]

While the *Diana* burned, Nixon's men sauntered through Chelsea in their dripping wet clothing, carrying their stolen treasures, driving the cattle and the horses and the worried sheep before them. Some of the men, the hungry and the greedy, paused to slaughter a few lambs to share with their messmates, or to sell in camp. They returned to Cambridge that morning, flush with victory and weighed down by their trophies. A hero's welcome awaited them. Better yet, a hero's reward: a pint of rum for each man who had gone "on Expedition."[28]

No one was more overjoyed than Old Put, who despite his advanced years was glowing like a teenage boy after pulling off a complicated and unlikely prank. Soaked from the waist down, Putnam proceeded directly to the Hastings House, and—with sodden shoes still oozing water—walked inside to find Artemas Ward and Joseph Warren waiting for his report. "I wish we had work like that to do every day!" Putnam chortled, craggy face red, damp, and grinning. Warren, who couldn't help but like the bullish man, grinned right back and made a revealing observation: the army, he remarked, needed both Putnam's daring and Ward's prudence. Indeed it did.[29]

Putnam and the men with him had every right to be proud of themselves. Once again they had stood their ground and fought British Regulars toe-to-toe, driven them back, and engineered the destruction of a royal warship. There had been no real battle plan, everything had been improvised, and yet nothing had gone awry. Pious Amos Farnsworth saw the hand of the Almighty at work in the events of the day: "Suerly God has A faver towards us: And He can Save in one Place as well as Another." And the haul was a rich one: perhaps four hundred sheep from Hog Island, plus five hundred sheep, over three hundred lambs, thirty head of cattle, and horses and hogs from Williams's property on Noddle's. From the *Diana*'s charred and smoking skeleton, Putnam's boys retrieved all the cannon and swivel-guns. Over the next few days, more parties of rebel soldiers returned to Noddle's to carry off or destroy everything that had been left behind. All told, between the day of the battle and June 10, the Americans destroyed three dwellings and a greater number of barns, plus Williams's "mansion house, with all the barns, corn-houses, and store houses, stores, provisions, goods, house furniture, wearing apparel, liquors, and utensils of all sorts, to a very considerable amount and value." All the property of an avowed "friend of the Cause."[30]

The rebels celebrated the victory with gleeful abandon. About a week after the battle, some Connecticut troops from Cambridge went to Roxbury Camp to parade a prized trophy: one of the *Diana*'s boats, with four hog-tied British prisoners aboard, which Putnam's boys had mounted on an oxcart. As the cart threaded its way through General Thomas's camps and around the Roxbury parade ground on Meeting House Hill, three Americans—sitting in the boat with the dejected prisoners—manned the oars, flailing them through the air as they pretended to row. It was a real treat for the Roxbury troops, bored and idle and homesick; they convulsed with laughter, and Thomas's engineer Rufus Putnam fired off one of the fieldpieces on the parade ground "for joy." Ward and Thomas should have taken heart, too. Even the men who had not been in the battle, even the men who had been miles away from it, laughed and joked and congratulated themselves over the scrap on Noddle's Island as if they *had* been there. It was a good sign—it meant that the army thought of itself as an army.[31]

Besides the boost to morale, Nixon's and Putnam's men garnered some valuable combat experience. As Putnam pointed out, the men were beginning to learn that cannonfire was never so dangerous as it looked or sounded. But there was something troubling about the whole affair regardless of the profits taken. The *Diana*, after all, had fallen victim to Putnam's boys not through any merit on their part, but simply because of accidents that were beyond anyone's control. Patriotic preachers thanked the God of Battles for the victory, all the sweeter for being so unlikely, but it was the God of Tides who had scourged the British. And the entire operation smacked more of unrestrained hooliganism than military precision. Ward, and Warren, too, could not help but be disturbed by the reports and petitions that filtered back to headquarters over the next few days: that the Americans marching through Chelsea had openly bragged about the "Verry fine Plunder" they had taken from Williams's farm; that soldiers, drunk on victory and possibly rum as well, had torched a house in Chelsea for no apparent reason; that no one seemed to feel any regret for having wiped out an honest citizen who had shown nothing but devotion to the Cause.[32] Despite the careful work of Ward and his lieutenants, despite the great progress in convincing the men to act as part of a genuine army, the men had behaved very much like the armed rabble that the British said they were. And leaders like Old Put, brave and honest and enterprising though he was, didn't help matters at all.

The American triumph in the "battle of Noddle's Island," as it came to be called euphemistically, may have been a qualified one. For the British, there was nothing positive about the experience at all. The loss of life had been slight; the Marines escaped unscathed, and there had been a smattering of casualties—two killed and a handful wounded—among the crews of the boats and barges that had attempted to carry the *Diana* off the sandbar that became her grave. The naval stores on Noddle's were not a total loss, either; Graves sent boats to retrieve what was left shortly after the battle. But in every other way the confrontation on the harbor islands was an unmitigated disaster. The Americans had stolen precious livestock from under the very noses of the British. Worse yet, their actions resulted in the destruction of a warship . . . not a very significant warship, to be sure, but the mere fact that one of the king's ships had suffered such an ignominious fate was an embarrassment that simply couldn't be assuaged. General Gage was not to blame—he had counseled Admiral Graves against sending ships or men to Noddle's, "supposing it to be a trap, which it proved to be," noted one of Gage's adjutants, Colonel Stephen Kemble—but that didn't mean he wouldn't be blamed, by his own men or by London. Lord Percy, who had as much respect for the Americans as anyone, captured the feeling at Province House with pungent understatement: "This is not the most agreable thing that could have happened."[33]

The three newly arrived generals were curiously silent about Noddle's Island. In a letter home, John Burgoyne called it an "insult," and that was about it. But as Howe, Clinton, and Burgoyne took stock of the overall situation and the prevailing mood in Boston, they were less than impressed—with the quality of the troops, or with the quality of Gage's leadership. To friends and connections back home, the three generals pointed out the army's failings and those of its commander. Clinton saw "nothing but dismay among the troops" from the moment he arrived. Sir Henry gasped in disbelief that no one had attempted to map the area of operations. Burgoyne's criticisms were much sharper. They were also mostly wrong. He was correct in noting that the troops were "still lost in a sort of stupefaction which the events of the 19th of April had occasioned," but when he secretly took Gage to task he lost sight of the general's predicament. Gage, Burgoyne claimed, had failed to arrest the ringleaders of the rebellion; he had neglected to occupy Dorchester or Charlestown; he had not trained his troops in American warfare. None of these was a valid charge. But the wordy would-be playwright didn't bother to probe the reasons behind Gage's conduct. Instead he killed the general with contemptuous, double-edged praise: Gage, he wrote, couldn't be blamed for being "unequal to his present situation, for few characters in the world would be fit for it."[34]

These were private carpings, not shared with Gage. Together they made a dour assessment of the tactical situation in Boston. Overall, though, the arrival of the major generals—and the reinforcements—had a salutary effect, breathing new spirit into Gage's army, lightening the gloom that had descended over every man and officer. "As our generals have now arrived," Lord Percy sighed with relief, "I take it for granted that something will be undertaken." Captain Harris of the 5th Foot longed to give the rebels "one good drubbing."[35]

Gage spent much of the next two weeks in consultation with the major generals, as a group and individually. They grew to appreciate his situation better, or at least Howe did, conceding that the force in Boston was "much too small" to suppress the rebellion, that it needed more men and warships and flat-bottomed transports, that the war could be fought much more effectively from New York. On these points, all of the generals agreed. And yet all of them wanted to do something *now*. They were eager for action. "Our elbows must be eased," Clinton wrote, in conscious imitation of Burgoyne. "Our own existence, the dignity of the nation, etc., requires Vigour, and that vigour will if anything can in the end prove Mercy." Charlestown and Dorchester, Sir Henry argued, must be taken, must be denied to the rebels.[36]

Gage became hopeful, too, with the reinforcements that nearly doubled the size of his force and with the friendly counsel of his new subordinates, and he succumbed to the infectious enthusiasm. After six weeks of enforced passivity, Gage wanted to take the war to the Americans.

The initial preparations for the as-yet unplanned offensive were subtle, not enough to arouse the suspicions of the Americans or even the Redcoats. As a first step, on June 4, Gage reorganized his army. He ordered each regiment to give up its elite "flank companies"— the light infantry and the grenadiers. The detached companies were to move their camps to Boston Common, where they would form two special, improvised battalions, one each of grenadiers and light infantry. The purpose, Gage stated in his general orders, was to allow the flank companies to practice special drills and exercises . . . but experienced officers knew that there was something more. Forming grenadier and light infantry battalions was something an army did before going on campaign.[37]

And then, on June 12, 1775, General Gage declared a war of words. For some obscure reason, Gage felt it necessary to signal the shift in strategy with an official proclamation condemning the rebellion. Perhaps he wished only to give the weak-hearted and indecisive one last chance to back away from the real troublemakers. Inexplicably, Gage let John Burgoyne do his talking for him. Gage was plain and blunt of speech; maybe he hoped that Burgoyne's self-trumpeted literary virtues would craft a stronger and more convincing case against the rebels. If so, it backfired, for the final product, purely in Burgoyne's words, was truly offensive. "Whereas the infatuated multitudes, who have long suffered themselves to be conducted by certain well-known incendiaries and traitors, have at length proceeded to avowed Rebellion," it began,

> and the good effects which were expected to arise from the patience and lenity of the King's Government have often been frustrated, and are now rendered hopeless, by the influence of the same evil counsels, it only remains for those who are invested with supreme rule as well for the punishment of the guilty, as the protection of the well-affected, to prove they do not bear the sword in vain.
>
> The infringements which have been committed upon the most sacred rights of the Crown and People of *Great Britain*, are too many to enumerate on one side, and are all too atrocious to be palliated on the other. All unprejudiced people . . .

will find . . . marks of premeditation and conspiracy, that would justify the fulness of chastisement. . . .

The authors of the present unnatural revolt . . . have uniformly placed their chief confidence in the suppression of truth; and while indefatigable and shameless pains have been taken to obstruct every appeal to the real interest of the people of *America*, the grossest forgeries, calumnies and absurdities that ever insulted human understanding, have been imposed upon their credulity. . . . From the popular harangues of the times, men have been taught to depend upon activity in treason . . . till, to complete the horrid profanation of terms and ideas, the name of *God* has been introduced in the pulpits, to excite and justify devastation and massacre.

A number of armed persons . . . assembled on the 19ᵗʰ of *April* last, and from behind walls and lurking holes, attacked a detachment of the King's Troops. . . . Since that period, the rebels . . . have added insult to outrage . . . and with a preposterous parade of military arrangement, they affected to hold the Army besieged. . . . The actions of the 19ᵗʰ of *April* are of such notoriety as must baffle all attempts to contradict them, and the flames of buildings and other property from the islands and adjacent country . . . spread a melancholy confirmation of the subsequent assertions.

With that, Burgoyne/Gage declared martial law, offering pardon to all rebels who would lay down their arms and return to obedience—to all, that is, except Sam Adams and John Hancock, "whose offences are of too flagitious a nature to admit of any other consideration than that of condign punishment."[38]

This was a truly awful document, and not only because of its self-consciously ponderous style, which in itself was sufficient cause for Burgoyne to feel shame. It also went out of its way to anger the rebels. Even in London the proclamation, once it reached England's shores, was the target of merciless ridicule in the press. "They *affect* to hold the army besieged[?]," wrote a critic in the London *Evening Post* a little over a month later. "Why, Master Gage . . . they do not affect it, they actually do besiege ye, in spite of your teeth."[39]

Little wonder, then, that in Cambridge and Watertown the response would be a mixture of rage and bemusement. But neither Gage nor Burgoyne lingered on the proclamation once published; the reaction to it was not of any great consequence to them or to the other generals. On the very same day that Gage sent it in to be printed, he met with his major generals at Province House to discuss how the rebellion might be crushed in the short term.

Despite the differences in their backgrounds and character, the generals at Province House—Gage, Howe, Clinton, Burgoyne, and Haldimand as well, though Haldimand had just been recalled and soon would be on his way to England—had no difficulty in arriving at a common plan of attack. The heights at Charlestown and Dorchester were obviously the points to be taken, but taking them simultaneously was beyond the capabilities even of Gage's recently enlarged force. Of the two, Dorchester was the more important. Its heights commanded the Neck, the Back Bay, and Boston itself. In a sudden strike, Howe would launch an amphibious assault on Dorchester, while Clinton would command the British center, Burgoyne conducting a cannonade from Boston Neck. "The operation must have been very easy," Burgoyne wrote, and given the sorry state of Thomas's defenses at Roxbury, Burgoyne was not boasting idly. The Redcoats would build two redoubts atop the Heights and launch another attack directly on Thomas at Roxbury. Once Thomas had been defeated and Roxbury secured, then and only then would Gage turn his attention to Charlestown. With Thomas gone and Charlestown in British hands, Cambridge would clearly be the next objective. "I suppose the Rebels will move from Cambridge, And that we shall take, and keep possession of it," observed Howe laconically.[40]

There was much work to be done. Transports had to be made ready, the organization of the attacking forces determined, food and ammunition and entrenching tools distributed. All this would take a few days, especially since the tasks would have to be done secretly, silently. Since the rebels were so enamored of their meetinghouses on Sundays, an attack on the Sabbath day seemed like a good idea. So the date was set: the transports and the men would move from Boston in the early morning hours of Sunday, June 18, 1775.

Gage and his generals were satisfied. The plan seemed almost foolproof. True, the Yankees had shown themselves to be enterprising, resourceful, and surprisingly brave. But numbers, bayonets, and artillery were what counted in the end. The American army, glowing with self-satisfaction from its little victory at Noddle's Island, could not possibly put up enough resistance to keep the Redcoats at arm's length for very long.

Six

* * *

A GOOD DEAL
OF A HUBBUB

For most of the men in the camps around Cambridge, Tuesday, June 6 was just another day. Some of them would labor on the forts; others would fetch firewood or refresh the latrines with spadefuls of dirt; most would loaf and gossip to pass the idle and uneventful hours. For a few of the regiments, this was a day of high ceremony. They paraded on the Common in mid-morning, muskets held high on the left shoulder, packs and bedrolls slung, looking as military as they could manage with tattered clothing, dirty faces, and grimy hands. The muster-master passed down the long lines of troops and between the ranks, taking casual notice of who was armed and who wasn't. It was a process called "passing muster," and though each soldier had been through it before, this time was different. Once the inspection was finished, the officers led the men in reciting the oath composed by the Provincial Congress. Whether or not the soldiers felt any change is impossible to say, but now it was official: they belonged to the army.

Part of the army was treated to a rare spectacle, not to be seen again during the siege of Boston: a prisoner exchange. The Provincial Congress, and Dr. Warren in particular, had taken great pains to ensure that the British prisoners taken on the Glorious Nineteenth were treated humanely. It was important to the Cause that the world know that Americans were not savages, unlike Gage's merciless brutes who had driven pregnant women into the streets and murdered old men in cold blood; it was important to Warren that the Americans show a little military pageantry. The Committee of Safety gave the assignment to, of all people, Israel Putnam. Just after noon, Old Put climbed into an elegant four-wheeled phaeton specially picked for the event and set off for Charlestown, where he would rendezvous with a British guard and nine American prisoners taken after the Concord fight. Following Putnam was a group uniquely fit for this kind of duty: Captain John Chester's company from Wethersfield, Connecticut, part of Spencer's regiment, dressed to a man in coats of brilliant blue turned up with red facings—the only company in the entire army wearing uniforms and not civilian clothing. The Wethersfield company marched down the roads to Charlestown, proud but not precise enough in their movements to keep their column orderly for very long, their captives—three officers and six enlisted men—paraded between them and Putnam's dapper coach. Dr. Warren, as always under some consuming compulsion to be everywhere at once, climbed into the phaeton with Putnam. Stocky Putnam seemed out of place being anywhere but on a horse, but he and Warren had a grand time. Old Put respected Warren; Warren, immaculately dressed and so poised as to appear almost effete, was not above chatting and joking with the good-natured Putnam.

At Charlestown the American party halted at the ferry, gave a signal, and a few minutes later the British sloop-of-war *Lively* lowered a boat, which rowed out to meet the Americans. The leader of the British party, Major James Moncrieffe, worked his way ashore and went straight up to Putnam. The two were old friends, having served together in the French and Indian War. The Briton's presence was one of the reasons that the doughty old Yankee was so eager to venture into this meeting which was in many ways so unlike him. It proved to be a cordial and pleasant little affair. The British enlisted men, all of them wounded, went over to the *Lively* for medical treatment, while Putnam, Warren, Moncrieffe, and the other British officers gathered for a "formal entertainment" and informal fraternizing. Soon the *Lively*'s boat returned with nine American prisoners—eight soldiers captured on April 19, plus a black servant named Caesar Augustus. The officers said their goodbyes, Chester's company formed into column and tramped down the road back toward the Neck, and Moncrieffe and his comrades rowed back to the *Lively*. They went back to being enemies and the war, such as it was, resumed.[1]

In the camps it was all the talk, because in the camps there hadn't been much worth talking about since the scuffle on Noddle's Island ten days before. The weather was clear and dry and very hot, hotter than it should have been in early June, broken only by a brief shower on June 13 that gave the men some respite from the broiling heat, and from the clouds of dust that caked their throats. On June 5, around noon, British guns in the fortifications on Boston Neck opened up on Roxbury, targeting a group of Thomas's boys who had ventured to the shore to dig clams.[2] There was an alarm at Cambridge, briefly, on the ninth, when it was rumored that the British had once again landed on Noddle's, and the following day some of the American boys went to the island one last time to burn everything that had so far escaped the torch.

Beyond that, there was only the ordinary pulse of life in the camps. A "bad woman" was apprehended for plying her trade among the troops at Cambridge. After being dunked in the Charles, saluted by the cheers and guffaws of the crowds of soldiers who looked on in mocking amusement, she was ceremoniously drummed out of camp. Also removed from Cambridge, by order of the Committee of Safety, was a "lunatic" from Boston named Daniel Adams, who "occasions great disorders in said camp." In Roxbury, two whores were driven from the camp of the Rhode Island boys. One of the companies in Thomas's command drew the unenviable chore of giving the smallpox-house a good scrubbing with soap and vinegar.[3]

Homesickness had begun to infect the men. Most of them had been in the field for five weeks or more, and since early May there were few opportunities to return home even for brief visits. General Thomas, who had more contact with his family than most, fretted over his wife's imminent visit, hoping that all three of their children could make the trip, too. "Let my Daughter know that I Dont forget her," he reminded Hannah Thomas. For some of the enlisted men, the fading sense of adventure was not enough to palliate despair. One soldier in Cambridge, "deeply in love, & wished to go home to see his *dear*," was denied a furlough by his captain; the heartsick man went into a barn and hanged himself. "I went down & saw him [then] I went hom & tuk a nap," Private James Stevens of Frye's Massachusetts regiment noted, laconically, in his journal.[4]

Sam Haws, a minuteman-turned-soldier from Groton, reported on the morning of the fifteenth: "Nothing remarkable this day."[5]

Yet there was something electric in the air, a feeling that something big was afoot, and in the camps at Roxbury and around Cambridge everyone could sense it. Of course there were alarms—there were always alarms, not just in the military camps but all through the region. Every time a British ship or two moored within sight of a coastal town it inspired terror, and it always proved to be nothing.

"My wife," General Thomas soothed his Hannah, who had heard that the British were going to burn Plymouth, "I should be Glad you would muster up that firmness & Resolution, which the Times we Live in Require[;] be not Terefyed at . . . the Chat of Every Timerious Person."[6] The arrival of the three British major generals was well known at American headquarters, and from that moment Ward and his subordinates were on high alert.

Plus more reinforcements were arriving in Boston. On June 12 and 13, three new regiments—the 35th, 49th, and 63rd Regiments of Foot—plus the 17th Light Dragoons debarked from their transports and onto the Long Wharf.[7] The British made no attempt to hide their arrival, and the Americans saw it all and worried. Gage's proclamation of June 12—that inexplicable document that blasted the "infatuated multitudes" for their "unnatural revolt"—lent a feeling of menace to the intelligence about the newly arrived Redcoats. The proclamation brought back some of the righteous fury that had animated the rebels right after the "murders" at Lexington and Concord. "A Blackguard thing," Salem merchant John Jenks called it, " . . . asserting for Truth what is known to every Child of 5 years to be an absolute lye . . . I think it had ought to be burnt by the common Hangman." On the thirteenth, the Provincial Congress formed a committee to respond to Gage word-for-word, and three days later it published the final product, which in like fashion offered peace to all except Gage, Graves, and the Tories; it was a marvelous document, for in polemic and inflated rhetoric even John Burgoyne couldn't hold a candle to the Patriot leadership.[8]

But that same proclamation, so unlike anything one might have expected from measured and moderate Gage, was also a source of disturbing uncertainty. Its hauteur, its venom and high-toned spite, hinted at something more than mere empty bombast . . . it hinted at action and at vengeance. Something was up, something big, something more than the occasional alarms that accomplished little more than breaking the monotony in camp. There were no telltale orders coming from headquarters, but the men sensed the change in the wind all the same.

They had good reason to be fearful even if unacquainted with the particulars. The British generals did not go to great pains to keep their operational plans a secret. Days before Howe and Clinton drafted their preliminary plans on June 12, word of an imminent British offensive had already filtered back through rebel spies to the Hastings House. Of this, the members of the Committee of Safety were absolutely certain: "Whereas, it is daily expected," they noted in their journal for June 13, "that General Gage will attack our army now in the vicinity of Boston, in order to penetrate into the country, it is of the utmost importance that said army be . . . prepared for action as soon as possible." The lunge might be aimed at Charlestown or at Dorchester, at both simultaneously or in rapid succession, but it *would* happen, and soon. They waited only for the specifics of when and how. In the meantime, they pressed General Ward to figure out just how many men he had under his command, and how many of them were actually armed with working muskets.[9]

If anyone gave away the suspicions of the high command, it was Artemas Ward himself. From his adjutant's pen flowed a new series of orders to guide his army of the godly: that the men attend prayer services twice daily, with muskets and accoutrements in hand "ready to march in case of alarm"; "that no Plays be Carried on of the Sabbath to Profane Holey Time"; "that Wood for the fire on Saterday be Prepared for the Sabboth." Battle, death, and oblivion were coming inexorably to scourge the enemies of the Lord's chosen people. It was time to get right with God.[10]

*I*ronclad confirmation of the planned British offensive came to headquarters late on the fourteenth. It came by an oddly circuitous route: from a "gentleman of undoubted veracity" who had left Boston on June 9. This gentleman informed the New Hampshire Committee of Safety, which then hurried the news along to Watertown. The British would attack on Sunday, June 18—first at Dorchester Neck, which they would fortify and hold, and then at Charlestown, pushing on from there to take Cambridge and drive away the rebels.

The rebel army had the advantage of numbers and enthusiasm. In every other way the British were their superiors. This was no trifling threat. The days of passively waiting for Gage to abandon Boston were over. Ward, Warren, and the Committee of Safety would have to act now.

The Committee of Safety convened the very next day, June 15, 1775. The question before the committee—how best to secure the heights at Dorchester and Charlestown, and therefore the colonial army and its stores—was not a new one. A month before, Benjamin Church and Colonel William Henshaw had scouted the area, recommending to the committee that a "strong redoubt" be placed on Bunker Hill, "with cannon planted there, to annoy the enemy coming out of Charlestown, also to annoy them by water to Medford."[11] Yet the Committee demurred, passing the decision to fortify or not to fortify back to the generals. Putnam was all in favor of taking the initiative. No subtle strategist, Old Put despised inactivity, fearing that without something to do the army would fall apart. Boredom and low morale would spread like a disease through the camps if there was no fight, he felt—and hence his almost churlish "demonstration" at Charlestown on May 13. So long as the men dug in, Putnam felt, they would be fine—a Yankee, he contended, feared for his shins and not for his head.

Thus far, Ward had disagreed vehemently—not just because the phlegmatic general was cautious to a fault but because he realized how much the army had to lose. An aggressive move toward

Charlestown or Dorchester would likely compel Gage to attack. Even if the odds were in the Americans' favor, the risk would be too great. Even if the army was not swallowed up by the British in one big bloody gulp, the stroke would certainly cripple the provincials, shred their morale, and leave the way open for a British attack on Cambridge. Ward, who had poured his all into assembling and safeguarding this fragile semblance of an army for nearly two months, was not about to see it sacrificed to satisfy Putnam's—or anyone's—reckless craving for action. And Warren, who for all his revolutionary ardor was an eminently practical man, had agreed with Ward.

As long as Gage remained inactive, the rebel high command could put the matter to the side while it dealt with the more immediate if mundane concerns of recruitment, supply, and discipline, but the recent news from Boston forced the American commanders to face the big strategic question squarely. The question was basically this: wait, provoke, or attack? Should the army sit tight in its camps in anticipation of the projected June 18 offensive? Or should it take some action now—to launch an outright assault on the British lines, or to goad the British into action?

Warren had come to believe that Ward's caution was no longer the best option, and once he had taken this truth to heart he embraced it enthusiastically. The Provincial Congress had, only yesterday, appointed the young doctor a major general of Massachusetts troops, conveniently forgetting its own distaste for delegates holding military rank. He hadn't received his commission yet—sadly, he never would—and though Warren had no military ambitions he was itching to put action behind his words . . . to fight the British "in blood up to his knees," as he once said without a trace of feigned bravado. Even Ward came to see the necessity of action. The loss of either prominence, of Charlestown or Dorchester, would deal the Cause a near-fatal blow. The loss of both would kill it.

On paper, the committee's response was swift and sure. Dr. Warren was in his element—he thrived under pressure—and under his guidance the committee fired off one stirring-sounding resolution after another. The Provincial Congress should authorize further recruitment; the militia—*all* of it, from one end of the colony to the other—was to be made ready to march at a moment's notice, each man armed and with thirty rounds of ammunition on his person. All men of military age were to go to church on Sunday with arms and accoutrements in hand; Sunday, after all, was the day appointed for the rumored British attack.

And—perhaps as a gesture to the esteemed Dr. Langdon, chaplain of the army and president of Harvard College—the Provincial Congress ordered that Harvard's library and all of the college's "scientific equipment" be removed from campus and stored, safely away from the fighting, in Andover.[12]

Most important, though, something had to be done about those hills.

" . . . [I]t appears of importance to the safety of this colony," the committee declared, "that possession of the hill called Bunker's hill in Charlestown, be securely kept and defended, and also, some one hill or hills on Dorchester neck be likewise secured." The former was simple: the committee recommended that "sufficient forces" be posted on Bunker Hill. Dorchester was the question mark. As "the particular situation of Dorchester neck is unknown to this committee," they left it up to the Council of War—meaning Ward, Warren, and the generals—to do what they deemed necessary "for the security of this colony."[13]

No one in Cambridge knew what, if anything, could be done about Dorchester. Communications between the headquarters at the Hastings House and John Thomas's command at Roxbury had never functioned well. Almost from his first day on the job, General Thomas had despaired about those hills so close to his camps.

He fully understood their strategic significance but never felt strong enough to take them. Nine days earlier, while Putnam and Warren attended to the prisoner exchange in Charlestown, Artemas Ward and Joseph Spencer had attempted to reconnoiter Dorchester Heights with John Thomas and William Heath. Wary British gunners in the lines on Boston Neck spotted the generals instantly; seconds after the Americans made their appearance on the Heights, three cannonballs whistled dangerously close, impelling a hasty retreat.

If four horsemen couldn't stand the heat on Dorchester Heights, there wasn't much chance of a regiment or two doing the same, let alone while digging in. But just to be sure, the Committee of Safety dispatched Captain Benjamin White and Colonel Joseph Palmer to accompany General Ward and others in a hurried junket to Roxbury to consult with Thomas and Heath. The men pounded down the road to Roxbury as fast as their horses could be spurred, but their effort was for naught. Thomas simply pointed out the obvious—what everybody knew already: there was no way that the Americans could take Dorchester Heights and hold them against a British onslaught, not with British guns on Boston Neck sweeping the Heights, not with less than three days' preparation, and not without cannon.

That settled it. Dorchester was, at least for the time being, a lost cause. Thomas couldn't hope to take and hold the Heights, and if the British did carry out their assault there on the eighteenth, there was little that Thomas could do about it. If the British pushed the attack on toward Roxbury, there was probably little that Thomas could do about that, either. He had virtually no artillery. There were plenty of heavy siege-guns sitting at Ticonderoga, but nothing had been done to transport them to Boston, and they might as well have been on the other side of the world. All John Thomas had to deter a British assault on Roxbury was a handful of small, pitiful earthworks.

So Ward would focus on Charlestown instead. It was a logical decision, really, since of the two critical points, Charlestown was the more vital for the survival of the rebel army. Cambridge was less than three miles away. In British hands, the hills of the Charlestown peninsula would present an immediate threat to Cambridge. Bunker Hill, which dominated the peninsula and the town, was out of range of most British cannon; only the Copp's Hill battery and the ships in the harbor could possibly reach it. Once taken and fortified, Bunker Hill could be readily defended against a British attack. Even if the Redcoats managed to overrun it, it would be no easy thing for them to move on and take Cambridge. Forts Numbers One and Two secured the river approaches to Cambridge, while Three guarded the main road between Cambridge and Charlestown. Charlestown was by far the less risky option . . . the only realistic option.

There was something else to be said for choosing Charlestown: taking a position there might disrupt Gage's plans for Dorchester. Gage might choose to ignore a rebel fortification newly dug on Bunker Hill, and follow through with his plans on the eighteenth, but then again he might not, and instead take the American move as a challenge. If that was the case, then the attack on Dorchester might be postponed. It might even be cancelled altogether.

All this was discussed within the solid walls of the Hastings House. None of the details filtered back to the men in camp, but even the most ignorant private could not help but notice that something big was about to happen. There had been a brief alarm in Cambridge that morning—"we were under Arms waiting for [the] Order to move forward Expecting to meet the Kings Troops"—and the men sensed something frantic in the way that their officers took stock of their numbers, of their muskets and ammunition. "Making all preparations for a battle," noted Caleb Haskell, of Moses Little's Massachusetts regiment, in his diary that evening. James Knowles, a sergeant in Chester's company, wrote to his wife in Wethersfield: "We've been in a Good Deal of a Hubbub."[14]

*T*hose preparations were impossible to hide for very long. On the next day, Friday the sixteenth, men began the work of moving the college library to safety from its temporary quarters at Harvard Hall, scooping up armloads of books and dumping them unceremoniously into waiting wagons. The bustle began very early in the day at the Hastings House, with officers entering and exiting the building in a seemingly constant stream, brisk and businesslike. Inside, the old steward's house was buzzing with activity. General Ward's minimal staff—which amounted to little more than an adjutant and a secretary—consulted nonstop with the members of the Committee of Safety, poring over maps, double-checking regimental returns, arguing, calculating. But the rough outlines of a plan had emerged relatively early in the day. Ward issued his orders that morning.

General Ward had, at Cambridge and the surrounding camps, about six thousand Massachusetts men, plus the New Hampshire regiments of Stark and Reed, Putnam's Connecticut regiment, and a portion of Spencer's. The Cambridge army totaled about eight thousand effectives altogether, not counting Thomas's right wing. It was a sizeable force, roughly two thousand stronger than Gage's entire army. Ward could not spare the entire force, or even the greater part of it, for a venture that he had come to accept only recently and even then with some reservations. Cambridge *must* be held, the army and its supplies *must* survive, whether or not the rebels could keep and hold Bunker Hill. The good news was that Ward probably wouldn't have to send off most of his troops. The purpose of the operation, after all, was not to provoke the British into an immediate battle.

Consulting with his generals in the Council of War, Ward decided to send the Massachusetts regiments of William Prescott,

Ebenezer Bridge, and James Frye—about a thousand men altogether—plus a detachment from Putnam's Connecticut regiment and a company of artillery from Gridley's artillery regiment. William Prescott would lead the expedition, accompanied by Colonel Richard Gridley, who would guide the construction of fortifications on Bunker Hill. These men would hold the hill for the first day. Late the next afternoon, three fresh regiments—Nixon's, Little's, and Mansfield's, all from Massachusetts—would march out to the hill to relieve Prescott's men.[15]

At precisely six o'clock that evening, in accordance with the general's orders, the men of William Prescott's, Ebenezer Bridge's, and James Frye's regiments filed through the towering elm trees onto Cambridge Common, wheeling clumsily into line opposite the Hastings House. The three understrength regiments each formed up into a faltering, uneven line two ranks deep. The man that Ward had chosen to lead them, Colonel Prescott, stood facing them, sizing them up. It was a moving and tense moment for the veteran Prescott, for he of all people knew just how much was riding on the successful completion of his assigned task. Here before him were a thousand sons of Massachusetts. A good number of them, and just about everyone in Prescott's regiment, had been in the field since the Lexington alarm, and they were a rough-looking set. The colony had not yet issued its promised "bounty coats" of brown wool, so the men were clad in a kaleidoscopic array of civilian clothing: homespun coats, waistcoats, and breeches in the dull earth tones imparted by walnut and sumac dyes, torn stockings, and linen shirts stiff and filthy from perspiration and dust. There was a variety of hats, too, but mostly the low-crowned, wide-brimmed round hats that passed for fashion in rural New England. Bits and pieces of military gear could be seen here and there, especially leather cartridge boxes, and since Ward's orders stipulated that each man should bring a blanket, just about everybody had some kind of bedroll. Tumplines—

blankets rolled into short, fat coils and slung over the shoulder with a rope or a leather strap—and sausage-shaped leather bags called "snapsacks" were most common. The weaponry was just as varied. Many of the men had brought from home long-barreled fowlers, simple but graceful weapons as long as a man was tall; others carried "the King's arms" used in the French war, and French-made muskets captured in that same conflict could be seen, too. A few—far too many—had no firearms at all, and bayonets were scarce.

A most unmilitary appearance, in other words. The untidy ranks highlighted that impression. Nor did the men compensate for their motley clothing and equipage with a soldierly bearing . . . Prescott's boys slouched and fidgeted in the ranks, holding their muskets at odd angles as comfort dictated. Yet there was a seriousness about them, an earnest sense of purpose that showed in their grim and smoke-smudged faces, "ready for a march somewhere, but we did not know where." They *knew* that they were setting out on some dangerous work, not a raucous jaunt like the one at Noddle's three weeks earlier. They suspected that, whatever lay before them, some of them would not be coming back. That didn't deter them or dampen their spirits. As Peter Brown, a private in Prescott's regiment, wrote without exaggeration, "we readly and cheerfully obeyed."[16]

And for those who might have been oblivious to the gravity of the moment, it was soon made crystal-clear to them. Dr. Samuel Langdon, the army's head chaplain pro tem, joined Prescott in front of the three regiments. The men formed an impromptu circle around the doctor, came again to a halt, and fell silent, so that only the singing of birds and the ceaseless din of the camps could be heard. They doffed their hats and bowed their bare heads as Langdon offered up a prayer on their behalf to their Creator. Langdon's young charges at Harvard College dreaded their president's tedious sermons, but no one could deliver a stirring prayer like the esteemed reverend. Only a couple of weeks before, he had opened the first session of the Third Provincial Congress with a prayer, moving the delegates to tears, and here, too, he was in high form. His brief blessing reassured his audience that the Lord of Hosts was on their side, that their Cause was a holy one. When he finished, the men donned their hats and re-formed their lines. The officers coaxed the men back into marching columns, and they set off into the dusk, right around eight o'clock.[17]

For the rest of the soldiers in Cambridge the day was already done, and with nothing else to do they emerged from their billets and from around their campfires to watch as the column passed by in the deepening gloom. This was no mere guard detail on its way to one of the outlying forts, and that knowledge was both stirring and dreadful. Prescott's regiment led the way, followed by Frye's and Bridge's, then the four horse-drawn fieldpieces from Gridley's artillery regiment. Bringing up the rear were wagons full of picks and spades, under the care of Captain Thomas Foster of Gridley's regiment. Foster had been ordered to gather all the entrenching tools he could find, and if anything, he had been overzealous in executing that order—he took every last tool from the ordnance store in Harvard Yard, exciting the officious ordnance-master there to fits of righteous anger.[18] At the head of the column marched two sergeants from Prescott's regiment, each carrying a lantern. A lantern could do nothing to penetrate the thick blackness of the falling night, but that was not their purpose—they were markers, hooded so as to be visible only to the troops behind, providing them with a guide lest anyone should lose his way.

With the sergeants strode William Prescott, tall and spare and gaunt. He was a hero to his Middlesex County boys, who worshipped him as if he were a warlike god. Prescott, forty-nine years old, was a farmer from Pepperell who had served in Massachusetts provincial forces in two wars. As a teenager he had been present at the taking of the French fortress at Louisbourg in 1745, and he saw action in the French and Indian War a decade later. His bravery had so impressed the king's officers that he was offered a commission in the royal army, which he declined. It is unclear just why General Ward picked him to command this all-important expedition, since Prescott's military experience was not exceptional. Perhaps it was because none of the Massachusetts generals was available: Heath and Thomas were needed in Roxbury, and Warren had so much business to attend to already. The only general near Cambridge was Israel Putnam. Putnam had his uses—no one could be counted on more than Putnam when there was fighting to be done—but the expedition to Bunker Hill needed a subtle touch and a quick mind. Ward was not about to let Putnam determine the time and place for a battle.

Prescott's column moved steadily westward, all but groping its

William Prescott's force marching to Charlestown, June 16, 1775.
(EMMET COLLECTION, MIRIAM AND IRA D. WALLACH DIVISION OF ART, PRINTS AND PHOTOGRAPHS, THE NEW YORK PUBLIC LIBRARY, ASTOR, LENOX AND TILDEN FOUNDATIONS)

way through the darkness, past the pickets at Fort Number Three and into the open farm country beyond. At Inman's Farm the group halted; there, waiting for them silently, patiently, was a portion of Putnam's Connecticut regiment, at least two hundred strong, maybe more. They filed into the gap between the Massachusetts infantry and Gridley's artillery. Putnam's most trusted captain, Thomas Knowlton, led the Connecticut men . . . *officially.* For waiting alongside Knowlton on the Inman's farm lane was none other than Israel Putnam himself. He had not been ordered, or even asked, to take part, but he knew what was going on, and it would take more than the absence of an engraved invitation to keep Old Put away from where the action was. That afternoon, while preparing for the night's work ahead of him, he sought out his sixteen-year-old son, Daniel. The boy must stay at Mrs. Inman's, his doting father warned him gently, and if the Inmans fled, then he should follow them to safety. The poor boy knew what that meant, knew that battle lay ahead, and pleaded with his father to let him come along. Putnam had no regard for his own safety, but he loved his son deeply and wouldn't allow it. "You can do little, my son, where I am going," he said softly, smiling, eyes welling. "And there will be enough to take care of me."[19]

Putnam joined Prescott at the head of the column and the march resumed, past the desolate marshy waste of Charlestown Common and onto Charlestown Neck, then taking the south road toward Charlestown village. Had the men known General Ward's orders, they might have been confused when they passed right by the looming bulk of Bunker Hill, which blotted out the stars in the sky to their left. Instead, they continued to trudge along through the falling darkness, following the main road toward the southeast, toward Charlestown and a smaller, gentler rise, unremarkable in comparison with Bunker's.[20] Old-timers knew it only as the southern part of Bunker Hill, while others thought of it as "Charlestown Hill"; locals were just beginning to call this lesser prominence by the name of the farmer whose cattle pastured on its slopes: Breed's Hill.*

*L*ike Boston, Charlestown was perched upon a bulbous peninsula connected to the mainland by a narrow neck of land, though Charlestown Neck was infinitely shorter than Boston's. The peninsula was roughly triangular in shape, bounded on the northeast by the Mystic River and on the southeast and south by the Charles River. On the southernmost corner of that irregular triangle lay Charlestown, once a thriving and tidy village of two thousand souls and four hundred shops and houses; now wholly deserted, a ghost town. Boston's North End lay only a few hundred yards away, across the waters of the Charles. The village took up only a very small portion of the peninsula. The rest was a mix of low, marshy ground, flat beach, and grassy pasturage.

And also like Boston, the Charlestown peninsula was hilly. There were three separate hills: to the north, Bunker Hill; to the southeast of Bunker was Breed's; and to the northeast of Breed's, on the easternmost and farthest corner of the peninsula, was Morton's (sometimes called Moulton's) Hill, rising up from the beach at Morton's Point. They, too, formed a rough triangle, but when viewed from Boston they appeared as a chain of three hills, descending in height from left to right. The largest, Bunker Hill, was named after George Bunker, an early inhabitant of the region. It was elongated, loaf-shaped, and rose 110 feet from the flat land at its base. Its ends, the narrow northwestern and southeastern slopes, were gentle, but the long southwestern and northeastern sides were quite steep.

---

* Traditionally it has been argued that Prescott halted his column at a crossroads closer to the Neck, at the base of Bunker Hill. The only detailed account of the march is Amos Farnsworth's; and though he wrote that the column halted "just before we turned out of ye rode to go up Bunkers-hill," he also thought that the Americans built their fortifications that night, and fought the next day, on Bunker Hill. Clearly he meant Breed's.

The choice to fortify Bunker Hill was properly made. It would be relatively easy to defend. It was high and steep enough to make an infantry assault a decidedly bad proposition. The hill was very close to the waters of the Mystic, but that river was shallow enough to keep larger warships at arm's length, and then, too, gun crews on land or on board ship would find it challenging to elevate their pieces enough to hit anything on the summit. The hill was safely distant from the British batteries in Boston and way out of range of the guns on Boston Neck. Of course, that meant that artillery placed on Bunker Hill couldn't do much damage to the British if they stayed put in Boston . . . but the hill commanded Charlestown, the entire peninsula, and the roads that led to Cambridge and Medford. If the British decided to make a go at Charlestown or Cambridge, a fort on Bunker Hill could make them think twice.

Plus the Yankees' work was already done for them, at least in part. On the night of April 19, as Percy's and Smith's Redcoats fled from the avenging rebels, Gage's engineer Montresor constructed a simple open-ended earthen fort, called a redan, to cover the retreat. It was hardly sufficient to suit the Americans' purposes, but it was a start.

The other two hills had little to offer. Morton's Hill, only thirty-five feet from base to summit, barely merited the name. Breed's Hill was much closer to Charlestown. It had one ad-vantage, and one advantage only, over Bunker Hill: it was close enough to Boston and to the Charles River that—if properly complemented with heavy guns—it could pose a serious threat to the British in Boston and the ships in the harbor. Its proxim-ity was a mixed blessing, though, for it also meant that Breed's was well within range of British batteries in the North End and of the warships, too, if they ventured into the shallow waters of the Charles. It did not command the peninsula the way Bunker Hill did. The hill was relatively steep to the west, where it came very close to Charlestown. Its northeastern side was protected by low, swampy ground and clay pits. The eastern and southeastern slopes, though, were open and gentle . . . except for the rail fences that separated the pasturelands of farmers Breed, Russell, and Green. Neither cattle nor sheep had grazed here in several weeks, on account of the war, and by mid-June the grass on the slopes of Breed's Hill would reach to a man's waist.

Prescott's orders reflected the month-old recommendations of the Committee of Safety: he was to take possession of, and fortify, Bunker Hill. William Prescott should have been clear on this point, but he may not have been—months later, Prescott would claim, erroneously, that his instructions stipulated Breed's Hill instead. Clearly there was some confusion, or some hidden agenda, for when Prescott halted his men near Breed's Hill that night he felt compelled to confer with Putnam and Richard Gridley about their objective. Why he did so is anyone's guess. Maybe Prescott felt a tad uncertain of himself as the critical moment drew nigh. Maybe—and perhaps more likely—Prescott either was confused about his orders or decided on his own to interpret those orders loosely. Either way, the three men engaged in a muted argument over *which* hill should be fortified. Gridley, who as an artillerist was the closest thing to an engineer in the party, favored sticking strictly to Ward's orders and marching directly up Bunker's steep slope. One of the other two men—Putnam or Prescott—agreed with Gridley, but the other vehemently insisted on changing the objective to Breed's Hill. And that argument won. The decision was made in short order: to move on to Breed's Hill and ignore Bunker.[21]

Tradition has blamed Israel Putnam for the error, an error that would cost the Americans many lives and come within a whisker's breadth of destroying the Cause. The assumption makes sense: Putnam the wolf-killer, Putnam the irrepressible man of action,

Putnam the eternal boy, wanted battle without thinking of the consequences. Prescott, on the other hand, was cool and logical . . . it seems unlikely that such a man would so flagrantly disobey orders, even if unintentionally. Yet there is evidence to the contrary. There is no denying that Putnam wanted a fight, but over the hours to come, Putnam deferred to Prescott in virtually everything, never pulling rank even though he was a general and Prescott a colonel. Putnam acknowledged Prescott's authority as commander of the expedition. And when the action began the next day, it was Putnam who took great pains to fortify Bunker Hill, on his own, while Prescott defended the earthworks on Breed's. There is no way of knowing just *who* was responsible for the fateful change in plans that night. But it is irresponsible to pin the blame on Israel Putnam just because the man's character *seems* to make him guilty.

The move from Bunker to Breed's was no trivial decision. It completely changed the nature of the American operation; it altered the dynamics of the contest. Placing a fort atop Breed's Hill in full view—in easy cannon range—of the British . . . *that* could be seen as nothing less than a challenge to Gage. Gage could ignore it if he wished, for the Americans did not yet have enough heavy artillery to make Breed's truly threatening, but it was highly unlikely that Howe and Clinton would let him do so. Putnam or Prescott, whoever made the choice of place, would have his bloody fight soon enough.

So Breed's Hill it would be. Prescott hoarsely ordered the men to attention, re-formed the column, and pushed them along again, this time toward Breed's. But first, the veteran colonel took an important precautionary measure. He called out Captain John Nutting, a Pepperell neighbor whom Prescott especially trusted, and told the captain to pick sixty men and take them right down to Charlestown itself. Nutting's men were to patrol the village and the beaches nearby, keep an eye on the British warships in the Charles ferryway, and take note if the British were alerted to the rebel activity on Breed's Hill. Nutting's men quickly flitted away into the night like ghosts, making their way through the dark and empty streets of the village. The captain posted sentries along the waterfront, sending the remainder of his men into the townhouse to rest but with "orders not to shut our eyes." Amos Farnsworth, the religious young man who so enjoyed a good sermon, was among them.[22]

By the time that Prescott's men reached the summit of Breed's Hill it was quite late, nearly midnight. Much time, much precious time, had been thrown away when the leaders of the expedition argued over their objective. And it was becoming increasingly apparent to officers and men alike just how little planning had gone into this outing. Yes, Gridley was a trained engineer with an adequate knowledge of field fortifications; yes, Putnam had reconnoitered the ground a month before, though it's impossible to say whether Old Put—not a man much given to reflection—actually took mental notes on the terrain. Regardless, the men were expected to build a fortification that could withstand British cannonballs and deter an attack by British infantry, and they were expected to do it by dawn—maybe only four hours away at this point—and in nearly pitch-black darkness. The moon sat low in the southeastern sky and cast almost no light on Breed's; all the men had was the weak, pallid light of the stars above.

The pressure was all on Richard Gridley's slumped shoulders now. It was a good thing that Ward had decided to send him. There wasn't a more experienced officer in the army, or in all of North America, for that matter. Like Prescott, Gridley had been at the triumphant siege of Louisbourg thirty years before, albeit in a much different capacity—as a provincial lieutenant colonel in command of the siege batteries there. He was one of those rare colonials honored with a commission in the British army. When war with the French broke out again in 1755, Gridley returned to military life, fighting actively throughout the war, serving under Loudoun and Amherst and Wolfe. Amherst thought the world of him. Since the war he had become an enterprising businessman, briefly operating a seal and walrus fishery (the animals were prized for their oil), and later an ironworks in his native Massachusetts.

Gridley was not politically active, but right after Lexington and Concord he offered his services to the Committee of Safety, who eagerly accepted—such a prize, especially when it came with knowledge of fortifications and siegework, was not to be taken lightly. One week after the Glorious Nineteenth, the Provincial Congress gave him his commission, complete with a hefty salary and a generous pension. He was the only officer in the provincial service to be so rewarded.[23] Sadly, Gridley did not entirely fulfill the promise that the rebels saw in him. At age sixty-five, he was past his prime, and the artillery regiment he raised exhibited some problems. His sons, Scarborough and Samuel, proved to be corrupt and incompetent, and their enlisted men came to resent them. Still, at Breed's Hill that night, the senior Gridley was a godsend.

And for that reason the aging cannoneer was fretful and nervous. He had to perform under almost impossible circumstances, without time or daylight to scout the ground. He did what he could, and he kept it simple. In what seemed no time at all, Colonel Gridley staked out the broad outlines of a redoubt. The redoubt took the shape of an irregular quadrangle: two long sides, each around eight rods—132 feet—in length, met to form a sharp angle that pointed due west. Two shorter walls, probably about half as long, joined in a shallower angle pointing east and connected the two longer walls. The men did not have the time, the tools, or the materials to fashion fascines or any other kind of obstacle, but a ditch that encircled the whole redoubt would make scaling its walls a difficult proposition for enemy infantry.

There was no time for fine points or for double-checking.

Gridley laid out the dimensions of the redoubt; the men stacked their muskets, dropped their bedrolls, took pick and spade in hand, and went straight at it. There was little direction, and if the men took any breaks it was only because there weren't enough tools for everyone, and it simply wasn't possible to fit a thousand toiling men, or even a few hundred, into so small a space. Prescott, nervous that the noise might attract unwanted attention from sentries across the Charles, or from the watches on the ships close by, sent yet another company to the waterfront. Captain Hugh Maxwell led his men to the beaches northeast of town, the spot closest to the battery on Copp's Hill; soon John Brooks, future governor of Massachusetts but now a major in Bridge's regiment, joined Maxwell. Prescott himself went to the waterfront a couple of times that night, thoroughly convinced that the British *must* have divined what his men were up to.

Prescott needn't have worried. Even if the sounds of digging, of picks ringing against rock, did carry across the water, even if the British correctly deduced that their enemies were entrenching near Charlestown . . . even if any of these things happened, there was very little that the British could do about it. Neither the land batteries nor the ships could fire their cannon blindly at a sound, without knowing for certain the precise source and location whence that sound emanated. Whether or not the Americans were discovered building fortifications by night, Gage would have to wait for daylight before he could act.

The British didn't react. Later it would be revealed that sentries on the Boston shore opposite Charlestown had heard Prescott's men working "with the utmost viger all night," though they didn't report it. When Major Brooks and Captain Maxwell patrolled the Charlestown beach—and later, when Prescott joined them—they heard nothing . . . nothing but the bells in Boston's church steeples chiming out the half-hours and the night watches aboard a warship in the ferryway shouting "All's well!" And all they could see were the twinkling lights of Boston, reflected in the dark waters of the Charles.[24]

*I*n his quarters—he lodged in John Hancock's opulent mansion, confiscated by the British—Sir Henry Clinton was unable to sleep that night. There was much to be done on the morrow if the attack on Dorchester Heights would be carried out, as planned, at daybreak on the morning of the eighteenth. On the seventeenth, only a few hours away, boats would have to be gathered for Howe's amphibious assault; in the garrison, ammunition would be issued and muskets inspected, rations cooked, everything put in order. Preparing for such a massive strike would take all day, because all of these things took time. But General Clinton had his blood up for the venture, and Clinton was a thinking man, not sociable, but reflective, and nervous, too. Something compelled him to go out "reconnoitring" that evening. Exactly where he rode he would never reveal to posterity. Maybe he rode down to Boston Neck, where the Sabbath-day attack would launch. Maybe he rode out to Copp's Hill or the beaches along Boston Common and the North End to get a glimpse of the mainland shore. He couldn't have gone to the mainland itself, let alone to Charlestown or its peninsula. That would have been dangerous; rebel pickets would have spotted him in no-time flat.

Something he saw or heard from his reconnaissance awoke Clinton's suspicions, and being a suspicious man by nature that wasn't hard to do. Later he would claim that "In the Evening of ye 16th I saw [the rebels] at work." Perhaps he did, but the only place where he could have *seen* the Americans digging that evening would have been at Roxbury—coincidentally, American pickets at Roxbury noted an unusual amount of activity in the British lines that very night.* Whatever Clinton glimpsed, it could not have been Prescott's men at work on Breed's Hill. They did not start digging until midnight or after; besides, they were too far away, and the night was too dark, to have allowed Clinton a look. Clinton could not have seen Putnam, Prescott, and Gridley leading their thousand up Charlestown Neck earlier in that evening, either. The general could not have *seen* anything that night, except at Roxbury.

We will never know what Clinton saw or heard on the night of June 16, 1775, but he sensed *something*, and it was well before midnight—before Prescott's men had even reached Breed's Hill—when Sir Henry roused Gage and Howe to tell them his news. He proposed to his two superiors an abrupt and drastic change in plans. "I . . . have strong suspicions that our C[harlestown] operations must preceed the other," he wrote later that night to a friend in England, and to that end he recommended immediate action: an amphibious assault on the rebels, wherever they were in Charlestown, whatever they were doing. Howe, Clinton later said, approved of the plan, but Gage demurred, cautiously—but correctly and wisely—pointing out that no one could say for sure what the rebels were doing or what they had in mind, not at this later hour. It would have been the height of folly for Gage to have chased after a shadow, to have sent an expeditionary force across the river to seek out and attack disembodied sounds in the moonless dark. Without knowing the broad outlines of the rebels' new positions on the peninsula—without knowing if there was indeed *any* rebel force on the hills—there was nothing that the British could do and still enjoy a reasonable hope of success. Clinton might not have liked the rejection of his proposal,

---

* Samuel Bixby, a private in Bolster's company, Larned's Massachusetts regiment, was stationed at Roxbury. On June 16, he recorded in his diary: "Firing by the regulars in Boston. Went on the Grand parade, where about 300 men were drawn for the Point Piquet, and about 600 to entrench the piquet. About 9 o.c. P.M. the regulars in Boston fired an alarm, and rung the bells. We heard them drawing the carriages to the neck, & the riding of horses with great speed up to their guard and back into Boston, and there was great commotion there. It was supposed they were preparing to attack us in the morning, but no special orders were issued. The town seemed to be alive with men marching in all directions." "Diary of Samuel Bixby," 286–87.

but he conceded that the army was unprepared and nothing could be done just yet. "If we were of active dispositions," he lamented to his English correspondent, "we should be landed by tomorrow morning at daybrake[;] as it is I fear it must be deferred till two."[25]

And so Sir Henry returned to his quarters, and Howe and Gage to their slumbers, but not because of laziness or contempt for their foes or an unwillingness to act. They did nothing because they had no choice. Until daylight revealed just what the rebels were up to, there could be no attack. Better to let the men rest now, to make careful but rapid preparations in the morning, than to lash out blindly at an unknown target. Without boats at hand, ready to ferry Gage's battalions across the river, it couldn't be done, anyway.

*A*ll the while the men atop Breed's Hill kept to their labors. Soon it was approaching four o'clock in the morning, the hour of daybreak, and the redoubt was nearly finished. *Nearly.* William Prescott, though not unfamiliar with battle, felt his chest tighten as he contemplated the firestorm to come. What made the anxiety worse was the fact that he felt all alone. Bridge was still with him, as was James Brickett, the lieutenant colonel of James Frye's regiment, yet they were "indisposed, [and] could render me but little service," Prescott reported afterward. Frye himself, crippled by gout that made walking or riding a nightmare of jagged-edged pain, had stayed behind in his quarters in Cambridge. Putnam was still somewhere in the vicinity, though God alone knew where, for the old man's energy was so boundless that he couldn't sit still for very long. And Gridley had gone off to check on the guns, which had still not come up to Breed's. Prescott felt his absence keenly. "The engineer forsook me," he noted with a trace of sadness in his account of the battle.[26]

There was nothing left to do, or rather nothing that Prescott could do. He sent out runners to fetch Nutting and Maxwell, to bring them back to dubious safety in the pit his men had scratched in the earth. Within minutes the hundred-some-odd men of the two shore patrols crested the hill, and heaving great gasping breaths they climbed laboriously over the parapet and dropped to the uneven floor below, panting. Spent. Everyone was spent. And the day was only just beginning.

At about five minutes past four o'clock the first feeble glow of dawn appeared on the horizon to the east-northeast, right over Noddle's Island and Chelsea, and the world around William Prescott exploded in smoke and flame and hot iron.

The thick darkness over Boston had just begun to dissolve with the first wash of daylight from the east, casting the hint of a glow over the rolling meadows of Noddle's Island. For nearly a week, Noddle's had been devoid of life, the Williams house and its outbuildings reduced to ash and charred jutting timbers, the sheep and horses and cattle all gone. But aboard the twenty-gun sloop HMS *Lively*, no one paid much attention to the dead expanse of land to the east-northeast. All eyes were fixed instead on the shadows off the port quarter, on the slopes near Charlestown, just a few hundred yards northwest of where the *Lively* rode gently at anchor in the Charles River ferryway.

Charlestown itself was no more alive than Noddle's, a mournful ghost of a village, its deserted houses and shops and its lifeless wharves shrouded in black silence. Or mostly silence. From the hills above the town floated sounds that were just barely there, not quite masked by the slap of the river against the ship's sheathing, by the creak of spars and tackle . . . the sounds of digging, the lurching rhythm of mattock and spade overturning parched rocky soil, carrying lazily down through the warm, pungent air above the Charles.

It was now just about four o'clock in the morning, eight bells, the hour when in more peaceful times the watch above decks would change. The sounds had begun some time after midnight. Clearly the provincials were up to some mischief on the Charlestown hills. But until daylight betrayed them, there was nothing that the *Lively* could do to interfere. No sense in throwing broadsides blindly into the dark toward an invisible foe. *That* would be a waste of good powder and shot.

Then the dim light of daybreak gave the lookouts aboard the *Lively* their first glimpse of the commotion on the hills. Hundreds of silhouetted figures scuttled around a great raw gash in the earth. A fort had emerged overnight atop the hill closest to Charlestown, in the tall, unkempt grass of the neglected cow pasture. No one could make out its shape or its dimensions—it was still too dark for that—but it was most likely a simple affair. Simple but definitely functional. And so purposefully audacious. The rebels could have thrown up fortifications elsewhere on the peninsula, sites that were safer, more defensible, sites that would have afforded some protection to the base at Cambridge. Yet they chose a hilltop within easy range of the *Lively*, tugging at her cable midstream. The fort was an overt challenge.

A couple of nights before, the *Somerset*—a sixty-four-gun ship-of-the-line that dwarfed the little sloop—had guarded the ferry-way, but Graves was so deeply haunted by the *Diana*'s fiery end that he'd ordered the *Somerset* withdrawn to the safety of deeper waters farther out in the harbor. The Charles River ferryway was narrow and shallow; there was just too much danger that the *Somerset* would run aground as the *Diana* had. The *Somerset* could not be allowed to share the *Diana*'s fate. On the sixteenth—just the day before—the *Somerset* left the ferryway and went to her new anchorage. The *Lively* would face the rebel challenge alone.

The *Lively*'s skipper, Captain Thomas Bishop, stood at the

quarter-rail with spyglass raised to his eye, but he did not take much time to marvel at the resourcefulness or daring or arrogant stupidity of his enemy. He would act, and act quickly. The captain's pride still smarted from the sharp blow it had received from Admiral Graves less than two weeks before. Bishop had had the great misfortune to become embroiled in a trifling dispute with the commander of the ill-fated *Diana*, Lieutenant Thomas Graves. Bishop had done nothing wrong—every officer on post knew it—but that hardly mattered when his accuser was the admiral's nephew. A court-martial was inevitable, and while the court sitting in judgment in the *Somerset*'s stateroom sympathized with Bishop, there was no way that the captain could evade the admiral's sputtering, foul-mouthed wrath. Bishop didn't want to endure *that* again. But he also knew an opportunity when he saw one, and an opportunity to redeem his bruised reputation was staring down on him from the heights of Charlestown.

The crew was no less eager. Here was a chance for action after months of dull routine, patrolling the waters off Boston and in the harbor as well. The noxious miasmas arising from the great stinking swamps of the Back Bay made the already grinding boredom unbearable. To a man, too, they were hungry for revenge. Each one of them knew precisely what had happened to the *Diana* three weeks earlier, even if they hadn't actually seen the last painful hours of her humiliating end . . . a king's ship, beached and rolled over on her beam ends, abandoned by her crew, Yankee thieves crawling all over her careening hull as they looted her. Even worse, they *burned* her. It was an insult to every ship and every tar in the fleet.

Bishop did not wait for orders from Graves. His crew was ready. Half of them had been awake and on deck, anyway, pursuant to the admiral's orders. The rest had since been piped up from below. The gun crews stood to their pieces, the sleek nine-pounders of the *Lively*'s starboard battery. Charged and shotted, ten black muzzles protruded menacingly from the gaping square maws of the gun ports. The rest of the crew scrambled to bring the ship about on her cable so that the starboard battery could bear on the hilltop fort.

Within minutes the *Lively* stood parallel to the rebel earthworks. Bishop studied the target one more time as the gun crews tried to get the range, and then he gave the order to open fire.

The explosion shook the placid dawn. The *Lively*'s entire starboard side erupted in a vivid sheet of flame, horizontal pillars of acrid white smoke cascading from each muzzle, merging to form a single billowy mass that drifted over the surface of the water, carried by the light morning winds toward the beach. The deck shuddered as the long nines, each gun and carriage weighing nearly a ton-and-a-half, leapt violently backward, slamming hard against the massive breeching ropes and tackle that absorbed the shock of the recoil. Nine-pound iron shot flew over the Charles with an unnerving screech, arcing invisibly—for unlike explosive shell, cast-iron solid shot did not trail a telltale corkscrew of flame and sparks.[27]

The battle for Charlestown had begun.

Seven

* * *

MASTERS OF
THESE HEIGHTS

*T*he captive inhabitants of Boston had become as accustomed
to the sounds of artillery as they had to the dearth of fresh
food. They had heard quite a great deal of cannonfire over the past
month, rattling their windows and crockery, disturbing their slumbers. It always came from the south, where British gun crews in the
Lines on Boston Neck tortured John Thomas's men, who could not
fight back. Still, the report of the *Lively*'s broadsides came as something of a shock, more so when the big twenty-four-pounders of the
New Battery on Copp's Hill joined in briefly. The sounds echoed
from an unexpected quarter and at the end of a tranquil and lan-
guorous night. After a while—it might have been an hour, or two,
nobody bothered to make a note of the time—the firing stopped,
ordered ceased no doubt by Admiral Graves.

The thunder of the guns easily roused Gage and Howe and Clinton, too, for none of them had slept very soundly after Clinton's revelation only a few short hours before. By the time the sun had cleared the eastern horizon, hinting at the promise of a cloudless and baking-hot day ahead, lieutenants and orderlies had gathered in small groups in the spacious yard that separated the façade of Province House from Marlborough Street. Wearing harried and serious faces, they flitted in and out of Gage's headquarters by the score. Headquarters was in ordinary circumstances a very busy place; today it was doubly so. For five days, the generals had assumed that the army would attack Dorchester Heights on Sunday the eighteenth, the very next day. The plan was straightforward and uncomplicated, but all such operations required careful logistical and tactical preparation anyway—if the mistakes of Lexington and Concord were not to be repeated. Even if everything had gone according to plan, the generals would have had their work cut out for them on the seventeenth. But things were most definitely not going according to plan.

The rebels had made the first move, at Charlestown rather than at Dorchester. It did not necessarily follow that the plans for Dorchester would have to be scrapped outright, but at the very least the situation demanded reappraisal.

So some time after sunrise, some time after the *Lively*'s long nines had fallen silent, Gage convened his chiefs at Province House. Sir Frederick Haldimand was noticeably absent—not that Gage had ever given his second-in-command much to do, but when Gage needed him most Haldimand was truly gone: in one of the great ironies of the battle, Sir Frederick had left Boston on a ship bound for England only the day before. Howe was there, and Clinton and Burgoyne. So, too, was Lord Percy. Scrawny, pinch-faced, and ugly, at age thirty-two, Lord Percy was one of the rising stars in the army who enjoyed the rare combination of political clout, great wealth, and undeniable brilliance. He kept his distance from Howe—the two men detested one another—and tactfully kept his silence, too, but Gage trusted Percy unreservedly. This, after all, was the man who saved Smith's column from disaster after Concord.

The *Lively*'s discovery was no big surprise. The Americans could be counted on to pull off a stunt like this, and Clinton's admonition had primed all of the generals for just this very circumstance. But Clinton's suspicions were not the same thing as firm intelligence. Now that the sun had risen, the generals could revisit their plans for the next two days.

Thus far, sunlight hadn't revealed all that much. Clinton and Howe could not entirely agree on whether the rebels had built a redoubt, a completely enclosed fort, or a redan, an open-ended fortification with no wall covering its rear. As yet there were no other earthworks guarding the approaches to Breed's Hill, at least none that were visible from the usual vantage-points in Boston. Still, the fort on Breed's posed a potential threat to British troops in the town and the shipping in the harbor. A *potential* threat. It had no artillery, no artillery worth mentioning anyway, and until it did, the fort was just so much displaced dirt as far as the British were concerned.

The choices before Gage and company were few, simple, and clear-cut. The British could have opted to ignore the rebels altogether and stuck to their plans for a Sunday assault on Dorchester. In retrospect, it might have been the wisest course of action—and the most daring. If Artemas Ward had sent a sizeable force to Charlestown, he would have no reinforcements to spare for John Thomas at Roxbury. Thomas's weak force could have been easily pushed aside and Dorchester Heights seized with little effort expended, and few lives lost. All the while, the Americans in that fort on Breed's Hill could do nothing to stop it. The fort was an unmistakable challenge to Gage—as it was no doubt intended to be—but in a tactical sense it was nothing more than an exposed outpost fairly begging to be taken.

Yet there was no telling what the Americans had in mind, or when they might find the artillery that would transform the earthwork from a glaring tactical mistake into a deadly gun platform, ready to rain all hell down on Boston and the fleet. It had been a full six weeks since Ethan Allen and Benedict Arnold had seized Ticonderoga and absconded with the heavy guns there. Gage knew it—all too well—but he had no idea where the guns were at the moment. His chief informant, Benjamin Church, was of no help at all in this moment. Church was still in Philadelphia at the Continental Congress.

For Gage, then, the practical choice, the prudent course, would be to shift direction: instead of attacking Dorchester first, as had been decided on June 12, the British would confront the Americans near Charlestown.

*T*he myth that enshrouds the story of Bunker Hill compels us to pin the blame for that bungled clash almost entirely on the British commanders. Gage and Howe, we are told time and again, were primarily responsible for the carnage on that hot June afternoon. Not because of their competence or lack thereof, but because of their attitude. They failed to appreciate—so the myth goes—the raw, unpolished genius, the spirit of enterprise, of the Americans, almost as much as they failed to understand that the art of war as practiced on the flat, unobstructed battlefields of the Old World had no place in the broken landscape of the New. Instead, Gage and Howe, like all British officers, dismissed the American fighting man as being beneath contempt, bereft of any and all military virtue. Any exercise of diligence or careful planning or anything that smacked of effort would be wasted on such rabble. It would "accord the rebels too much respect."[1]

And so, according to this time-honored story, the British

generals—Sir Henry Clinton notably excepted—were intentionally lethargic as they made their plans to deal with Prescott's men
on Breed's Hill. Everything Gage or Howe did was invariably accompanied by a haughty sneer, for the task of fighting against provincials was so utterly lacking in dignity that it scarcely merited any
kind of consideration. One comes away with the impression that
the British commanders—not just at Bunker Hill, but throughout
the Revolution—made a point of making questionable decisions
and taking ridiculous chances just to show the world the shameful
ennui they must have felt when confronted with such contemptible
opponents.

Like most myths, this one has at its heart a kernel of truth. The
British officer corps had a reputation for xenophobia that extended
as much to their European allies and foes as it did to their American
cousins. Young, inexperienced officers, full of youthful bravado and
hot air and little else, certainly no wisdom or perspective, cheerfully
and mindlessly groused about the "Yankey scoundrels," the "rascals
and poltroons," who kept them cooped up in Boston. They bewailed
their misfortune in having to fight such "scoundrels, for one only
dirties one's fingers by meddling with them."[2]

These, however, were the empty words of would-be warriors. Officers who had seen much service, or those who had fought side-by-
side with Americans in the previous war, knew better. They knew
from experience exactly what the rebels could do. Those who didn't
know before Lexington and Concord certainly did afterward. Bitterly they complained about the unfair advantages that the rebels had
during the bloody retreat from Concord, and they couldn't help but
decry the rebellion as "despicable." But still they recognized in the
American army a formidable and resourceful opponent, one whose
abilities should never be underestimated. "During the whole affair [of
April 19] the Rebels attacked us in a very scattered, irregular manner,
but with perseverance & resolution," wrote Lord Percy after Con-

cord. "Whoever looks upon them as an irregular mob, will find himself much mistaken. They have men amongst them who know very well what they are about . . . nor are several of their men void of a spirit of enthusiasm . . . for many of them . . . advanced within 10 yds. to fire at me & other officers, tho' they were morally certain of being put to death themselves in an instant."[3] Howe and Gage shared that view. Indeed, Gage's apparent passivity over the previous two months was based on just this—the notion that no matter what he tried, the rebels would find some way of frustrating him.

Perhaps more important, Gage was painfully aware that his army was highly flawed, wanting in experience, discipline, and self-confidence. It may have been superior to Ward's army in organization and training . . . but only by degrees in some instances, and it had thoroughly demonstrated that it was not the well-tuned fighting force that it should have been. Officers and men were eager for a fight—the "one good drubbing" that Captain Harris longed for—but that didn't mean that they were any better prepared for a general engagement than they had been two months earlier. Gage could not afford—Britain could not afford—to take the chance that the army might come completely undone in the midst of an operation that promised to be infinitely more trying than the fumbled expedition to Concord.

So when Gage, Howe, Clinton, and Burgoyne sat down to discuss their options at Province House that morning, they were not guided by dismissive contempt, but by a realistic appraisal of the opposing armies, tempered by a healthy respect for the myriad unseens and unknowns that lay beyond the hilltop fort across the river, just out of sight.

Clinton made the first and—on the surface—the most alluring proposal. He was bleary-eyed from fatigue—he had not slept a wink since his evening reconnaissance—but no less sharp-witted than ever. What the rebels had given the king's troops at Charlestown,

Sir Henry argued, was a rare and wondrous opportunity: a chance for a full envelopment of the American position. The redoubt on Breed's Hill was not impregnable, not even close, and it lay at a considerable distance from Charlestown Neck. The pencil-thin Neck was the only viable escape route from the fort, from anywhere on the peninsula, for that matter, and the only passage by which Ward's reinforcements could arrive from Cambridge.

This would be the Americans' undoing, Clinton went on. If Gage were to send a body of troops across the Charles by boat, taking the beach on the tip of the peninsula, and then Clinton were to lead a smaller amphibious force up the Mystic River to make landfall close to the Neck, then for the Americans all would be lost. The men on Breed's Hill would be sealed off, with no hope of escape, no hope of relief. It wouldn't take a huge force to accomplish this: only one thousand, fifteen hundred maybe, to hit the beaches in the main assault, and another five hundred for Clinton's movement near the Neck. Or the British could land the entire force at Charlestown itself, march it through the town's deserted streets, bypass the American fort, and accomplish the same objective. The defenders of the fort would be doomed. "By this movement," as one of Clinton's admirers later described it, "we [would have] shut them up in the peninsula as in a bag . . . they must have surrendered instantly or been blown to pieces."[4]

Although Clinton had no prior experience with amphibious operations, he was a literate soldier with a firm grasp of tactical theory. He was no fool, and he knew quite well—unlike later historians—that no matter how quickly the army moved, an amphibious assault on the peninsula was not something that could be let loose that very instant. Boats would not just appear on their own at Boston's wharves; troops could not be supplied with ammunition and cooked rations in a matter of minutes. The army was not capable of descending instantaneously on the Charlestown beaches to overwhelm a surprised enemy. Preparations for an amphibious operation would take *hours*, not minutes, to complete in a satisfactory way, even if hurried beyond all prudence.

What Clinton suggested, then, made perfect sense, especially since the army was gearing up for an offensive the next day anyway. If Gage issued the marching orders *now*, then the Redcoats could be brought across the Charles and in position to attack at "day brake," in Clinton's words, *the next day*, on Sunday, June 18, 1775.

Historians and armchair strategists have consistently hailed Clinton's plan as the only logical solution offered by a British general that day. Partly that admiration comes from the mistaken assumption that when Clinton said "daybrake," he meant *that* morning, Saturday the seventeenth. Of course he did not; daybreak had passed, and the vicissitudes of logistics would not allow an immediate attack anyway. Even then, Clinton's plan was not practical. Executing a true envelopment was a tricky business in the best of circumstances. If the enemy held substantial forces in reserve—as Ward did at Cambridge—then it was a recipe for disaster. A well-timed movement from Cambridge, a couple of battalions sent headlong up the Neck and crashing into Clinton's flank or rear, and all would be over for Clinton. The Redcoats, and not the rebels, would be the ones squeezed in the bag.

Gage was aware of the risks, was aware of just how quickly the predator could become the prey in an envelopment, and knew enough about the Americans to know that they shouldn't be counted on to sit still while a portion of their army was cut off and destroyed. His impetuous subordinate's plan made the fatal error of assuming that the rebels would wait passively in Cambridge. So Gage shot it down. And Howe backed him up.

Sir Henry accepted the rejection gracefully. Outwardly he had no choice but to bow to Gage's judgment. Inwardly, however, he felt the sting of rejection and blamed it all on snobbery. Clinton was not a man to be easily convinced that he could be wrong. And he was the only one of the group—except for Burgoyne, who hardly counted—who had learned the military art in the German states, fighting the *real* war against the French. Gage and Howe had been trained in "the American school," and therefore "affected to despise" veterans of the European campaigns like himself.

Once again, Gage had exercised appropriate caution. Clinton's proposed stratagem, Gage pointed out to his youngest major general, went against an essential tactical principle: it would divide his forces and put a small portion of them in between two larger enemy bodies. Only five hundred Regulars standing between the Yankee fortifications and Ward's main body? With those kinds of odds, it mattered little how poorly trained the Americans were; Clinton's small division—only a single battalion, really—would likely be crushed as soon as Ward got wind of what the British were up to. Clinton had not been there in April to see how the rebels had confidently swarmed all over Smith's men retreating from Concord, how the men and boys had materialized out of every farm and field and copse of trees as if conjured by magic, how they had made the trek back a living hell for the poor confused grenadiers and light infantry. Gage had seen it, and he wasn't going to risk seeing it again.

Then Billy Howe spoke up. His proposals were not so well developed as those of his junior colleague Clinton, nor were they so bold. Later critics would find Howe's plan singularly lacking in imagination and subtlety, not precisely the thing one would expect from the man who had scaled the Heights of Abraham, the man who had championed light infantry and irregular warfare. In fact, at this stage Howe's suggestions were so embryonic that they really don't deserve to be called a "plan" at all. Yet they were the more prudent, the more practical, given the circumstances. What Howe recommended was this: get troops to the southeastern tip of the peninsula, as many as possible, as quickly as possible. The specifics of the attack could be determined then, when the British forces were on the ground facing the Yankee fortifications. For the moment, Howe was fairly convinced that the work atop Breed's Hill was a mere redan—"incompleat no flanks, neither picketted pallasaded or ditched"—and therefore only poorly defended in the rear and on the flanks. "The hill was open and of easy assent and in short it would be easily carried." Most likely it could be taken by a "turning" movement.[5]

Turning movements were all the rage among eighteenth-century tacticians, and with good reason: they worked, and worked well. The foremost soldier of the age—Frederick the Great of Prussia— had used them to dramatic effect. The "oblique order of battle," as Frederick called it, had given the Prussians the single greatest victory of the Seven Years' War, and indeed the greatest upset of any eighteenth-century battle: at Leuthen in December 1757. In the simplest terms, it involved nothing more complicated than a feint—a "demonstration in force"—against the center of the enemy line, one of its flanks, or some other weak point. When that feint drew the enemy's attention, and his reinforcements, to that sector of the battle-line, the attacker would slip as many troops as he could around an unguarded flank, change front to face the enemy on that flank, deploy into line of battle, and come crashing down on the unsuspecting enemy. The results could be grimly breathtaking. At Leuthen, Frederick's vastly outnumbered army of 36,000 exhausted Prussians had outflanked, routed, and crushed a far superior army of more than 80,000 Austrians.

Such an attack required great stealth and speed, but it could be done. Howe was a passionate proponent of this kind of tactic. On Breed's Hill he saw a perfect opportunity to put it into practice.

What Howe most definitely did *not* propose was "a frontal assault in the best tradition of Europe's battlegrounds."[6] And unlike Clinton, who was willing to wait for the next day, Howe insisted on immediate action. If the British acted at that instant, forgoing the Dorchester operation set for the following day, they just might be able to scrape together enough boats, muster the men, and row them across the Charles in time for high tide, roughly around two o'clock that afternoon. It would be the ideal time to make landfall. If need be, the infantry could be ferried across during ebb tide—the boats could stop short of the beaches and the men made to jump out and wade through the last few yards of waist-deep surf. But the artillery was an entirely different animal. No amount of coaxing would persuade a six-pounder fieldpiece, more than a ton of brass and oak and iron, to do the same.

Howe's ideas held sway, for they were the only viable ideas. Gage gave his assent. Clinton expressed his concern that the Americans, once confronted, would be able to escape. "I feared that there was a double stone wall with a lane between by Which they could retire safely," he pointed out . . . though he had no evidence at hand to suggest that such a wall or lane actually existed. It was typical Clinton. He worked alone, planned alone, and once his mind was made up he was unshakably convinced of the superiority of his ideas.[7]

Later, hoping to repair the damage that the American war had done to his reputation, Sir Henry would lodge all sorts of shrill objections to the decisions made that day. He would pout that "My advice was not attended to." But at Province House he went along with his colleagues.

So much for Charlestown. There were other matters to be discussed, quieter matters, but still vitally important. The attack on Dorchester would not take place as planned five days before, but there was no sense in letting the rebels know that. Best to keep them guessing. Accordingly, Gage directed Lord Percy to take charge in "the Lines" on Boston Neck.

The council adjourned some time before seven o'clock that morning. William Howe would be responsible for nearly the entire plan of action on which the generals had settled. If the assault force was to be ready and well on its way to Charlestown in six hours—a true feat of rapid planning and execution—then Howe would have much work to do in the next couple of hours.

General Howe issued his orders at seven. All of the "flank companies"—meaning the light infantry and grenadiers, encamped together as a body on the Common—plus five infantry regiments and one of the Marine battalions were to be dressed, armed, and ready to march to one of two embarkation points in the city.

Now for transportation and naval support—both essential components of a successful amphibious assault. Samuel Graves did not attend the Council of War at Province House that morning. Most likely Gage intentionally left him out; the two men did not get along well, and Gage didn't need the admiral's input anyway. But Howe did. The two men met aboard the *Somerset*, then moored in the harbor.

Graves had been awake even before the *Lively*'s first broadside, catching up on correspondence and routine paperwork, so both he and Howe were already quite tired at the very beginning of what promised to be a long day. Still it was an amicable and productive meeting. Howe hoped very much that the *Somerset* and the other larger ships, the *Boyne* and the *Asia*, could bring their guns into play, and Graves hoped so, too: the massive thirty-two-pounders on the *Somerset* and *Boyne* could wreak havoc on the rebel fortifications . . . *if* they could reach them. All of the third-raters drew too much water; it was dangerous to send them in the shallows of the Charles and the Mystic, and even then it was doubtful that the lower-deck batteries on these big ships could be elevated high enough that their projectiles would hit the crest of Breed's. Graves reluctantly conceded that the big ships would be of no use that day, except for the boats, men, and ammunition they could supply. So the *Somerset*'s skipper detailed thirty-eight tars to man the armed transport *Symmetry* and her battery of eighteen nine-pounders; another twenty left the *Somerset* to handle the sloop *Falcon*, while men from the flagship *Preston* took over the tiny sloop *Spitfire*. All was improvised; nothing was as Graves or Howe would have preferred it. "As this Affair was sudden and unexpected," Graves noted sadly, "there was no time for constructing floating Batteries, or Rafts of real Service, as any such would have been a work of some days."[8]

The remaining craft—the sloops *Lively, Glasgow, Falcon,* and *Spitfire,* the transport *Symmetry,* and a handful of smaller vessels— would perform the primary task: covering the landing. If the ships could destroy or substantially damage the rebel fortifications, that would be a big plus, but the essential thing was to keep the rebels pinned down so that they didn't make trouble for the Regulars when they waded ashore. Charlestown itself was another consideration. Howe felt that the rebels could take cover in the deserted buildings and harass the British as they deployed. The ships could guard against that, too.

Could Howe and Graves have made better use of their ships? Undoubtedly. As events would prove, a couple of smaller craft placed in the Mystic estuary could have done great damage to the rebels, and perhaps even changed the course of the battle. But Howe and Graves were reacting to what they knew that morning, and their disposition of the warships reflects that. Still, it is impossible not to find a trace of fault with the general and the admiral for not considering the possibility.

The ships alone, though, could not win the battle, no matter how they were situated around the Charlestown peninsula. Ships could not take ground. If the British wanted the heights, no matter how many tons of cast-iron shot the warships hurled at the Americans, sooner or later foot troops would have to land on the peninsula and take physical possession of them.

So everything, the success or failure of the British attack, would come down to the individual Redcoat—his resilience, his fortitude, his courage, his discipline and obedience. Yet even the common British soldier suspected, just as Gage did in his heart of hearts, that the king's army was shockingly unprepared for what lay in store for it that day.

*W*hile the British generals pondered their next move, Prescott's men on Breed's Hill were not idle. Scared, perhaps, but not idle.

Daybreak that morning had been full of surprises on both sides. The first rays of pallid light had betrayed to the *Lively*'s crew the source of the sounds they had heard since midnight. It also revealed to Prescott's exhausted, dirty Yankees just how daring their action had been . . . or possibly how poorly their leaders had considered the consequences of their bold but ill-advised move.

For the redoubt that they had fashioned at such great pains and with such great stealth was badly sited, and dawn made it plain to all just how badly. The redoubt, by itself, was an imposing edifice, more substantial by far than Montresor's redan on Bunker Hill, that relic of the April battles that seemed so very distant now. But that was in essence the problem: the redoubt stood by itself. It was exposed on both flanks. The Americans' right flank—the approaches to the redoubt from the west-southwest, in the direction of Charlestown—was *almost* secure. Any force attempting to take the fort from that direction would have to work its way through the streets of Charlestown, emerging at the base of the hill well within musket range of the redoubt. And even then it would have to pass through some truly difficult terrain. A mere handful of infantry nesting in

Charlestown's empty houses and shops could make it very hot for a British force trying to move on the fort from that direction. The American left flank, though, was a different story.

Nothing really guarded the left flank, no earthworks, no impassible terrain. A four-hundred-yard stretch of open land separated the earthen walls of the redoubt from the shore of the Mystic River. True, there was swampy land at the hill's northeastern base, and there were the rocks and holes and fence lines that could complicate the movement of troops through any farmland in rural New England. But these were impediments, not guarantees, and the men recognized this as clearly as if their God had inscribed their doom upon the landscape.

It didn't help at all that the men who had bowed reverentially to Dr. Langdon's imprecations to that God only nine hours before were drained, physically and emotionally. Few had any water left. "No drink but rum," noted Peter Brown, though there was a short-lived water supply somewhere within the redoubt. There was not much food, either. Artemas Ward had tried to prevent the latter discomfort: on the general's orders, the commissary had issued three days' worth of rations to the Massachusetts men the day before. Either the officers had not troubled themselves about getting the food to the men or the men themselves neglected to stuff their haversacks. Or they may have thrown away their extra rations on the march to lighten the load, as inexperienced soldiers often did.[9]

Now it hardly mattered whose fault it was. The men on Breed's Hill were calorie-starved, their cracked lips and parched, dust-choked throats rebelled against their braver intentions. And they were deprived of rest as well. They were already tired out from the night march when they got to Breed's at midnight or thereabouts. By daybreak they were barely able to function, let alone think or fight.

They were men who had begun to understand the rigors of

military life and the frequent senselessness of orders, but they had not yet fully made the transition to soldiers. Prescott's troops were not yet so robbed of individuality and skepticism that they could not openly question the motives and even the intelligence of their officers. Their exhaustion amplified their fears, almost to the point of paranoia, as they surveyed the brightening meadows around them and perceived how exposed, how very vulnerable, they were in their naked hilltop perch.

Even before the guns on the *Lively* opened up, grumbling began to ripple through the mass of men in the redoubt. Surely this was no accident. Surely their officers had led them to this spot to die, to be sacrificed for some purpose they themselves couldn't discern, some end in which their individual lives counted for no more than so many hogs led to the pens at Cambridge Store. "We saw our danger, being against 8 ships of the line and all Boston fortified against us," fumed Peter Brown, still angry as he recounted the events more than a week later. "The danger we were in made us think there was treachery, and that we were brot there to be all slain, and I must and will venture to say that there was treachery, oversight or presumption in the conduct of our officers."[10]

Perhaps Brown waxed theatrical. There were no "8 ships of the line" facing Charlestown, no eight ships of the line in all of Boston Harbor. The danger was not quite so dire as Brown thought. Nor did the American officers intend anything insidious, nor any stratagem that required the wholesale sacrifice of American lives. There had only been the sins—the grievous sins—of poor thinking, ill-conceived planning, and amateurish generalship. The American commanders had bitten off more than they could chew. And, amazingly, those commanders never fully grasped the fatal depth of their collective mistakes and miscalculations until it was just about too late.

As the maddening, paralyzing suspicion of treachery infected the men in the redoubt, the storm broke over the river.

It was not a surprise to the men, for all knew that the British would not let their deed go unpunished. But for men who had never before experienced an artillery bombardment—at least not one aimed directly at them—it was still a great shock. Those who had been fearfully watching the *Lively*'s silhouette hulking ominously in the Charles ferryway first saw the flash, the oddly silent explosion of orange blossoming for a fleeting moment along the sloop's starboard side. Then, almost in the same instant that the deafening report of the nine-pounders buffeted their ears, the balls came flying among them.

In broad daylight, solid shot from medium and larger cannon were perfectly visible—their size, the laziness of their flight, and the arc of their trajectory made them appear almost harmless to the uninitiated. More accurate—or luckier—shots might whistle past their ears, or bury themselves harmlessly into an earthen parapet. Shot that fell short of its target was just as likely to skip along the ground, continuing its flight in a series of bounds until inertia or a substantial target halted it.

But in the half-light of daybreak, the invisibility of the nine-pounder shot made them truly terrifying. Men whose fears were already magnified by hunger, thirst, and fatigue found the experience all but unbearable.

Mercifully, the *Lively*'s initial bombardment caused scant physical damage, injuring no one and wrecking nothing of value. The moral effect, though, was not trifling. The bombardment left the redoubt's defenders dazed; they would have proven to be utterly useless if put to the test at that moment. Many if not all of them might have sought refuge in flight. Thank God they were not left to their own devices.

For Prescott had also perceived the trap into which he, Gridley, and Putnam had led their men, at just about the same time that Peter Brown and his friends began to suspect treachery. To his credit,

Prescott did not waste time nervously dithering between possible choices. He was no great tactical genius, but he knew something of fortifications and siegecraft from his time at Louisbourg, and most important, he was level-headed and calm. He was inured to the sights and sounds of artillery fire, and his cool presence in the redoubt that morning kept the American fighting men from surrendering to sheer unreasoning panic.

During the *Lively*'s cannonade, Prescott kept his men low and under cover, but as soon as the firing stopped the veteran colonel acted without hesitation. Correctly adjudging the redoubt's right flank as the lesser concern, he immediately set the men to work on shoring up the exposed left flank. He laid out a line that extended approximately 165 feet from the redoubt, running from the crest of Breed's Hill, anchoring in a swamp at the hill's base.

Somehow his boys summoned up the strength and the will to pick up their tools again, to hack at the unyielding soil. Daylight made the task easier, but fatigue made it harder. Enervated muscles protested at every swing of a mattock; joints cried out in pain every time a shovel blade struck rock with a jarring ring. The men were on the cusp of physical collapse. Only desperation—and Colonel Prescott—drove them on, and at a fevered pace.

As they dug the deep trench, Prescott's men cast nervous glances behind them and seaward. Behind them they hoped to find relief or reinforcements, but they saw none. Looking seaward, just around eight A.M., they spied something even more disheartening. The *Lively* had shifted position: Captain Bishop had turned the sloop around again, warping it down the channel and dropping anchor off Morton's Point. Two more sloops had joined her—the *Falcon* and the *Spitfire*—in the channel between Boston and Charlestown. Another two, the sloop *Glasgow* (armed with twenty nine-pounders) and the armed transport *Symmetry* (with eighteen nine-pounders), had worked their way well up the Charles so they could rake Charlestown Neck with artillery fire. It was not an ideal point for such a task; a milldam kept the ships some distance from the Charles River shore. Hovering nearby were several small "gondolas" or *scows radeaux*, small gunboats each armed with one twelve-pounder.[11]

The ships surrounding the peninsula were but yapping pups when compared to the big third-raters like the *Somerset* and the *Boyne*. The *Spitfire*'s main armament of six three-pounders was laughably puny for this sort of work. To the Americans looking down at the smaller craft from Breed's Hill, though, it seemed as if half the king's navy was ranged against them . . . eight men-of-war, Peter Brown claimed to see, but given the circumstances, Brown can be forgiven a little hysterical exaggeration. Standing out in the open as they dug the new trench line—the "breastwork," as it came to be known—the Americans on Breed's felt horribly unprotected.

Then it began all over again: the flash, the shuddering boom, the thud of solid shot hitting packed earth, only this time it came from several ships and several directions at once. The big twenty-fours of the Copp's Hill battery joined in about an hour later. The former Admiral's Battery was much stronger now; during the morning, British soldiers had dragged three more twenty-fours and a large siege mortar up to the battery. Copp's was too distant for the guns to have much effect on the redoubt or the breastwork, or to have much chance of hitting the men, but still the cannonade worked its dark magic.[12]

*T*hirty-five-year-old Asa Pollard was one of the Massachusetts boys who toiled on the breastwork as the hail of shot rained down on the gentle slopes of Breed's Hill. Five weeks before, he had enlisted in Captain Stickney's company in Bridge's regiment, and since then he had been in the camp at Cambridge, twenty-odd miles from his farm in Billerica. There was nothing especially remarkable about Asa Pollard . . . and yet all by himself he almost brought Prescott's efforts to a halt.

While Pollard hacked at the dirt amid the flying iron, a nine-pounder shot from one of the British ships smacked into the forward slope of Breed's Hill. Throwing up a cloud of dirt and grass from its point of impact in the pasture, the ball bounded gracelessly along the ground toward the half-completed breastwork. No one noticed it any more than they noticed any one of the individual cannonballs that came in their direction. After the last bounce it sailed just a few feet off the ground, directly at Asa Pollard, and before Pollard's comrades had had so much as a chance to suspect that anything was amiss, the four-inch iron sphere struck him squarely on the head.

The people of eighteenth-century America were accustomed to death in a way that few of us today could fully appreciate. They lived with death. They were raised in a society where child mortality was shockingly high, where fatal accidents were commonplace, routine illnesses frequently fatal, and medical care rudimentary. But no amount of exposure to death in its more peaceful forms could prepare a man for the sight of death by artillery fire. Canister and grapeshot at close range could tear entire ranks of men to bloody ribbons. Solid shot was especially insidious. Harmless though it looked, if it chanced to hit a living target the damage was unspeakable. It could eviscerate a horse or cut a man in two, and not neatly, for no wound made by artillery was neat.

That shot killed only Pollard—the poor man had not even had the chance to collect his forty-shilling promissory note from the Provincial Congress—and only those standing next to him were spattered with his brains and gore. Only a very few men actually saw Pollard's splayed and mangled corpse drop awkwardly to the ground in front of the breastwork. In a way, it was a merciful death, quick and unexpected; there were far worse ways for a man to die in battle. Yet the effect on the entire force on Breed's was no less than if a hundred men had fallen. And that was the value of artillery. Like the bayonet, artillery fire was a moral weapon, inefficient and statistically almost harmless but capable of shattering men's nerves and reducing the stalwart to quivering jelly. The tons of iron thrown at that grassy hillside by British cannon caused no more than a handful of casualties and barely made a dent in the fortifications. But the solitary ball that took away Asa Pollard's head spread such febrile terror through the ranks that no man would pause to consider how unlikely it was that he might suffer the same fate.[13]

William Prescott saved the day, or at least the hour. One of his subordinates implored him to allow Pollard a proper Christian burial, complete with some semblance of liturgy. Prescott curtly refused, ordered that the corpse be interred immediately without ceremony, and rebuffed a parson who offered to conduct the services. The curious who pushed in to catch a glimpse of the shattered body were gruffly told to return to work.

It seemed cold to men who were new to soldiering, but Prescott knew what he was about. All night he had been encouraging the men, driving them on to dig, dig, dig. Now terror threatened to finish off what fatigue had started, so Prescott did what any veteran officer would do to keep the respect of his men and hold terror at bay. He climbed to the top of the parapet, standing upright in the teeth of the firestorm, striding up and down the line of the breastwork. In complete disregard of the flying shot, Prescott doled out gentle and encouraging words, reminding the men that the cannonade was all noise and nothing more.

Prescott's simple act of physical courage kept the men at their urgent task. If they hadn't known the grim but fatherly colonel before this day, didn't recognize on sight the black broad-brimmed hat and the long linen frock that covered his long, lanky frame, they did now. To his boys, Prescott seemed to embody everything strong and martial and sure, and his presence alone was what assured them that perhaps they might have a chance of surviving the day.* One of Prescott's veterans, recalling the scene in his dotage, summed it up: "Had it not been for Colonel Prescott there would have been no fight."[14]

But even Prescott's presence was no guaranteed palliative against fear. Asa Pollard's death was but a taste of things to come. Sometime, sometime soon, the slopes and meadows would be crawling with Redcoats, bayonets glinting in the sun, demanding to be quenched in blood . . . *their* blood. Ahead of them lay only the grim business of war, and each of the men knew full well that in this business the Redcoats were their betters. That knowledge killed morale, no matter how fearless the colonel showed himself to be. The force that Prescott and Putnam had led to this spot was, only a few hours earlier, enthusiastic, even cocky. But *these* men, the ones who had been toiling all night and dodging cannonballs all morning, were tired, haggard, fearful, and cowering.

Bereft of hope, they began to leave. Not in large bodies, not scampering in headlong flight, but quietly, furtively. By twos and threes they shuffled off toward the Neck, half ashamed and half relieved. The men in Prescott's regiment held on, for the most part, but those from Bridge's and Frye's regiments didn't feel the same sense of obligation. Colonel Bridge was gone, and Lieutenant Colonel Brickett—Frye's second in command—had suffered a minor wound during the cannonade. With their leaders gone, the two regiments began to fall apart.

---

* Virtually every written history of the battle of Bunker Hill relates the following anecdote in one way or another: General Gage had left Province House to observe the progress of the battle. While watching through his spyglass the effects of the cannonade, Gage saw Prescott standing tall atop the redoubt's parapet. The general handed the spyglass to Abijah Willard, a prominent Loyalist and Prescott's brother-in-law, who was standing with him. Willard recognized Prescott. Gage asked, "Will he fight?" and Willard responded, "Yes, sir; he is an old soldier, and will fight as long as a drop of blood remains in his veins!" (In Richard Ketchum's version, the response is "I cannot answer for his men, but Prescott will fight you to the gates of hell.") It's a stirring anecdote, to be sure, but undoubtedly apocryphal. The closest Gage could have been to the fighting was on Copp's Hill—and if he was there, neither Clinton nor Burgoyne remarked upon it. And at that distance—over one thousand yards lay between Copp's Hill and the summit of Breed's—the idea that Willard could have seen and recognized Prescott, given the primitive optics of the day and the amount of gunsmoke that must have hung in the air, seems implausible at best. Frothingham, *Siege of Boston*, 126; Ketchum, *Decisive Day*, 127.

Prescott felt understandably alone. The force at his command, the force that would soon face a British onslaught, was melting away before his eyes, dwindling when it needed to be growing. A few hundred drained, glassy-eyed soldiers, propping themselves up against the walls of the redoubt and the breastwork and trying hard just to keep themselves awake, were not likely to hold up for very long. They needed relief, they needed reinforcements, and desperately.

Artemas Ward had actually made provision for reinforcements, or rather for relief: Nixon's, Little's, and Mansfield's regiments were already under orders to relieve Prescott late that afternoon. Late, perhaps, given the new and unexpected circumstances, but until the thunder of the guns reached Cambridge that morning, Ward had no way of knowing that Prescott would disobey his orders and fortify Breed's instead of Bunker Hill. Prescott knew not to expect relief until evening, but still he hoped that perhaps Ward would sense the danger and send reinforcements to him earlier. Throughout the morning Prescott glanced longingly to the northwest, wanting to see the telltale clouds of dust that would signal the approach of a marching column from Cambridge. There was none. Prescott's officers and men were just as cognizant of that sad fact as the colonel was himself. One by one his officers importuned him: send a courier; ask General Ward for more troops.

At first, pride blinded Prescott to the obvious need. He wanted reinforcements; only a fool would have desired to face the British with the shrinking and exhausted force then manning the earthworks. But the colonel countered his officers' pleas with a ridiculous assertion: "the men who have raised these works are the best able to defend them."[15]

It was a stupid argument, for the unvarnished truth was that the men who had built the redoubt were probably those *least* suited to defend them. Maybe with a few hours' sleep, maybe if fed and watered . . . maybe things would have been different. But Prescott's men were in no condition to fight, and there were far too few of them. Either Prescott's judgment was impaired by his own almost unimaginable fatigue or it had given in to petulant, prideful resentment of Ward for not backing him up. He clung stubbornly to his position: there would be no relief, nor would he ask for any.

William Prescott and common sense, however, were never long parted, and only a little while after the British cannonade resumed he caved in. He turned to one of the more valuable officers in his little command, Major John Brooks of Medford, then ranking officer in Bridge's regiment. Brooks would go on to a distinguished career in the Continental Army and, much later, as seven-term governor of Massachusetts, but in 1775 he was a twenty-three-year-old physician who took his duty very seriously. On Prescott's order, Major Brooks started on his way out of the redoubt to get to Ward's headquarters in Cambridge—and only then realized that he needed a horse if he didn't want his errand to consume the entire day. Where, Brooks asked Prescott, might he find a horse? "Get one from the artillery," came Prescott's typically clipped reply. That didn't work; the gunners, anxiously eyeing the redoubt's exit, were not about to part with their transportation under any circumstances. And so John Brooks was put in a position so ridiculous that it would have been funny if the lives of hundreds of men weren't at stake: he set out for Cambridge on his urgent mission—one might say the *most* urgent—on foot, compelled to walk the three-and-a-half-mile trek to the Hastings House.[16]

Israel Putnam beat him to it.

*T*he morning had just begun and already the Hastings House was in an uproar. That a battle had broken out was known throughout Cambridge; there was no mistaking the sound of British cannon. Only gradually did the specifics filter back to Artemas

Ward, and the timing could not have been worse. Ward had had a sleepless night of worry, and his bladder stones had returned with a vengeance. The general was not at his best. Nor was Joseph Warren, who had awoken that morning with a pounding migraine. For most of the morning Warren would be useless, confined to bed in the old college steward's house while he tried to nurse his throbbing head.

Israel Putnam had checked in with Ward much earlier in the morning. With nothing to do at Breed's, and with no official position there, Putnam had left Prescott on his own and spent what was left of the night at Mrs. Inman's house. He woke to the sound of the *Lively*'s guns, dressed as fast as he could, and in a flash was mounted and riding out to assess the situation on Breed's Hill. The sun was barely clear of the eastern horizon when Putnam turned his horse about and galloped back to Cambridge to tell Ward about the British cannonade. He rode back to Breed's to see Prescott again, and once he had inspected the redoubt, the inexhaustible Connecticut Yankee doubled back and drove his poor horse to Cambridge again.

It was nearly nine o'clock when Old Put, red-faced and perspiring heavily, leapt from his horse this second time and burst unceremoniously through the front door of the Hastings House. Prescott, he announced to Ward in his bluff and plain-spoken manner, was hard pressed, his men starving and exhausted and some of them retreating without orders.[17]

Inwardly, Ward fumed at Putnam's words. No one, it seemed, had followed his orders. He had made sure that the men Prescott led to Charlestown had plenty of food: hadn't Commissary Pigeon issued more than three thousand rations—well over a ton-and-a-half of meat and the same quantity of bread, with thousands of pints of beer to wash it down—to the one thousand men of Bridge's and Frye's and Prescott's regiments before they set out that evening? How could they be without food or drink . . . unless someone had disobeyed his orders? Worst of all—why did Prescott take Breed's

Hill and not Bunker? Maybe it was an honest mistake, but his intentions made no difference now. If Prescott had done as he had been told, then the relief scheduled for that evening would have been adequate, and Prescott would not need reinforcements now.

There was no time to cast blame, only time to react to changed circumstances. Ward listened patiently to Putnam's half-shouted news, summoned his adjutant, and made out new orders. John Stark was to send two hundred men from his New Hampshire regiment from their camp at Medford to Prescott at Charlestown. Until Ward had a better idea of just what the British intended to do, that was all he could spare. The orders being issued, Putnam flew out the door as quickly has he had entered, mounted his horse, and set out again, thundering down the road back to Charlestown.

Making his way onto Charlestown Neck, Old Put passed right by Major John Brooks, walking down the road in the opposite direction as fast as his legs could carry him. Neither of the men had any idea that they were on the same errand.

Brooks arrived at the Hastings House about an hour after Putnam left. He looked like hell, having been awake for nearly thirty hours and having just walked nearly four miles on a hot morning. Brooks was immediately ushered into Ward's forbidding presence. Ordinarily, Artemas Ward was among the most pleasant of men—not courtly and extroverted like Warren, but earnest and kind to a fault. Not today. Pain, worry, and disappointment had made Ward irascible. Brooks did his best not to waste the general's time and got straight to the point. The British, he said, were most assuredly getting ready to undertake something big, probably at Charlestown, and Prescott was in a bad spot. Brooks had little to add to what Putnam had already told Ward, except for an air of pained desperation that was etched plainly on his features.

Now Ward was genuinely worried. He could not ignore Prescott's plight, even if he or Putnam or Gridley had brought that predicament upon themselves by their disregard for orders. But neither could he fully commit to Charlestown, not yet. The responsibility was simply awful, and so Ward—a man firmly dedicated to the idea that the army served the people and not the other way around—turned to the only authority he could: the Committee of Safety, which had given its blessing to the Charlestown operation before Reverend Langdon had bestowed God's.

The Committee was, like Ward, immersed in problems stemming from Charlestown. Belatedly—unforgivably so—the amateur warmakers scrambled to attend to affairs that *should* have been given top priority on Thursday night, not put off until Saturday morning. They alerted the counties and towns nearby to muster whatever militia they had left, pleaded with local officials to send every last grain of gunpowder they could scrounge to the depot at Watertown, and wrung their hands that David Cheever and the Committee of Supplies had virtually nothing more to send them—sixteen halfbarrels of powder today, after six half-barrels the day before, not a bad amount but not enough to make Ward feel any safer. And no horses. In a countryside full of horses, the Committee of Safety was finding it difficult to secure a few mounts for its couriers.

While Warren recuperated from his debilitating headache, Richard Devens presided over the Committee, and it was to him that Ward, with Brooks in tow, presented his dilemma. Prescott needed reinforcements, and no one would argue with that . . . but what if the British bombardment of Breed's Hill were only a diversion? What if Gage or Howe or Clinton attacked at Dorchester and Roxbury as originally planned? What if the British had something else in mind, like a landing at thinly defended Lechmere's Point, allowing them to stab directly at Cambridge while bypassing both Charlestown and Roxbury? Sending too many reinforcements to Prescott could leave Cambridge vulnerable; sending him too few could be equally disastrous.

Fortunately the members of the Committee were all of one mind: Prescott must be relieved, but Cambridge could not be stripped of troops. Satisfied, if maybe a bit unhappy, Ward thanked Devens, returned to his office, and dictated the new orders. Nixon, Little, and Mansfield were still scheduled to relieve Prescott, but in the meantime the remaining companies of Stark's regiment, plus Colonel Reed's New Hampshire regiment, would join the portion of Stark's command that had already received its marching orders.

In his own day, Artemas Ward's handful of enemies—including James Warren of the Committee of Safety, who took an inexplicable dislike to him—thought that the general was unforgivably cautious, sending far too few men out to help Prescott. And in the generations since then, historians and writers have raked Ward over the coals for his reticence. "To make his experiment a success," wrote historian Allen French in 1934, "Ward should have been bold."[18] But the taking of Breed's Hill was not Ward's "experiment." It was Prescott's, or Putnam's, not Ward's, and if Prescott and Putnam had followed Ward's orders, reinforcements would not have been necessary—or at least not so desperately necessary. To have been "bold" in that moment, on the morning of June 17, would have been irresponsible to the army, to the colony, and to the Cause. Until Ward knew where Gage would land his crushing blow, there was no sense at all in sending troops out and obliging the British, weakening the defenses around Cambridge in order to oppose a mere feint. Ward was only doing what a responsible commander should have done.

*A*cross the ferryway in Boston, the pace was equally frenetic, but purposeful and directed. If the British were to land troops near Charlestown that afternoon, as William Howe insisted, then there was simply no time to lose.

Like Ward, Howe has been repeatedly accused of negligence—

and in Howe's case that means lethargy: that Howe succumbed to "the eighteenth-century leisure," a steadfast refusal to rush or be rushed, a mindset that made instant action impossible. The truth is, though, that Howe was hurrying the preparations as much as was humanly possible. Even Clinton, a man usually judged to be more aggressive than Howe, believed that an attack on Charlestown would have to wait until the next morning. Howe wanted it done by high tide—around two to three o'clock that afternoon.

That was a tall order indeed. Fortunately the British army was more adept at amphibious operations than any other army in Europe. There was a great deal of ill-will between the army and the fleet most of the time, but during the Seven Years' War the two services worked together well enough, with several successful amphibious landings to their credit in Europe and in America. Howe himself had been party to one: James Wolfe's brilliantly executed assault on Quebec in 1759. Few other officers in Gage's army could claim the same experience, but the army as an institution was thoroughly familiar with the process.[19]

The key to a successful amphibious attack was careful planning. There was no other way, no shortcut; this kind of operation simply couldn't be improvised in a matter of moments. Boats, boat crews, munitions, horses, artillery, and all of the considerable but indispensable paraphernalia necessary to transport and support an infantry force of 2,300 men . . . these things didn't just materialize on the spot. It took a huge investment in elbow grease, logistical gymnastics, and above all *time*. To have everything ready to go in five hours or so was stretching the limits of physical possibility. To have attacked the rebels *immediately* that morning—and so many armchair generals have insisted that this is what Howe *should* have done—was something that went well beyond those limits.

In their tent cities on the slopes of the Trimountain and on the Common, the business of preparation proceeded without delay or diversion or leisure. Salt meat and peas had to be cooked, muskets scoured, worn flints replaced with fresh ones. This was not mere primping for show, for in battle a rusty musket, a plugged vent hole, or a tired flint could well mean the difference between life and death for the individual foot soldier. The common matrosses, the artillery crews, had to be doubly diligent in preparing their cannon for transport by boat. Surgeons assembled their field kits while company officers inspected each man, his weapon, his gear, and his ammunition load. Everyone had urgent tasks, and they consumed most of the morning. For the men of the 52nd Foot, encamped on the Common with the flank companies, the morning schedule was especially rushed: today they would receive new muskets. It took some time for the men to turn in their older weapons and get their hands on their glittering new firelocks. They were still test-firing their muskets when the order came to fall in on the parade. Reassuringly, there was not a single misfire.[20]

And then there were the boats themselves, after the infantry the most vital components of the operation. Gage did not have enough of them, despite frequent appeals to London for flat-bottomed, shallow-drafted craft built for the express purpose of ferrying troops.[21] Howe would have to make do with whatever Graves could give him. That meant the ships' boats, the tenders, cutters, launches, dinghies, and yawls that could be found lashed to the upper decks of all naval ships. Such boats weren't intended to carry infantry in large numbers, or to bring them ashore in pounding surf. They most certainly were not meant to carry the massive and awkward bulk of six- and twelve-pounder fieldpieces. But they were all Howe had to work with. Preparing them for crossing the Charles took the better part of the morning. It would take even more time to get the boats to the designated embarkation points at the North Battery Wharf and the Long Wharf.

By noon the boats were ready. The sailors took the oars, the coxswains the tillers, and at the admiral's signal they pushed off and rowed to their assigned wharves.

*T*he foot troops were ready to march at eleven-thirty that morning, in accordance with General Howe's orders. The sun had not yet reached its zenith, but the angry heat was already stifling, only slightly appeased by mild breezes. The troops picked for the assault, lined up in parade formation at their camps through-out Boston, seemed unfazed by the high temperatures. They were accustomed to wearing several layers of linen and coarse, tightly milled woolen clothing, shirts, breeches, waistcoats, and regimentals in all sorts of weather.

Howe's force was not a large one, less than half of Gage's army—2,300 men altogether, at a time when European field armies on campaign frequently topped 80,000. But there was something singular, something breathtaking, about the spectacle when Howe's Redcoats formed up on parade that day. The most impressive assemblage was on Boston Common, the camp of the flank companies. On the Common's eastern edge, where the beaten, dusty expanse of the former pastureland met the ordered streets of the town, the grenadiers and light infantry stood in perfectly ordered lines, two ranks deep: the tall, burly grenadiers, their height exaggerated by the massive bearskin hats they wore; and the shorter and more lithe men of the light infantry companies, not quite so ferocious-looking as the grenadiers but still sharp. They formed an undifferentiated mass, each man standing at attention, bayonetted muskets planted butt-first on the ground, every piece of gear worn in precisely the same manner, every man in the same posture, brass and burnished steel glaring bright in the intense sunlight . . . uniform, silent, menacing. The captains and lieutenants stood proudly beside their companies. Not a man wavered, not a man talked or so much as coughed. Perfect stillness. If there was excitement or fear or dread in their hearts, their stone-hard faces didn't betray it.

It was a spectacle of martial splendor such as had never been seen before in Boston or anywhere in America, not since the French war. But General Howe had no intention of simply overawing the enemy with pomp. Ever the light infantryman, Howe wanted his troops to be as unburdened as they could be, knowing that the day's work would be hot, knowing how important it was not to tire the men before that vital moment—the final seconds and last yards of the assault, when the lines would dash themselves against the enemy with bayonets leveled. Speed would count then, above everything else. So each man was to be stripped of all but the bare essentials: " . . . with their Arms, Ammunition, Blanketts and the provisions Order'd to be cook'd this Morning"—just one day's rations. All of the other impedimenta usually carried in the knapsack would be left behind in the tents, where specially detailed guards would watch over them.* Howe's men were ready for business.[22]

At precisely eleven-thirty the field officers took their places in the line, and with a shouted order the men in the ranks faced smartly to the left. One by one the companies of light infantry and grenadiers stepped out onto the Common Street, then onto Tremont Street, in a long, narrow column two men abreast. With colors cased, fifes skirling and drums beating a lilting march, the column turned right onto the broad expanse of King Street. As beaten as they felt from hunger and martial law and the paralyzing fear of the smallpox, in that moment the people of Boston forgot their troubles, ignored the awful sounds of cannonfire that had been assailing their

---

* Traditionally, historians have agreed that Howe ordered his men to take three days' cooked rations with them to Charlestown—the implication being that Howe, by burdening his men so, was either impractical or indifferent to their sufferings. Yet Howe did not order this; his orders stated only that the men were to carry "the provisions Order'd to be cook'd this Morning." And his orders for the following morning included the reminder that "Tents and provisions may be expected when the Tide admits of Transporting them to this side" . . . in other words, food was on the way the next day—an unnecessary measure if the men had actually been issued three days' rations. Stevens, *Howe's Orderly Book*, 1–3.

ears for hours, and gave no thought to the blood that was undoubt-edly going to be spilled on the hills across the river. They watched instead in childlike wonder, gape-mouthed, lining the streets and peering through unshuttered windows, as the column made its way onto the Long Wharf, halted, and dressed its lines.

The clocks in Boston had just chimed the noon hour when the Redcoats took their places at the Long Wharf. There were nearly 1,100 of them: ten companies of light infantry, ten of grenadiers, and the battalion companies of the 5th and 38th Regiments of Foot. A further seven hundred men—elements of the 35th, 43rd, 52nd, and 63rd Foot and the 1st and 2nd Battalions of Marines—filed into the square near the North Battery. Here they would wait for the boats, already en route from every ship in the squadron. There were not enough boats to carry them all at once; even without accounting for the "reserve" that Howe would keep at the North Battery, the boats would have to make two trips.[23]

By one o'clock the soldiers had begun to climb into the boats. It was always an awkward procedure for landsmen, doubly so when they were burdened with knapsacks and muskets, so it took time. On the *Preston*'s mizzen a blue pennant climbed the peak halyard, the signal for the advance, and the oarsmen shoved off from the Long Wharf and headed out into the harbor, rowing counterclock-wise around the city and finally rounding the North End before heading straight for the Charlestown beaches.

Eight

* * *

THE ENEMY'S
ALL LANDED AT
CHARLESTOWN!

*W*illiam Howe could be satisfied, at least so far. The amphibious operation, despite all its potential complications and foul-ups, had proceeded without a hitch. The neat lines of boats passing around the North End and pressing toward Charlestown said it all: the British had the situation well in hand.

On Breed's, William Prescott rubbed his weary eyes and waited anxiously to see what would happen next. A measure of hope had arrived in the form of artillery. Some time during the forenoon hours, the cannon he thought he had—the cannon that had accompanied his column from Cambridge the night before—finally showed up. What the gunners had been up to in the meantime was anyone's guess. The guns that Ward had sent along, probably four-pounders, were really not necessary at this point in the battle. They were far too light to do any damage to the British ships or the battery on Copp's . . . even if Ward had given Prescott all the cannon at his disposal, and Thomas's guns, too, it would not have been enough to drive the British away. Besides, if there was anything that the Americans lacked more than gunpowder, it was trained artillerists. But if the British landed at Charlestown, *then* the small fieldpieces could be put to good use. Even a handful of four-pounders could disrupt an assault or destroy enemy morale. Prescott would need the guns when—if—the fields in his front filled up with red-coated targets.

Captains John Callender and Samuel Gridley—the latter one of Colonel Gridley's less-than-competent sons—brought up their two sections and manhandled them into the redoubt. But Prescott and engineer Gridley had made a curious omission: in their haste to build the redoubt, neither had remembered to cut out embrasures for the cannon, and the expedition had neglected to bring wood planks for gun platforms. There was no time to correct this mistake now, so the gun crews improvised, blasting makeshift embrasures through the earthen walls with the cannon themselves.[1]

It proved to be a wasted effort. The gun crews fired a few rounds in the general direction of Copp's Hill. John Burgoyne, watching the action from Copp's in the company of Henry Clinton, was more bemused than concerned as one of the four-pounder balls whistled harmlessly overhead. A couple of rounds were enough for Callender and Gridley. "The captain [of the artillery] fired but a few times," observed Private Peter Brown in evident disgust, "and then swang his hat round three times to the enemy, then ceased to fire."[2] Deciding that their services were not needed—or that their presence wasn't worth the danger of being hit by a British cannonball—Gridley, Callender, and the gun crews abandoned their guns and left the redoubt, not the least bit ashamed to be deserting Colonel Prescott in his hour of need.

Israel Putnam put in an appearance or two on Breed's. Old Put was everywhere that day, now on the road to Cambridge, then checking on Prescott, later trying to rally the stragglers who had fled the redoubt and were walking leisurely toward the Neck. As usual, the Connecticut Yankee was unconcerned about his personal safety and oblivious to danger; he rode through the smoke and thunder of the British bombardment, even across Charlestown Neck where the salvos of the *Glasgow* and the *Symmetry* made passage uncomfortable, without so much as batting an eye. Putnam's main concern, though, was Bunker Hill. Either he understood that Bunker would make a good rallying point if the British forced Prescott off Breed's or he feared that the British would attempt an envelopment such as Clinton had proposed . . . or it had been Prescott, and not Putnam, whose decision it was to fortify Breed's, and Putnam was now doing his best to make good that mistake. Either way, he bent himself to the task of elaborating on Montresor's old redan and building it into something substantial, a stronghold that could withstand a British advance from Breed's toward the Neck. On Bunker Hill, Old Put was a dynamo, a stout and roaring figure who rode from one end of the hill to the other, grabbing slackers, pushing tools into their hands, forcing them to go to work. He knew how to shame men into action while encouraging them, and there on Bunker Hill, Putnam had some luck.[3]

At one point in the late morning, Putnam came to Prescott, looking to get his hands on the entrenching tools that were now mostly lying idle. Couldn't the colonel detail a few men to bring the spades and picks off Breed's and on to Bunker? Prescott didn't need them anymore, but Putnam did, and there was no sense leaving them in the redoubt for the British to capture later. Prescott demurred, pointing out that once he gave his men an excuse to leave the redoubt they would never return. But he finally gave in, and some of the men leaped at the chance to absent themselves legitimately from the hail of solid shot. Tools in hand, they left the redoubt, along with many others who felt obliged to accompany their comrades on this arduous task; one would think that the tools were so heavy that it would take no fewer than two or three men just to lift them.

And Prescott was right: the men never came back.[4]

Putnam's ceaseless activity was part of his character. It was also a sign of the great fatal flaw in the American army that day: nobody was actually in command. There were two commanders on the field that day—Prescott and Putnam—and Ward, ensconced in Cambridge, tried his best to oversee *all* American defenses, since there was no telling just what Gage or Howe or Clinton was up to. Prescott commanded in the redoubt, but his gaze and his authority extended no farther, and even he couldn't do everything that needed to be done there—including preventing the artillery from leaving. Putnam tried to see to the overall defense of the peninsula . . . and to the arrival of reinforcements, to the rallying of the hundreds of men who abandoned the redoubt, and to a thousand things that he shouldn't have had to do but did anyway because he had no staff. Prescott and Putnam did not quarrel and did not contend over rank, since neither man was pompous or self-important in the least. But that is not the same thing as having an overall commander to look at the big picture, to delegate important tasks, and to move men about as the situation required.

But then, the American army had not been in action before, and no one in Cambridge had anticipated *this*.

As the noon hour approached, it was a moot point anyway. There was no time to fashion a command structure. It was far too late for that. All the Americans on the heights of Charlestown could do was dig, wait . . . and pray.

It was right around noon, in fact, when Americans watching Boston from Charlestown spotted the first portents of their doom. The Redcoats were marching, entire battalions of them, down to the

North Battery. All knew what that presaged: the British were going to take to their boats, and that meant an attack.

Within moments, a mounted courier—there were far too few of those, and far too few horses, for that matter—spurred his horse into a full gallop onto the road to Cambridge with the news.

*T*he report from Charlestown did not come as a big surprise to Artemas Ward or anyone in the Hastings House. The bombardment alone—and it had gone on for *hours* now—was enough to signal, plainly, that Gage had something planned, something big. But knowing that the British were on the move didn't answer many questions. In particular, it didn't tell Ward what he wanted, what he *needed*, to know: *where* were the British going to attack? Most of the signs pointed toward an attack on Charlestown . . . most, but not all. Colonel Paul Dudley Sargent, keeping watch near Lechmere's Point, saw a schooner—with four to five hundred Redcoats aboard, or so he thought—trying to ply its way into Willis Creek. A landing there would mean a direct attack on Cambridge, the very thing that Artemas Ward feared above all else.[5] Regardless, if the army at Cambridge were to have any use at all in the battle or battles to come, it would have to be set in motion *now*, if indeed it wasn't already too late.

Around one o'clock in the afternoon the alarm sounded in Cambridge. The bells in Christ Church clanged out their tocsin as officers rushed to take charge of their commands. Stephen Jenkins, adjutant of Little's regiment, drove his horse into camp and shouted to his men, "Turn out! Turn out! The enemy's all landed at Charlestown!"[6] Soldiers dropped whatever they were doing and hurried to their companies. They grabbed their muskets and accoutrements, and what little ammunition they had; most had been issued cartridges only the day before, but not very many, and there was no time now for the officers to check cartridge boxes or redistribute ammunition. One by one, the regiments marched out of Cambridge as they received their orders from headquarters. The fifers and drummers of Doolittle's regiment struck up a novel tune, one that British musicians liked to play in mockery of their homespun foes, and now adopted by the rebels as their own: "Yankee Doodle."[7]

In Hastings House, Ward did his best to make sense of the situation, writing out orders that were a tad short of explicit, intending to send sufficient reinforcements to Prescott while keeping Cambridge, Roxbury, and all points in between safe from a possible British thrust. Ward ordered Gardner's regiment to join Patterson's at Fort Number Three, guarding the army's far left flank; Ward's own regiment, under the command of Lieutenant Colonel Jonathan Ward (no relation to the general), marched to Lechmere's Point to reinforce Paul Dudley Sargent's detachment. Cautious Ward may have been, but he all but stripped Cambridge bare of troops that afternoon—only two companies of Bridge's regiment remained behind to guard headquarters. In the confusion of the moment, regimental commanders misunderstood the directions given them, and individual soldiers and entire companies got lost in the muddle and failed to march with their regiments. Understandably so, for the orders themselves could be confusing to commanders who could hear the cannonfire near Charlestown and yet were supposed to march in a different direction.[8]

Experience Storrs, lieutenant colonel of Putnam's Connecticut regiment, followed Ward's orders and led part of his unit to Fort Number One, guarding the Charles River approaches to Cambridge. It would be an important position should the British break through at Roxbury and march on Cambridge, but Storrs was more concerned about Putnam and the rest of the regiment. Eventually, Storrs left Fort Number One and headed toward Charlestown, too late to take part in the battle then raging on Breed's Hill.[9]

Colonel James Scammon received orders—or sincerely thought he had—to take his regiment to Lechmere's Point. Scammon's regiment had traveled a long way to get to Boston; the men were all from Maine, which was still part of the Bay Colony. There, at Lechmere's, Scammon met John Whitcomb—who had just been appointed general by the Massachusetts Provincial Congress on the same day as Joseph Warren, and like Warren had yet to receive his actual commission—and Whitcomb's regiment. Whitcomb was baffled by Scammon's sudden appearance, and asked in some confusion why Scammon had bothered to bring his men to Lechmere's. Scammon was himself befuddled, and he said so, pathetically asking Whitcomb where *he* thought that Scammon should go. Whitcomb was no less in the dark than Scammon. "I told him to go where he could do the most service," he testified afterward, and Scammon for some reason believed that he was supposed to go to a "little hill"— probably Cobble Hill, just east of Cambridge.[10]

Ward and the Committee of Safety were especially worried about Thomas. They did not ask Thomas to send any regiments toward Charlestown—they knew well enough that soon Thomas might need *their* help rather than the other way around—but there was precious little they could offer him, either. Alerting him to the intelligence that British troops were about to land near Charlestown, the Committee of Safety let Thomas know, subtly, that he was on his own: "You are to judge whether this is designed to deceive or not. In haste leave you to Judge of the Nesesaty of your movements." To Ward's credit, part of Moses Little's Massachusetts regiment was ordered to be sent close to Boston Neck. At any rate, Thomas knew, long before the Committee wrote to him, that the British were on the move; the sound of the guns on the Charles made it fairly clear. He did the only thing he could: he put his entire force on alert. Samuel Haws, a private in Joseph Read's Massachusetts regiment, listened to the cannonade and the battle that followed from his "alarm post," where he remained all night, watching for signs of an attack on Roxbury.[11]

By two o'clock, Cambridge was all but stripped of troops and "quiet as the Sabbath," a visitor to Ward's headquarters observed.[12] The greater part of the regiments were on the move, marching toward Charlestown, taking posts outside Cambridge, or wandering about in fretful bafflement. Many of them would not see any action that day. The uproar and uncertainty at headquarters, added to the lack of a proper staff and the near absence of horses, meant that Ward's orders often arrived at their destinations unconscionably late. Arguably the worst instance involved Stark's New Hampshire regiment. Ward's second command to Stark—to send out the remainder of his regiment—came on the heels of the general's meeting with John Brooks, and could not have been written much later than eleven o'clock or so. Stark received the orders some time around two P.M.[13]

John Stark's regiment fell into all sorts of difficulties. Earlier that morning, Colonel Stark had received Ward's order to send two hundred men to Prescott's relief. Stark chose his lieutenant colonel, Isaac Wyman, to lead the detachment to Charlestown. Stark's regiment was extraordinarily blessed in having superb officers, and Wyman was no exception. A fifty-one-year-old tavernkeeper from Keene, New Hampshire, Wyman had survived two of the most horrific slaughters of the French and Indian War—the 1757 massacre of British troops outside Fort William Henry, and Abercrombie's frontal assault on Fort Carillon the following year. As Wyman prepared his detachment for the march, he and Colonel Stark discovered that the men had virtually no ammunition. It shouldn't have come as a surprise. The day before, the ordnance officer at Cambridge Store had issued ammunition to most of the regiments there; to Stark, he gave one hundred pounds of powder, four thousand musket balls, and five hundred flints. For a regiment of nearly six hundred men, it wasn't much, but it was more than any other regiment received from the ordnance stores that day. No one in the regiment had taken stock of the ammunition; no one had bothered to make up the loose powder and ball into paper cartridges. So that morning, as Wyman's men were supposed to depart their camp at Medford, Stark issued out all his ammunition to the men, amounting to no more than a cupful of powder, fifteen balls, and a flint to each man. The men broke from parade and sat down to roll paper cartridges—a waste of valuable time.[14]

Wyman's two hundred were slightly delayed by the ordeal. But the rest of the regiment was ready to go when Stark received his summons at two o'clock, and within minutes the Hampshiremen were swinging down the road from Medford to Charlestown.

*On Breed's Hill, the imminent arrival of Howe's water-borne assault force was heralded by the guns of the fleet. They had been firing for quite some time now, but as the boats rounded the North Battery and hove into view, the cannonfire intensified. Every gun in the squadron was trained on the redoubt and the breastwork, and it seemed as if their crews were loading and firing them twice as fast as before. Three-, six-, and nine-pound balls crowded the air as the sloops in the ferryway zeroed in on the rebel earthworks; the much bigger shot from the twenty-fours on Copp's Hill rent the air over the Charles and slammed into the hillside. The barrage did little apparent damage—one of the advantages of soft earthen fortifications is that they tend to absorb projectiles—but with the greater profusion of shot, greater casualties were inevitable. The men in the redoubt and along the breastwork scarcely seemed to notice. They were transfixed by the spectacle that lay before them, the sweeping panoramic vision in the sparkling waters of the Charles. Twenty-eight boats of various shapes and sizes, all that Graves's squadron could spare, plowed majestically through the waters of the Charles in lines so straight and orderly as to be beyond belief. The boats were crammed with men—anywhere from thirty to forty soldiers, plus the oarsmen; very uncomfortable men, inadvertently poking each other with muskets and knapsacks and bayonet scabbards that always seemed to protrude at the most inconvenient angles, jostled about by the motion of the boats through the current and the surf. Yet from a distance the sight was glorious to behold, an explosion of color that glided inexorably across the face of the waters, the madder red and white of the uniforms, wreathed lightly by the dry white smoke drifting from the guns of the *Lively* and the *Falcon* . . . a young boy's dream-fantasy of war. Civilians in Boston sat on rooftops and climbed Beacon Hill to watch it; the soldiers who stayed with Colonel Prescott couldn't take their eyes off it.

The boats made their landing on the beach at Morton's Point, on the extreme northeastern corner of the peninsula. Almost simultaneously the first line of boats hit the beach, the crews shipped their oars, and the soldiers scrambled out with such grace as they could muster, ascending the beach on unsteady legs. And once the boats had been emptied, their crews turned them about again to get the rest of the main force at the North Battery, and the artillery at the South Battery.

The Americans did not contest the landing, not at first. The British had landed far out of musket range from the breastwork. In desperation, still waiting for reinforcements, William Prescott figured he ought to do *something*. Most of his artillery was gone—Captains Gridley and Callender had already deserted the redoubt, dragging their four guns with them—but Captain Samuel Trevett and his section of two fieldpieces had just arrived. Prescott ordered Trevett to take his two four-pounders in the direction of the beach and see what havoc they could cause to the British at Morton's. To protect

Bostonians watching the Battle of Bunker Hill, June 17, 1775. Note Charlestown ablaze across the Charles River. Military necessity prompted the British to set the town afire, but the American rebels were outraged by what they saw as wanton cruelty.

them, Prescott sent along Captain Thomas Knowlton and his men from Putnam's regiment.

Knowlton, his Connecticut men, and Trevett's gunners hurried down the face of Breed's and quickly out of sight. Prescott lost track of them: the guns "followed a different course, and I believe those sent to their support followed, I suppose to Bunker's Hill."[15] The hard-bitten Massachusetts colonel was dead wrong. Knowlton, though only thirty-four, was as seasoned a veteran as Prescott; he had fought in the French and Indian War at the age of fifteen, was commissioned as a provincial lieutenant before he reached twenty, and was with Israel Putnam during the miserable British attack on Havana in 1762. And apparently he had an eye for good ground. Instead of confronting the British at Morton's Hill, he led his men to a ditch north-northwest of Breed's Hill, just east of Bunker Hill. The ditch paralleled the course of Prescott's breastwork, but lay about two hundred yards behind it, and ran from a country lane north of Breed's to the south bank of the Mystic River. The ditch was exceptionally well suited for a defensive fight: before it ran a "fence half of stone and two rayles of wood." Knowlton positioned his men behind this fence; they grounded their muskets and stripped rails from another fence nearby, building a second, parallel fence in front of the one along the ditch. At their captain's direction the men cut down the hay in front of their improvised wall—the hay had not been mown in quite some time, and with flintlock muskets flashing amidst it there was good reason to fear it as a potential fire hazard—which they then packed into the space between the two parallel fences. Sod, tree limbs, rocks, too. The result was a bulletproof wall, not immune to artillery fire but good enough to provide cover when the British decided to launch their assault. To soldiers, both American and British, Knowlton's line would become immortalized as "the rail fence."[16]

The Americans were about as ready as they would ever be.

Almost. For there were, yet unnoticed, two gaping holes in the American defenses. The first was at the northern extreme of the zig-zagging rebel line, between the end of the rail fence and the beach along the Mystic. The second was more obvious: a yawning chasm between the northern end of Prescott's breastwork and the southern end of the rail fence. Much of the ground in between the two defensive lines was swampy, but not impassible. Prescott could assure himself that his position was infinitely more secure than it had been ten hours before, when the redoubt stood alone and exposed on Breed's. But there remained major flaws in the American position, flaws that a clever tactician—like William Howe—would most certainly exploit if given the chance.

*C*opp's Hill proved to be the perfect vantage point for watching the movements in and around the hills of Charlestown. Burgoyne would spend almost all day in the battery on Copp's; Clinton would join him until the course of events demanded his presence elsewhere. William Howe was there, too, for a while. From Copp's he could clearly see the outlines of the redoubt and the breastwork. He could see that they were but thinly defended, and that if there was any artillery it wasn't firing. Howe could not make out the rail fence, since Breed's Hill itself blocked his view, but he had a fair idea of how he could carry out his assault. The turning movement he'd had in mind since early that morning would still work, and the rebel left flank was the weakest spot in the line. Concentrate on that, Howe knew, roll it up, and the rebels would scamper from the breastworks in no time at all. Raw troops simply could not withstand even the prospect of being overrun, front, flank, and rear.

Howe came ashore with the second wave. With him was Sir Robert Pigot, who would be commanding the left wing in the attack. There were not enough boats—that was probably the most damning problem—and so not all the men waiting at the North Battery for the boats to return were able to go with the second wave. The battalion companies of the 43rd and 52nd Foot, plus the flank companies of the 35th, could be accommodated, but the six flank companies of the two Marine battalions and the 63rd Foot would have to wait with the reserve, to be called upon if needed. But once the second wave had landed, Howe had nearly 1,600 foot troops on the ground at Morton's Point, plus the artillery—four light six-pounders, four light twelves, and four 5¼-inch field howitzers.[17] That should be enough, he thought. The rebel earthworks were sparsely manned, and the constant artillery barrage must have softened them a bit.

But as he surveyed the American lines from Morton's Hill, General Howe had second thoughts. From here the rail fence was perfectly visible, and although it, too, was thinly manned—Knowlton's boys, perhaps two hundred strong, covered a line about 250 yards in length—it was something the British commander hadn't counted on. He would need to gather the reserve from the North Battery, all seven hundred and more. It was the prudent thing to do. Perhaps an immediate assault, without waiting for the reserve to come up, might have done the trick, but something told Howe that he needed more men. And unless the Americans could, or would, bring more men into the fight, there wasn't much that they could do to make their line any stronger. Best to wait and be sure.

So while he waited for his request for the reserve to make its way back to Gage, Howe prepared for the attack. He formed his men atop Morton's Hill facing the redoubt on Breed's. Two wings, three lines each: the grenadiers and the light infantry in the front, the 38th and 5th Foot in the center, the 43rd and 52nd in the rear, their backs to the beach. Each line was formed in two ranks, for although the regulations still called for the men to fight in three ranks, like most officers with American experience, Howe preferred the thinner formation. The day was turning out to be a hot one, and the men would need their strength for the struggle ahead of them, so there was no sense in keeping them at attention while they waited on the reserve. With Howe's kind permission, the Redcoats on Morton's Hill broke ranks. They sat down and relaxed, grabbing a quick bite to eat from the cooked provisions in their haversacks.[18]

It was during this oddly peaceful interlude, with the soldiers sitting down to a meager repast while the guns continued to thunder over the water, that Howe noticed something disturbing, something that might put a crimp in his plans. On the large hill to the west—Bunker Hill—there was a mass of rebel troops, apparently milling about in confusion, some digging, others loafing . . . none of them inclined, so it appeared, to move on toward Breed's and beef up the forces in the earthworks. But all of a sudden, right around three o'clock, two bodies of men—two regiments, one might guess from their size— descended the hill and—before Howe's very eyes—moved up to the fortified fence just in front of the base of the hill. They fanned out to their left, toward the Mystic beach, filling in the gap on the rebel left flank. That flank was no longer floating in the air. Turning it, driving it back toward the earthworks, might prove to be tougher than the general had anticipated.

Tougher, but not impossible. The position was still thinly held. A quick rush with the light infantry, with the bayonet only, could still carry the rebel left by sheer impetus alone.

With that in mind, Howe made his first move. He ordered Lieutenant Colonel George Clark of the 43rd Foot, commanding the provisional Light Infantry Battalion, to move his elite troops along the beach in the direction of the rebel left. They advanced to within four hundred yards of the fortified fence. Under the cover of a steep earthen bank, nearly nine feet high, the light infantrymen went to ground, prone, to keep their position as secret as possible. They would spearhead the attack. Upon them hinged every hope of a quick victory.

What William Howe had witnessed on Bunker Hill was the arrival of the Hampshiremen.

John Stark did not waste any time when he received his orders from Ward's headquarters, inexplicably delayed, at two o'clock. Ammunition, such as was to be had, had already been handed out, and the men had been on the alert ever since, so the remaining four hundred men of the regiment set out on the road from Medford immediately.

Stark drove his men hard, and they loved him for it. Nobody in the army, not even Old Put, came closer to fitting the ideal of the rugged American frontiersman. Not quite forty-seven years old at the time of the battle, John Stark was gaunt, and despite his comically bushy eyebrows, his hatchet-face and piercing eyes showed a man who was all business. There were many veterans among the of-

John Stark. This touchy and proud New Hampshire leader was adored by the men who served under him. His impulsive decision to take possession of "the Rail Fence" probably saved the rebel forces from a quick and humiliating defeat.
(EMMET COLLECTION, MIRIAM AND IRA D. WALLACH DIVISION OF ART, PRINTS AND PHOTO- GRAPHS, THE NEW YORK PUBLIC LIBRARY, ASTOR, LENOX AND TILDEN FOUNDATIONS)

MAJ. GEN. JOHN STARK.

ficers of Ward's army, but Stark was a true soldier, well acquainted with conventional tactics but born and bred in the irregular warfare of the frontier. At age twenty-four, he was taken captive by Abenaki Indians while trapping, kept prisoner in Quebec, and adopted into the tribe after enduring a brutal beating by gauntlet. He and all three of his brothers joined Rogers' Rangers at the outset of the French and Indian War in 1755. John, who considered Robert Rogers a close personal friend, rose to the rank of captain in that distinguished band. His skill as a woodsman and as a tactician earned him the admiration of none other than George, Lord Howe, William's older brother. Stark marched alongside both George Howe and Thomas Gage—and Israel Putnam and Artemas Ward, too—during the attack on Fort Carillon in the summer of '58.

John Stark was the kind of soldier who earned admiration effortlessly, though never seeking it. He had a gift for leadership, a common touch, and yet was surprisingly literate and cultured beneath his rough and forbidding exterior. His favorite book was Voltaire's biography of Charles XII, the great Swedish warrior-king, and he habitually carried a copy with him. Stark had the talents of a born commander, but not the kind of personality that makes for a successful general. Blunt, sharp-tongued, touchy, and proud, Stark had little regard for politicians and even less for their authority.[19]

A successful entrepreneur at the time of the Lexington alarm—sawmills were his stock-in-trade—John Stark raised a regiment almost instantly; eight hundred men, it was said, flocked to join him in a matter of hours. The regiment entered the service of Massachusetts that April because New Hampshire had yet to establish its own army. The Provincial Congress recognized his talents and granted him a colonel's commission, with the condition that New Hampshire would take over the regiment, and Stark, too, once the colony had settled its affairs. Several weeks passed before the New Hampshire legislature summoned him to Exeter; when he finally made the trip, his disrespectful behavior practically guaranteed an unpleasant reception. The legislature baldly informed Stark that it had given overall command of the troops—and, worse, command of Stark's own regiment—to Nathaniel Folsom, a man with limited military experience but good political connections. The old ranger was incensed. Stark openly ridiculed the decision. Why should Folsom command the regiment that he, Stark, had raised and trained himself? Had the delegates at Exeter found "any way of making a child that was born today older than one that was born six weeks ago?" Only with great difficulty and many concessions could Stark be persuaded to accept a commission from his native colony. That kind of insubordination made John Stark a hero to the men he led, but it would prove fatal to any military ambitions he may have cherished.[20]

The entire leadership of Stark's regiment was distinguished by great talent and greater popularity. Stark tended to attract men like himself—unpretentious, capable, and fearless. Isaac Wyman was one; Andrew McClary, the regiment's major and "the handsomest man in the army," was another. Like Stark, McClary was a product of the frontier, a former Rogers' Ranger, and a successful entrepreneur; unlike his colonel, he was extroverted and gregarious, just as popular as Stark but more likeable. The son of an Ulster Irish immigrant, Major McClary was a mountain of a man six and a half feet tall, with a great, booming voice that carried over even the din of battle.[21]

Stark and McClary hurried their four hundred Hampshiremen down the road from Medford and up to Charlestown Neck, where a traffic jam of sorts blocked their way. The British vessels moored off the Charlestown milldam were lobbing solid shot across the Neck, hoping to discourage reinforcements from reaching Breed's Hill, and thus far they had had their intended effect. A couple of Massachusetts regiments were held up on the mainland side of the Neck, afraid to cross for fear of the flying iron, and so, too, were a few horse-drawn wagons, sent by headquarters to bring rum, beer, and provisions to Prescott's beleaguered troops. Stark was annoyed by the clogged road, to say the least; he had been ordered to get to Charlestown, and he would, by God—no cannonfire or cowardly militia would stop him. He motioned to McClary, who strode forward toward the hesitating Massachusetts boys, politely—but very loudly—asking if they would be so kind as to yield the road to Colonel Stark's regiment. McClary was not a man to be refused; the Massachusetts regiments quickly stepped to the side to let Stark and his men pass by. Stark paid no heed to the cannonballs flying, bounding across the Neck, but one of his captains next to him did: Henry Dearborn, a slight-built twenty-four-year-old physician—the army was full of doctors, it would seem—later to be a general and secretary of war under President Thomas Jefferson, tried to step up the pace and get to the other end of the Neck as quickly as possible. Stark quietly, calmly, told Dearborn to slow down. The men needed to save their strength, Stark observed, and "one fresh man in action is worth ten fatigued men."[22]

What Stark found once he had made his way onto the peninsula was utter chaos. Small groups of soldiers were picking their way back, having deserted the earthworks, while others milled about atop Bunker Hill as Old Put did his damnedest to get some work out of them. Leading his regiment up the slopes of Bunker Hill, Stark soon encountered Isaac Wyman and the rest of the regiment, and within a few minutes the much smaller New Hampshire regiment of James Reed caught up with Stark's men.[23] Putnam was there, too, but Stark ignored him. He had no reservations about obeying Artemas Ward, but he didn't recognize Putnam as a superior, even if they were old comrades from Rogers's legendary outfit.

John Stark instead studied the ground from the far end of Bunker Hill. With his trained eye, he was the first officer on the scene to recognize the fatal flaw in the American defenses. What he did next was probably the single most important action taken by any American leader that day.

In Stark's front, down the gentle slope from where he stood, was the rail fence, now held by Knowlton's Connecticut boys. It was, of course, barely manned, with each soldier occupying a full yard or two along the length of the barricade. That was bad enough; worse, though, was the fact that the far end of the line was completely unoccupied, including the Mystic beach itself. And just a few hundred yards away, on the small hill that lay just off to his left in the distance, were the Redcoats. Whole battalions of them.

Stark did not consult with Putnam; he did not wait for or ask for orders. He acted. Pushing his men forward, Stark moved toward the far left flank, behind the rail fence. Here he halted the regiment—with Reed's not far behind—and gave a quick and businesslike speech. Stark wasn't one to speak extemporaneously or at length, but he could turn a phrase when he had to, and in his typically brisk manner he reminded the men of their duty and assured them that they would do just fine, so long as they held their ground and listened to their officers. With that the men gave three loud huzzahs and rushed the last few yards to the rail fence.

Reed's regiment took its place in the line next to Knowlton's boys; Stark's went farther to the left, filing into the gap between Reed's and the bank of the Mystic. And Stark, sizing up the situation before him, caught another potentially fatal oversight. The rail fence ended, abruptly, a few yards short of the beach. There was a point at which the grassland ended in a miniature bluff, dropping some nine feet to the muddy beach below. That beach was itself only a few feet wide . . . just wide enough to allow the passage of an infantry column. Stark saw it, and without skipping a heartbeat he pushed his men toward the beach. They jumped down the bank onto the beach, and within moments they were building up a chest-high barricade using stones they had pilfered from fences nearby.[24]

With that action, the American defenses were complete, mere moments before Howe would launch his first assault. The right was anchored by the Breed's Hill redoubt, formidable if primitive and poorly manned; then the breastwork, running northward down the slope of Breed's. Falling back almost two hundred yards, the line resumed with the rail fence and trailed away to the Mystic shore to the north. There was one hole remaining, and it was a big one: that two-hundred-yard gap between the breastwork and the rail fence. Swampy ground there added some security, but not enough.

Some enterprising soul saw this gap and corrected it, just in the nick of time. Before Howe's battalions began their steady advance, three arrow-shaped fortifications appeared as if by magic, in a staggered line along the swampland between the rail fence and the breastwork. No one ever claimed credit for the deed; most likely Thomas Knowlton had his troops throw them together from fence rails. More than either the redoubt or the breastwork, these little *flèches* would almost prove to be Howe's undoing.

*T*wo distinguished visitors, unheralded and unexpected, came out to the American position to volunteer their services right before Howe launched his first attack. The first was Seth Pomeroy. Nearly seventy years old, Pomeroy was one of the five men first nominated for generalship by the Massachusetts Provincial Congress, ranking right after Ward. He was a gunsmith by trade, but it was his soldiering that caught the Congress's attention: he was in the siege lines at Louisbourg in 1745, where he served under engineer Richard Gridley, and he saw action during the French and Indian War, too, commanding a Massachusetts provincial regiment. He had never received his general's commission from the Congress, probably because he never coveted the position. Pomeroy had been relaxing at his home in Northampton when he learned of the Committee's intent to seize Charlestown Heights; at midday on the sixteenth, he packed a few belongings and an old musket he had built himself, leapt onto a borrowed horse, and practically flew down the road to Charlestown, nearly a hundred miles to the east. Putnam greeted the old gunsmith as his superior officer, but the modest Pomeroy had no interest in leading troops that day. He left Putnam, descended Bunker Hill, and joined the New Hampshire boys at the rail fence.[25]

Old Put, no doubt, would have been happy to let someone else take over. He was to be doubly disappointed, for no sooner had Pomeroy left him than Joseph Warren came riding up Bunker Hill to see him. Warren had risen from his sickbed in the Hastings House when the alarm had sounded in Cambridge, sipped some chamomile tea to soothe his throbbing head, and went downstairs to find the house all but deserted—General Ward and his staff were out and about, supervising the reinforcements, and only Warren and Mrs. Hastings remained. Accompanied by his student, David Townsend, Warren set out on foot for Charlestown. He had been at Grape Island and Noddle's Island, and he wasn't about to miss another chance to kill a few of Gage's murderous Redcoats. Somewhere along the route, Warren borrowed a horse and rode the rest of the way to the peninsula. He stopped at the Sun Tavern, a public house between Bunker Hill and Charlestown Neck, where surgeons had already set up an improvised field hospital. Warren, armed only with a walking stick, borrowed a musket from Colonel Brickett of Frye's regiment—Brickett, too, was a physician—and spurred his horse toward Bunker Hill.

Putnam was delighted to see Warren and offered his friend command, which Warren gently refused; the doctor went on to the redoubt, where Prescott made the same offer, and again Warren declined. He was a major general—the Provincial Congress had said so—but he had no commission, and anyway Warren wanted to *fight*. And so he took his place in the redoubt, fashionably attired in a light cloth coat with silver buttons, his hair "curled up at the sides of his head and pinned up," borrowed musket in his hands.[26]

*B*y three o'clock, Howe was just about ready. Robert Pigot led the two battalions of his left wing, the 38th and the 43rd Foot, off Morton's Hill and along the beach toward Charlestown. Then the anticipated reserve arrived: boats quickly scraped onto the beach, offloading the flank companies of the 2nd Marines and the 63rd Foot, who had had no time to recover from their trip when they were ordered up to join Pigot. More boats, carrying the 47th Foot and the 1st Marine Battalion, landed right afterward, on the beach facing Breed's Hill. To John Burgoyne and Henry Clinton, watching the operation unfold from their perch at the Copp's Hill Battery, Howe had done everything right. "Howe's disposition was exceedingly Soldier-like," Burgoyne wrote approvingly, "in my opinion it was perfect."[27]

Howe still had some last-minute preparations to attend to before sending the men forward. Naval artillery support, directed against the rail fence, might be of some use, he thought, and so he sent back a request that the gondolas then raking Charlestown Neck with solid shot be withdrawn, brought back through the ferryway, and redeployed in the muddy shallows of the Mystic. But the timing was poor for such a movement: although it was just about high tide, it would be a chore getting the gondolas up the Charles, and by the time they reached the Mystic, the ebb tide would be working against them. Had it been possible to retrieve the gondolas quickly, the battle might have gone very differently. There wasn't much that Howe could do about that, unfortunately, and he certainly couldn't wait very long for the gondolas.

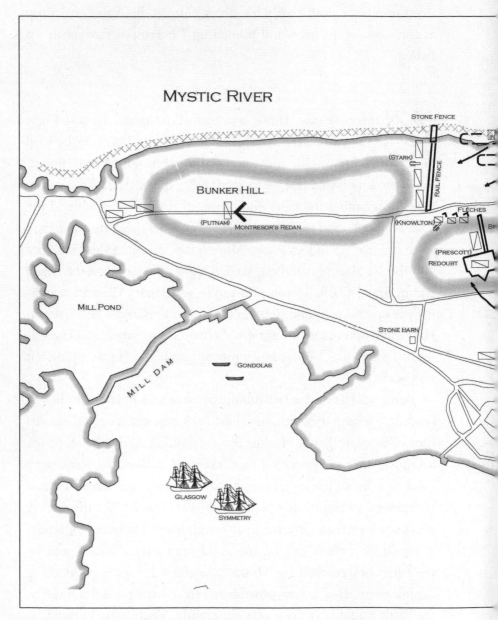

MYSTIC RIVER

STONE FENCE

(STARK)

RAIL FENCE

BUNKER HILL

FLÈCHES

(PUTNAM)   MONTRESOR'S REDAN

(KNOWLTON)

BR

(PRESCOTT)
REDOUBT

MILL POND

STONE BARN

MILL DAM   GONDOLAS

GLASGOW

SYMMETRY

The Battle of Bunker Hill, June 17, 1775, 3 P.M.

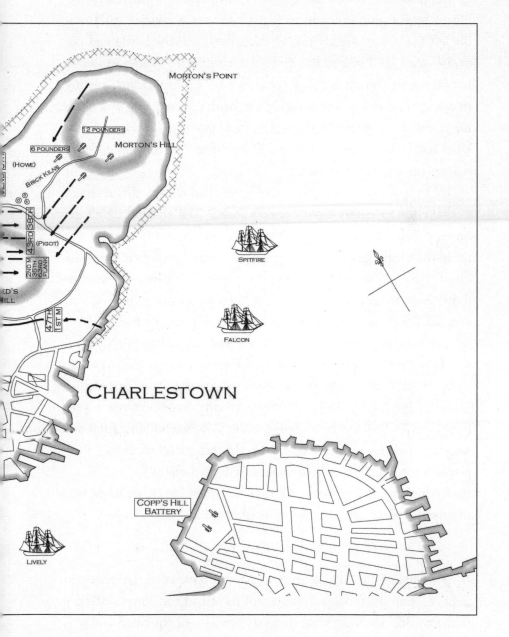

MORTON'S POINT

12 POUNDERS

6 POUNDERS

MORTON'S HILL

(HOWE)

BRICK KILNS

38TH

43RD

(PIGOT)

2ND M

35TH

63RD

FLANK

ED'S
HILL

47TH

1ST M

SPITFIRE

FALCON

CHARLESTOWN

COPP'S HILL
BATTERY

LIVELY

But he could do something about Charlestown, which was proving to be a major annoyance. Pigot had sent a courier to Howe: his left flank was already taking casualties, and the battle had not even begun yet. Prescott had sent a detachment into Charlestown to harass the British should they come close. The Americans, nesting in a few buildings in town, facing the beach, were firing at Pigot's men, who were "exceedingly hurt by [the] musketry."[28] Howe knew what had to be done; Graves and Haldimand had recommended it before: the empty town must be destroyed.

By happy coincidence, Samuel Graves had chosen this moment to make his appearance on Morton's Point. The admiral didn't get on very well with Gage, but he had no problems with Howe and was more than willing to help the general. When he offered his assistance, Howe responded instantly: burn down Charlestown. Graves didn't have to be told twice. He had been anticipating this request, and the sloops in the Charles had been heating cannonballs red-hot for just this very purpose. Graves sent out his orders to the ships, and Howe sent a messenger to relay the request to the gun crews on Copp's Hill. Within minutes, hot shot from the ships and "carcase"— primitive incendiary shells—from the twenty-fours on Copp's were flying across the water into Charlestown. Wooden buildings and dry weather made for a quick result. "We threw a parcel of shells," Burgoyne wrote, "and the whole was instantly in flames."[29]

Everything was in place. All that remained for Howe to do was to give the order, and the assault would begin.

*T*hough the British army might not have been the largest in Europe, though it might not have had the "finest infantry in the world," the individual Redcoat was as well equipped and well armed as any soldier in the Old World. His uniform—regimental coat, waistcoat, breeches, and stockings—might seem tragically ill suited for combat, tight, confining, and hot as it was, but it was no more "diabolically contrived" than that of any European soldier of the period. Nor was the gear that he carried all that burdensome. It has been claimed that the individual British soldier carried nearly 125 pounds of gear into battle at Charlestown in 1775—difficult to accept when the typical British recruit probably weighed little more than that, naked and stripped of everything. In reality, the total weight of gear when in heavy marching order—that is, with everything a soldier would need on campaign—was probably closer to sixty pounds. Howe, though, had considered even *that* burden far too heavy for battle: only musket and bayonet, ammunition, blanket, and rations would be carried, a total load that probably didn't exceed thirty pounds. The Redcoats did not labor under any unusual or unaccustomed burdens that afternoon on the Charlestown peninsula. British soldiers, after all, had worn similar uniforms and carried similar gear before, on scores of battlefields in Europe and in North America.

And the Redcoat carried a good weapon. Though a shorter musket had been authorized only seven years before, Gage's men were all equipped with the Long Land musket of the 1756 pattern, often called "the King's arm" but more familiar today as the Brown Bess. Its 46-inch-long barrel threw a spherical lead musket ball, nearly three-quarters of an inch in diameter; weighing ten and a half pounds, the weapon's overall length was 62½ inches, but its socket bayonet increased its length by a further 17 inches. In general quality of workmanship, it was undoubtedly superior to the antiques and fowling-pieces used by the American troops, but its basic characteristics were little different. The flintlock firing mechanism was fairly reliable but touchy, especially in damp weather, and when it came to ballistics a musket was a musket. Smoothbore weapons firing lead balls were wildly inaccurate beyond 150 yards, a little less so at seventy-five to one hundred yards, but absolutely devastating at fifty yards or less. Accuracy, though, was not all that vital when firing at large masses of men in tightly packed ranks. There is no evidence that any of the rebels at Charlestown had much more accurate, though slower-loading, rifles; and since the British soldiers in Gage's command had gone through a fair amount of marksmanship training, the Americans did not have a significant edge over the British in accuracy of fire. All in all, the two sides were probably about evenly matched.

To be brilliantly successful, a turning movement, like the one Howe had in mind, needed speed and stealth. For Howe, stealth wasn't guaranteed. The lay of the land didn't allow him to hide his movements from the enemy. So speed—accompanied by overwhelming force—was the key.

Howe's plan of attack was simple. Pigot's left wing would make a "demonstration"—a feint—against the redoubt and the breastwork. It would keep the rebels uncertain about Howe's true intentions; more important, it would keep them from shifting forces to meet a threat elsewhere on the line. The real attack would come from the British right, directed toward the rail fence. The light infantry would move quickly up the beach along the Mystic, hitting the far American left, hitting it *hard*. Once the line was forced at that point, the defenders rousted from behind the rail fence, the grenadiers and the rest of the right wing could exploit whatever success the light infantry might have.

No matter how they hit the American line, the Redcoats were going to be marching straight into enemy fire. To modern eyes, these tactics appear costly, even suicidal. But eighteenth-century tacticians knew a different truth, a truth that had been proven again and again on European battlefields: bayonet charges worked, even in a frontal assault, even against an entrenched and determined enemy. To make a successful bayonet charge, the attackers had to maintain cohesion, had to keep their formations tight. They had to move without stopping, not even to shoot, not even to return the enemy's fire. They had to press on, ignoring the men falling around them, disregarding the blood and the screams and the mangled bodies of their comrades. There would be casualties, many casualties; the faster the charge, however, the less time for exposure to enemy fire. But once the attacker was upon the enemy with bayonets leveled chest high, the defenders would almost always break and run for their lives. For the bayonet was, above all, a moral weapon, a weapon of terror. It took a truly formidable soul to face a bayonet and not quail in abject fear.

But it demanded much from the attacker. Keeping formation under fire was difficult enough; but the worst was fighting the temptation to fire back once the balls began to fly. Veteran officers knew that this was an instinctual response, common with raw or untrained soldiers: "young troops . . . never having seen service," wrote Lieutenant Richard Williams of the 23rd Foot, "foolishly imagine that when danger is feared they secure themselves by discharging their muskets, with or without aim."[30] It took discipline, the kind of discipline that reduces men to unthinking, unfeeling automatons, to carry a bayonet charge through to victory.

Training and discipline, and not weapons or equipment, were the things that distinguished the British from the Americans, or so one would assume. The behavior of the individual soldier would be the deciding factor. Here, Howe had a great deal to worry about. On the retreat from Concord, the Redcoats had not done their best, not by a long shot. Howe knew that the battle facing his army would prove a much sterner test than Concord. Would the rank-and-file of the army meet the challenge this time, or would they fall apart in confusion and fear as they had two months ago?

The soldiers themselves were pondering that very same question.

Nine

* * *

GRASS BEFORE
THE SCYTHE

"They advanced towards us in order to swallow us up,
but they found a choaky mouthful of us . . ."

PETER BROWN, PRESCOTT'S REGIMENT, JUNE 28, 1775

*W*illiam Howe gave the order to attack at around half-past three. The twelve-pounder guns on Morton's Hill opened fire on the breastwork, and the battalions moved forward. The grenadier battalion led the way, marching straight toward the rail fence. Following them were the battalion companies of the 5th and the 52nd Foot. At the same time, Pigot led the battalions of his wing from the Charles River shore toward the base of Breed's Hill, directly opposite the redoubt.

In the redoubt and in the breastwork, and all along the rail fence, the Americans watched with awe as the long red lines—about five hundred yards away—moved slowly in their direction. They were tired and hungry, and all but overcome by the broiling heat, for although some of the men had stripped to their shirtsleeves, many still wore their rough woolen coats. The few barrels of rum and beer that Ward had sent were not enough to assuage their unbearable thirst. They had been waiting for what seemed to be an eternity. For Prescott's men in the earthworks on Breed's it was nearly that— they had been awake for thirty-six hours, and working hard for the past sixteen. No matter how exhausted and scared they were, they couldn't help but stare in wonder at the majestic sight before them . . . the thudding of the drums, beating out the cadence, the glittering of the sun off polished bayonets and burnished buttons, the slow pace of the red-coated battalions. Some of them had fought the Regulars before, at Concord and at Noddle's, and they knew that the British were not invincible. But in that moment, as they wiped the sweat from their foreheads and gazed at the impossibly formal approach of the enemy, that knowledge didn't count for much.

Even as the attack was in motion, reinforcements were arriving in the American lines, piecemeal and disorganized but reinforcements all the same. Ward sent some of them—Paul Dudley Sargent's detachment and Jonathan Ward's regiment received their orders to leave Lechmere's Point and go to Charlestown at about four o'clock—while other regimental colonels simply responded to the sound of the guns and took it upon themselves to march their regiments to the scene. Scammon, frustrated at being sent to Lechmere's and then to Cobble Hill, ordered his men to march as soon as he heard the din of small-arms fire to the north. With no real commander to guide them, the newcomers went wherever they chose. On Bunker Hill, Israel Putnam managed to bully some of the soldiers loitering there into moving on toward the coming battle. They took their places in the line, randomly, primed and loaded their muskets, and waited . . . staring at the British formations advancing, slowly, inexorably.

The progress of the grenadier battalion was indeed slow, almost maddeningly so. Of course, the beginning of an assault was supposed to proceed slowly. There was no sense in tiring out the men when they were well outside musket range; better to save their strength for the last few yards, when speed and strength and impetus really counted. They had to halt frequently, too, because Howe wanted time for the field artillery to wreak some havoc. His lighter guns, four six-pounders, were moving forward with the grenadier company of the 35th Foot, and they were finding it difficult. At the base of Morton's Hill was an old clay pit, not far from a group of kilns for firing brick, and the ground there was swampy—not exactly ideal conditions for moving cannon by hand. All the toil ended up being for naught: the gun crews, it was alleged, found that the ammunition boxes bolted to the trails of their gun carriages contained not six-pound balls but twelve—and since twelve-pound shot were fully an inch bigger in diameter, they were useless.[1] Word got back to Howe, who ordered up more six-pound shot, but for a while the six-pounders would be able to do nothing of service.[*]

The terrain itself impeded the grenadiers. Even at the measured marching pace of seventy-five steps per minute, crossing the fields toward the rail fence that stretched out before them in the distance was a grueling chore. Small hidden holes abounded, tripping the unwary. Waist-high grass filled the unmown fields, whipping at their tightly buttoned gaiters, catching at their clothing, leaving seeds and burrs clinging to their legs. Then there were the rocks . . . the damnable, huge, sharp-faced rocks, which lay in profusion across the line of march as they did in every field in this part of the country, barely visible beneath the untamed grass. But the fences were the most obdurate hindrance. They crisscrossed the fields every few yards,

---

[*] It has been alleged that the error in the ammunition supply occurred through the carelessness of the British artillery commander, Lieutenant Colonel Samuel Cleaveland—" . . . from the dotage of an officer of rank in that Corps, who spends his whole time dallying with the schoolmaster's daughters. God knows he is old enough—he is no Sampson—yet he must have his Delilah." The schoolmaster was Lovell of the Boston Latin School; one of his sons, Benjamin, was clerk of artillery stores for the garrison, while the other—James—was a Whig. There is no other evidence to support the allegation, yet Cleaveland certainly came under fire for the blunder. French, *First Year*, 749.

or so it seemed, and these were not the kind of fences that could be trampled down and stepped over. They were good, stout fences, Yankee fences, and soon the hands of the grenadiers were torn and bleeding from the task of dismantling the obstacles. The heat was hellish. Wool coats and waistcoats amplified it; sweat poured from beneath the heavy bearskin hats the grenadiers wore proudly, stinging their eyes and drawing a flood of muttered curses. It was only a few hundred yards. It seemed like miles.

To the right of the grenadiers, the light infantry was already well on its way. They had lain hidden in the shelter of the sunken Mystic beach when the light companies got the command to move forward. Their commander, Lieutenant Colonel George Clark, gave the word; the men rose nimbly to their feet, and they were on the move. The narrow beach would not allow them to go forward in long, thin lines, so instead they advanced in column, four men abreast, one company column following another. In their lead was the light company of the 23rd Foot, the Royal Welch Fusiliers. The Royal Welch was perhaps the most storied of British regiments, made legendary for its gallant conduct against a superior French force in the August 1759 battle of Minden. About half of the 23rd's officers were "Minden men," veterans of that bloody German battlefield, including Captain Lieutenant Thomas Mecan, the thirty-six-year-old Irishman who led the Fusiliers' light company this day. But the rank-and-file were raw, almost to a man, like just about all the Redcoats here. And all were conscious of a nagging uncertainty that had haunted them for two months: that during the retreat from Concord, they had panicked while under the fire of these very same farmers and tradesmen in homespun clothing. They were anxious to prove themselves, but apprehensive that they would not.[2]

Behind the stone wall they had thrown up only minutes before, Stark's New Hampshire boys waited, breathlessly, for just the right moment. They were packed behind the stone wall, three deep. They were not trained men, but Stark had prepared them well. He had planted wooden posts into the soil, on the beach, and in front of the rail fence, about fifty yards out . . . firing markers, so that even the most anxious soldier knew exactly when to fire—wait, wait, until the Redcoats get to that post. *Then* fire. Stark, Wyman, and McClary walked quietly behind their men, soothing them in hushed voices, calming them, reminding them: aim low, aim at their legs and not at their heads, but keep your fingers off your triggers until they get *really* close.

Onward the light troops pushed, not pausing, not stopping to fire, but fully intent on rushing in with the bayonet as they were trained to do. Finally they were so close that the New Hampshire boys could make out their faces and even the distinctive facings and insignia of the Royal Welch. Then the oncoming red mass drew up to the markers.

There was a shouted command, then the ragged explosion, which seemed to crackle desultorily at first and then crescendo into a long, drawn-out *boom*. Flame leaped from a score of muskets. Then came a continuous, spastic roll of gunfire as the men loaded and fired as fast as they could without waiting for commands. The Hampshiremen gaped in disbelief as the head of the British column vanished from sight; the survivors staggered and fell back, reeling from the shock of the volley. For a while the Redcoats continued to push on toward the stone wall. The Royal Welch light company had disappeared; the light infantrymen of the 4th Foot—the "King's Own"—stumbled over the wounded and the dead to get at the wall, where they were met with more musketry. More experienced veterans might have kept going, since the stone wall was so *close*, but these Redcoats were not veterans. As a body, the light companies turned and fled, not in a panic but not slowly, either, streaming all the way back to Morton's Point. Their officers—those left standing—hurried to the rear, brandishing their light fusils like batons as they tried to rally the men. On the beach behind them, lying amid pools of blood, among cartridge boxes and muskets and hats, the detritus of battle, strewn promiscuously about, were the dead . . . nearly one hundred of them. And many, many more were wounded, moaning, screaming, desperately crawling toward the rear through the tangle of dead bodies.

The grenadiers on the field above the beach must have heard the unrestrained shouts of triumph that drifted over the riverbank from the stone wall, where Stark's men rejoiced and congratulated themselves on their unlikely victory. But the grenadiers didn't ponder its import. They had problems of their own. Repeated encounters with strong pasture fences slowed them, forcing them to stop and dress their lines more often than should have been necessary. This was the kind of work that pioneers—soldiers specializing in construction or demolition—were meant to do, but the only pioneers in the garrison had been left in the care of the artillery commander, Colonel Samuel Cleaveland; so while the grenadiers kicked and cursed and battered at the stubborn fences, the pioneers sat in Boston, useless.

Ninety yards out from the rail fence, the grenadiers came upon yet another fence line blocking their advance. Once again they tried to bash it down, clamber over it, or scurry under it, but it was so strong that the brawny grenadiers had to "ground arms"—lay their muskets down—so that they could go at it with both hands.[3] But this time they were within musket range of the American lines. They were still stuck there when, all along the rail fence, the New Hampshire and Connecticut boys leveled their muskets and fired. The volley was more annoying than anything else— some of the grenadiers fell, not in heaps as with the light infantry on the beach—but the shock troops had had enough. They were angry, weary, and distracted, and despite their orders to press on with the bayonet only, they succumbed to the instinct to defend themselves by firing back at their tormentors. Crowding together

around the partly demolished fence, their neat and straight align-
ment completely gone, the grenadiers loaded and fired with the
fury of men possessed, ignoring their officers' attempts to re-form
the lines and resume the advance. And the rebels fired back. The
difference was that the Americans, behind the rail fence, had reasonable cover, while the grenadiers were standing in the open,
massed together, perfect targets even for inaccurate smoothbores.
The grenadiers suffered; the Americans did not.

Meanwhile, Howe's second line, the 5th and 52nd Regiments,
advanced in support of the grenadier battalion as they had been ordered. Blinded by smoke and sweat, the officers of the two regiments

*The Rail Fence. Here soldiers from New Hampshire and Connecticut inflicted the
heaviest casualties in the British ranks, and prevented Howe from simply
swarming Prescott's redoubt and the breastwork.*

didn't notice the grenadiers halted in their front until it was too late. The 5th and the 52nd literally stumbled right into the backs of the frustrated grenadiers as the American musket balls whizzed about them. Neat lines of infantry collided with disorganized clumps of men, and any semblance of organization came undone in an instant. The rebels kept pouring heavy fire into the packed and confused muddle while Redcoat officers from all three battalions shouted and waved their swords, vainly endeavoring to extricate their men from the tangled mess. Finally the whole body, with no hope of re-forming for the assault, found itself compelled to march back out of range of the rebel musketry.

Howe did not shy away from the action. Nobody would ever accuse William Howe of a lack of physical courage, not at this point in his career, and in the fighting before the rail fence Howe was at his reckless best, staying imprudently close to the advancing troops. But the general had lost control of his right wing. The direction of the fighting in this sector was in the uncertain grasp of the battalion commanders and the company officers. It was at their initiative, and not at Howe's command, that the attack resumed.

Once the lines had been set straight and dressed, and the gaps torn by the musket-fire from the rail fence filled in, the assault began again. It shifted slightly to the left, closer to the arrow-shaped *flèches* that connected the rail fence to the earthen breastwork. Some of the fences were down, destroyed by the grenadiers in their earlier attempt, but the going was no easier the second time around.

So the grenadiers came on toward the rail fence once more, the battalion companies of the 5th and 52nd backing them up, and if the Redcoats hadn't felt the fury of the American defenders before, they would surely feel it now. The cannonade from the ships and from Copp's had ceased for the time being—there was too much danger of the solid shot ripping through the British ranks, so close to the American lines now—and the field in this quarter fell oddly silent. Only the tramping of feet and the occasional shouts of the officers and the sergeants penetrated the thick quiet. Behind the rail fence, nothing could be heard but the whispered encouragement of Stark, McClary, and Knowlton, reminding the men again and again to hold their fire.

Far to their left, the men in the advancing battalions caught view of an awe-inspiring sight, a vision so terrible that it made the unnatural quiet doubly ominous: Charlestown was ablaze. Graves had done his job and done it well. The ghost town, a tinder box in these conditions, went up in flames so quickly that observers were shocked by the suddenness of the conflagration. Houses, shops, the skeletal hulls of half-built ships . . . everything was on fire, and from the spires of Charlestown's churches fingers of flame reached into the heavens. Black smoke rose in clouds, sometimes blotting out the sun. It painted an apocalyptic backdrop for the scene playing out on the hills and pastures adjacent, an omen of horrors.

The grenadiers and their support pushed closer this time, maybe to within fifty yards, before the explosion came. Once more the smoke and flame followed in a ragged volley; once more the sheet of lead flew from the rail fence ahead, but at a range so close that no shot could fail to hit home. Bits of cloth, madder-red and white, and of pipe-clayed leather lofted into the air as the volley tore into the packed ranks. Like the light infantry on the beach, the entire front rank of the grenadiers, officers and men alike, seemed almost to melt into the ground . . . *almost*, for the violence of the blow was palpable. Some of the men in the first rank collapsed with scarcely a whimper, their awkward bearskins toppling precipitously before their feet; others were flung backward and hard, as if recoiling from a bodily punch. The ground over which they advanced filled quickly with dead bodies, arranged in all the ghastly and contorted postures that a dark imagination could conjure. After the first volley, the guns were briefly silent, the screams of wounded men and the shouts of officers filling the air. After a few seconds the firing began again. The rebels behind the rail fence were priming, loading, and firing as fast as their trembling hands could move. "An incessant stream of fire poured from the rebel lines," one British officer reported. "It seemed a continued sheet of fire for near thirty minutes."[4]

The Redcoats before the rail fence and abreast the *flèches* then did precisely what they were not supposed to do, what they had done in their earlier feint: they stopped. Their officers screamed at them, beat at them with the flats of their sword blades, to get them moving again, but under that kind of fire obedience to orders was not of paramount concern to the British soldiers. Elite the grenadiers may have been, but only in relative terms. It took true veterans to press onward into that kind of fire and consummate the advance with the push of bayonet. These Redcoats were not veterans. No one on earth could have convinced them that a quick rush across those last few yards would actually have *saved* lives. They responded the way neophyte soldiers usually did in such circumstances. They gathered together in clumps, furiously firing and loading, firing and loading, wildly and without aiming. "The fire of the enemy was so badly directed," wrote Henry Dearborn, with Stark at the rail fence, "I should presume that forty-nine balls out of fifty passed from one to six feet over our heads, for I noticed an apple tree, some paces in the rear, which had scarcely a ball in it, from the ground as high as a man's head, while the trunk and branches above were literally cut to pieces."[5]

Samuel Trevett's two four-pounder cannon soon joined in the fray. They had left the redoubt much earlier, when Prescott ordered Trevett and Knowlton to oppose the landing on Morton's Point, but Trevett ended up with Knowlton when the Connecticut officer occupied and fortified the rail fence. They were here now, and at nearly point-blank range. A four-pounder was hardly the most destructive gun in the world, but at this range, with grape and canister, it could do damage.

The nightmare was just beginning for the Redcoats firing pointlessly at the rail fence. No one, not even Howe, seemed to have noticed the *flèches* before. Some of Knowlton's men had posted themselves there, and now they had a chance to complete the near annihilation of the British assault. From this point they could fire on the flanks of the grenadiers, what was called "enfilade fire," and few things were more terrifying, even to veteran troops, than being fired on from the front and the flank simultaneously.

As the grenadiers and the supporting battalions withered and fell from the maelstrom of musket balls and grapeshot, the light infantry came to their support on the right. Clark and some of the surviving company officers—including Thomas Mecan of the Royal Welch, who had somehow emerged unscathed from the killing zone on the beach—rallied the shattered remnants of the light battalion and led them back into action, but toward the rail fence instead. Like the support battalions in the earlier movement, the light battalion got confused in the smoke and the din, and moving up from the far right flank they came up close behind the grenadiers. The men of the light company panicked, mistook the smoke-obscured grenadiers for the rail fence, and opened fire—straight into the backs of the grenadiers. They realized their mistake, but not before felling a substantial number of their own comrades.[6]

The assault was beyond all hope now. About half an hour after the shooting had begun, the Redcoats streamed back from the field, to the cheers of the Connecticut and New Hampshire boys, toward the beach where their few remaining officers would try to piece together companies that had virtually ceased to exist. The battalions, especially the grenadiers, were irreparably shattered. Among the fallen was Lieutenant Colonel James Abercromby, Gage's adjutant general and temporary commander of the grenadier battalion, mortally wounded by the murderous fire from the rail fence.* A forty-three-year-old veteran of many battles, Abercromby had served in North America during the French and Indian War. In his dying moments, as his men carried him from the field, Abercromby recalled one of the friendships he had made during the French war, and frantically he called out to his men, "If you take General Putnam alive, don't hang him for he's a brave man!"[7]

Someone else, only a few yards away behind the rail fence, also knew Abercromby from the previous war. Abercromby had once reprimanded an officer in Rogers' Rangers over the poor discipline of his men . . . a Ranger officer from New Hampshire, one Captain John Stark.[8]

*R*obert Pigot's left wing was seeing its fair share of action— and death—too.

Pigot's role was to provide a diversion for the main attack, which was to come on the right, from the battalions of Howe's wing. The redoubt and breastwork were Pigot's responsibilities, but not taking them—only pressing on them just enough to keep the rebels there occupied, and maybe to tease them into wasting their precious ammunition in a futile long-range firefight. The 1st Marine Battalion and the 47th Foot sidled along the base of Breed's Hill, circling the southern and eastern faces of the redoubt; the 38th and 43rd Foot, plus the flank companies of the 35th, 63rd, and 2nd Marines, moved directly on the breastwork.

It wasn't long before Pigot ran into trouble. Charlestown was just beginning to go up in flames, and Prescott's flankers stationed there had fled the burning buildings . . . only to take up new posi-

---

* Colonel Abercromby should not be confused with General James Abercrombie, who commanded British troops in the French and Indian War, and who bore the greatest share of the responsibility for the bloody and unsuccessful attack on Fort Carillon in 1758.

tions in a stone-built barn that lay between town and the redoubt. From here the rebel marksmen continued to fire on Pigot's left flank, never inflicting many casualties but clearly annoying, even unsettling, the Redcoats of the 47th Foot and the 1st Marines.

Still, it was nothing like what Howe's men had had to face so far, and the desultory sniping from the stone barn didn't deter Brigadier Pigot from his assigned task. Pigot led his men to within extreme musket range of the works, probably a little over one hundred yards. Here he halted all the battalions and ordered them to open fire. Prescott's men responded in kind, and for several minutes the two sides engaged in a ferocious-sounding musket battle. Despite the smoke and the noise, the fight took very few lives on either side. William Prescott correctly deduced that Pigot was not yet up to anything especially threatening, and that his own men—about 150 in the redoubt, by Prescott's estimate, probably more than in the breastwork—were diminishing their limited stocks of ammunition to no good purpose. Prescott quietly ordered his men to cease fire and to maintain silence. Don't fire, he cautioned, until the Redcoats draw within thirty yards of the walls. He may—*may*—have uttered the immortal words, "Don't fire until you see the whites of their eyes." The phrase has been attributed to Stark and Putnam, too, but it makes little difference who said it or even if it was said at all. It was common sense, and all the veteran commanders in the American lines would have said the very same thing in different ways.

From his vantage point at the base of Breed's Hill, Pigot could not see up into the interior of the redoubt, and even when the rebels were firing it was rare to see anything protrude from the thick earthen walls other than a musket barrel or a hat brim. Once the firing had stopped, Pigot convinced himself that the redoubt must have been abandoned. He sent all his battalions up the hill, slowly but confidently. Perhaps the rebels *had* given up. Perhaps the day wouldn't demand a blood sacrifice.

And when the Redcoats reached Prescott's thirty-yard perimeter, right about the same time that Howe's grenadiers came within range of the rail fence, the musket barrels appeared over the parapet, a nasal Yankee voice shouted an incomprehensible command, and a volley thundered down the side of the redoubt, to be followed by successive volleys from all along the breastwork. Again the shattered, bleeding ranks, milling in confusion, officers trying to push the men together and fill up the lines. Again the repeated volleys from the hill, the rebels firing so quickly that "we did not take the trouble to return ram rods but dropped them by our sides as we reloaded."[9] Pigot's men, though, didn't stay and fight back as Howe's did. Their assault was only meant to be a feint. Pigot and his troops fell back, in good order, leaving corpses and writhing wounded men in the bloody grass behind them.

*W*illiam Howe was stunned. He was accustomed to battle, calloused to the awful sights and sounds and nauseating smells of violent death, but now—only an hour or so after the first waves of troops had set out on their steady march toward the American positions—he was practically in shock. A few brief minutes before, he had been surrounded by eager young staff officers, waiting on him, following alongside him as he plunged into the fray behind the grenadiers. Now there was nobody left. All of his staff, all twelve of them, had been hit. Page, his engineer, was wounded and unable to stand, a musket ball having shattered his leg. Lieutenant Jorden, who had been standing by Howe's side earlier that morning when he and Gage and Clinton had hammered out their plans, was dead. From the redoubt, Colonel Prescott looked down during this lull in the fighting and saw Howe there, a lonely, sad man surrounded by a cluster of dead and wounded officers.

As he watched the pitiful remnants of the grenadiers and the supporting battalions limp wearily back toward him, Howe simply could not believe what his tired eyes told him: his right wing, especially the elite troops of the flank companies, were all but annihilated. Grenadier companies, once nearly forty strong, were now eight or nine men led by a sergeant. And there were noticeably fewer officers than there had been an hour ago.

It was not just the carnage that assailed Howe's mind. It was the behavior of the troops, something that he had not anticipated but probably should have. The demise of the light infantry on the beach was the most perplexing, the most disturbing. He had trained light infantry—he had trained many of these very same men at Salisbury Plain only a year before—and though brave, they had behaved as if they were week-old recruits. The grenadiers, too. It was not that there was something unusually deadly about the American musketry. There was good reason to admire the rebels, for disciplined or not they had demonstrated almost unbelievable restraint in holding their fire until the critical moment—not the kind of thing one would expect from a half-trained militia. Yet musketry was musketry, and the American volleys were no more and no less destructive than volleys fired by any entrenched enemy. The grenadiers and the light infantry had withstood that fire, very courageously in fact. But they had not done what veteran troops should do in an assault, not done what they had been ordered to do, not done what their officers had importuned them to do. They did not keep advancing with the bayonet across the danger zone. Instead they stopped and fired, ineffectually, and made themselves easy targets for the rebels lurking behind the walls and the fences.

The plan had seemed so simple when he proposed it at Province House less than twelve hours ago. But now the assumptions on which that plan had been crafted—that the light infantry and the grenadiers could be counted upon to break the American line, with the bayonet and superior discipline—had been proven wrong. The revelation was profoundly unsettling. "It was a moment," he later confessed painfully, "that I never felt before."[10]

So what should he do now? What *could* he do now? He could not simply give up, and not only because of honor. Honor might be a compelling reason, but more important, his force had already sacrificed so much in blood and sweat—and under his command—that it would be unconscionable to leave the field to the rebels. It would be a blow from which Britain would never recover. If left to another day, the rebels would have that much more time to prepare and perfect their defenses.

Howe had no choice. There would have to be another assault.

The battle raging around Breed's Hill was watched like few other battles in history; spectators outnumbered participants by a wide margin. All over Boston, civilians and off-duty Redcoats strained to see the event from rooftops and church steeples, from attic windows and from the summits of the Trimountain, even from fields and hills along the coastline. Reverend Peter Thacher, a young preacher from Malden, rushed from his home to witness the battle from the Chelsea shore, taking careful notes and later penning a report for the Provincial Congress—a report chock full of interesting but questionable details, seen as they were without a spyglass and from nearly a mile away from the battlefield.[11] Morbid curiosity may have compelled some—after all, how often does one get to see a battle?—but for the most part, those who watched the spectacle were genuinely fearful of its outcome and its consequences, of how the bloodletting would disrupt *their* lives. The sight of the brilliant red-and-white ranks advancing in perfect order at the opening of the assault, set off by the contrasting black smoke issuing in vast clouds from burning Charlestown, the puffs of snow-white smoke from the ships crowding the peninsula and from the battery on Copp's, all the pageantry that populated the dreams of restless youths when they ached for adventure . . . but then the awful vision of the defeated red mass, dragging itself away like a cowering wounded beast, leaving behind it a spotty blood trail of the dead and the nearly so. Whig and Tory shared the same dread, for no matter how the battle ended, it meant an end to any hope of peace. An optimist could dismiss Lexington and Concord as mere disturbances, where overzealous men got carried away in defending their homes and their property against a distrusted soldiery, but the battle unfolding before their very eyes could not be so characterized. It was a point of no return, and even if it wasn't "the decisive day . . . on which the fate of America depends," as Abigail Adams wondered, it most certainly marked the end of an era.[12] And *that* was a terrible thing to know.

Even where the struggle couldn't be seen with the naked eye, the percussive sounds of the battle were audible for miles around. Mrs. Adams heard them, and trembled, as she watched the battle from Penn's Hill in Braintree with her seven-year-old son—the future president, John Quincy Adams—and poured out her worry, her excitement, and her heartbreak in a letter to her husband, John, then in Philadelphia celebrating the creation of the Continental Army and the appointment of George Washington.

The battle could be heard in Roxbury, too, and from the upper-story windows of General Thomas's headquarters perched on Meeting House Hill, the action around Charlestown could be clearly seen. It was "at too great a distance for the naked eye to discern what was doing," wrote John Trumbull, adjutant of Spencer's Connecticut regiment and later to become one of America's first great painters. "Charlestown, which lay full in our view, was one extended line of fire."[13] The men in Thomas's command knew that a pitched battle raged to the north, but they had plenty of troubles of their own to keep them occupied. Around noon that day a signal gun sounded the alarm, the bells of the Meeting House clanging in response. The men rushed to their posts, and Thomas immediately dispersed the individual regiments through and around the town. One of them occupied the forward outpost, the "Burying Ground Redoubt," that guarded the intersection where the road to Dorchester branched off from the Roxbury-Boston highway. Spencer's Connecticut regiment and Learned's Massachusetts regiment rushed to the gun emplacements near the parade ground on Meeting House Hill. Thomas didn't have many men to work with, and Ward certainly had none to spare. Thomas was on his own. If the British decided to send the remainder of the garrison in a direct assault on Dorchester Heights, or straight into Roxbury, then it was pretty plain that they couldn't be stopped. But Thomas would make sure that the Redcoats would pay for every inch of ground: he had his men fell apple trees across the streets of the deserted town to form crude barricades, anticipating a last-ditch effort to fight the British house-to-house.[14]

Just what Thomas Gage meant to do at Dorchester and Roxbury isn't exactly clear. He may have planned nothing more than to keep Thomas's command pinned down, unable to come to Ward's aid; he may have intended to keep Ward guessing, to make the rebels think that he just *might* launch a full-scale assault from the Neck that very afternoon. But there is a tantalizing possibility that he had every intention of attacking there—that day or the next, as originally planned. Gage remained at Province House so that he could supervise the day's operations, *all* of the operations, and he kept at his disposal a couple of troopers from the 17th Light Dragoons to act as runners between "the Lines" and headquarters. Gage clearly wanted to keep close tabs on Percy's progress. One wonders if Gage, before it became painfully obvious that the assault on the heights of Charlestown wasn't going quite as planned, might have been seriously contemplating a near-simultaneous offensive from the Neck.

Whatever Gage's intentions were, he hit Roxbury and hit it hard.

Lord Percy commanded the troops at Boston Neck, including the 35th Foot and other regiments not presently with Howe or Pigot. As soon as he spotted Spencer's regiment standing in formation on Meeting House Hill, in full view of the British positions, the effete but highly skilled Percy gave the order and the heavy siege guns along the base of the Neck opened up. They kept up "a pretty smart cannonade . . . in order to amuse the Rebels on that side," Percy reported with characteristic understatement, but to Thomas's boys it was anything but amusing. Big shot from the siege guns flew in profusion from the British batteries and screamed down into Roxbury. Not just solid shot but explosive shell and carcase, too, "with intent to burn that town," according to General William Heath, who was there with Thomas. Fortunately the town didn't catch fire. As a private in Learned's regiment watched in terror, "the balls whistled over our heads and through the houses, making the clapboards and shingles fly in all directions." Spencer's regiment, exposed on the hill, came under direct fire and retreated down the hill and on to the next one. As Adjutant Trumbull brought up the rear, pushing stragglers along, a solid shot flew right by him—"I heard the rush of a heavy ball," he said—and hit a stone wall over which Spencer's men were clambering in panic. The impact knocked a stone loose and drove it straight into the chest of one unfortunate who had just gotten over the wall. He fell, cried out that he was killed, and died in a few minutes. "There was no external wound," Trumbull recalled, "but the body over the region of the heart was black from extravasated blood."[15]

He was, remarkably, the only casualty. But Percy's guns kept up their bombardment all afternoon and well into the night, and there was little Thomas could do but have his men sit tight and wait it out. Late in the afternoon, an enterprising group of his soldiers rolled forward a couple of light fieldpieces and deployed them near the abandoned farmhouse of Enoch Brown, about halfway between the American lines and the British, but the Redcoats easily drove them back.

*T*he cannonade at Roxbury went on unabated, but following the failure of Howe's and Pigot's first attacks a lull descended on the battlefield outside Charlestown. Along the Charles shore, where Howe's shattered battalions tried to take stock of their loss and regroup, shock, mourning, and anger prevailed. Surgeons and surgeon's mates did their best to take care of the wounded, though the numbers were overwhelming. The walking wounded and those who had been dragged from the field by their comrades were quickly ushered into the waiting boats, to be taken back to the military hospitals in Boston. Most, though, lay where they fell, and not even the most dedicated surgeon was about to walk into that no-man's land.

From their observation point at the Copp's Hill battery, John Burgoyne and Henry Clinton had been intently watching the carnage across the river. Even though they saw that "Howe's Left were staggered," Burgoyne was typically confident and buoyant, while Clinton was dour and worried. Gage had given them the responsibility for noting Howe's progress and taking action should he need assistance. Howe had in fact asked Clinton for help. Sir Henry responded, dispatching the 2nd Marines and the 63rd Foot. Clinton and Howe watched as the boats carrying the two battalions crossed the Charles and landed their occupants on the beach. But the new arrivals didn't go anywhere, though they were clearly needed, and both men became concerned: "We perceived them on the beach," Burgoyne reported, "seeming in embarassment which way to march." Clinton didn't hesitate: without asking Gage or Howe for direction, he begged Burgoyne to send his apologies to Gage for leaving without orders, went down to the North Battery wharf, hitched a ride on a boat, and crossed the Charles. Americans troops, in or near Charlestown, targeted Clinton's boat and fired at it. But Clinton landed unscathed, gathered up all the stragglers and lightly wounded men he could find near the beach, and after forming them up into an improvised battalion, led them in column back toward Pigot's wing.[16]

In the rear of the American line, the confusion was at its worst; bravery and cowardice stood side by side. Regiments and individual companies were still making their way toward the battle, but the shot sweeping Charlestown Neck terrified them—one cannon-ball bisected three men in a row in full view of hundreds of their comrades. Many of the reinforcements, including Colonel John Mansfield's regiment, hovered on the mainland side of the narrow isthmus and refused to cross. Hundreds of men loafed or paced aim-lessly on Bunker Hill while Putnam tried to cajole them into moving forward. Putnam had too many irons in the fire, though, and he could scarcely do anything about the frightened or indifferent sol-diers milling near the earthworks that he was still hoping to finish. Colonel Samuel Gerrish led his Massachusetts regiment up the slopes of Bunker, a feat that very nearly destroyed the out-of-shape colonel, "unwieldy from excessive corpulence." Corpulence wasn't Gerrish's only flaw: as soon as he saw the Redcoats re-forming in the distance, he shook in a fearful tremor, and between his gasping breaths he bellowed, "Retreat! Retreat! Or you'll all be cut off!" Gerrish's men, already frightened, had had their fill without even coming close to the action. A few of them kept their cool and fol-lowed their adjutant, a recent Danish immigrant named Christian Febiger, into the battle. The rest scampered back down the hill and toward the Neck. Putnam came up to scold Gerrish for his shameful display of cowardice but was unable to rally the fleeing men.[17]

Old Put's chief role that afternoon, it seemed, was to rally the disheartened and bully the recalcitrant. He rode from one position to another, his sweating red face a storm cloud of fury, a couple of pickaxes and spades lashed to his saddle. At one point he came upon the two artillery sections led by Samuel Gridley and John Callender. Both men, with all four of their guns and the gun crews, were tearing for the rear as fast as they could drag the cannon. Putnam drew up to them and brusquely ordered them to return to the fighting. One of the captains replied that they were all out of ammunition; Putnam, skeptical, leapt from his horse and went straight to one of the guns. He opened one of the side-boxes and found it full of cartridges. Enraged, the red-faced old warrior threatened to kill the artillery officer if he didn't about-face and take his fieldpieces into action. The officer complied, and led his section up Bunker Hill . . . but as soon as he could avoid Putnam he and his men bolted for the rear once again, abandoning the cannon on the hill. The other officer did the same. Of the artillery sent by Ward the day before, only Trevett's two guns remained on the field and ready for action.[18]

Captain John Chester, of Spencer's Connecticut regiment, finally made it to the field after a long and tiring march. Chester's company was the one that had followed Warren and Old Put to the prisoner exchange in Charlestown less than two weeks before. Then, their snappy blue and red uniform coats had befitted the occasion, but now Chester feared that those same uniforms would make his men conspicuous targets. So before leaving their barracks at Christ Church in Cambridge, Chester ordered his men to cover their uniforms with dingy homespun "frocks and trousers." By the time they reached Charlestown Neck, Chester's boys, wearing so much clothing, must have been nearly done in by the heat.

What Chester found as he marched his company out onto the peninsula and up to Bunker Hill shocked him. There was no order, no steady flow of reinforcements up to the lines. Instead, there were only small scattered bands of men, some moving up, most moving back, away from the action. "They were scattered some behind rocks and hay-cocks, and thirty men, perhaps, behind an apple-tree." Shirkers were using any excuse they could find to absent themselves: "frequently twenty men round a wounded man, retreating, when not more than three or four could touch him to advantage." Some of the cowards made no excuse at all; others claimed that they had been ordered to the rear because they were exhausted. One entire company, officers and all, was marching shamelessly back toward the Neck. Chester called to their commander, and getting no response, he grew so incensed that he halted his company and ordered them to cock and level their muskets at the offending troops. Without a word of protest, the retreating men turned around and marched with Chester.[19]

In the lines ahead, the stalwarts remained. They had been giddy, drunk with victory, only minutes before. They had withstood two attacks by the Redcoats. Actually, Howe had ordered only one assault; what the Americans perceived as a second assault was really the second half of the first attack, as the grenadiers and light infantry re-formed and went at it again on their own volition. It made little difference. Cheer after cheer had sounded from the rail fence, the breastwork, and the redoubt, as the rebels watched the vaunted grenadiers and the rest turn their backs and run toward the beach, indifferent to the dead and maimed bodies they stepped on as they hurried to safety. In their ardor, some of the American troops behind the rail fence tried to leap out from behind the barrier and pursue the fleeing Redcoats until their officers prudently stopped them. That euphoria had passed, though, as the lull in the fighting gave the men opportunity to reflect on what might happen next. They were tired and sore, almost drained; their musket barrels were so hot from the prolonged firing that they could scarcely be touched without burning a hand. And as they searched their pockets and their cartridge boxes for the next round, it dawned on them that they couldn't hold out forever. They were down to their last few rounds. Frantically they scrounged cartridges here and there from the boxes of the few men who had been killed or wounded. In the redoubt, Colonel Prescott—who had feared this moment—found a few charges intended for the fieldpieces there, long since gone. He broke open the linen bags and doled out handfuls of gunpowder to the men clustered around him.

They would need every round they could get. As they watched in mounting dread, the amorphous clusters of Regulars were forming into assault columns.

Howe's original stratagem—turning the rebel left flank—didn't work, and there was no sense trying *that* again. Once Howe's mind had cleared, he decided to change his tactics slightly. The rail fence was *deadly*. The defenders were thicker here than at any other sector of the rebel works, as far as he could tell; by no means could it be considered the weak point anymore. The *flèches* had proved murderous. Now he would concentrate his strength, or what was left of it, on the breastwork, while Pigot went up against the redoubt again, and the light infantry performed a feint—not a true assault—toward the rail fence.

And this time Howe would dispense with the long, thin lines of infantry. That had been necessary at first. Infantry in line was an easy target for musketry, to be sure, but it was a less satisfactory target for artillery. Deeper columns presented artillery with rich opportunities for carnage, as a single solid shot could pass through a column front-to-rear, tearing men apart as it passed. After the first attack, though, Howe could say for certain that the rebels had little effective artillery. An assault in column—the preferred formation for such an attack, as the most advanced tactical theorists of the day averred—had great advantages. It could move more quickly, especially across the danger zone within musket range of the enemy; and unlike a line, it did not have to be kept straight and dressed. If infantry in line were to lose its precision, all would soon fall into disorder,

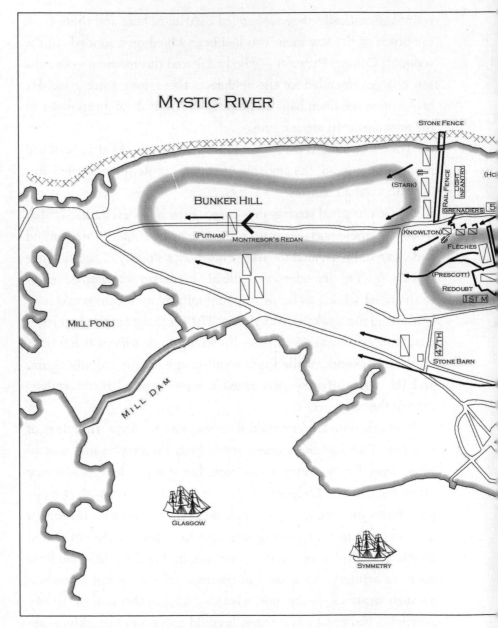

MYSTIC RIVER

STONE FENCE

(STARK)

BUNKER HILL

(PUTNAM)   MONTRESOR'S REDAN

RAIL FENCE

LIGHT INFANTRY

(Ho

GRENADIERS

5

(KNOWLTON)

FLÈCHES

(PRESCOTT)

REDOUBT

1 ST M

MILL POND

47TH

STONE BARN

MILL DAM

GLASGOW

SYMMETRY

The Battle of Bunker Hill, June 17, 1775, 4 P.M.

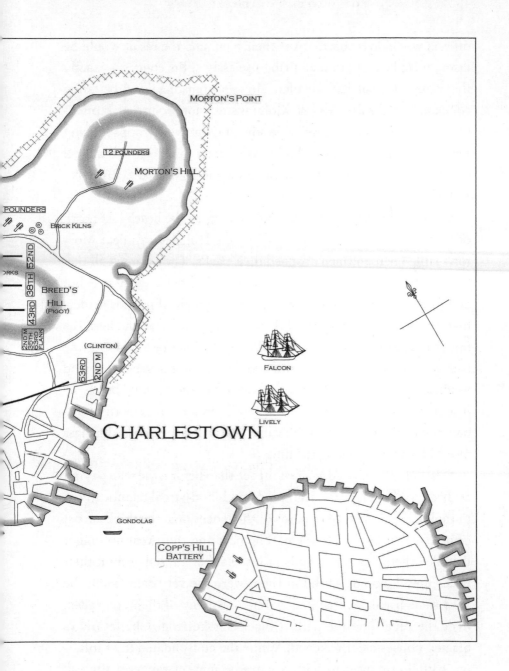

MORTON'S POINT

12 POUNDERS

MORTON'S HILL

POUNDERS

BRICK KILNS

52ND

38TH

ORKS

43RD

BREED'S
HILL
(PIGOT)

2ND M
35TH
63RD
FLANK

(CLINTON)

63RD

2ND M

FALCON

LIVELY

CHARLESTOWN

GONDOLAS

COPP'S HILL
BATTERY

officers would lose control over their men, and the result would be disorganized clumps of men firing uselessly at the enemy—exactly the same fate that had befallen Howe's grenadiers and battalion companies in the first assault. Columns did not require such precision. And there was an intangible advantage as well: troops moving forward quickly in column had a weight, an impetus, that was all but impossible to slow down without defending artillery. Just what Howe needed, in other words.

So the columns formed up, Pigot's wing on the beach just north of Charlestown, near the base of Breed's Hill; Howe's near Morton's Hill. There the men dropped their packs. They weren't all that heavy, containing a blanket and nothing else, but the day was hot and so was the work, and shedding only a couple of pounds made a man feel refreshed. Despite all their exertions and fear and loss, the men were ready as never before. The rebels had tasted blood; the battered Redcoats positively thirsted for it, and for vengeance and vindication. The grenadiers, what was left of them, could barely be held back, shouting "Push on! Push on!" in a red rage born of impatience and hate.[20] Then the drums beat the cadence and the mass moved forward, all along the line.

The columns moved at a faster pace than before, the men paying no heed to the tall grass, trampled and blood-streaked, nor to the potholes, the destroyed remains of the fences, and the thick carpet of bodies that lay before them. The heat and the sweat no longer troubled them, and the clouds of insects that buzzed around their heads they ignored. Ahead of them were the very same men, the very same firelocks, that had claimed so many of their comrades; over the rebel line the pall of black smoke from Charlestown's blazing houses had thickened. While the consolidated light infantry battalion moved to within extreme musket range of the rail fence, the grenadiers and the 5th Foot marched alongside them, then suddenly wheeled toward the *flèches* and the left flank of the earthen breastwork. Two more battalions, the 52nd and 38th, drove straight toward the breastwork; the 43rd moved on the redoubt, and the 47th Foot and the 1st Marines sidled around Breed's Hill to take the redoubt from the south. The artillery—finally— could be put to some good use. The six-pounders had their proper ammunition now, and well out of range of the American muskets, the fieldpieces began to lob solid shot and grape into the exposed left flank of the breastwork.

For some reason, the defenders in the American line found this sight as breathtaking as the first assault: the columns, eight men across but spread out, "the men often twelve feet apart in the front, but very close after one another in extraordinary deep or long files." The slight afternoon breezes had already cleared the field of the smoke from the previous firefight, so the Redcoats were plainly visible. "They looked too handsome to be fired at," one Massachusetts soldier later recalled, "but we had to do it."[21]

The Redcoats met with the same reception they had before. They were close to the rebel positions, so close that in the breastwork they could make out hats and the ominous black muzzles of muskets and individual faces . . . and then the shouted commands, and the ripping volleys flaming from the earthworks. Some of the Redcoats, predictably, stopped to fire, but for the most part they held together and stuck to their path, despite the gaps being torn in the columns. "As fast as the front man was shot down, the next stepped forward into his place; but our men dropt them so fast, they were a long time coming up," one rebel wrote. "It was surprising how they would step over their dead bodies, as though they had been logs of wood."[22] All along the line, the Americans kept loading and firing, loading and firing, until the barrels of their weapons practically glowed. It was tougher work for the rebels now, not for lack of targets, but because by now musket barrels were becoming fouled by the tough, hard residue that comes from burning black powder, and greasy hands could not grip ramrods hard enough to force musket balls down the fouled barrels. Most of the men had fired quite a few rounds during the engagement; one man who had been with Prescott in the redoubt later reported that he had fired at least thirty.[23]

This time the Redcoats would not be deterred. They kept moving, on and on, to the deep ditch that surrounded the redoubt and the very wall of the breastwork. They dropped to the ground by the score, for still the withering fire came from the earthen walls above, and the casualties on the left of the redoubt were the worst. Adjutant Waller, with the 1st Marine Battalion, recalled: "When we came immediately under the work, we were checked by the severe fire of the enemy, but did not retreat an inch. We were now in confusion, after being broke several times in getting over the rails, etc." The 1st Marines suffered grievously. While Waller tried to re-form the two right-hand companies of the Marines—they had stopped dead in their tracks and began to fire up at the redoubt above them, to no effect—a captain, a subaltern, a sergeant, and "many of the privates" were killed by musket-fire from Prescott's men.[24] Worse: the Marines' commander, Major John Pitcairn, was down, mortally wounded. A fair and judicious officer, loved by his Marines, Pitcairn was well known to the men on the other side of the wall—he was the one who led the Redcoats onto Lexington Green on the morning of April 19. A musket ball fired from the redoubt hit Pitcairn in the chest; he collapsed right into the arms of his nineteen-year-old son, Lieutenant Thomas Pitcairn. Later, it would be claimed that Peter Salem, a free African-American man in Nixon's regiment, was the one who fired the fatal shot, but given the distance and the confusion, it is impossible to be certain.

Even now, as the British assault drew to its murderous climax, American reinforcements were still running up to the works and taking part in the battle, without so much as pausing to catch their breath. Chester's Connecticut company hurried down the forward slope of Bunker Hill to watch the grenadiers and the 52nd wheel toward the breastwork. During their descent from Bunker they endured heavy fire from small arms and artillery. "Good God, how the balls flew," Chester's lieutenant Samuel Webb exclaimed. "I confess, when I was descending into the Valley from off Bunker's Hill side by side of Capt. Chester at the head of our Company, I had no more thot of ever rising the Hill again than I had of ascending to Heaven as Elijah did, Soul and Body together."[25]

But all the troops in Cambridge could not stop the British now. Howe's six-pounders raked the breastwork from end to end in a vicious storm of grape and solid shot; the remaining defenders—a patchwork group of men from Prescott's, Doolittle's, Nixon's, and Ward's regiments, and undoubtedly many others, too—either fled outright toward the Neck or desperately scaled the north wall of the redoubt to take shelter there. Redcoats swarmed over the breastwork and toward the redoubt. The end was near.

If the Americans defending the line had had enough, so, too, had the British. These men were not fresh troops. The only unbloodied units on the field, the 63rd Foot and the 2nd Marines, were not brought into this attack. They remained, idle, near the beach where Clinton had left them. The men now storming the breastwork and approaching the redoubt were the very same men who had watched their file mates drop to the ground in heaps during the previous attack. Their blood was up, but they were exhausted and in shock. And in many cases they were all but leaderless. The previous assault had taken a dreadful toll of officers. A sergeant led the grenadier company of the 63rd Foot, as all the officers were down; the 35th's light infantry company had only six privates left, and no officers or NCOs, and so the eldest of the six acted as their commander.

So as the Redcoats reached the base of the redoubt for the last push, their discipline once again began to unravel. All around the outside of the redoubt, the soldiers jumped the ditch and found foothold on the berm, the broad, flat step just in front of the steep walls. It was a safe zone—the rebels in the redoubt could not shoot down at them without making themselves vulnerable to enemy fire; the Redcoats stayed there, cowering, unwilling to move up the wall but knowing that certain death awaited them if they retreated. Their officers begged them, implored them, shouted at them, beat at them, and still they would not move. Here and there a captain or a lieutenant would grab a man by his cartridge box belt and hoist him bodily to his feet, but upon standing would be shot down in an instant. Other officers tried to lead by example, scrambling up the walls to the parapet and calling for their men to follow; they, too, were shot down.

One of these was George Harris, captain of the 5th Regiment's grenadier company. He scaled the north wall of the redoubt, beckoning to his men and shouting for all he was worth, "Come on, come on" . . . but nothing would get them to leave the safety of the berm, and so Harris returned to them, spoke a few inspiring words, and climbed again. Still no response. He repeated the action, but the third time he mounted the parapet an American in the redoubt was waiting for him. The rebel leveled his musket and fired. The ball grazed the top of Harris's head, knocking off his hat and fracturing his skull. Harris toppled backward, unconscious, plummeting right into the waiting arms of his lieutenant, Francis Rawdon. Somehow the skinny twenty-year-old Irish aristocrat managed to catch Harris. Shaken back to consciousness, Harris moaned, "For God's sake, let me die in peace," but his lieutenant wouldn't allow that. Rawdon detailed four men to carry Harris out of the action, which they did—but almost as soon as they left the berm and crossed the ditch, enemy fire struck down three of the four men, one mortally.

Eventually, Captain Harris made it back to the shore and onto a waiting boat. Wrapped in a borrowed blanket, he reached Boston, where surgeons performed a trepanning operation on his contused skull. Though in some discomfort, Harris found the whole thing fascinating. "[The surgeons] indulged me with the gratification of a singular curiosity—fixing looking-glasses so as to give me a sight of my own brain."[26]

With Harris gone, Lieutenant Rawdon took over the company. He made an odd spectacle—skinny, pale, and delicate, his thick black eyebrows contrasting sharply with his immaculate pow-dered wig, topped off by a favorite vanity, an informal round cap made from catskin—but that moment was his first stride toward a long and distinguished career as a general, a politician, and one of the most influential men in British India. Rawdon brought the men to their feet. They hadn't followed Harris, but they did follow the young Irish lord, up the wall and onto the parapet, leaping down on top of the stubborn defenders of the redoubt. Rawdon sur-vived, miraculously, though a ball did punch a hole right through his catskin cap.[27]

And so it was all around the redoubt. On its south, east, and north walls, British Regulars finally got the nerve to make the last push, up, over and down into the fort, just as the Americans inside had exhausted their ammunition. Their once formidable musketry died "like an old candle,"[28] and the Redcoats were upon them. The Regulars had been through hell, several times over, in fact, to get to this point, and had seen their comrades and their officers fall. They had become murderous beasts, all their humanity and compassion having been driven from them. They lunged and thrusted with their bayonets, screaming and roaring as they stabbed and slashed at the provincials in their front. "Nothing could be more shocking," wrote Adjutant Waller, who helped to lead the 1st Marines and the 47th Foot into the redoubt, "than the carnage that followed the storming [of] this work. We tumbled over the dead to get at the living."[29]

A handful hung on in the redoubt, and although few had bay-onets—and even if they had, they would not have been terribly proficient in their use—Prescott's men fought back with what they had, swinging clubbed muskets or hurling rocks. But it was all over. Stark, still at the rail fence, contemplated leading his men over the fence and against the exposed British right flank, but thought better of it—the light infantry was yet in his front, and in an open battle against the infuriated Redcoats his Hampshiremen wouldn't have had a chance. In the redoubt, Prescott finally gave the order to abandon the work, and while the brave or reckless few slugged it out with the British, purchasing time at the cost of their lives, the remainder fled precipitously through the narrow exit in the rear of the fort, while clouds of dust and powder smoke hung in the air, practically obscuring the interior. As they retreated, the British around the redoubt poured a deadly fire into them, restrained only by the Redcoats' fear that they might hit their own men. Peter Brown ran for his life: "I was not suffered to be toutched . . . I jumped over the walls, and ran for about half a mile where balls flew like hailstones and cannons roared like thunder." Amos Farnsworth, who like Brown had been with Prescott from the beginning, was not so fortunate. He "retreated ten or fifteen rods; then I receved a wound in my rite arm, the bawl gowing through a little below my elbow breaking the little shel bone."[30] In their desperation, men shed themselves of everything—muskets, knapsacks, even hats and coats—that might impede their flight to safety.

Abel Parker was one of those who fought to the last possible moment. He was a twenty-five-year-old private in Captain Nutting's company in Prescott's regiment, the very same company that had patrolled the streets of Charlestown while the others dug the redoubt. During the first assault he had taken position in the breastwork, and during the firefight he was wounded, a musket ball entering his leg but not completely disabling him. Like many of the men defending the breastwork, he retreated to the redoubt when the flanking movement came, and just as the Redcoats crested the parapet on the final assault his musket fouled, so choked with powder residue that he couldn't ram down another final charge. He picked up the firelock by the muzzle, crushed a couple of British skulls with the butt-end, and when Prescott shouted the order to retreat he ran for the exit. As Parker wriggled through the narrow port, Redcoats climbed the rear wall of the redoubt to fire on the retreating men. A ragged volley thundered; the man on each side of him stumbled and fell headlong, dead, and a ball passed through his shirtsleeve as he hobbled along, using his useless musket as a crutch. Limping down the steep hillside, by some minor miracle Parker got away to the Neck and safety.[31]

Prescott left last of all . . . calmly, unhurried, backing his way out of the dim and smoke-wreathed interior of the earthen fort as Redcoats came at him with their bayonets. He parried their thrusts with his sword and made his escape, following his men toward Bunker Hill and the Neck.

There weren't very many dead left behind in the redoubt. Howe thought that there might be about thirty. Among them was Joseph Warren, the major general who fought as a private. Warren had stayed until the last, finally getting his wish to fight the British in blood up to his knees. The British were not likely to let him escape. To the Redcoats and their officers he was the most dangerous incendiary in all America, worse than Hancock or Sam Adams, and it was easy for the soldiers to pin upon him the blame for all the horror and blood and pain they had lived through that day. Many of the British knew his face, and Warren's elegant dress contrasted jarringly with the rough work clothing worn by everyone around him. Up until the very last, he stayed in the redoubt, walking calmly behind the men and shouting encouragement, but eventually even he had no choice but to beat a hasty retreat.[32] As he left the redoubt a British musket ball smashed through the back of his skull. Patriotic orators of another generation liked to envision Warren giving a stirring speech in his dying moments, expressing his devotion to American liberties and exhorting all who heard him to similar acts of valor. There was no speech. Warren fell, silently and headlong, facedown in the dirt just outside the redoubt. Of all the men who fell on Breed's Hill, he was the one that the Cause could least afford to lose.

The American retreat from the field was a jarring contrast of discipline and panic. The defenders of the redoubt and the breastwork fled for their lives. They had little choice, as the Redcoats were upon them and firing into their backs as they ran. Stark's and Knowlton's men left as a body, in good order, facing about from time to time to fire at their pursuers, taking cover behind every fence and stone wall that lay in their path, bringing their wounded with them as they withdrew. Chester's company and their comrades at the stone wall behind the main line kept up a steady fire until the retreating men passed them, and then they, too, fell back, not running, but calmly. At the choke-point of Charlestown Neck, though, the masses of rebels—no longer organized into regiments or even companies, but a huddled, frightened mass—created a logjam, as the men tried to get through the narrow passage and away from the peninsula as fast as they could. Somehow, Samuel Trevett, despite all the confusion, managed to extract one of his two fieldpieces from the field. It was the only American cannon saved that day; Trevett's other gun, plus the four guns from Gridley's and Callender's sections, fell into British hands.

Sixteen-year-old fifer John Greenwood was marching toward the battle with his unit, Paterson's Massachusetts regiment, as the first wave of fleeing soldiers reached Charlestown Neck. "Everywhere the greatest terror and confusion seemed to prevail, and as I ran along the road leading to Bunker Hill it was filled with chairs and wagons, bearing the wounded and dead, while groups of men were employed in assisting others, not badly injured, to walk," he recalled years later. "I felt very much frightened, and would have given the world if I had not enlisted as a soldier; I could positively feel my hair stand on end." But as he gaped in terror at the horrific sights, Greenwood saw something that brought back his resolve—a black man, badly wounded in the neck and bleeding profusely, walking calmly away from the battlefield. In awe, Greenwood asked the man if he was in pain. The soldier replied that it didn't hurt much; he only intended to "get a plaster put on it," and then "he meant to return."[33]

The British, by this point, were too exhausted to take the pursuit very far. Howe himself was spent, almost in a daze, an awful sight, with blood from the grass streaked on his snow-white stockings. At this moment, Henry Clinton reported to Howe, bringing with him his contingent—the improvised battalion he had scraped together from the beach, plus the 63rd Foot and the 2nd Marines. Clinton had been watching the action all day and he wanted a piece of it. Howe confessed, sheepishly, that his left flank was all but gone, and then the two generals discussed their plans for the follow-up. Clinton wanted to push the Americans as hard and as far as he could; Howe was understandably more cautious, and only wanted the peninsula swept clear of rebels. His ardor checked, Sir Henry left one hundred men to guard Prescott's redoubt on Breed's, and with all the remaining troops close at hand he marched down the hill toward Bunker, rousting out a few rebels who had taken shelter in houses nearby. As the British advance guard crested Bunker Hill, Clinton momentarily feared that he would find the works there— Montresor's old redan, since slightly improved upon by Putnam— full of diehard rebels. But the fort was empty, and Clinton halted his troops. He sent for Howe's artillery, which came up in short order. Clinton set his men to digging, bolstering up the redan, and there they spent the night.

Opposite them, on Prospect and Winter Hills, the retreating Americans took a stand, digging like demons with the very few entrenching tools that had been saved. "Flung up by morning an entrenchment 100 feet square," Experience Storrs, lieutenant colonel of Putnam's regiment, reported. "Done principally by our regiment under Putnam's directions, had but little sleep the night."[34]

The fighting ended there, but not the casualties. A few rebels strayed a bit forward, onto the Neck, to see what the British were about, and to make sure that their comrades had all made it off safely. Stark's regiment had taken up a position on Ploughed Hill, directly northwest from Bunker Hill. Andrew McClary thought he spotted the British on Bunker Hill preparing for an advance, so he ordered Captain Dearborn to take his company forward toward the Neck and observe. The British guns on Bunker Hill had been firing in the general direction of the rebels, and the ships near the milldam had been firing at the retreating Americans for some time. Dearborn obeyed, going as far as the entrance to the Neck, and there McClary joined him. McClary satisfied himself that the British were not intending to attack and ordered Dearborn to retire to Ploughed Hill. Major McClary was walking back toward Dearborn when a ninepound ball, fired from the *Glasgow* off the milldam, bounded along the ground and hit him right in the back. The hulking McClary had always seemed invincible to his men, but not even he could survive a direct hit from a solid shot. The ball perforated him and sent him sailing three feet into the air, arms and legs flailing crazily, and then he dropped dead, facefirst in the dirt.[35]

Ten

* * *

A GREAT THO DEAR
BOUGHT VICTORY

*O*n both sides, there were leaders willing, even eager, to fight
on. Clinton was restrained only by Howe's appropriate caution. Israel Putnam, on Winter Hill, at one point rallied his men and
formed up for the assault. Putnam should have known better, but he
was not one for worrying about odds. Fortunately for the American
army, a few shots from Howe's twelve-pounders on Bunker Hill dis-
suaded Putnam. William Prescott was at least as anxious as Putnam
for another brawl. Reporting to the Hastings House on the night of
the battle, he offered to rally the army and make an assault on Howe's
positions on Bunker Hill. It would have been suicidal if the Americans
could even have traversed the Neck without suffering ghastly casualties. Ward, who knew better than anyone how exhausted the men
were, and how little powder there was, turned down Prescott's offer.[1]

Tension remained high on both sides for the twenty-four hours following the battle. Individual rebels moved forward from their positions on Prospect Hill during the evening and night of the seventeenth, firing from cover on the 52nd Foot, posted on Charlestown Neck.[2] The British guns on Boston Neck continued to bombard Roxbury into the wee hours of the next morning. The greatest concern at Ward's headquarters, though, was that Howe would push toward Cambridge on the morning of the eighteenth. At Ward's command, one thousand Massachusetts and Connecticut troops set out from Roxbury for Cambridge very late on the seventeenth. They took up positions in the new fortifications on Prospect Hill very early the next morning, crowding them. "We are Reinforc'd by Multitudes which we Don't want," complained Sergeant Knowles of Chester's company, "any more will be a Disadvantage to us."[3] The Americans on Prospect and Winter Hills didn't get much sleep on the night of the seventeenth. They looked to the east, toward the orange glow of Charlestown's smoldering ruin, and waited anxiously for an attack they were sure would come but never did.

*L*ong before the smoke cleared from the redoubt, long before the Redcoats settled in for the night on Bunker Hill, anyone could see that it had been a costly day for the British. No fewer than 226 officers and men had been killed, and a further 828 wounded, of the 2,300 or so who had shoved off from the wharves early that afternoon. Of the injured, about 250 died later from their wounds. The percentage loss appears staggering: some 10 percent killed outright, in excess of 40 percent total casualties. The battle at the rail fence—not at the redoubt—was the true meat-grinder of the affair, for it was the flank companies who suffered most. All of them were shattered, and some had simply vanished: in the grenadier company of the 4th Foot, only four men emerged unscathed; all of the grenadiers of the Royal Welch had fallen save three. Gage's command, so recently and so dramatically strengthened since May, was just about at the level it had been at the time of Lexington and Concord.[4]

To modern eyes, the losses seem almost beyond belief, but it must be remembered that—for that time period—while they were above average, they were actually well within the norm for a pitched battle. It was a small battle, even by the standards of later battles of the Revolution, with fewer than three thousand engaged on each side. Despite the pageantry, and what looks like the formal and slow choreography of battles in the Age of Reason, eighteenth-century warfare was almost unimaginably bloody. British losses in the battle of Bunker Hill were roughly the same, proportionately, as those inflicted on the army of Frederick the Great when it was defeated by a larger Austrian army at Kolin in June 1757. Still, the battle was far bloodier than anything that most Americans had ever seen, and the relatively few veterans in the British ranks who lived through Minden knew—without checking the official numbers—that the battle outside Charlestown was much, much more brutal. The most remarkable thing about the British casualty figures was the unusually high proportion of officers among the dead and wounded: nineteen dead and seventy wounded. Of all the British officers who would fall in battle in the eight years of the Revolution, nearly one-quarter did so at Bunker Hill.

The steady, mournful procession of the wounded into Boston that day, that night, and into Sunday morning quickly removed any doubt as to the awful cost. Loyalists in the town might have been, like Ann Hulton, momentarily "exulting in seeing the flight of our enemies, but in an hour or two we had occasion to mourn and lament."[5] No sooner had the battle ended than the "friends to government" pitched in, sending their "coaches, chariots, single-horse chaises, and even hand-barrows" to the waterfront, where they met the boats coming across the Charles, filled to the gunwales with the wounded and the dying, awash with their blood. John Clarke, a lieutenant in the Marines, watched in horror as a sad and grisly parade of carriages passed by him in the street, full of dead and dying officers. Women—the wives of the slain and the mortally wounded—crowded the streets, wailing over the loss of their husbands and over the sad fate that awaited them, as penniless soldiers' widows, back home in England. The army itself went into mourning, too, over the loss of popular officers. Thomas Pitcairn, weeping over the lifeless body of Major Pitcairn, cried aloud, "I have lost my father!"; some Marines standing in a circle around the pair rejoined, "We have lost *our* father."[6]

Gage's medical service was not prepared for anything like this. The army hospitals in Boston had been designed to handle the demands of a peacetime garrison and little more. The steady influx of grievously wounded men quickly overburdened the existing medical facilities. At the town almshouse, at the workhouse, and in abandoned or vacant shops throughout the town, regimental surgeons established improvised hospitals, but even those were inadequate to the task at hand. Over the next few days, wounded men would perish in the streets for want of care, as the surgeons worked day and night at the grim task of removing musket balls and amputating limbs that had no chance of being saved. An inordinate number of the victims would lose both of their legs. British surgeons found cause for outrage in the course of the countless operations. From many of the wounded soldiers, they had extracted projectiles of a kind they had never seen before: "old nails and angular pieces of iron." The Americans, one surgeon complained bitterly, "had either exhausted their ball, or they were determined that every wound should prove fatal." Rumors soon began to fly around the town that the Americans had even coated their musket balls with a "white crusted matter"—a poison, by which means "an uncommon rancorous suppuration has followed in almost every Case." "The army,"

Adjutant Waller observed, "is . . . full of rage and ferocity at the rebellious rascals who both poisoned and chewed the musket-balls, in order to make them more fatal."[7]

Still, Howe had won a victory, and a significant one. Howe and his men had taken the hill, rousted the rebels from their holes, and put them to flight; with a larger and less bruised force at hand, Howe and Clinton could have easily swept the enemy from Cambridge and Roxbury, too. But the prevailing feeling in Province House and throughout the officers' lodgings in Boston was one of loss . . . not so much of missed opportunities, of errors, but rather that the battle on Charlestown Heights presaged worse things to come, a bloody and indecisive war.

Thomas Gage waited over a week to put to paper his reflections on the battle. It was not until June 25, when he had given up hope of an attack on Dorchester, that he made his official report to Lord Dartmouth. It was a lightly detailed and laconic report, and honest, noting that the victory over the rebels was "dear" and regretting the high losses among the officers. The very next day he penned a much more personal account to his friend Barrington, one that practically dripped frustration and anguish. "The loss we have Sustained, is greater then we can bear," he lamented. "Small Army's cant afford such losses." New York would be much better suited as a base for suppressing the rebellion, he said, and clearly he was just plain fed up with Boston. "I wish this Cursed place was burned!"

Although two very different letters—one measured and cautious, the other personal and open—they shared a striking similarity. Both to Dartmouth and to Barrington, Gage expressed his frustration that nobody in London seemed to realize how much it would take to vanquish the American rebels. For months he had been relating to his superiors that—no matter how much he despised the disaffected colonials—the Americans were resourceful and resilient, a tough opponent, and it would take much, much more than Gage's little army in Boston to subdue them. He knew these things already; the king and his ministers just wouldn't listen. To Dartmouth: "The Rebels are not the despicable Rabble too many have supposed them to be. A recent military spirit, joined with an uncommon degree of Zeal and Enthousiasm, has made them otherwise." And to Barrington: "These People shew a Spirit and Conduct against us, they never shewed against the French, and every body has Judged of them from their former Appearance, and behaviour, when joyned with the Kings Forces in the last War; which has led many into great mistakes. They are now spirited up by a Rage and Enthousiasm, as great as ever People were possessed of." Bunker Hill had proven that beyond a shadow of a doubt, and now it was time that the policy-makers in Britain recognize it and act accordingly. "You must proceed in earnest or give the Business up," he concluded to Barrington.[8]

But Gage saw things from a different perspective than any of his fellow officers in Boston. As governor and military commander, he had to consider the implications of the battle for British policy in North America, and the grand strategy involved should the government truly desire to put down the rebellion.

For Howe, Clinton, and the hundreds of field and company officers in the garrison, the chief thing they noted was the losses the army had suffered, and the negligible profit that could scarcely compensate for those losses. John Burgoyne saw only glory in the day; though he would concede that the battle had been "a complication of horrour," in his mind's eye it appeared as a great and terrible *drama* that had played out on the hills of Charlestown. Burgoyne waxed eloquent about the appearance of the British assaults, the sound and the fury of Charlestown in flames, everything but the hideous sight of the hillside littered with the dead, the maimed, and the crawling wounded. Howe and Clinton didn't see what had so bedazzled their junior colleague. Both concurred with Gage about the losses. "This unhappy day," Howe called it. "I freely confess to you," he wrote to Adjutant General Harvey, "when I look to the consequences of it, in the loss of so many brave officers, I do it with horror. The success is too dearly bought." "A dear bought victory, another such would have ruined us," concluded Clinton.[9]

The officers beneath them in the chain of command were decidedly less circumspect. To them, there was nothing redeeming about the battle at Charlestown. "The victory has cost us very dear," one of them spat, " . . . nor do I see we enjoy one solid benefit in return, or are likely to reap from it any one advantage whatever."[10] These officers, who had seen their men "cut down like grass before the scythe," as Abigail Adams described it, were not inclined to be forgiving of their superiors for their mistakes, whatever they were.[11] Gage, predictably, took his share of the blame, even if he hadn't been present at the battle—and indeed *because* he hadn't been present. Gage hadn't seized Bunker Hill in May, when it was known that the rebels intended to take it for themselves; he neglected to make adequate arrangements for hospitals afterward. Those were the arguments, and if they were a tad unfair it was because Gage's popularity had never been high within his command. Now it would sink even lower.

The most damning indictments, though, were directed at William Howe. Howe drew surprisingly little criticism for his conduct of the battle. He was popular, after all, and anyone who knew him—anyone who had caught a glimpse of him at the end, all alone, bloodstains on his stockings and his face transfigured by shock— knew that his conscience was just as tormented by visions of carnage as anyone's. But those who felt that Howe was to blame didn't hold anything back . . . and they tended to lionize Clinton, arguing that if Sir Henry had been in command, the day would have ended much differently. If Gage and Howe had followed Clinton's advice, landing troops in the rear of the redoubt while pummeling the rebel left with cannonfire from ships in the Mystic, one officer opined, then the Americans "must have surrendered instantly or been blown to pieces. But from an absurd and destructive confidence, carelessness or ignorance, we have lost a thousand of our best men and officers and have given the rebels great matter of triumph by showing them what mischief they can do us." For that, he argued, Howe was to blame: "We are all wrong at the head. . . . This madness or ignorance nothing can excuse. The brave men's lives were wantonly thrown away. Our conductor as much murdered them as if he had cut their throats himself on Boston Common." And then a chilling line: "Had [Howe] fallen, ought we to have regretted him?"[12]

Gage's officers liked to say that at Bunker Hill they had "taken the bull by the horns," and Gage himself had written the same thing to Barrington, adding optimistically that his army was "[a]ttacking the Enemy in their strong parts." One of Clinton's close friends, the artillerist Colonel William Phillips, used Gage's words to mock him and Howe as typical graduates of the unimaginative "American school" of tactical thought. "A *German*," he wrote Clinton, "would have taken the *Bull* by the *ribs* . . . and not by the *Horns*."[13]

It was easy and normal to blame Howe. Whether he deserved the blame or not was a different matter, but since it was he who had both planned and carried out the attack, there was no way he could completely escape the wrath of embittered subordinates and rival generals. Yet as they reflected on their experience, as they talked in hushed tones among themselves and compared notes, the British officers who had been in the fighting on June 17 came to a truly disturbing, if not altogether surprising, conclusion. The *real* failure on that bloody day was not one of command, but of discipline; those at fault were not the leaders, but the men in the ranks. Very few would question the bravery of the individual Redcoat. Yet the men didn't listen to orders; they panicked at the first volleys; they allowed the rebels to force them into futile firefights, clustering together like scared sheep in the open, succumbing to the instinct to fire back rather than following the commands to move on with the bayonet. "Like young soldiers, [they] halted under the enemy's fire, and [they] severely suffered for it," observed one officer. Adjutant Waller saw it as he tried to coax his flustered Marines past the fences before the redoubt. Rawdon saw it, too, and it troubled him: "Our confidence in our own troops is much lessened since the the 17th of June. Some of them did, indeed, behave with infinite courage, but others behaved as remarkably ill. We have great want of discipline both amongst officers and men."[14]

Such remarks filtered upward, through the ranks to the generals themselves, and the knowledge truly shook them. Howe hinted at it in his official report—"not with the greatest share of discipline," he remarked about the muddled attack of the grenadiers on the rail fence—but Clinton and Burgoyne came right out and uttered the unthinkable truth. "There is a melancholy reason" for the disproportionately high officer casualties, John Burgoyne wrote. "Though my letter passes in security, I tremble while I write it; and let it not pass even in a whisper from your Lordship to more than *one* person: the zeal and intrepidity of the officers . . . was ill seconded by the private men. Discipline, not to say courage, was wanting. In the critical moment of carrying the redoubt, the officers of some corps were almost alone; and . . . all the wounds of the officers were not received from the enemy." Clinton was so unnerved by this truth that, even in the many notes he scrawled to himself, he felt compelled to write this one in cipher: "All was in Confusion officers told me that they could not command their men and I never saw so great a want of order."[15]

It was with good reason that Burgoyne asked for secrecy and Clinton hid the thought from everyone's eyes but his own. In Britain, the opposition Whigs were on the lookout for anything that might bolster their stance against the war; an army that was similarly opposed to the war was about the best counterargument they could muster. "I do not mean to convey any suspicion of backwardness in the cause of Government among the soldiery," wrote Burgoyne, "which ignorant people in England are apt to imagine; and as little would I be understood to imply any dislike or ill will to their officers."[16] The notion itself could topple the war effort.

But the idea that the men couldn't be controlled was unsettling in a purely tactical sense, too. Lexington and Concord had pointed to it; and instead of redeeming the Redcoats' already besmirched reputation for poor discipline, Bunker Hill only confirmed it. All of the officers, all of the high command in Boston, found the huge losses of June 17 shocking, but the really shocking thing was that the men couldn't be trusted. *This*, and not the depth of the slaughter, was what so haunted Howe as he watched his nearly broken army flee back to the beach . . . "a Moment I never felt before."

On the other side of the Charles, the Americans didn't know exactly what to make of the battle. Clearly, it hadn't been a victory. The British had won the day—and not because there was some kind of silly notion prevalent in the eighteenth century that the army that physically held the battlefield once it was all over was the victor. The British had accomplished what they had set out to do: they took Breed's Hill, Bunker Hill, and the entire Charlestown peninsula, and drove the Americans back to Cambridge. *That* was a victory.

But American casualties were light, at least in comparison with Howe's: about 139 killed, 278 wounded, and thirty-one captured. The heaviest losses, not surprisingly, took place in the redoubt and the breastwork near the battle's end. Prescott's regiment lost forty-three killed or missing, forty-six wounded; Bridge's, seventeen killed and twenty-five wounded; Frye's, ten killed, thirty-eight wounded, and four missing. Stark's regiment, at the rail fence, lost fifteen killed and forty-five wounded. The small number captured is significant: even in the chaos of the retreat, the rebels managed to drag off most of their wounded, leaving behind only those so severely injured that they couldn't move—or be moved—to safety in time. Most of them would die in British captivity. Burgoyne had suggested releasing them, but British surgeons had no choice but to treat their ghastly wounds. The shock and infections that followed amputations were their killers, not the British. One captive who survived was dragged along when the British evacuated Boston and sailed for Halifax; he wasn't released until precisely one year after the battle, when he made his way back to Massachusetts to demand his back pay![17]

The losses among the officers were not particularly high, either, but were significant enough. Colonel Thomas Gardner was mortally wounded as he led his Massachusetts regiment into action at the breastwork, stoically commanding his frantic son—his lieutenant colonel—to take over. At the end of the battle, four men removed him from the field on an improvised stretcher fashioned from blankets and poles; he would die on July 3, after a final visit from his son. Moses Parker, the lieutenant colonel of Bridge's regiment, fell when a musket ball shattered his knee. The British took him prisoner and carried him back to Boston, where he died after surgeons removed his wounded limb. Major Willard Moore led Doolittle's regiment into action near the close of the engagement; he was hit twice—in the thigh and through the torso—in the hail of musketry that swept the peninsula as the British swarmed over the rebel earthworks. Andrew McClary was perhaps the most promising soldier to die on the field; his grisly end robbed the soon-to-be Continental Army of one of its potentially greatest leaders. Four other colonels—Ebenezer Bridge, John Nixon, Jonathan Brewer, and Richard Gridley—were wounded but survived. There was no dearth of physical courage in Artemas Ward's army.[18]

The death most keenly felt, though, was that of Joseph Warren. He "fell . . . with as much Glory as Wolfe on the plains of Abraham," lamented his friend and colleague James Warren, "after performing many feats of Bravery, & exhibiting a coolness & conduct which did Honor to the judgment of his Country in appointing him a few days before one of their Major Generals." For days, no one knew for sure that the great incendiary was dead, though there were persistent and conflicting rumors to that effect. No one, no American at least, had witnessed his sad end. His younger brother John rode to Cambridge as soon as he heard the sound of the cannonfire, and was told at Medford early the next morning that Joseph was missing. "I went immediately to Cambridge enquired of almost every Person I saw . . . Some told me that he was undoubtedly alive and well; others that he was wounded; and others that he fell on the field." Later, a British officer, who had been supervising burial details on Breed's Hill after the battle, confirmed that he had "stuffed the scoundrell with another Rebel into one hole and there he and his seditious principles may remain." Even in death, Warren was hated above all others by the Redcoats. It wasn't until many months later that Warren's brothers and a handful of friends, including a silversmith and prominent Patriot named Paul Revere, went to Charlestown to look for Dr. Warren's remains. They found a corpse that seemed to fit with the evidence they had—it bore a bullet-hole through its skull—and Revere examined it closely. There, in its mouth, were two artificial teeth and a silver wire . . . placed there, in the spring of 1775, by Revere himself. It is possibly the first postmortem identification by dental records in American history.[19]

It would be impossible to replace Joseph Warren. For two months he had almost single-handedly supervised the war effort, acting as a bridge between the Provincial Congress, the Committee of Safety, and the generals. Respect for the doctor was universal, and hence he wielded great power without exciting the distrust of either the military leaders or the politicians. Yet the Provincial Congress *had* to replace him. On Monday, June 19, the delegates in Watertown elected James Warren of Plymouth as president in the doctor's stead. The next day they promoted William Heath to the rank of major general to fill the vacancy in the command structure. Heath was probably better suited to the post than Joseph Warren had been, but the choice of James Warren as president of the Congress was hardly an ideal choice. Although James Warren was a good and honest man, close to the late president and to the Adamses, he had no regard at all for Artemas Ward, a fact that did not bode well for the future of Massachusetts and its army.[20]

James Warren's dislike of Ward was so intense that he actually blamed the general for the failures at Bunker Hill. "Had our brave men, posted on Ground Injudiciously at first taken, had a [Charles] Lee or a Washington Instead of a General destitute of all military ability & skill to command them," he fumed to John Adams in Philadelphia, "it is my opinion the day would have terminated with as much Glory to America as the 19th of April." Everything, in fact, that was wrong with the army was Ward's fault. "You would tremble to be possessed of the true state of [the army]," Warren wrote Sam Adams four days after the battle. "Fine fellows you know our countrymen are; and want nothing but a general of spirit and abilities to make them a fine army. . . . Could you believe, [Ward] never left his house on Saturday. . . . I wish that was the worst of it."[21]

But James Warren was alone in his censure of Ward. Sam Adams, writing from Philadelphia, reproved Warren for his words: "Take Care lest Suspicions be carried to a dangerous Length. Our Army have behavd valiantly. There may have been an Error: but that Error may have proceeded not from a Want of Spirit but a Want of Judgment." If the harried commander-in-chief didn't get any credit for whatever good came from that day, he didn't take any blows for it, either, and undoubtedly anyone who even vaguely understood the events of the seventeenth could see that Ward's caution likely saved the army from a truly irreparable disaster. Still, as the participants thought back on those events, the missed opportunities and the dangerous flirtation with catastrophe, they couldn't help but dwell on the might-have-beens . . . and those responsible for keeping victory just out of reach. Men who had been in the breastwork and the redoubt faulted the Connecticut and New Hampshire boys at the rail fence for not pouncing on Howe's exposed right flank during the final assault. Those at the rail fence felt just the opposite: "Had the province [i.e. Massachusetts] Troopes supported our Connecticut [men] we should have made a longer Stand," thought James Knowles, a sergeant in John Chester's company.[22]

The Committee of Safety wanted to make some sense of the battle, too, and immediately it launched an investigation to determine what, if anything, had gone wrong on the Charlestown hills. It eschewed any regional bickering, yet found that there were indeed villains to be punished. In the month following the battle, four officers stood before courts-martial at Cambridge to answer for their conduct. Samuel Gerrish was found guilty of cowardice for his embarrassing loss of self-control on Bunker Hill, as was John Mansfield; John Callender—who had earned a redoubtable enemy in Israel Putnam—was likewise condemned for his role in withdrawing his fieldpieces from the redoubt at the height of the action. Gerrish, Mansfield, and Callender were cashiered; Callender, to his credit, would later join the Continental Army and redeem his tarnished reputation. James Scammon was also court-martialed, but the court could not find any fault with him—he had followed his confusing orders as he had understood them, and Scammon was acquitted accordingly. Scammon had the proceedings of his court-martial published, hoping to vindicate himself. Yet his performance in the battle permanently soiled his record. Over a year later, he would petition the Massachusetts government, offering to raise a regiment for Continental service. He wanted to "shew his

Country that he is ready at all Times to risque his Fortune and Life in defence of it."[23]

Both the Provincial Congress and the Committee of Safety shied away from making any larger accusations of failure or incompetence. The men who were probably most responsible for the failures of June 17—William Prescott and Israel Putnam, if it were indeed one of them who chose Breed's Hill over Bunker—drew no rebukes for their mistakes. The Committee mentioned only that the two men, plus Gridley, had fortified Breed's Hill "by some mistake"; James Warren, writing in confidence to John Adams, likewise remarked that the hill was "Ground Injudiciously at first taken." But that was it. The bravery of Prescott and Putnam had been so remarkable as to put everything they did, even if poorly thought out, well beyond reproach. Prescott had said that if his men had had more ammunition, they could have held off the British indefinitely. The tough old colonel surely believed it. Whether it was true or not the members of the Committee thought it made perfect sense, so in their analysis *that* was the reason that their forces had been driven from the field.[24]

Overall, though, the American reaction to the battle was one of euphoric jubilation. "I think yesterday was a Glorious Day to N[orth] America," wrote James Knowles of Chester's company, who saw in the resilience of the defenders "proof of Yankey Bravery." John Stark, not one for hyperbole or overstatement, reported to the New Hampshire Provincial Congress that "we remain in good spirits as yet, being well satisfied that where we have lost one they lost three." Nathanael Greene quipped, "I wish [we] could Sell them another Hill at the same Price as we did Bunkers Hill."[25]

Most ascribed the good fortune of the day to the hand of the Almighty God. But God had help that afternoon on Breed's Hill, and if there had been villains and cowards, there were many more heroes who had worked to further His inscrutable will—Prescott above all. No one would deny Prescott's coolness under fire and his unpretentious heroism. Stark, too, and Putnam, but in the rosy afterglow of the battle, it was Prescott who got the accolades, rightly or wrongly. And even in the confusion of the action, where so many witnesses could not recall exactly what they had done and seen, and when they had done it or seen it, the courage of a few individuals stood out. None received more praise than Salem Poor, a private in the company of Captain Benjamin Ames, in Frye's regiment. Poor was a former slave from Andover who had purchased his freedom at the age of twenty-one for an enormous sum of money. He was twenty-seven when he fought at the breast-work with Frye's regiment, where he performed so well that no fewer than three colonels—Jonathan Brewer, Thomas Nixon, and Prescott himself—and eleven other officers felt compelled to peti-tion the Provincial Congress for his recognition. "Under Our Own observation, Wee declare that a Negro Man Called Salem Poor . . . in the late Battle at Charlestown, behaved like an Experienced Of-ficer, as well as an Excellent Soldier. To Set forth Particulars of his Conduct Would be Tedious, Wee Would Only begg leave to say in the Person of this Sd. Negro centers a Brave & gallant Soldier— the Reward due to so great and Distinguisht Caracter, Wee Submit to the Congress." Poor was only one of at least 103 non-whites— eighty-eight African-Americans and fifteen Native Americans—in the American fortifications on June 17.[26]

The triumphant defeat at Breed's Hill, and the heroes it created, worked like a tonic on the morale of the Grand American Army. That army had not been without hope; at Lexington and Concord, on Grape Island and Noddle's, American soldiers had driven away the vaunted and hated Redcoats. But in the battle at Charlestown, the American army had been in a *real* battle, not just a skirmish, and although they could not hold their ground indefinitely they had indeed held their ground longer than anyone—British or rebel—

would have expected. It was probably more of a surprise to the Americans than it was to Gage and his officers.

In a way, that was a bad thing, for one of the lessons the American rebels took from the battle of Bunker Hill was an unsubstantiated faith in themselves. Not that they were poor fighters; the British would freely acknowledge that the Americans proved themselves fierce, determined, and brave. That faith was misplaced because it put too much stock in the virtues of half-trained, poorly disciplined amateurs. The men under Prescott, Putnam, and Stark did not understand that the British Regulars they met on June 17 were only slightly less inexperienced than themselves, and it was that inexperience that kept the battle from turning into a bloody and humiliating defeat for the American army.

*T*here was another lesson that Americans took from the battle, and it was a lesson that had much greater importance in the moment: fortifications, the rebels learned, are good.

Even the most ardent believer in the martial superiority of American citizen-soldiers had to admit that the troops around Charlestown held out so long because they had dug in. An open battle against the British Regulars, under almost any circumstances, would have ended much differently. And so, from the night of the seventeenth to the end of the siege nine months later, the men at Cambridge and Roxbury took up the spade and the mattock with a vigor bordering on mania. Putnam had started with the fortifications on Winter Hill only hours after the retreat from the Charlestown peninsula. Soon redoubts, redans, primitive *flèches*, and lines of trench rose from the ground as if summoned by God, surrounding Chelsea, Malden, Medford, Roxbury, and Dorchester. The "Brookline Fort" watched over the mouth of the Charles, reinforcing Fort Number One near Cambridge; trench lines popped up on the Dorchester hills closest to Roxbury; and in Roxbury itself, Thomas had his men build the formidable "Roxbury Fort" on the rise immediately behind Meeting House Hill. Virtually every swamp, creek, and meadow near the approaches to Cambridge and Roxbury was graced with some kind of fort, and as often as possible, with light fieldpieces to give them some bite. Sometimes the men took it upon themselves to dig in, without direction or command, exhibiting more zeal than common sense. General Thomas protested when Greene's Rhode Islanders began entrenching— without his authorization—near their Jamaica Plain camp, and ordered them to stop. The Rhode Islanders "swore that they would not, and [Thomas] thought best to let them go on with the work."[27]

In the main, though, the new fortifications—if somewhat randomly and overeagerly placed—went up under the scrutiny of engineers who, if amateur, nonetheless proved to be highly talented. One of them was Lieutenant Colonel Rufus Putnam of David Brewer's Massachusetts regiment. Putnam, distantly related to Old Put, had seen some action in the French and Indian War, but his knowledge of engineering came solely from his successful career as a millwright. Assisting him was a young man who would go on to great things. Just approaching his twenty-fifth birthday, Henry Knox was an ardent patriot with no military experience whatsoever. In his hometown of Boston, Knox ran a small bookstore, where he stocked—and read—many volumes on strategy and tactics, on artillery and siegecraft. One of his more noteworthy customers was none other than Nathanael Greene, who whiled away more than a few hours discussing the military art with the eager and charismatic proprietor. Knox left Boston sometime after Lexington and Concord, eloped with his love, Lucy Flucker, the daughter of prominent Boston Tories, and moved with her to Worcester. But more often than not, the big man—over six feet tall and of a gigantic build, tending toward obesity but not quite there yet—could be found in and around Cambridge, though he held no military rank. He may have been with Richard Gridley on the night of the sixteenth, assisting with the placement of the Breed's Hill redoubt. In the days following the battle, he was much in demand as an engineer. What he knew of building forts came exclusively from books, but clearly Knox had a talent and a zeal that more than compensated for his lack of actual experience.

The Committee of Safety understood that there was much more that had to be done if the army were to be prepared for a further British offensive, which everyone this side of the Charles assumed was a foregone conclusion. The army's combat losses had been minimal, but Ward and Thomas were still short of men, and even worse, they were short of supplies and munitions. Three days after the battle, the ordnance master at Cambridge Store estimated that there was about 2¼ tons of gunpowder in the depot, nearly half of which he had to send to Watertown by order of the Committee of Safety—the Committee, it seems, worried that the supplies in Cambridge were just too vulnerable to capture by the Redcoats.[28] The scarcity of muskets was greater than before, as many of the men flying up Charlestown Neck had thrown away their weapons as they ran for their lives. For several weeks following the battle, the Committee pulled out all the stops in its search for usable muskets. There was absolutely no cloth ing to be had in Watertown, and blankets remained a crying need. General Ward probably fumed over the blanket shortage more than anything else. "If our men must be in the rain without covering," he asked the Committee of Supplies, "and we should be attacked Immediately after . . . what are we to Expect? Destruction."[29] There was no immediate remedy, it seemed, for the army's lack of bayonets, and many—including Prescott—firmly believed that the men in the redoubt and the breastwork would have made a better account of themselves if they had had bayonets like the Redcoats did. Supplying them would be a troublesome business—the Yankee troops carried so many different kinds of firearms, many of which would have to be altered, and the bayonets themselves would have to be individually hand-fitted. As a stopgap expedient, General Ward proposed that the Committee procure simple spears, with an iron head surmounted on a twelve-foot wooden shaft. It was a desperate measure, to be sure, but one that the Committee heartily adopted, as did the Provincial Congress. They were in such haste to get these relics of a bygone age into the hands of the troops manning the lines that the Congress even authorized the blacksmiths contracted for the work to labor on the Sabbath day.[30]

Finding men to bolster the siege lines evolving around Boston was, if anything, harder than equipping them. The Committee of Safety had called up the militia "in the neighboring towns" on the day of the battle, and the day after, but sent them home promptly, and no new recruits were forthcoming. Despite the boost to morale after the battle, entire units were leaving the army without apology. When Ward mistakenly had Samuel Trevett—the artillery captain who had performed so well—arrested for misconduct, his entire company deserted, returning only after the Committee of Safety intervened and ironed everything out. A company from Salem followed their lieutenant when he left the army; another from Bradford deserted as a body and went home. Fortunately the Provincial Congress stepped in, strong-arming the individual communities to punish and return all men who left the camps without leave.[31] The other colonies failed to furnish many more men, the plaintive appeals of the Congress notwithstanding. Connecticut raised more troops, but kept them close by, fearing a British invasion of New York; Rhode Island forwarded a few men; and New Hampshire raised a third regiment, under Enoch Poor, and sent it on to Boston. Even then, disputes over rank threatened to gut the New Hampshire contingent. Stark again refused to bow to the authority of Nathaniel Folsom, the elected commander of all New Hampshire forces, and vowed that he would "take his pack and return home (and meant, I suppose, to take his men with him)," Folsom griped.[32]

Faced with such troubles, the Provincial Congress fretted and worried about prosecuting the war. The delegates feared an attack on Cambridge, and even though the British were bombarding Roxbury almost daily, they ordered Thomas to send a regiment to reinforce Ward. Ward, thankfully, pointed out that Thomas was undermanned, and the Congress relented. Then the Congress ordered two regiments from Plymouth to come to Cambridge, but the authorities in Plymouth wailed that their nearly inaccessible harbor was most assuredly bound to be assaulted by the British, so Congress let them keep the troops and even sent more to shore them up. The delegates at Watertown sorely missed Joseph Warren's calming voice and guiding hand.

*I*t was well that the British remained so quiet in the weeks after Bunker Hill. Gage and Howe had resigned themselves to sitting tight and waiting to see what the Americans were up to. Only Clinton pushed for action, and he was relentless about it. Sir Henry saw no reason why the attack on Dorchester Heights, planned earlier, should be aborted after the bloody day at Charlestown. On the day after the battle, he urged the taking of Foster's Hill, on the western edge of the Dorchester peninsula; if the Americans were to place batteries on Foster's, Clinton argued, then the British positions on Boston Neck—indeed Boston itself—would be untenable. Gage's engineers and artillerists shot him down—in the unlikely event that the Americans had the nerve to take Foster's themselves, then British guns on land and on sea would "blow them to atoms." But Clinton nagged, and Gage relented. There would be an attack on Dorchester Heights on the next Saturday, June 24, with Clinton leading the main force in an amphibious assault. Admiral Graves would supply the requisite naval support, and William Howe would push on the new rebel lines nearest Charlestown Neck to provide Clinton with an appropriate diversion. Two thousand Redcoats—more than five full battalions, plus a couple of artillery companies—were armed and provisioned and ready to go Friday evening. They waited by their boats all that night; by six o'clock that morning, the swarms of boats and armed gondolas were moving stealthily toward Dorchester Point. But Gage had a change of heart before the flotilla made landfall. He ordered Clinton to abort the attack, compelling Sir Henry to send a courier by boat in order to recall the troops.[33]

It would be the last time the British would attempt a large-scale attack during the long siege of Boston.

Eleven

* * *

NEW LORDS,
NEW LAWS

*I*n the last few days of June, the siege of Boston was finally beginning to look something like a siege. The new British earthworks on and around Bunker Hill were finished, and they were impressive, fronted by ditches, fraises, and chevaux-de-frise. Putnam's three original forts protecting Cambridge were now joined by dozens of others. Howe's Redcoats and Ward's rebels stared at one another from their respective redoubts and redans and *flèches*, occasionally engaging in firefights that served to break the boredom and little else.

The real action, if indeed there was any, was to the south, around Roxbury and Boston Neck. John Burgoyne commanded the British lines there. The British had mounted no serious attempt to force Thomas's lines at Roxbury since the aborted amphibious assault of

June 24, but in the meantime they did their best to make things hot for the Americans. The main British and American fortifications were about eight hundred yards apart; the forward picket posts were separated by a mere 250 yards, close enough to allow British and American pickets to shout insults, good-natured and otherwise, at each other. Roxbury itself had become a doleful sight. The inhabitants had long since fled; "the once busy, crowded street is now occupied only by a picket-guard. The houses are all deserted, the windows taken out, and many shot-holes visible. Some have been burnt, and others pulled down to make room for the fortifications."[1]

Every couple of days, the British guns in the Lines would open up for a few hours, throwing "balls, bomb-shells, carcases, & stink pots" into the American forts or right into the dilapidated houses in town. Sometimes the sloops in the harbor chimed in, too. The Americans rarely responded, for although a few medium and heavy guns had been dragged into Roxbury Fort and some of the advanced works, ammunition was scarce and there was no sense wasting that precious commodity by throwing it away on the British works. Collecting spent British ammunition continued to be one of the main activities for Thomas's boys. They found it a lucrative pastime. General Thomas had promised a reward for each cannonball recovered and brought to his headquarters, as much as two gallons of rum for a twenty-four pounder. It wasn't without its dangers. Men unfamiliar with artillery fire would try to stop the slow-moving shot with their feet, "by which means several brave lads had their feet badly crushed."[2]

There was some sparring between the rival pickets. The house and shop of Enoch Brown became a point of contention, as the Redcoats often sent pickets there to watch the rebels and fire on their work details. The Americans tried repeatedly to destroy the house, resulting in several sharp skirmishes, until finally on July 8, the rebel batteries opened fire on it—a rare occasion—and on the floating batteries that had drawn close to retaliate. Brown's house burned to the ground. Three days later the Americans managed to destroy Brown's shop, too, and then life in the lines—in Cambridge and in Roxbury—reverted to its previous routine: parading, cleaning barracks, digging entrenchments, alarms, bombardments, more alarms and more bombardments.

Almost nobody noticed when, on Sunday, the second of July, George Washington came to town.

*G*eorge Washington left New York City on June 26, 1775, with Charles Lee and his staff, leaving behind Philip Schuyler to take care of military affairs in his native New York. Washington was in a hurry, for although the news of the battle near Charlestown was encouraging—militia *could* stand up to British Regulars after all—there were a million things that had to be attended to, and until he got to Cambridge he really had no idea what was expected of him. But his arrival was a cause for great celebration throughout New England, and Washington didn't have the heart to show anything but humble gratitude for the way that every town he passed through lionized him and Lee. The party rode through New Haven—where a crowd of Yale students escorted him from the town—and into Massachusetts, where he stopped at Springfield. Here, Dr. Benjamin Church and Moses Gill (a key member of the Committee of Supplies) greeted him, and at the order of the Provincial Congress, the two men chaperoned Washington and his entourage through Worcester and on to Watertown. At Watertown, Washington and Lee were obliged to make an appearance at a session of the Provincial Congress, on Saturday, July 1.

The Congress was delighted to see the two generals. Massachusetts was not so jealous of its army or its war effort that it could not rejoice in seeing the Virginian and the Englishman taking over its direction. John Hancock, who had as much reason to resent Washington as anybody, generously set the example: "he is a Gent[lema]n you will all like," Hancock had written to Joseph Warren on June 18.[3] The delegates were genuinely relieved that the Continent had rallied around New England, that it had adopted the Cause and the war with little hesitation. James Warren, of course, was happy that somebody—*anybody*—would supersede Artemas Ward; but most delegates, though not sharing Warren's jaundiced estimation of their own Ward, still understood that the transfer of power was all for the best.

That afternoon, after discussing recruitment and powder supplies, the delegates at Watertown treated Washington and Lee to a hospitable address. They thanked Washington for his ardor and zeal, for his sacrifice in setting aside a comfortable life to hazard all for the Cause. But they were also painfully honest with the new commander-in-chief. The army outside Boston was not what it should have been, and they wanted to prepare Washington for the shock. "We wish," they confessed, "you may have found such regularity and discipline already established in the army, as may be agreeable to your expectations. The hurry with which it was necessarily collected, and the many disadvantages, arising from a suspension of government, under which we have raised and endeavored to regulate the forces of this colony, have rendered it a work of time." Disciplining the army to Washington's satisfaction, then, would have to be done by Washington. And, they warned the general, the soldiers themselves were still not really soldiers. "The greatest part of them have not before seen service; and although naturally brave, and of good understanding, yet, for want of experience in military life, have but little knowledge of divers things most essential to the preservation of health and even life. The youth of the army are not possessed of the absolute necessity of cleanliness in their dress and lodging, continual exercise, and strict temperance, to preserve them from diseases frequently prevailing in camps, especially among those, who, from their childhood, have been used to a laborious life."[4]

Washington must have found the speech disconcerting, but he had no time to make a formal reply, aside from briefly thanking the Congress for its hospitality. A detailed response would have to wait for a few days. Lee also made a short address, uncharacteristically modest for the self-promoting soldier: "You may depend . . . gentlemen, on my zeal and integrity; I can promise you nothing from my abilities."[5]

The next morning, Washington and Lee set out for Cambridge, three miles away.

Cambridge had been waiting for them. Ward waited, too, and without a trace of jealousy or dread, but rather relief: the burden he had borne for more than two months was about to be lifted from his exhausted shoulders. The entire camp had known about Washington's appointment for nearly a week. On the morning of the twenty-ninth, Ward celebrated the news—subtly—in his orders for the day: the "parole" (password) throughout the army was to be "Washington," the countersign "Virginia." Ward wanted to impress Washington: in the very last orders he issued as commander-in-chief, Ward demanded that the barracks be swept clean and repaired, that the soldiers refrain from profane language, and that lewd women be removed from the camps.[6]

The new generals rode into Cambridge around noon on the second, a Sunday. Ward had planned a grand reception for them: several of the Cambridge regiments were to parade on the Common, accompanied by a corps of twenty-one drummers, to salute General Washington and to witness the formal transfer of command. But heavy rains fell late that morning, driving the paraded regiments to scamper for cover, and the ceremony had to wait for the next day. The bad weather didn't discourage Artemas

Ward, who was so elated by his imminent demotion that he cast his Puritanical reserve to the side and threw a spectacular party for his senior officers that night, with General Washington as the guest of honor. In Mr. Hastings's long, narrow dining room, Washington, Lee, Ward, Putnam, and the rest reveled and joked over wine and punch into the wee hours of the morning. At one point, the members of this distinguished assemblage grabbed Caleb Gibbs, the young adjutant of Glover's Marblehead regiment, and hoisted him—while still seated—atop the dining table, chair and all, and they howled with laughter as Adjutant Gibbs regaled them with bawdy drinking songs. The sentries posted on the Common probably couldn't believe what they saw in the wide-open windows of the candlelit dining room at headquarters—the pious General Ward and the grave, stately newcomer behaving like common hard-working, hard-drinking farmers, like *men*.[7]

But on the next day, the third, it was back to business. Washington and Ward appeared on the Common before a formation of infantry drawn up in a hollow square, where Washington delivered a brief and unmemorable speech, read the text of Psalm 101—*I will sing of mercy and judgement unto Thee, O Lord*—and that was it. The soldiers barely took notice of Washington's arrival or of the ceremony. "This morning we preaded [paraded] to receive the new jeneral. it rained & we wos dismissed. the jenral com in about nune," James Stevens of Frye's regiment recorded in his diary on the second. And the next day: "Nothing hapeng extroderly." His comrade, Phineas Ingalls, wrote: "A new general from Philadelphia."[8]

Washington's appearance at Cambridge meant just short of absolutely nothing to the common soldiers in the ranks. They remarked little on the comings and goings of generals in their diaries and letters—unless it was some great adventure, and the deeds of Old Put were always worthy of comment—so there was no particular reason to say anything about this new general. They didn't know Washington and probably knew very little of his reputation. Until Washington did something to change their daily routine, they would reserve comment and judgment. The daily routine would be the same regardless of who was in command. Or so they thought.

If the tepid reaction of the enlisted men troubled Washington or Lee, neither of them commented on it. Both men knew that they had much to do, not only to make the army *theirs*, but also to make it functional in the way that they would prefer. The army was no longer Massachusetts's, no longer New England's, but the army of all America.

George Washington takes command of the army at Cambridge, July 1775. This portrayal, reflecting American patriotic myth, turns Washington's first appearance before what would soon become the Continental Army into a dramatic and moving occasion. In reality, the rebel troops outside Boston barely took notice when their recently appointed commander-in-chief arrived. But within a few weeks they would all feel the effects of his leadership.

What Washington didn't know was the extent to which he would have to rebuild that army.

*B*efore attending the unremarkable little ceremony on Cambridge Common, Washington had the opportunity to meet with the commanders at Cambridge. Ward and Putnam, eager to see the imposing Virginian, extended their hospitality, and showed the new generals to the headquarters allocated to them by the Provincial Congress: the house of Dr. Langdon, the president of Harvard College, very close to Cambridge Common. Langdon had not abandoned the house; the Congress generously allowed the army chaplain a single room for his lodging. The rest now belonged to Washington, Lee, and their staffs.

One of the first items of business that Washington attended to was to give Ward and Putnam their commissions. Ward accepted his graciously, Putnam with obvious joy. But the two men then intimated to Washington that not everyone was content with the choices that the Continental Congress had made when establishing the leadership for the army. In fact, Congress had truly botched the job, and the generals they had appointed were unhappy. To Washington, who knew little about the complicated command system in the Grand American Army, this all came as a big and unpleasant surprise.

In June, after selecting Washington as commander-in-chief, the delegates at Philadelphia fleshed out the command structure of the Continental Army with four major generals and eight brigadiers. Everyone, even—and perhaps especially—the Massachusetts representatives, understood the reasons for Washington's appointment and agreed with them: his credentials as a southerner were pleasing to those who feared that the army would be dominated by New Englanders; in terms of military experience he ranked toward the top of those suitable for command; and unlike Lee he was an American born and bred. No one, or very few, disputed those facts. But if all of the thirteen colonies were to be made to feel welcome in this union, then the remaining twelve generals would have to be carefully chosen, distributed among the other colonies so that no one felt left out. Politics, more than ability, would be the determining factor.

That, perhaps, was unavoidable, as has been the case—and probably always will be—when democracies go to war. What the members of Congress didn't understand was that the order of the appointments—and the implication of seniority—would be an issue with the appointees. The first major-generalship went to Artemas Ward. There was little dispute about that; Ward had stepped up when nobody else had, and since April 20 he had built and commanded the army. It was an appropriate reward for faithful and dedicated service. Next was Charles Lee. Again, a solid choice. Lee was the most experienced soldier in America, and was second only to Washington in popularity with Congress. Only Lee himself felt any resentment at his selection. Inwardly he fumed at being ranked behind the amateur militia general Artemas Ward, but most of the time Lee kept his mouth shut about his hurt pride. Third was Philip Schuyler of New York. Schuyler, a forty-one-year-old patrician from Albany had only negligible military experience— during the French and Indian War, he had served as a quartermaster in the provincial forces—but he was intelligent, soft-spoken, and well liked. Schuyler ranked high in New York political circles; his appointment was a necessary nod to New York, whose support would be vital in the coming war. The fourth major-generalship was given to Israel Putnam. Old Put was the most famous soldier in New England, and his exploits at Noddle's Island had been the talk of the Continental Congress. Here was a fighting man if ever there was one. Even if soldiers like John Thomas or John Stark surpassed

Putnam in tactical judgment, it didn't matter. Putnam was a man of action, and Congress wanted men like him in command.

And that was where the difficulties began. The eight brigadier-ships were handed out, in descending order, to Seth Pomeroy of Massachusetts, Richard Montgomery of New York, David Wooster of Connecticut, William Heath of Massachusetts, Joseph Spencer of Connecticut, John Thomas of Massachusetts, John Sullivan of New Hampshire, and Nathanael Greene of Rhode Island. In its generalship, then, the Continental Army remained a largely New England army, and though that would change over time, it wasn't the troublesome issue. It was the order of the commissions that raised hackles among the appointees. Putnam had been promoted over the heads of Spencer and Wooster, his superiors in the Con-necticut service. Pomeroy, who had done little during the siege, and Heath, recently promoted to major general in Massachusetts to fill the vacancy left by the death of Joseph Warren, were first and fourth on the list of brigadiers . . . while John Thomas, who as lieutenant general ranked next to Ward in the Massachusetts army and who held an important independent command at Roxbury, was ranked seventh. Wooster, Spencer, and Thomas felt sorely aggrieved, as if they had been personally slighted; Heath, promoted over his friend and superior Thomas, felt just a bit embarrassed.

Thus, George Washington would have his first brush with a problem that would plague him for the remaining eight years of the Revolution: talented men putting personal gain and petty hubris above the needs of the Cause. He would have been sympathetic to the plight of the offended generals if only they had reacted with a mea-sure of forbearance. But two of them—Wooster and Spencer—did not. Wooster, then commanding a Connecticut contingent hovering near New York City, returned his commission to John Hancock, churlishly remarking that "I have already a commission from the assembly of Connecticut." A militia officer he was, and a militia officer he'd stay, if the alternative meant subordinating himself to the likes of Israel Putnam. Joseph Spencer simply left Roxbury in a huff, without bothering to tell Washington where he was going and what he intended to do, and returned home to Connecticut. His officers—at his instigation—protested to the Connecticut Assembly, asking that Spencer be begged to return. Governor Trumbull pleaded with Spencer to stay, and with Washington to redress Spencer's grievances. Washington, though, had no sympathy for Spencer; "I should hope every Post would be deemed honourable which gave a Man Opportunity to serve his Country," he growled to the governor. Trumbull appealed to Spencer's patriotism and sense of duty, and finally the touchy brigadier returned to camp and accepted his place. Wooster, however, stubbornly refused to have anything to do with his Continental rank.[9]

There remained only Thomas, and it was Thomas who most concerned Washington, Lee, and the Massachusetts leadership. From James Warren, Washington had a pretty good sense of the old soldier's worth. "His merits in the military way have surprised us all," Warren had recently glowed to his friend Sam Adams. Thomas was, in Warren's estimation, far superior to Ward. "I can't describe to you the odds between the two camps [Cambridge and Roxbury]. While the one has been spiritless, sluggish, confused and dirty, I mean where General Putnam and our Friend [Joseph] Warren's influence have not had their effects; the other has been spirited, active, regular and clean. [Thomas] has appeared with the dignity and abilities of a General." Thomas made good on Warren's commendation: unlike Spencer, he stayed at Roxbury and did his duty. Washington wrote to him personally, urging him to stay; so, too, did the entire officer corps at Roxbury. Most revealing, though, was the letter sent to him by Charles Lee, who traveled to Roxbury and discussed the situation with Thomas over dinner. "You think yourself not justly dealt with in the Appointments of the Continental Congress," wrote

Lee, after their meeting. "I am quite of the same Opinion; but is this a Time, Sir, when the Liberties of your Country, the Fate of Posterity and the Rights of Mankind are at Stake to indulge our Resentments for any ill Treatment we may have Received as Individuals?" Lee then turned, craftily, to his own dispute with Ward. "I have myself, Sir, full as great, perhaps greater Reason to complain than yourself. I have passed through the highest military Ranks in some of the most respectable Services of Europe . . . I ought to consider at least the preference given to General Ward over me as the highest Indignity—but I thought it my Duty as a Citizen and Asserter of Liberty, to wave every Consideration of this Nature."[10]

But John Thomas had no intention of leaving. And even if he had, Washington and the Massachusetts political leaders were so determined to get Thomas to stay that they quickly arranged things to his satisfaction. James Warren suggested the expedient to Washington: Seth Pomeroy, the seniormost brigadier, had left the army and gone home, giving no indication whether or not he would accept his commission. So . . . what if Thomas were to be given Pomeroy's slot? Without waiting for approval from Philadelphia, Washington made the switch and elevated Thomas. William Heath, much relieved at being extricated from his uncomfortable dilemma, heartily agreed.

One suspects, though, that Thomas was looking, half-heartedly, for a way out. His poignant letters to Hannah, full of barely suppressed longing, revealed how deep his homesickness had become. "You write to me about Comeing Home I should be glad to Comply with your Request," he wrote her on July 4. "I hope the Time will Come befor Long that I may Return to my family." He craved the company of his wife and his children infinitely more than the chocolate and snuff he constantly asked Hannah to send him. Life at home was, he said, "the only happy way of life that I am acquainted with." Yet he soldiered on, and there is good reason to believe that he would have accepted his earlier commission even without Washington's gracious intervention.[11]

*D*ealing with the touchy new Continental generals consumed the better part of Washington's first month in Cambridge. It was a sad and disturbing portent of things to come—for the rest of his military career, Washington would have to spend countless hours assuaging the egos of prickly, volatile subordinates—and it impeded him in his more important task of reorganizing the army and preparing it for combat. The spirit of insubordination could not help but trickle downward. Even the colonels contested their ranking. John Stark, arguably the touchiest of all, protested his commission. To him it was an unforgiveable slight that Congress ranked above him two colonels who had held lesser rank than he during the French and Indian War![12] Washington hoped to cultivate in the army a sense of higher purpose, of stoic self-sacrifice and obedience in this holiest of causes. His officers were setting a poor example.

Undeterred by this puerile behavior, Washington went straight to work on the enlisted ranks and the junior officers. Starting on the very day of his arrival, he visited the camps around Cambridge, inspected the fortifications all around the Bay, and spent some time assessing the situation in Roxbury. What he found disturbed him. Washington assumed that he would not find anything remotely like a professional army, and he had told the Provincial Congress so when he sent a formal reply to their welcome address: "The course of human affairs forbids an expectation, that troops formed under such circumstances, should, at once, possess the order, regularity, and discipline of veterans." But the conditions in the disorderly camps went far below his lowest expectations. The army, Washington told his brother John Augustine, was little more than "a mixed multitude of people . . . under very little discipline, order, or government." When

Philip Schuyler complained of the state of the troops in New York, Washington scoffed, "mine must be a portrait at full length of what you have had in miniature. Confusion and discord reigned in every department, which in a little time must have ended either in the separation of the army, or fatal contests with one another." The soldiers were slovenly, the camps filthy and putrid, the officers inattentive and shiftless. The sporadic gunfire that sounded from the camps at all hours of day and night still persisted, despite all of Ward's efforts to curb the offense, and it absolutely shocked the Virginia general. Tents, clothing, blankets, muskets . . . all these vital commodities were lacking. Record-keeping, so far as Washington could see, was nonexistent, and therefore no one in the army seemed to have known what supplies were in store, what had been issued, or how much ammunition or artillery there was. On July 3, he published his first general orders to the army, requiring all colonels to submit exact returns for their regiments. It should have taken no more than an hour, Washington later fumed, but instead it took eight days for the information to get back to headquarters. What kind of colonel, he wondered, didn't know—each and every morning—how many men were in his regiment?[13]

Charles Lee was even less forgiving than Washington. "We found everything exactly the reverse of what had been represented," he wrote on July 4. "We were assured at Philadelphia that the army was stocked with engineers. We found not one. We were assured that we should find an expert train of artillery. They have not a single gunner and so on. So far from being prejudiced in favor of their own officers, they are extremely diffident in 'em and seem much pleased that we are arrived."[14] The Yankee engineers, Lee believed, were singularly incompetent: "I really believe not a single man of 'em is [capable] of constructing an Oven."

Washington, and Lee especially, exaggerated just a bit. The New England army was blessed with a well-functioning supply system; if there was any fault in record-keeping, it was with the regimental commanders and not with the commissary. But certainly Washington can be forgiven for this minor oversight. The enormity of the task he had accepted had been dropped on him all at once, and to him it must have seemed that he had been charged with doing the impossible.

But just as with the fracas over generalships, Washington pushed on, venting occasionally about the obstacles in his path but working bullheadedly to remedy the ills. Orders regulating the conduct of the army flew in profusion from the pens of his clerks. The men were to keep themselves and their camps clean and tidy. Slackness—in sentry duty, in fatigue details, in *anything*—would not be tolerated; drunkenness and games of chance simply had to go. Soldiers who disobeyed their officers, or who caused disruption in the camps, would be punished severely. Whippings, usually in the time-honored dose of thirty-nine lashes, became a daily event, imposed for everything from verbal abuse toward officers to stealing from civilians; "riding the wooden horse"—a brutal punishment, in which the condemned soldier was forced to sit astride a rail in excruciating pain, his legs pulled by weights lashed to his ankles—had also been used when Ward was in command, but under Washington it, too, became a regular occurrence.

Washington was, if anything, even more concerned with the behavior of the officers. Early on, the new commander-in-chief made it clear that he expected everything about the officers to be beyond all reproach. Joseph Hawley, a member of the Provincial Congress who became one of Washington's most valuable advisers, pointed out that while Massachusetts had brave officers, "yet there are too many, and even several Colonels, whose characters, to say the least, are very equivocal with respect to courage." It was a very subtle observation about the performance of people like Samuel Gerrish at Bunker Hill. "There is much more cause to fear that the officers will fail in a day of trial, than the privates." Observing that "if the officers will do their duty, there is no fear of the soldiery," Hawley went on to suggest that bravery should be rewarded . . . but that "every officer who . . . shall act the poltron [and] dishonour his General and . . . betray his Country" should be punished without mercy.[15]

Washington took Hawley's advice to heart; it was very close to his own view of an officer's honor and calling. He would have to make examples. Washington had not been at Bunker Hill to see the cowardice that Hawley had hinted about, but fortunately there were several candidates at hand that had already been all but condemned by the Massachusetts leadership. Hence Samuel Gerrish and John Mansfield, the two colonels who had behaved with something less than bravery at Bunker Hill, were cashiered. Samuel Gridley somehow escaped justice for his poor performance with his artillery, but not John Callender. Callender's dismissal was Washington's cue. On July 7, the general proclaimed in his orders for the day: "It is with inexpressible Concern that the General upon his first Arrival in the army, should find an Officer sentenced by a General Court Martial to be cashiered for Cowardice—a Crime of all others the most infamous in a Soldier, the most injurious to an Army, and the last to be forgiven."[16]

Physical courage was only one of the qualities that Washington expected his officers to have. They were also to be professional and responsible. Officers, he reminded again and again in general orders, must pay close attention to their men, enforce obedience to orders, and not tolerate shirking, misbehavior, or disrespect. Furloughs could not be granted frivolously; company commanders were not to allow more than two men to be on leave at any time. The egalitarian friendliness between officers and enlisted men, so common in the New England regiments, was destructive to proper discipline. Officers must maintain instead a well-defined, professional distance from the men under their command. It was important, too, that officers *look* like officers. They must be readily identifiable so that the men knew when to show respect. Uniforms, perhaps, were out of the question, so Washington came up with a simple system of insignia—colored "ribbands," or sashes, worn diagonally across the chest for generals, colored cockades for the hats of field and company officers; NCOs were to wear epaulettes or strips of colored cloth on the right shoulder of their coats.[17]

And then there was the paperwork, always paperwork. Virtually every day, it seemed, headquarters reminded all officers of the necessity of keeping accurate records of the number of men in their commands, the number of men sick or absent, the quantities of food and equipment and ammunition issued. An army, as Washington frequently observed, simply could not function without precise record-keeping.

In none of these regards—except for the rules on officers' insignia—did Washington do anything that Artemas Ward hadn't already tried. Ward, too, had reminded the officers to enforce obedience to orders and to obtain and present accurate returns, and commanded the enlisted men to keep themselves and their immediate environs clean. Nothing was new here . . . except in the manner of application. Where Ward reminded, or maybe nagged, Washington threatened. Where Ward occasionally had a soldier or two whipped for disobedience, Washington had several flogged daily. In all fairness to Ward, he was at a disadvantage when compared to his successor. He had virtually no staff, and the men who made up his rudimentary staff were well-intentioned amateurs, as was Ward himself. Washington, on the other hand, had considerable experience both in leading militia on campaign and in the daily operations of a professional army. Moreover, he had the advice of Charles Lee, a lifelong professional soldier of high rank—as Lee would tell anyone who cared to listen—and of Horatio Gates. Gates, like Lee, was British by birth and a former officer in the king's army who had fought in Europe during the War of the Austrian Succession and in America during the French and Indian War. He had retired with the rank of major and moved to America, where—again like Lee and Washington, too—he took up the life of a Virginia planter. He had known Washington for years—both men, besides Thomas Gage, had been with Braddock in the Monongahela disaster—and the two became reacquainted in the 1770s. Washington respected Gates for his experience and knowledge. When the Continental Congress filled out its generalships, it honored Washington's recommendation and appointed Gates as adjutant general of the army, with the rank of brigadier general.

It also worked to Washington's advantage that he was an outsider. He had no ties to the men he commanded, and had no reservations about ramming discipline and obedience down their throats. Ward couldn't bring himself to do that. The soldiers were his neighbors, and regional loyalty softened his heart and stayed his hand.

That same regional loyalty worked in just the opposite way for Washington. Maybe his status as an outsider helped him as a disciplinarian, but it didn't endear him to his army. The New England soldiers, accustomed to officers who were not much better than they in social origins, viewed the aristocratic slave-owner with suspicion. And Washington, for his part, never warmed to this first Continental Army, either. He saw some potential in them, at least at first—"materials for a good army," he wrote of them in mid-July, "a great number of able-bodied men, active, zealous in the cause, and of unquestionable courage." But it wasn't long before he found that he really didn't like Yankees. "Their officers," Washington wrote in late August, "generally speaking are the most indifferent kind of People I ever saw. . . . they are by no means such Troops, in any respect, as you are led to believe of them from the accts. which are published, but I need not make myself Enemies among them by this declaration, although it is consistent with the truth." The men would fight well, he thought, if only they had good officers, but that didn't mean that he thought much of the rank-and-file, either. "They are an exceeding dirty and nasty people." To Richard Henry Lee, he complained that "it is among the most difficult tasks I ever undertook in my life to induce these people to believe that there is, or can be, danger till the Bayonet is pushed at their Breasts; not that it proceeds from any incommon prowess, but rather from an unaccountable kind of stupidity in the lower class of these people. . . ." Nathanael Greene, who worshipped Washington, couldn't help but sense the general's hostility toward the New England men. Washington, Greene rationalized, "had not had time to make himself thoroughly Acquainted with the Genius" of the Yankees.[18]

George Washington would never be happy with the results of his "reformation" of the army. The regularity and precision he sought, especially in administration, would have to wait for the Valley Forge winter and the arrival of the Prussian émigré Steuben in 1778. He stewed constantly over what he saw as his failure to bring the army in line, and on at least one occasion very nearly lost his temper. Early in August, as he discussed operational plans with his generals, he found that the Committee of Supplies had committed a grave error in its bookkeeping. The Committee had earlier informed the general that it had over *three hundred* barrels of gunpowder in store; just as he sat down with his Council of War to talk strategy, it was made known to him that the actual supply was only thirty-six barrels. "Almost the whole powder of the army was in the cartridge-boxes," wrote Washington's secretary Joseph Reed, "and there not twenty rounds a man." When the facts were made plain to Washington, "the General was so struck that he did not utter a word for half an hour."[19]

Yet there was a change in the army, in its spirit and in its daily activities, and everyone felt it. A preacher from Concord visited the army in mid-July and saw it plainly: "There is great overturning in camp, as to order and regularity. New lords new laws. The Generals Washington and Lee are upon the lines every day. . . . The strictest government is taking place, and great distinction is made between officers and soldiers. Everyone is made to know his place and keep in it."[20]

New lords new laws, and it was only natural that Washington should bruise some egos and tread upon a few toes as he pushed this new order on the army with vigor, showing little patience for those who didn't care for the myriad little brutalities of military life. But the Whig leadership in Massachusetts fell in love with the man. "You had prepared me to entertain a favorable opinion of General Washington," Abigail Adams gently chided her husband John, the man to whom Washington owed his rapid ascendancy, "but I thought the half was not told me. Dignity with ease and complacency, the gentleman and soldier, look agreeably blended in him. Modesty marks every line and feature of his face." So, too, did many of the officers in camp, especially the younger ones who had grown impatient with the slow progress of discipline. "General Washington fills his place with vast ease and dignity," Henry Knox glowed to his Lucy, "and dispenses happiness around him."[21]

For their part, the men in the ranks might have taken exception to this early hero-worship, but they accepted the new order with good grace and little grumbling. Most of the men who kept diaries had little to say about Washington or the reforms he authored. Within a matter of weeks, this first incarnation of the Continental Army was already showing Washington's personal imprint . . . but it would be a while before the men would see Washington as *their* general. He had yet to prove himself in the way that Old Put and Stark and Prescott had, and until he did, until he shared with them all the terrors of battle, Washington would still be little more than "a new general from Philadelphia."

*A*nd that was indeed what Washington wanted—a chance to share those dangers with his men. He didn't come to Cambridge just to build, or rather rebuild, an army. He came to *fight*. And from what he had learned from the scattered and confusing reports of what had happened on Breed's Hill in June, it seemed that the men were ready for a scrap, too. The businesslike air that now permeated the camps did not dampen the men's spirits. They were just as enthusiastic as they had been on the Glorious Nineteenth, maybe even more so, now that the rebellion had taken on a less haphazard, more solid form. On July 6, the Continental Congress had issued its radical declaration on the "Causes and Necessity of Taking Up Arms" against Great Britain, and a little more than a week later, all the regiments in Washington's new command stood at attention on their respective parade grounds as their colonels read the long declaration to them, word-for-word. Written on behalf of what they called "the United Colonies of North-America," the document listed all of the evils that British ministers had visited upon the king's hapless and devoted American subjects, who didn't want independence, only a say in their affairs and their fate, but vowed not to lay down their arms until the "Aggressor" did so first. It was hardly a document meant to speak to ordinary farmers, to stir the blood of the unlettered, but the men in the camps outside Boston responded with one unrestrained cheer after another. In Putnam's regiment, camped on Prospect Hill, the men went wild when Old Put himself concluded the ceremony by unfurling a brand-new regimental standard, bearing the devices "An Appeal to Heaven" and "Qui transtulit sustinet" (He who transplanted us, sustains us). The warlike roaring of Putnam's men stirred up some concern among the British troops in the entrenchments near Charlestown, who instantly prepared for a Yankee assault. "And the Philistines on Bunker's Hill," wrote Nathanael Greene, "heard the shout of the Israelites, and, being very fearful, paraded themselves in battle array."[22]

Something else boosted the high spirits of the army that summer: the arrival of the Continental riflemen. Back in June, the Continental Congress had authorized the recruitment of rifle companies in Maryland, Pennsylvania, and Virginia. They started to arrive in Cambridge in late July, some of the units making truly heroic marches to get to the scene of the action: the Virginia company commanded by Daniel Morgan, later to be one of Washington's most trusted subordinates, marched the six hundred miles from Winchester, Virginia, to the Cambridge camp in a mere twenty-one days. The rifle companies quickly became the talk of the camps. New Englanders, accustomed to inaccurate smoothbores, were astounded by the newcomers' skill with the long rifle, their ability to hit tiny targets at unheard-of distances. The appearance of the riflemen was equally amazing: their fringed linen hunting frocks, their buckskin trousers and moccasins, made them look more like Indians than white men to the settled, civilized New Englanders.

Unlike the New England farmers, these were true frontiersmen, accustomed to hunting, tracking, and living in the woods, men who relied upon their firearms for their sustenance and for their very survival. But the riflemen, despite their initial promise, quickly wore out their welcome. Without orders from above, daily they would creep out in front of the American lines to snipe at Redcoats in the lines at Bunker Hill or Boston Neck. They took very few lives and wasted a great deal of the army's dwindling powder supply, so in October, Washington called a halt to the practice. Worse yet, they set back Washington's attempts to instill discipline. Even more so than the Yankees—whom they disliked, thinking them soft and effete, and they were absolutely befuddled by the presence of so many African-Americans in the New England ranks—they were egalitarian, and hence they refused to acknowledge the authority of any officer, even their own. They thought of themselves as an elite, an attitude encouraged by the way they had been lionized on their arrival. They would not perform routine fatigue duties. Attempts to discipline them, often triggered by their frequently riotous and drunken behavior, were met with sullen resentment and even outright mutiny.

Washington could not afford to wait to make his army perfect. While his "reformation" of the army was yet under way, he prepared for action. He tidied up the army's command structure, something that had been needed for a very long time. On July 22, he divided the army into three wings: Artemas Ward took over the right wing, at Roxbury, joining his subordinates Thomas, Heath, and Greene; Charles Lee would command the left wing, centered on his headquarters at Medford; Israel Putnam got the center at Cambridge, where Washington would supervise the entire army from his new quarters at the Vassall House. In all three wings, the men went straight to the task of reinforcing the already considerable noose of fortifications, tightening the American chokehold on Boston. Where Ward had employed hundreds of men in digging fortifications, Washington detailed thousands. By fall, the American lines from Roxbury to Medford and Chelsea were thick and forbidding.

In the meantime, the men found outlets for their enthusiasm. They provoked occasional skirmishes with the British outposts near Charlestown Neck and forward of the lines at Roxbury, sometimes taking prisoner a Redcoat or two to pump for intelligence. And they pulled off a couple of daring raids reminiscent of the attack on Noddle's Island. On the night of July 20, a party of Yankees set out in whaleboats from Nantasket, landing at Boston Light in the outer harbor; in full view of the British warships, they set fire to the lighthouse and returned to Nantasket unharmed. Admiral Graves immediately sent carpenters to repair the light, escorted by a couple of companies of Marines, and the Americans responded that night. Under the direction of the enterprising Major Benjamin Tupper, about four hundred rebel troops in thirty-three whaleboats hit the island and attacked the Marines, many of whom were in their cups from rum which the carpenters had smuggled ashore. The Marines fled. Tupper's force retreated once Graves sent reinforcements, but not before killing or capturing some fifty British Marines . . . and burning the lighthouse again.[23]

Like the incident at Noddle's, these minor affairs boosted American morale, but Washington wanted more. He wanted to do what he had set out to do: to free Boston. Before he had left Philadelphia, the Continental Congress had presented him with instructions that were frustratingly vague. Washington must assess the size of the army and the quantities of its supplies, estimate the size of the enemy force in Boston, and fight anyone who opposed his army. He could not disband the army outside Boston, but neither could he augment it to more than double the size of Gage's force—the latter a ridiculous stricture, reflecting the almost total dearth of military experience among the members of Congress. And he could not act without first consulting his generals, assembled in a council of war.

These instructions didn't require that he move offensively against Boston, but they didn't tell him not to, either. Besides, Congress hoped that Washington would take the initiative. So once his reform program was well under way, Washington called his generals together. On September 8, he presented them with a bold proposal: to attack Boston by boat, while Ward's right wing moved on the British lines on Boston Neck. The generals took three days to make their response. Since Gage's force was estimated at 11,500 effectives— far in excess of the actual numbers—and the Americans had, at most, 16,000, "it was not expedient to make the attempt at Present at least."[24]

So there would be no attack on Boston, not in 1775 at least. All that Washington could do was to sit tight and hope that the British would attempt another large-scale offensive, so that the American forces could satisfy Nathanael Greene's heartfelt desire to "sell them another hill at the same price"—but the British showed no signs of complying. Fortunately, Washington had found something to occupy his attention and soothe his restlessness. After originally rejecting the idea, in July, the Continental Congress revisited the bold plan to take the war into Canada. At the very least, an invasion of Canada would divert British resources from Boston and points south; at best, the supposedly disgruntled French-speaking *Canadiens*—and maybe even the Indians nearby—would rally to the American cause, thereby making it all but impossible for King George to suppress the rebellion. Congress handed the task to Major General Philip Schuyler, who would be seconded by Richard Montgomery of New York, a capable longtime veteran of the British army. Washington quickly warmed to the idea. Benedict Arnold, frustrated but still ambitious after his less-than-satisfactory role in the taking of Ticonderoga, came to Washington with an even bolder proposition: Arnold offered to take a thousand men north via the Kennebec River, through the Maine wilderness and into Quebec province, while Schuyler and Montgomery invaded farther west and attacked Montréal. The Virginian saw great potential in Arnold's proposition. In late August, Arnold began to recruit his hand-picked little army in the camps outside Boston, and on September 11, 1775, they departed on their great northward trek . . . toward glory, defeat, and oblivion.

*W*hat Washington and his generals didn't know was that in Boston, the British had it almost as bad as they did. The American army recovered from Bunker Hill quickly and almost painlessly. It wasn't so easy for the British. The shock of the loss from the June 17 battle was in itself enough to paralyze both Gage and Howe; the pitiful scenes in the crowded military hospitals, the almost daily burials of men who finally succumbed to festering wounds, all served to remind the generals of the unbearable cost of the attack. Only when troop transports began to bring in reinforcements from Ireland later in July did the Boston garrison manage to achieve its prebattle size. By summer's end, Gage had under his command no more than 6,500 effectives, and that number would gradually diminish instead of growing. The food shortage, only an inconvenience early in the summer, became perilous in the last weeks of the season. Fresh meat and vegetables—when they could be had—cost anywhere from eleven to fifteen times the price they had commanded in early June. Even the salt provisions were running low. For the sick and wounded remaining in the hospitals, broth made from fresh mutton or beef was a rare luxury; most of the convalescents, even the officers, had to get by on broth made from salt pork—an expedient as repugnant to regimental surgeons as it was to the sick. More frightening yet, the dreaded scourge of smallpox reappeared with a vengeance in the town. By and large the British troops were inured to smallpox, but it was a threat nonetheless, and the growing number of civilians infected with the pox put a heavy demand on hospital resources.

Morale had already been low among the Redcoats before Bunker Hill. Now it plummeted to depths that most officers had never before witnessed. Company officers noted that their men had become despondent, contentious, surly, *beaten*, and with such men—no matter their numbers—any kind of large-scale operation against the impudent Yankees was bound to fail. Far from redeeming the weak self-confidence of the army, the battle at Bunker Hill only served to shatter what little pride the men in the ranks once had.

Gage—and Howe, who would soon replace him—had no intention of taking the offensive. Howe concurred with Gage that the only sensible strategy was to sit still, dig in more deeply, and wait for approval from London to abandon the town. New York City, both men fervently believed, was far more defensible, and had a much larger population of men and women loyal to the king; the British would find welcome there, and those who refused to welcome them would either leave or be cowed into obedience. Only once during that summer did the British attempt anything like a breakout, and that was primarily Clinton's doing. At the very end of July, while Howe kept up a steady cannonade from the new fortifications near Charlestown, Sir Henry led a nighttime bayonet assault on the advanced American posts outside Roxbury, nearest the Boston Neck lines. Clinton succeeded in breaking through with a very small assault force, but as there was no thought of following up his success with a full-scale attack, he ultimately had to withdraw. Clinton groused and grumbled about the lost opportunity, and the only result of the inconsequential operation was to show the American defenders where their weak points were . . . so they could be strengthened later.

Thomas Gage, meanwhile, had politics to worry him. He had not led the troops at Bunker Hill, nor were the losses there really his fault. The main failing of the British army there had been the failure of the enlisted men to follow their officers, but the responsibility was his regardless. Because of Lexington and Concord, Gage's reputation and career were already hanging by a thread. In London, the demand for his recall had grown stronger. On the very day of Bunker Hill, a disgraced but ambitious politician, Lord George Germain, decided to lend his voice to the rising chorus ranged against Gage. Gage was not equal to the job, Germain claimed, and was capable of nothing more than obeying orders to the letter; his men, moreover, had no faith in him as a leader.

Bunker Hill sealed Gage's fate, and Gage knew it even before he heard the home government's reaction to the news of the battle.

In late August, he sent his wife and children to England aboard the *Charming Nancy*, one of the transports carrying the wounded and maimed from the battle to the grim and indifferent fate that awaited them at home. Gage was certain that he would be joining his family soon. His own report on the battle was honest—he made no effort to hide or minimize the losses of that day—but regardless, there was much to damn him in the king's eyes.

Gage's main failing was that he had been correct all along. The rebellion could not be suppressed with an army of six thousand men trapped in Boston; it would require tens of thousands to venture beyond the seacoast and into the countryside, and preferably from New York rather than Boston. Howe agreed, and so—more or less—did Clinton. The king and Dartmouth and Lord North had not listened, believing Gage's warnings to be the product of a timid man with an overly fertile imagination. Bunker Hill had proved Gage right. And when the news of Bunker Hill reached England late in July, the popular outcry and the reaction of Parliament meant that Gage would be punished for being so.

So Thomas Gage would have to go. Fortunately, George III liked him, as did most men who knew him personally, and the king was determined to "let him down easy." What Gage received on September 26, 1775, was not official condemnation, but a summons—since there would clearly be no more substantial fighting in 1775, the general was to consult with the king and his ministers on his strategic plans for 1776. Gage was no fool. He knew full well that his career in America was over, but he didn't complain, or gripe, or give vent to any bitterness. Over the next two weeks he set his affairs in order, packed his belongings, and consulted with Howe, who would take command—temporarily, or so it was said officially—in his absence. On October 10, with no fanfare, no tear-filled goodbyes, and possibly little regret, Thomas Gage boarded the transport *Pallas*, bound for England, never to return.

Gage wasn't the only political victim of Bunker Hill. Samuel Graves would soon follow. He was not nearly so incompetent, passive, or corrupt as modern historians like to think he was, but neither was he as assertive as he could have been. Even if he had been entirely blameless, Graves—much like Gage—would still stink of failure. His was the command, his was the responsibility, and after the squadron's humiliations at Noddle's Island and Boston Light the admiral was doomed. In January 1776, Vice Admiral Richard, Viscount Howe, William Howe's older brother, arrived in Boston to take Graves's place.

*I*f the politicians in London assumed that putting William Howe in command would bring about a more vigorous prosecution of the war—which they did—then they were to be sorely disappointed. Howe's view of the situation in Boston was not much different than Gage's. He looked forward to the day when he might abandon Boston, honorably, and try to crush the rebellion from New York. Throughout the fall and into the winter, Howe's immediate concerns had little to do with strategy. If he were to leave Boston, then he would have to do something about the thousands of hungry, gaunt, hope-starved Loyalists who depended upon him for protection. For reasons both humanitarian and political, the loyal subjects of the king could not be abandoned to the questionable mercies of their rebel neighbors. Howe thought that they might be suitably housed in New York; Clinton suggested a temporary home for them in Halifax.

In the meantime, Howe had to take care of his despondent troops. Naval raids along the coast had been able to acquire some livestock and fodder. In early November, he sent a small expeditionary force by boat to Lechmere's Point, capturing nearly one hundred head of cattle before being driven off by alert rebel troops.

Such raids did not provide a reliable supply of food, though—certainly not enough to meet the needs of the entire army. Fresh food was not to be had. What little could be found went to the hospitals, and even salt provisions were running low. Not only smallpox, but scurvy, too, ate away at the garrison, and there was little that Howe could do about it.

Washington also was beset with a thousand mundane problems that required his personal attention: the perennial issues of supply, of gunpowder in particular, and the constant and annoying political demands of his office. To get what he wanted, be it munitions or recruits, Washington had to deal with local authorities in Massachusetts, keep the Continental Congress apprised of his every coming and going, and maintain cordial relations with the governors and assemblies of the other colonies. He had, in short, become the chief diplomat of the army as well as its military commander. Washington did the job well. He could be courtly when he needed to be, a talent that would serve him well over the next seven or more years. The Massachusetts leadership never lost its fondness or respect for Washington. Not all of Washington's generals were so lucky. Charles Lee, initially greeted as a kind of martial savior, wore out his welcome in short order. His coarse language and boorish manners repulsed James Warren and discouraged visitors to his Medford headquarters, which Lee appropriately nicknamed "Hobgoblin Hall." Lee's habit of keeping two dogs—one of them "a native of Pomerania, which I should have taken for a bear had I seen him in the woods," wrote one wag—with him at his table when he dined struck proper Yankees as more than a bit odd. Abigail Adams, visiting Hobgoblin Hall in December, patiently indulged General Lee when he pulled up a chair and told his dog Spada to climb up. Spada seated himself in the chair and obediently lifted up a paw toward Mrs. Adams. "I could not do otherwise than accept it," Abigail told her husband John.[25]

The army's medical service weighed heavily on Washington's mind, too, and with good reason: the burgeoning smallpox epidemic in Boston was threatening to spill over into the American camp. Gage and Howe, already burdened by the demands of an overpopulated city and a hungry garrison, were allowing, even encouraging, the departure of poor Bostonians. Some of these castaways were undoubtedly infected. Fearing that a weakened, pox-ridden army would likely be too tempting a target for the British to resist, Washington wisely eschewed mass inoculations for the troops in favor of quarantines. He set up a new smallpox-house near Fresh Pond. Medicines, like everything else, remained in short supply, and the new medical department of the Continental Army had more than its share of troubles. By early fall, complaints—mostly from regimental surgeons—were flooding into Washington's headquarters about the department's inefficiency, and most of them pointed to the man he had just appointed as the army's first surgeon general: Dr. Benjamin Church of Boston.

Church's competence as a medical administrator wasn't the only questionable thing about the man. Dr. Church, a forty-one-year-old physician, ranked among the foremost Boston Whigs. Like Joseph Warren, he was cultured and charming, with a gift for eloquence, and he had served on virtually every committee or revolutionary council in existence. He was a delegate to the Provincial Congress and a trusted member of the Committee of Safety, privy to every sensitive secret of the Cause and the war effort. But he was also brazenly unfaithful to his English-born wife, and his taste for high living cost more than he could afford. Sometime before the outbreak of hostilities in the spring of 1775, he found a source of ready cash to supplement his income: General Gage. Throughout that spring and summer he passed sensitive military information along to Gage, so skillfully concealed that none of his colleagues suspected a thing about his activities. In July 1775, though, a former mistress whom he had employed to carry his correspondence accidentally left one of his treasonous letters with a Whig friend, and in short order his secret was out. He was tried, convicted, expelled by the Provincial Congress, fired by Washington, and condemned by the Continental Congress to house arrest. In 1778, he left the country; his ship was lost at sea, and Church—America's first traitor—was never heard from again.[26]

*I*n some ways, Church's treason was more insidious than that of Benedict Arnold four years later. Unlike Arnold, Church had no reason to be aggrieved at the Cause he served; his betrayal was colder, more calculated, more self-serving than Arnold's. But the affair bothered Washington surprisingly little. "The army and country," he concluded, "are exceedingly irritated." He didn't have time to spare for a matter that was already over and done with. The army absorbed all his attention.

If the "reformation" of the army had been Washington's only concern, it would have been enough. But there were worse problems—far, far worse—lurking just around the corner. Washington knew it was coming, everyone knew it was coming, and no one wanted to acknowledge it. The army was going to fall apart, and the date for this catastrophe was already set: January 1, 1776.

Congress called it the Continental Army, but its composition had barely changed. It was still an army of New Englanders, with the small and irritating exception of the rifle companies from the middle colonies. The men didn't sign any new enlistment papers when Washington arrived in July; they were bound only by the terms they had agreed to when volunteering for their respective colonies. And the end of their service wasn't far off. The Connecticut troops were slated to go home on December 10, 1775. The Massachusetts, Rhode Island, and New Hampshire regiments would follow on

December 31. Washington's army, then, was not only too small to attack Boston—it was going to go away at the end of the year.

Late in September, Washington wrote to the Continental Congress of his concerns and needs. He painted a stark but concise and unexaggerated picture of the situation in Boston, and his news couldn't have been encouraging to the delegates in Philadelphia. The army was short of everything, as usual, powder of course, but also all the things that the men would need once cold weather set in: blankets, warm clothing, even firewood. And money, too. The men had to be paid, provisions had to be purchased. There was no way that he could force the British out, and the army would dissolve by year's end. Congress, hoping as Washington had that the army could end the siege before winter, was alarmed, and sent a three-man committee—including one Benjamin Franklin—to Boston to confer with their general.

The congressional committee arrived in Boston in October. Soon they came to understand why Washington was stymied. Just to make his points clear, Washington convened his Council of War for the committee's benefit, asking for his generals' recommendations for an attack on Boston. The answer was the same as before: no attack under the present circumstances. Franklin's committee agreed, and they also concurred that the army had to be beefed up with new recruits. No fewer than twenty thousand would do, Washington had argued, and the committee believed him.

But all these things were more easily said than done, especially recruitment, and it was in recruitment and reorganization that Washington encountered his most obdurate stumbling-blocks. The structure of the regiments would first have to be made standard. Each of the four New England colonies maintained different sizes for their regiments. Washington proposed a consolidation: reducing the present forty-odd regiments in the army to twenty-eight. That in itself presented the high command with a tough obstacle:

although the total number of men in the army would stay the same, consolidation meant that some officers would have to give up their posts. But most of the New England officers were unwilling to do so, and their men likewise were loath to serve under unfamiliar officers. The Yankees stubbornly resisted any and all attempts to change their present, comfortable arrangement.

There were many advantages to be derived from consolidation. It gave Washington the opportunity to drive out incompetent or lazy officers, and to bring in fresh talent from outside New England. This was, to Washington's thinking, a *Continental* army, representing *all* of the colonies. The individual colonies, therefore, should be willing to work together for the common good and put regional prejudices to the side. The Yankees didn't see it that way, and their provincialism drove Washington to distraction. "Connecticut wants no Massachusetts man in her corps," he wrote in November. "Massachusetts thinks there is no necessity for a Rhode-Islander to be introduced into hers; and New Hampshire says, it is very hard, that her valuable and experienced officers, who are willing to serve, should be discarded, because her own regiments . . . cannot provide for them." Two of the Massachusetts colonels set a great example for the officer corps: when Asa Whitcomb lost his regiment and his command, he graciously accepted the inevitable, vowing that he would fight on as a private soldier if that was to be his fate. Jonathan Brewer was so moved by Whitcomb's action that he voluntarily gave up his regiment to Whitcomb. Washington was touched by this unvarnished display of honest patriotism, so much so that he gave Brewer the new post of barrackmaster, promising him the next regimental command that opened up.[27]

Most officers didn't manifest the same kind of "noble sentiments" as Whitcomb and Brewer, and the enlisted men were even worse. Recruitment proved to be unexpectedly tough. The men, most of whom had been in the camps since late April or early May, were not interested in prolonging their service in the name of what their generals called "the Continent." Their pay was in arrears, and Congress refused to offer any kind of enlistment bounty as an incentive. For the Massachusetts men, the Continental service meant losing money: Congress would pay the men once monthly by the calendar month, while Massachusetts had paid them by thirteen "lunar months" of twenty-eight days. They would lose a full month's pay in a year. But mostly they were gravely homesick. They had done their time and their duty, and saw no particular reason why they should stay. "The pulse of a New England man beats high for liberty," Governor Trumbull mused. "His engagement in the service he thinks purely voluntary; therefore, in his estimation, when the time of inlistment is out, he thinks himself not holden without further engagement."[28]

Washington believed that the men would rise to answer their country's call, but few of the enlisted men thought of themselves as being part of a united America. The first week of reenlistments, in November 1775, produced fewer than a thousand enlistments in eleven regiments. At that rate, Washington would have no more than 2,500 men in the ranks on January 1. Late in November he exhorted the men to reenlist, emphasizing the easy conditions of their service—"never were soldiers whose duty has been so light, never were soldiers whose pay and provision has been so abundant and ample"—and pointing out that if they abandoned their country and their Cause *now*, the result would be catastrophic.[29]

The appeal moved virtually no one. In fact, as the end of old enlistments drew near, the men got downright surly about what they saw as their right to leave. The Connecticut regiments proved the most difficult. Their terms ended on December 10, but most of the men were under the impression that the date was instead December 1. On the morning of the first, Charles Lee paraded the Connecticut troops in their encampment at Winter Hill in an effort to convince the skeptical soldiers that they still had nine days to serve. Lee ordered the men who insisted upon leaving immediately to form up separately, in a hollow square, and as soon as they found their places he walked into the center of the square and lost his temper. "Men, I do not know what to call you," he shouted at them, "you are the worst of all creatures!" "And [he] flung and curst and swore at us," recalled one of the recalcitrant Yankees, Simeon Lyman of Webb's Connecticut regiment. Lee was not above threats: he would immediately, he promised, send them out to attack the impregnable British lines on Bunker Hill if they would not stay on for at least a few more days. Some of the soldiers, shamed by Lee's tirade and by the pleas of their own officers, gave in; others stubbornly refused. These men Lee swore he would imprison. They, too, then gave up. Only one man continued in his refusal to stay. Lee dashed up to him, grabbed the man's musket, and promptly hit the gawking soldier on the head.[30]

But on the tenth they all left, all of the Connecticut boys, with only a handful signing the Continental enlistment papers. The Rhode Island troops itched to follow them, despite Nathanael Greene's efforts and to his infinite embarrassment: "I was in hopes . . . that ours would not have deserted the cause of their Country. . . . It mortifies me to Death, that our Colony and Troops should be a whit behind the Neighbouring Governments in private Virtue or Publick Spirit."[31]

It was a crisis, a terrible crisis, and one of the most shameful moments in the history of the American army. The men were fully within their rights to walk off, but it did not speak well of their patriotism. The generals, Washington in particular, had little sympathy for the departing soldiers. They, too, had sacrificed a great deal, and had gone without the comforts of home and family . . . though it was true that the generals lived better than the men—Washington's military "family" at the Vassall House in Cambridge consumed in excess of twenty-five pounds of meat each day.[32] They had harangued the troops almost daily, with increasing fervor as December wore on, but nothing they said or did, nothing they promised or threatened, could move more than a tiny minority of the men to hang on for the Cause.

Privately, Washington raged. Martha had come to stay with him in mid-December, but even the presence of his wife couldn't brighten his mood. "Such a dearth of public spirit, and such want of virtue, such stock-jobbing, and fertility in all the low arts," he wailed to his secretary Reed, "to obtain advantages of one kind or another . . . I never saw before, and pray God's mercy I may never be witness to again. What will be the end of these manœuvres is beyond my scan. I tremble at the prospect . . . such a dirty mercenary spirit pervades the whole that I should not be surprised at any disaster that may happen. . . . Could I have foreseen what I have, and am like to experience, no consideration upon earth should have induced me to accept this command." And in another letter to Reed: "I have often thought, how much happier I should have been, if, instead of accepting a command under such Circumstances I had taken my Musket upon my Shoulder & enterd the Ranks, or, if I could have justified the Measure to Posterity, & my own Conscience, had retir'd to the back Country & livd in a Wigwam."[33]

These were rare moments of self-pity for Washington, perfectly forgivable self-pity, and in truth he was only venting his frustration and bitterness to his young secretary. But this was also one of Washington's finest moments. Despite his anger and profound disappointment, he kept his cool and stayed on. Philip Schuyler and Richard Montgomery, leading the invasion force through the Champlain corridor toward Montréal, endured the same conditions that Washington did. The troops were mutinous, the New York and Connecticut regiments were constantly at odds, and the Connecticut men were equally determined to leave at the end of their enlistments in

December. But where Washington accepted the difficulties and did his best to work with what he had, Schuyler and Montgomery succumbed to despair. The flaws of their army weakened their personal resolve. "Habituated to order, I cannot, without the most extreme pain, see that disregard of discipline . . . which reign so generally in this quarter," Schuyler wrote Washington, "and I am therefore determined to retire." And Washington, mired in bigger troubles of his own, still managed to muster up some encouragement for his colleague from New York. "When is the time for brave men to exert themselves in the cause of liberty and country, if this is not? God knows, there is not a difficulty, that you both very justly complain of, which I have not in an eminent degree experienced . . . but we must bear up against them, and make the best of mankind as they are, since we cannot have them as we wish."[34]

And that was one of the many qualities that made Washington great, that transcended his occasionally questionable skills as a strategist and tactician: his perseverance, his resolve, his utter devotion to the Cause, his willingness to bear all. Much lay ahead of the man, more trials, more battles, more clashes of wills with politicians and with his own officers and soldiers. But this first trial was in some ways the worst of all, more trying than the defeats of 1776–77 and the Valley Forge winter, and Washington passed it. Less than six months after taking command at Cambridge, the Virginian had proven himself equal to his task.

*F*ortunately for Washington and for America, the army did not come apart at the seams. By mid-January, about 8,200 men had enlisted, though because of generous furloughs—granted by Washington in a desperate effort to bribe the Yankees into signing on again—and because of the camp illnesses that always worsened in the winter, only about 5,600 were actually healthy and ready for action. Drafts of militia from Massachusetts and New Hampshire helped to fill the ranks during this critical time, while one army faded away and another, brand-new one slowly came to take its place. Some of the departing troops, like Bridge's Massachusetts regiment, graciously offered to stay on a while longer, even if they had refused to sign up for another full year. By March, there were upward of ten thousand men under Washington's command.

Washington still ached for a dramatic assault on Boston. Halfway through February he proposed a full-scale attack, up Boston Neck and across the ice of the frozen Back Bay, but sagely his generals shot down the idea. The rejection stung Washington, but it was all for the best, for his army was not so strong as he thought, nor was Howe's force so weak. Still there was some hope of victory. Henry Knox, the Boston bookseller turned engineer, provided the means. Knox, who replaced the old and ailing Richard Gridley as commander of the army's artillery train, had gone to New York in late autumn, intending to get his hands on the vast stores of guns and ammunition secreted away in Fort Ticonderoga. New York's colonial legislature hemmed and hawed about giving up the prize; they had yet to receive reimbursement for some gunpowder they had handed over for Continental use, and since they considered Ticonderoga their property they were not about to sacrifice the heavy ordnance there for nothing. But ultimately Knox convinced the legislature, and early in December, he and his men began the laborious process of loading the heavy guns onto ox-drawn sledges. In an epic trek of fifty-six days, Knox brought the ponderous train of heavily burdened sledges eastward through the forbidding, ice-clad passes of the Berkshire Mountains and eventually to Cambridge. Powder might still be in short supply, but the rebels had plenty of guns now.

With the blessing of his generals, Washington decided to put the big guns to use in late February. Dorchester Heights would be the venue. Gage and Howe hadn't troubled themselves about the hills near Dorchester since Gage had called off Clinton's June 24 assault. Perhaps the Britons feared another confrontation like Bunker Hill; perhaps Howe intended to evacuate Boston soon anyway, and didn't see the need to cast away lives for an unnecessary goal. For whatever reason, the hills remained unoccupied. If the Americans were to seize and fortify the high ground beyond Roxbury, they would have to do so under cover of darkness and in one night, as they had with the redoubt at Breed's, but the frozen winter ground was far too hard to permit that kind of digging. Rufus Putnam came up with a brilliant expedient: the Americans, he suggested, could build portable, modular fortifications and put them atop the Heights in a matter of hours.

Washington approved the plan, so for several days in the late February chill the men fashioned prefabricated wooden gun emplacements, called "chandeliers," plus hundreds of prickly fascines and earth-filled gabions. To cover the preparations, American batteries along the shoreline kept up a steady fire on the British for a couple of nights, and then—on the night of March 4, 1776—John Thomas led a force from Roxbury up the hills of Dorchester, while horses and oxen dragged the prefabricated fortifications behind. By the next morning, the fortifications were complete enough to withstand a British counterattack—and complete enough, too, to bombard Boston into oblivion.

In Boston, Howe knew that the Americans were up to something on Dorchester Heights, but it was already too late. The sudden appearance of the rebel batteries, bristling with heavy siege cannon, took him and his army by surprise. Howe's initial instinct was to take a swing at the new American positions, and on March 5, he put his army in readiness for an all-out assault on Dorchester Heights. At the last minute, after considering the heavy casualties that such an attack would inevitably entail, he called off the operation. He was going to leave Boston anyway, eventually, and he couldn't justify the high cost of an assault if all it would accomplish was to save British honor. A brutal storm hit Boston that night, and that was all the justification he needed. The time was right for Howe to leave and cut his losses while he could.

Promising Washington that he would not set the town alight if the Americans would allow the Redcoats to evacuate unhindered, Howe set his garrison to the sad task of abandoning Boston. For several days, the soldiers collected all the provisions they could take, destroyed what they could not, rounded up those loyal Americans who wanted British protection, and prepared to embark for friendlier shores. One by one, the regiments filed onto the waiting transports while the Americans watched with a mixture of curiosity and jubilation from a safe distance. Late in the morning of the seventeenth, the last transport cast off its moorings and sailed out into the harbor, bound ultimately for British-held Halifax.

General Washington waited until the next day to venture into Boston with part of his army. The British transports were still in view then; they would not depart Nantasket Road for more than a week. But the celebration began immediately. After a siege of nearly eleven months, Boston had been liberated, and with very few lives lost. No one—no one in Boston, at least—knew that while the Redcoats would never again set foot in or near that city, they would be back, in greater numbers, with greater resolve, with greater skill and perseverance. No one knew of the great trials and heartbreak and near calamity that would visit them over the next seven long years. The American army had earned its first great victory, and Washington his first laurels, but the war had just begun.

Epilogue

※   ※   ※

*B*oston had fallen and it was a matchless day. No one in Massachusetts could recall one quite like it, in their own lifetimes or in the dimly remembered tales of their parents and grandparents. There was nothing with which it could be compared, not in all the wars against the French. It was immaterial that Knox's trek through the treacherous Berkshires, or that Thomas's nighttime seizure of Dorchester Heights—stirring deeds performed by valiant men— only hastened the inevitable. Howe would have left sooner or later, regardless. That didn't matter to the rebels. Boston was free, George Washington was its liberator, and the Continental Congress was so elated with the turn of events that it had a special commemorative medal struck to honor its champion.

For some it was a day of reflection, too, as the Continental

Army cautiously left the security of its siegeworks and moved into the deserted British lines, carefully working its way into Boston itself. Some of the men walked out to Charlestown Neck and onto Bunker Hill. There, Howe's fortifications awaited them. None of the Americans had been on this ground since the seventeenth of June, and the sight that greeted them was eerie beyond description. Wind whistled over the otherwise silent redoubt and the trenches flanking it; standing on the parapet were grotesque and motionless figures—dummy sentries, placed there by the Redcoats before their hurried departure. From their skeletal frames hung weatherbeaten British uniforms, their empty tattered sleeves flapping in the breeze.

Among the Americans who strolled from Bunker Hill to Breed's—casually, as if they were tourists indulging a morbid curiosity—were Colonel John Stark and a spare, eager young staff officer from Maryland, one James Wilkinson. At nineteen, Wilkinson was active and ambitious, not yet tainted by the rumors of scandal and graft that would plague his rocky political career later in life. He listened and watched in rapt hero-worship as Stark—normally taciturn, but today lighthearted, sentimental, even chatty—pointed to features in the landscape and recounted the events of June 17 in indifferent sequence. It was *there*, where the rail fence once stood, that his New Hampshire boys had dealt out death to Howe's steadily advancing battalions. *There* was the stone wall, built in frantic desperation by those same Hampshiremen across the width of the Mystic beach, only moments before the light infantry had dashed itself to pieces against it. *There*, on the grassy slopes ahead, the British dead "lay thick as sheep in the fold." And *there*, to the right, was the hill where Prescott made his lonely stand, his Massachusetts men firing until the last moment, until the last round.[1]

It all seemed so very long ago, that battle, and to Wilkinson—a veteran but still callow—the events of that day appeared as a great and fabled contest from a distant time, a Homeric struggle acted out in rural Massachusetts, even if most of the giants from that epic yet walked upon the earth. And in a way the battle for the heights of Charlestown *had* been so very long ago, so very far away. That battle had been fought in a different time, by a different army. True, the new army had kept many of the trappings of the old; many of the names—Ward, Putnam, Prescott, Stark, Thomas, Heath—were still present. A fair proportion of the veterans of Bunker Hill had reenlisted in the Continental service . . . many, though by no means enough. But the army that had come together outside Boston in the fevered outburst of patriotic emotion after Lexington and Concord, the army that had reveled in its boyish adventurism on Noddle's Island, the army that had fought and bled on Breed's Hill . . . *that* army, the first American army, had faded forever from sight.

As the army changed, its leaders walked off, one by one, into the mist. None of them was, like Thomas Gage, a political or moral casualty of the battle. Yet none of them really fit into the new order of things, into the professional army that Washington and his coterie of generals had been striving to build since the previous summer. The old leaders would reappear, individually, to play lesser, forgettable roles in the Revolutionary drama.

Israel Putnam emerged from Bunker Hill a hero. That, and his reputation for courage and action, earned him a place at Washington's side. He stayed with Washington, who never had reason to doubt Putnam's value . . . until the Continental Army saw its first real combat. Old Put did not perform especially well in the campaigns around Long Island and New York City in 1776, and the following year, he drew some criticism for his actions in the Hudson Highlands, where he gave up two important forts to the British. General Washington came to learn what anyone should have seen in 1775: Putnam was a valiant fighter, a charismatic leader of men, with physical courage that none could possibly match, but he did not have a mind for grand strategy and complicated maneuvers. Old Put's service in 1776–77 confirmed that unfortunate truth. Washington had already relegated Putnam to the sidelines when the redoubtable old Yankee farmer was felled by a debilitating stroke in 1779. He died eleven years later at his Connecticut home. His reputation was such, though, that despite his mediocre showing after the siege of Boston, it never suffered.

Neither did William Prescott's, whose fame rested entirely on his performance at Bunker Hill. But then neither did Prescott participate much in the war after the liberation of Boston. He continued on in command of his Massachusetts regiment—now called the 7th Continental Regiment—through the New York campaign the following year, and then he backed away. He never held a rank higher than colonel. After the war he returned to public life, serving in the Massachusetts General Court, taking up the sword once more when Massachusetts mobilized its militia to put down the rebellion of Daniel Shays in 1785–86. Later generations of Massachusetts patriots would see in Prescott, though, the true hero of Bunker Hill. As the fiftieth anniversary of the battle approached, Prescott partisans fought a sharp and surprisingly nasty war of words with the admirers of Israel Putnam, debating which one held overall command during the battle . . . even arguing over which one might have uttered the possibly apocryphal words, "Don't fire 'til you see the whites of their eyes!" Prescott did, however, make an outstanding if inadvertent contribution to history, or rather to the writing of history. His grandson was William Hickling Prescott, the early and influential scholar of Spanish and Latin American history. The younger Prescott would marry a woman with a parallel pedigree, one Susan Amory. Miss Amory's grandmother was one of the Inman girls, on whose farm Putnam lived prior to Bunker Hill; her grandfather was an officer in the Royal Navy—Captain John Linzee, who commanded HMS *Falcon* during the war. Amory's grandfather, in short, had directed his ship's guns to fire on Prescott's grandfather on that hot June day.[2]

John Stark's military career lasted somewhat longer than Prescott's. His sensitivity and bullheaded pride, though, restrained him from rising as far as his considerable talents merited. He served in the Continental Army into 1777, when he resigned in protest because fellow Hampshireman Enoch Poor was promoted to a generalship over Stark. Stark's greatest moment—after the stand at the rail fence, that is—came during the Saratoga campaign. Commanding New Hampshire militia—he stubbornly refused to have anything to do with the Continentals—he scored one of the unlikeliest victories of the war: near Bennington, in present-day Vermont, Stark attacked outright a contingent of Brunswicker mercenaries from General John Burgoyne's army, capturing the entire body and making possible Horatio Gates's triumph over Burgoyne at Saratoga. Stark loved the soldier's life, but after the war he retreated completely from public scrutiny, returning to his life as a farmer. He died on his farm in Derryfield, New Hampshire, in 1822, only a few weeks short of his ninety-fourth birthday.

The generals commanding at Roxbury fared only a little better, for the most part. William Heath, the only general officer to take part in the battle at Concord, continued in the Continental service throughout the war. But the portly Heath never distinguished himself, never gained Washington's trust, never found the opportunity to prove himself. Washington did, however, recognize the considerable military talents and patriotic devotion of John Thomas. Congress trusted him, too, and sent Thomas northward to take charge of American military operations against Quebec as soon as Boston fell. Thomas's homesickness had not abated; he missed his family beyond words when he was but a few miles away from them, and now that he would be sent to Canada, his longing for home became almost more than he could bear. But Thomas was always the dutiful soldier, dedicated rather than ambitious or self-seeking, and he went, hoping against hope for that reunion with his family—"Never shall [I] Injoy my Self untill that Happy Day Shall Come but as my Country Calls me I must obey."[3] That "Happy Day" never came. When he arrived at Quebec in April 1776, he found the smallpox-ridden army there a shambles and ordered its withdrawal. On the trip south, Thomas contracted smallpox, and on June 2, he died at Chambly. His was the kind of devotion to country and colony that kept the Cause alive, and in return for his sacrifice of family and the comforts of home he suffered a painful and lonely death in the wilderness, hundreds of miles from his "dearest Hannah."

Of all the leaders of the Grand American Army, none was more poorly served—by his contemporaries and by posterity—than Artemas Ward. He was the first to go and the least remembered. Despite the generalship conferred upon him by the Continental Congress, and the divisional command given him by Washington, Ward had no place in Washington's army. He had been eager to cede his command to the Virginian, but somehow the relationship between the two men soured during the long autumn months of the siege. Both James Warren and Charles Lee disliked Ward intensely, and Warren and Lee had Washington's ear; for his part, Ward bristled at Washington's scathing and tactless criticisms of the New Englanders. "Some have said hard things of the officers belonging to this colony, and despised them," Ward wrote, sadly, to John Adams later that autumn. "But I think, as mean as they have represented them to be, there has been no one action with the enemy which has not been conducted by an officer of this colony."[4] General Ward was proud of the army he had led, and Washington's complaints—just or not—could not help but sting the Yankee churchwarden's pride. He had done the best he could with what he had, and under the constraints placed upon him by the Provincial Congress. When the Continental Army left Boston, Ward remained behind as commander of what was called the Eastern Department; Washington had no use for the man, and Ward's health prevented him from taking the field anyway. A year later, he resigned his commission. His bladder stones made life away from home positively miserable for him.

But Ward's character would not permit him to withdraw from service to the colony, and then the state, he loved so well. He had an active political career—in Massachusetts, in the Continental Congress, and finally serving two terms in the U.S. House of Representatives—and a full life, dying at his home in Shrewsbury just a few weeks shy of his seventy-third birthday. No one outside of his family would ever remember him as a hero of the Revolution. Few would even remember his name. The reward he gained for his selfless dedication to public service was ignominy. Over the years, even in scholarly histories of the Revolution, Artemas Ward would appear as the anti-Washington, and almost as comic relief because of his fabricated shortcomings: lethargic, incompetent, indifferent to the sufferings of his men, a political general so fat from high living and indolence that he couldn't ride a horse, the man whose lack of foresight damned the New England army to failure at Bunker Hill. Historians should know better. Ward was the first commander-in-chief of the American army in the Revolution. He sought no laurels, demanded no advancement. He took his generalship from Massachusetts—reluctantly—because it was his duty. He had none of Washington's advantages but all of the great man's dedication to the Cause, and perhaps even more. While Washington was still tending to his business at Mount Vernon, Ward had already taken upon himself the terrible responsibility of command in the most dangerous of times. Artemas Ward was not a talented general, but then he never claimed to be. Without his patient persistence, it is unlikely that the troops gathered outside Boston in late April 1775 would have been around to greet Washington less than three months later. At Bunker Hill, his caution saved, rather than destroyed, the rebel army.

None of these men would be elevated into the pantheon of Revolutionary heroes; none of them would be granted admittance to George Washington's small band of trusted lieutenants. They, along with the army they created and led, had served their purpose, and once that purpose had been fulfilled they passed into history.

*F*or the British there was no such upheaval. The army that left Boston for Halifax in March 1776 would return to the fray, most of its regiments serving in one theater or another for the remainder of the American war. And while Bunker Hill had dealt the death blow to Thomas Gage's reputation and his military career, it did little or no harm to the rest of the British high command. William Howe actually profited from the battle. Maybe some of the junior officers held Howe responsible for nearly wrecking the army on June 17—"our conductor as much murdered them as if he had cut their throats himself on Boston Common"—but the court of George III didn't share that feeling. Howe had, after all, won a victory at Bunker Hill, and Gage had absorbed most of the blame for nearly everything that had gone wrong during the siege of Boston. Howe was knighted for his services, and shortly after the flight to Halifax, his appointment as commander-in-chief in America was made permanent. In the summer of 1776, the general—now *Sir* William Howe—finally acted on his long-held belief that New York, and not Boston, should be made the center of British operations in the colonies. Thus began Howe's year-and-a-half duel with George Washington and the Continental Army, a contest that proved Sir William to be a talented but erratic commander. He took New York and administered a series of stinging defeats to the still-raw Continental Army, but missed at least one golden opportunity to destroy the main rebel army. In 1777, Howe outmaneuvered Washington, hit the Americans hard at Brandywine, and repulsed Washington's counterattack at Germantown, ultimately taking and occupying Philadelphia . . . but made no attempt to pounce on the weakened, dispirited American army encamped at Valley Forge in the winter of 1777–78. Loved by his officers and his men like few British commanders were, Howe nonetheless failed to exhibit the spirit of enterprise and daring that had made him famous as a light infantry officer under the sainted Wolfe. In 1778, he tendered his resignation from his post in North America. The king granted it without protest.

William Howe's heart was not in the war. It probably never was. Evil-tongued critics gossiped that the general's attentions and energies had been drawn elsewhere . . . namely to Elizabeth Loring, the beautiful—and willing—wife of prominent Boston Loyalist Joshua Loring Jr. Even Howe's friends couldn't help but notice how distracted the general was when Mrs. Loring was present. Later generations of historians have asserted that it was the experience of Bunker Hill that blunted Howe's martial drive and ruined the soldier, if not the man. Something, they argue, shocked Howe to his core: maybe it was the immense loss of life under his command, maybe the disproportionately high share of officer casualties. Perhaps it was the speed with which the army came undone on the very first assault against the rail fence, that moment that he "never felt before," watching in near disbelief as the elite troops of the light infantry and the grenadiers broke apart like raw recruits. It was not a matter of Howe's physical courage, for again and again during the remainder of his time in America, he demonstrated cool disdain for enemy fire and utter disregard for his personal safety. There is nothing to prove that Bunker Hill made Howe cautious, indecisive, lacking in confidence and the will to send his troops in harm's way. The theory has been widely accepted through constant repetition and nothing else, certainly not because there is any firm evidence to back it up. And Howe, it should be remembered, had gone to fight in America with the greatest reluctance.

When Howe resigned, it was Sir Henry Clinton who took his place, and Clinton would serve as commanding general until the very end of the war. His role at Bunker Hill, limited though it was, did wonders for his reputation. The traits he manifested in the Council of War on June 17, 1775—the predilection for tactical envelopment, the casual dismissal of conflicting opinions, the insistence that his own way was the only correct way, the truculent reaction when his opinions were not adopted—would make their mark on his generalship from 1778 onward. And his sensitivity, too: when Gage wrote his final report on Bunker Hill for the king, he showered Clinton with genuine, heartfelt praise, but made the mistake of remarking that Clinton had "followed" the final reinforcement into battle. The statement was technically correct, and Gage meant nothing by it. But to Clinton it seemed as if Gage had called his bravery and competence into question—to think that he would "follow" rather than lead—and the junior general was so upset that he repeatedly petitioned Gage to rectify the alleged error.[5]

Though he led the main British army into larger battles, and though he presided over the final failure of British arms to force the issue in the rebellious colonies, Sir Henry Clinton obsessed over Bunker Hill until the end of his life. His personal papers, especially the notes he compiled as he wrote up his personal *apologia* in the twilight of his career, reveal a man who could not stop thinking about what he did, what he hadn't done, and how others had failed in the battle for Charlestown Heights. There was something about Bunker Hill that clutched at his heart and soul. Perhaps he still rankled over the rejection of his proposed plan of attack, even years later. Perhaps he sensed in the disastrous operation a missed opportunity, for Britain and for his career.

The real change for the British came, instead, from the reaction at home. The news of Bunker Hill offended George III, now more determined than ever to crush the rebellion and punish its leaders. And so Gage would go, and Graves with him. So, too, would the man charged with the direction of the war effort from home: Lord Dartmouth, the mild and reasonable secretary of state for the American Department. He had done nothing wrong, but then neither had Gage, and it didn't matter. Lord North and the king were set on shaking up the establishment, and so out went Dartmouth and in came Lord George Germain. Germain was hardly the most talented man in the world, and had come back from a dead political and military career. At Minden, Britain's last major European engagement in the Seven Years' War, Germain had commanded the army's cavalry, but he disobeyed orders and was cashiered by an angry King George II. George III, though, liked Germain, who like him was all in favor of a heavy-handed approach to the American rebellion. "The dye is cast," George III wrote, and he meant it. The army in North America would be expanded to ten thousand men. In December, British diplomats would begin signing treaties with a handful of minor territorial states in the Holy Roman Empire, ruled by German princes who actively engaged in the practice of *Soldatenhandel*—the soldier trade. Several thousand German mercenaries, soon to be known as "Hessians" because the bulk of them came from the landgraviate of Hessen-Cassel, would be on their way to America later in 1776.

It was an unpleasant irony that every single measure that the king and Lord Germain took in response to the American rebellion that fall and winter accorded precisely with the recommendations that Thomas Gage had made more than a year before.

*A*nd that was perhaps the most significant repercussion of Bunker Hill: it condemned the colonies and Britain alike to a long war. There was no turning back, and those who had hoped to appeal to the king's sympathy would soon find themselves without a shred of hope. There could be no olive branch now that the rebels had taken such a fearsome toll of the king's soldiers. Prior to Bunker Hill, the notion of independence was something that only a handful of radicals—like the Adamses of Massachusetts—entertained, and even then they only whispered the word among themselves for fear of alienating the moderates in the Continental Congress. After the battle, though, the idea of an independent American nation didn't seem quite so ludicrous. It was all or nothing now. Few colonial politicians would, as George Washington's military secretary Joseph Reed put it, risk their lives for "half treason." They were already traitors in the king's eyes. No sense in courting death for compromise when the risk was no greater if independence were the object.[6]

That war would continue for nearly eight more years after the rebels made their stand on Breed's Hill, and during those eight years the Continental Army would endure much more trial and loss than the New England army had experienced in the spring of 1775. There would be signal victories, but more losses, and many times the Cause would teeter dangerously on the brink of absolute collapse. Washington would barely hold the army together through it all; his constant struggles with the Continental Congress over every aspect of the conduct of the war contrasted starkly with the relatively harmonious relationship between the first American army and the political authorities in Massachusetts. The legacy of Bunker Hill would haunt Washington for the rest of the war. To many observers, the battle had proven a dubious truth: that untrained American citizens, if zealous in the Cause and adequately equipped, could frustrate the most vigorous efforts of a professional British army. It was the argument that Patriots, drunk with the self-satisfied fervor of the *rage militaire*, had been touting since before the war began, and it would repeatedly cause Washington grief as he tried to create a professional American army capable of meeting the British on equal terms. If patriotic militia could do what Ward's army did at Bunker Hill, then why *should* America risk the expense and trouble and potential dangers that came from a standing army?

And the foe that Washington and his generals faced after the liberation of Boston was much more formidable than Gage's army of 1775. From Howe's invasion of New York in the summer of 1776 to Cornwallis's surrender at Yorktown in 1781, the British army was larger, leaner, better trained, more capable, and more determined than before. The struggle metamorphosed into a war of attrition. That required great stamina on the part of the Continental Army, the Continental Congress, and the Americans who supported them . . . a stamina that was not always readily at hand.

It was fortunate, then, that the army outside Boston, the first American army, exited the stage after Washington's arrival in Cambridge. As an institution, it was not cut out for the kind of long-term commitment that the war would demand. It was, after all, an army of militiamen, despite the best efforts of Ward and company. George Washington required something else entirely, an army created in his own image, and little by little, the Continental Army would become something very like the competent, efficient, professional force that the Virginia generalissimo had in mind. *That* was the army that won the Revolution. But the leaders and men of the first American army served a purpose that was just as necessary. Before Americans thought of themselves as a united people fighting for their rights and liberties, and ultimately for their independence, that army held the line until America adopted New England's struggle as its own. It stayed in the field for little thanks and less recompense, and though it was far from perfect, it bought precious time for the thirteen colonies to respond as one to the actions of Great Britain. The army that fought at Bunker Hill kept the Cause alive until Americans could decide just what that Cause was, and precisely what it was that they were fighting for.

Notes

* * *

PROLOGUE
1. A. Levasseur, *Lafayette in America in 1824 and 1825; or, Journal of a Voyage to the United States*, vol. 2 (Philadelphia, 1829), 200–206.
2. William B. Sprague, *Annals of the American Unitarian Pulpit* (New York, 1865), 85–86.
3. Daniel Webster, *The Bunker Hill Monument Orations*, ed. Albert F. Blaisdell (New York, 1892), 8–28.

ONE: MASSACHUSETTS'S WAR
1. John Thomas Papers, Ms. N-1663, 171.1.10.5, Massachusetts Historical Society, Boston (hereafter cited as MHS).
2. John R. Galvin, *The Minute Men: The First Fight: Myths and Realities of the American Revolution* (Washington, DC, 1996), 106–231; David Hackett Fischer, *Paul Revere's Ride* (New York, 1994), 184–260.
3. Charles Martyn, *The Life of Artemas Ward, the First Commander-in-Chief of the American Revolution* (New York, 1921), 89–91.
4. Allen French, *The First Year of the American Revolution* (New York, 1934), 23–25.
5. John Cary, *Joseph Warren: Physician, Politician, Patriot* (Urbana, IL, 1961), 174–99.
6. French, *First Year*, 26–27.

7. Walter Muir Whitehill, *Boston: A Topographical History*, 2nd edition, (Cambridge, MA, 1968), 1–46.

8. Edward Barrington De Fonblanque, *Political and Military Episodes in the Latter Half of the Eighteenth Century, Derived from the Life and Correspondence of The Right Hon. John Burgoyne* (London, 1876), 148.

9. William Lincoln, ed., *The Journals of Each Provincial Congress of Massachusetts in 1774 and 1775, and of the Committee of Safety* (Boston, 1838), April 5, 1775, 120–29.

10. Galvin, *Minute Men*, 6–88; Fischer, *Paul Revere's Ride*, 151–56.

11. French, *First Year*, 22–31, 43–55.

12. Peter Force, ed., *American Archives*, 4th Series (Washington, DC, 1837–46), 2:372–73; Richard Buel, Jr., *Dear Liberty: Connecticut's Mobilization for the Revolutionary War* (Middletown, CT, 1980), 33–39.

13. Lincoln, *Journals of Each Provincial Congress*, April 21, 1775, 520; April 23, 1775, 148–49.

14. French, *First Year*, 57–75.

15. Force, *American Archives*, 4/2:384.

16. "Amos Farnsworth's Diary," *Massachusetts Historical Society Proceedings*, 2nd Series, 12 (1897–99), entry for April 26–29, 1775, 78–79; Justin Florence, "Minutemen for Months: The Making of an American Revolutionary Army before Washington, April 20–July 2, 1775," *American Antiquarian Society Proceedings*, 113 (2005), 69–73.

17. French, *First Year*, 60; Force, *American Archives*, 4/2: 580–81, 609–10, 675, 752, 914.

18. French, *First Year*, 61; Lincoln, *Journals of Each Provincial Congress*, April 26, 1775, 523.

19. James Warren to John Adams, May 7, 1775, in Massachusetts Historical Society, ed., *Warren-Adams Letters: Being Chiefly a Correspondence Among John Adams, Samuel Adams, and James Warren* (2 vols., Boston, 1917–25), 1:47.

TWO: YOUNG SOLDIERS WHO HAD NEVER BEEN IN ACTION

1. Quoted in William B. Willcox, *Portrait of a General: Sir Henry Clinton in the War of Independence* (New York, 1964), 54 n. 7.

2. Frederick Mackenzie, *A British Fusilier in Revolutionary Boston: Being the Diary of Lieutenant Frederick Mackenzie, Adjutant of the Royal Welch Fusiliers, January 5–April 30, 1775*, ed. by Allen French (Boston, 1926), 42.

3. John Richard Alden, *General Gage in America* (Baton Rouge, LA, 1948), 15.

4. Elizabeth Ellery Dana, ed., *The British in Boston: Being the Diary of Lieutenant John Barker of the King's Own Regiment from November 15, 1774 to May 31, 1776* (Cambridge, MA, 1924), 5.

5. Thomas Gage to Viscount Barrington, December 14, 1774, in Clarence Edwin Carter, ed., *The Correspondence of General Thomas Gage* (2 vols., New Haven, CT, 1931–33), 2:663.

6. Thomas Gage to Viscount Barrington, November 2, 1774, in Carter, ed., *Correspondence of General Gage*, 2:658–59.

7. Alden, *General Gage in America*, 235–36.

8. On the state of the British army in 1775, see the remarkable study by Matthew H.

Spring, *With Zeal and With Bayonets Only*: *The British Army on Campaign in North America, 1775–1783* (Norman, OK, 2008). On life in the British army during the Revolution, see Sylvia R. Frey, *The British Soldier in America*: *A Social History of Military Life in the Revolutionary Period* (Austin, TX, 1981).

9. Frey, *British Soldier in America*, 54–55.

10. Spring, *With Zeal and With Bayonets Only*, 76–83.

11. Stephen Brumwell, *Redcoats*: *The British Soldier and War in the Americas, 1755–1763* (Cambridge, MA, 2002), 191–263, 290–314.

12. Thomas E. Crocker, *Braddock's March* (Yardley, PA, 2009), 207–56.

13. Brumwell, *Redcoats*, 261–63; Spring, *With Zeal and With Bayonets Only*, 57–62.

14. Mark Urban, *Fusiliers*: *The Saga of a British Redcoat Regiment in the American Revolution* (New York, 2007), 1–33; Spring, *With Zeal and With Bayonets Only*, 104–24.

15. Dana, *British in Boston*, 7.

16. Orders for June 14, 1775, Orderly Book, 1st Battalion Marines, Orderly Book Collection, MHS.

17. Mackenzie, *British Fusilier in Revolutionary Boston*, 28–29; Spring, *With Zeal and With Bayonets Only*, 207–208.

18. Richard Williams, *Discord and Civil Wars*: *Being a Portion of the Journal Kept by Lieutenant Williams of His Majesty's Twenty-Third Regiment while Stationed in British North America during the Time of the Revolution* (Buffalo, NY, 1954), 22.

19. Dana, *British in Boston*, 32, 39; French, *Diary*, 1:25–26.

20. Spring, *With Zeal and With Bayonets Only*, 121.

21. John A. Tilley, *The British Navy and the American Revolution* (Columbia, SC, 1987), 22.

22. Ibid., 3–21.

23. Ibid., 26–27.

24. Dana, *British in Boston*, 39.

25. R. R. Gale, *"A Soldier-Like Way"*: *The Material Culture of the British Infantry 1751–1768* (Elk River, MN, 2007), 85.

26. Francis S. Drake, *The Town of Roxbury*: *Its Memorable Persons and Places* (Roxbury, MA, 1878), 70–73.

27. George Harris to Mrs. Dyer, May 5, 1775, in S. R. Lushington, *The Life and Services of General Lord Harris, G.C.G., During his Campaigns in America, the West Indies, and India* (London, 1845), 38.

28. Tilley, *British Navy*, 28.

29. Force, *American Archives*, 4/2:747; Alden, *General Gage in America*, 255; French, *First Year*, 120–23.

30. William B. Willcox, *Portrait of a General*: *Sir Henry Clinton in the War of Independence* (New York, 1964), 45.

31. Dana, *British in Boston*, 43.

32. George Harris to Mrs. Dyer, May 5, 1775, in Lushington, *Life and Services*, 39.

33. Williams, *Discord and Civil Wars*, 5.

34. George Harris to Mrs. Dyer, June 12, 1775, in Lushington, *Life and Services*, 40.

35. Paul David Nelson, *Francis Rawdon-Hastings, Marquess of Hastings: Soldier, Peer of the Realm, Governor-General of India* (Cranbury, NJ, 2005), 24–28.

THREE: THE GRAND AMERICAN ARMY

1. Buel, *Dear Liberty*, 36–37.

2. John Thomas to Hannah Thomas, May 4, 1775, John Thomas Papers, Ms. N-1663, 171.1.10.10, MHS; Artemas Ward to John Thomas, May 8, 1775, John Thomas Papers, Ms. N-1663, 171.1.7.26, MHS.

3. James Warren to John Adams, May 7, 1775, in *Warren-Adams Letters*, 1:47.

4. Diary of Samuel Haws, Greaton's Regiment, in *Military Journals of Two Private Soldiers, 1758–1775* (Poughkeepsie, NY, 1855), 53.

5. Ibid., 54; "The Revolutionary Journal of James Stevens of Andover, Mass.," *The Essex Institute Historical Collections* 48 (1912), 43–44.

6. James Ferrell Smith, "The Rise of Artemas Ward, 1727–1777: Authority, Politics, and Military Life in Eighteenth-Century Massachusetts" (dissertation, University of Colorado, 1990); Martyn, *Life of Artemas Ward*, 3–50; Florence, "Minutemen for Months," 74–79.

7. Orders for May 2 and June 1, 1775, Artemas Ward Orderly Book, Ward Family Papers, Ms. N-1724, MHS.

8. French, *First Year*, 177, n. 50.

9. Drake, *Town of Roxbury*, 271; "The Revolutionary Journal of James Stevens," 44.

10. James Murray to Elizabeth Murray Inman, May 23, 1775, James Murray Robbins Papers, Ms. N-801, MHS.

11. John Pigeon ledger, 1775–1833, Ms. N-719, MHS; "Provisions delivered various Regiments—1775 / Capt Hales Book," Commonwealth of Massachusetts State Archives, Boston (hereafter cited as COMSA); "Records of Cambridge Store," blotter 1 (April 21, 1775—May 17, 1775), COMSA; "Records of Roxbury Store," COMSA.

12. Orders for April 21, 1775, Artemas Ward Orderly Book, Ward Family Papers, Ms. N-1724, MHS.

13. Orders for May 4 and May 8, 1775, Artemas Ward Orderly Book, Ward Family Papers, Ms. N-1724, MHS.

14. French, *First Year*, 184; "Records of Roxbury store, 1774," COMSA.

15. Force, *American Archives*, 4/2:739–40; Isaac J. Greenwood, ed., *The Revolutionary Services of John Greenwood of Boston and New York 1775–1783* (New York, 1922), 9.

16. Philip Cash, *Medical Men at the Seige* [sic] *of Boston* (Philadelphia, 1973), 40–49.

17. "Statement concerning fire-arms lately at Harvard College," May 5, 1775, Revolution Letters Miscellaneous 146:48, COMSA; "Return of Colo Ruggles Woodbridges Regt, Cambridge, June 14th A 1775," Revolution Military Miscellaneous 146:195a, COMSA.

18. "List of Cannon at Roxbury camp," May 7, 1775, Revolution Military Miscellaneous 146:51.

19. Joseph Warren to Elbridge Gerry, May 2, 1775, Elbridge Gerry Correspondence, MHS.

20. French, *First Year*, 80–82.

21. Ibid., 300.

22. Bounty Coat Rolls for Little's Regiment, Revolutionary War Muster Rolls, vol. 56, COMSA.

23. Galvin, *Minute Men*, 66–67.

24. Lincoln, *Journals of Each Provincial Congress*, May 20, 1775, 553.

25. George Quintal, Jr., *Patriots of Color*: '*A Peculiar Beauty and Merit*': *African Americans and Native Americans at Battle Road & Bunker Hill* (Boston, 2004), 21–36.

26. Massachusetts Provincial Congress to the "Eastern Indians," May 15, 1775, Revolution Letters Series, 193:194, 195; Cary, *Joseph Warren*, 208–209; French, *First Year*, 62–63.

27. John Thomas to Hannah Thomas, May 1, 1775, John Thomas Papers, Ms. N-1663, 171.1.10.8, MHS; Bounty Coat Rolls for Paterson's Regiment, Revolutionary War Muster Rolls, vol. 56, COMSA.

28. Artemas Ward to the Provincial Congress, May 19, 1775, Revolution Military Miscellaneous 146:76, COMSA.

29. Lincoln, *Journals of Each Provincial Congress*, May 20, 1775, 248.

30. "Report of the Com^ee of Safety relative to New England Army," June 2, 1775, Revolution Military Miscellaneous 146:153, COMSA.

31. "Report of Com^ee on the impropriety of having officers of the Army members of Congress," May 18, 1775, Revolution Military Miscellaneous 146:72, COMSA; Lincoln, *Journals of Each Provincial Congress*, June 28, 1775, 580–81.

32. Hannah Jones to John Thomas, May 1, 1775, John Thomas Papers, Ms. N-1663, 171.1.7.88, MHS.

33. Force, *American Archives*, 4/2:720–21; Joseph Warren to Samuel Adams, May 26, 1775, in Richard Frothingham, *The Life and Times of Joseph Warren* (Boston, 1865), 495.

34. Force, *American Archives*, 4/2:791.

FOUR: THE FIERCEST MAN AMONG THE SAVAGE TRIBES

1. Theodore G. Tappert and John W. Doberstein, eds., *The Journals of Henry Melchior Muhlenberg* (3 vols., Philadelphia, 1942–58), 2:699–700; Charles Royster, *A Revolutionary People at War* (Chapel Hill, NC, 1979), 25–53.

2. Timothy Pickering, *An Easy Plan of Discipline for a Militia* (Salem, MA, 1775), 11; Tappert and Doberstein, *Journals of Henry Melchior Muhlenberg*, 2:700.

3. Edmund Cody Burnett, *The Continental Congress* (New York, 1941), 64.

4. Douglas Southall Freeman, *George Washington, A Biography* (7 vols., New York, 1948–57), 3:420.

5. Allen French, *The Taking of Ticonderoga*: *The British Story* (Cambridge, MA, 1928).

6. Eliphalet Dyer to Joseph Trumbull, June 10, 1775, in Paul H. Smith, et al., eds., *Letters of Delegates to Congress, 1774–1789* (25 vols., Washington, DC, 1976–2000), 1:472; Burnett, *Continental Congress*, 73.

7. Silas Deane to Elizabeth Deane, June 3, 1775, in Smith, *Letters of Delegates*, 1:437; John Adams to Abigail Adams, June 10, 1775, in Charles Francis Adams, ed., *Familiar Letters of John Adams and His Wife Abigail Adams, During the Revolution* (New York, 1876), 62.

8. Lincoln, *Journals of Each Provincial Congress*, May 16, 1775, 229–31.

9. French, *First Year*, 136.

10. Lincoln, *Journals of Each Provincial Congress*, May 16, 1775, 231.

11. Joseph Warren to Samuel Adams, May 26, 1775, in Frothingham, *Life and Times of Joseph Warren*, 495–96.

12. John Adams to Abigail Adams, May 29, 1775, in Adams, *Familiar Letters*, 59.

13. John Adams to James Warren, June 27, 1775, in *Warren-Adams Letters*, 1:67.

14. John Adams to James Warren, July 24, 1775, in *Warren-Adams Letters*, 1:89; Theodore Thayer, *The Making of a Scapegoat: Washington and Lee at Monmouth* (Port Washington, NY, 1976), 16.

15. Edward G. Lengel, *General George Washington: A Military Life* (New York, 2005), 19–80.

16. Ibid., 81–84.

17. Eliphalet Dyer to Joseph Trumbull, June 17, 1775, in Smith, *Letters of Delegates*, 1:500–501.

18. Don Troiani and James L. Kochan, *Don Troiani's Soldiers of the American Revolution* (Mechanicsburg, PA, 2007), 101.

19. Eliphalet Dyer to Joseph Trumbull, June 17, 1775, in Smith, *Letters of Delegates*, 1:500–501; Freeman, *Washington*, 3:426.

20. Burnett, *Letters of Members of the Continental Congress*, 1:130–32.

21. Eliphalet Dyer to Joseph Trumbull, June 17, 1775, in Smith, *Letters of Delegates*, 1:500–501.

22. Worthington C. Ford, et al., eds., *Journals of the Continental Congress, 1774–1789* (34 vols., Washington, DC, 1904–37), 2:92.

23. Freeman, *George Washington*, 3:440.

24. Lincoln, *Journals of Each Provincial Congress*, June 20, 1775, 365–66.

FIVE: ELBOW ROOM

1. Dana, *British in Boston*, 40.

2. Buel, *Dear Liberty*, 38.

3. Nathanael Greene to Jacob Greene, June 2, 1775, in Richard K. Showman, et al., eds., *The Papers of Nathanael Greene* (6 vols., Chapel Hill, NC, 1976–present), 1:85.

4. "Amos Farnsworth's Diary," 79.

5. Charles Coffin, *The Life and Services of Major General John Thomas* (New York, 1844), 5–8.

6. John Thomas to "My Son Natte," June 25, 1775, John Thomas Papers, Ms. N-1663, 171.1.10.33, MHS.

7. John Thomas to Hannah Thomas, May 24, 1775, John Thomas Papers, Ms. N–1663, 171.1.10.20, MHS.

8. John Thomas to Artemas Ward, May 18, 1775, John Thomas Papers, Ms. N-1663, 171.1.7.29, MHS.

9. Lincoln, *Journals of Each Provincial Congress*, May 10, 1775, 540.

10. There is no good modern biography of Putnam. One must rely on the questionable veracity of older works: William Cutter, *The Life of Israel Putnam* (New York, 1850); Increase N. Tarbox, *Life of Israel Putnam ("Old Put"), Major-General in the Continental Army* (Boston, 1876).

11. French, *First Year*, 187.

12. "Amos Farnsworth's Diary," 79.

13. Dana, *British in Boston*, 46–47.

14. Orders for May 30, 1775, Orderly Book, 1st Battalion Marines, Orderly Book Collection, MHS.

15. F. A. Whinyates, *The Services of Lieut.-Colonel Francis Downman, R.A., in France, North America, and the West Indies, Between the Years 1758 and 1784* (Woolwich, 1898), 23.

16. Dana, *British in Boston*, 44.

17. Abigail Adams to John Adams, May 24, 1775, in Adams, *Familiar Letters*, 56.

18. "Amos Farnsworth's Diary," 80.

19. Dana, *British in Boston*, 49.

20. French, *First Year*, 199.

21. Sir Henry Clinton to unknown, June 13, 1775, quoted in Henry Clinton, *The American Rebellion: Sir Henry Clinton's Narrative of His Campaigns, 1775–1782*, ed. by William B. Willcox (New Haven, CT, 1971), 18 n.1.

22. French, *First Year*, 201.

23. Dana, *British in Boston*, 47–48; "Revolutionary War Journal, Kept by Phineas Ingalls of Andover, Mass., April 19, 1775–December 8, 1776," *The Essex Institute Historical Collections*, 53 (1917), 83; Anne Rowe Cunningham, ed., *Letters and Diary of John Rowe, Boston Merchant* (Boston, 1903), 295.

24. Statement of Israel Putnam, March 21, 1776, Noddle's Island Papers, Ms. S-678, MHS.

25. Phillips Payson to Henry Williams, February 16, 1786, statement of Caleb Pratt, no date; and statement of Abijah Hastings, no date, Noddle's Island Papers, Ms. S-678, MHS; petition of Ebenezer Ingersol of Watertown, January 2, 1776, Revolution Petitions Series 180:278, COMSA.

26. "Amos Farnsworth's Diary," 80–81.

27. "Description of a skirmish at Hogg Island and Noddle's Island," May 27, 1775, Revolution Military Miscellaneous 146:131; William Bell Clark, et al., eds., *Naval Documents of the American Revolution* (11 vols., Washington, DC, 1964–2005), 1:544–47.

28. Statement of Caleb Pratt, no date, Noddle's Island Papers, Ms. S-678, MHS; entries May 1–May 31, 1775, John Pigeon ledger, 1775–1833, Ms. N-719, MHS.

29. French, *First Year*, 193.

30. "Amos Farnsworth's Diary," 81; statements of Moses Gill, no date, and Thomas Cheever, no date, Noddle's Island Papers, Ms. S-678, MHS; petition of Henry Howell Williams, June 12, 1775, Revolution Petitions Series 180:44–45, COMSA.

31. Drake, *Town of Roxbury*, 275.

32. Petition of Alexander Shirley of Chelsea, March 1, 1776, Revolution Petitions Series 180:332, COMSA; statement of Thomas Cheever, no date, Noddle's Island Papers, Ms. S-678, MHS.

33. "The Journals of Lieut.-Col. Stephen Kemble," *Collections of the New-York Historical Society for the Year 1883* (New York, 1884), 43; Lord Percy to Henry Reveley, May 1775, in Charles Knowles Bolton, ed., *Letters of Hugh Earl Percy from Boston and New York 1774–1776* (Boston, 1902), 55.

34. De Fonblanque, *Political and Military Episodes*, 140, 144; Willcox, *Portrait of a General*, 45.

35. Lord Percy to Henry Reveley, May 1775, in Bolton, *Letters of Hugh Earl Percy*, 55;

George Harris to Mrs. Dyer, June 12, 1775, in Lushington, *Life and Services of General Lord Harris*, 52.

36. French, *First Year*, 202.

37. Dana, *British in Boston*, 54.

38. Force, *American Archives*, 4/2:968–70.

39. French, *First Year*, 204.

40. William Howe to General Harvey, and to Richard Howe, June 12, 1775, in *Report of the Bunker Hill Monument Association* (Boston, 1907), 109–111, 115; Force, *American Archives*, 4/2:1094.

SIX: A GOOD DEAL OF A HUBBUB

1. Force, *American Archives* 4/2:920.

2. "Diary of Samuel Bixby," *Proceedings of the Massachusetts Historical Society* 14(1875–76), 286.

3. Samuel A. Green, ed., *Paul Lunt's Diary, May–December 1775* (Boston, 1872), 6; Lincoln, *Journals of Each Provincial Congress*, June 14, 1775, 566; Diary of Samuel Haws, 57; "An account of Provision &c Issued to the Provincial Troops in Roxbury Camp," June 10, 1775, Records of Roxbury Store, COMSA; entry for June 8, 1775, diary of Nathaniel Ober, Ms. S-200b, MHS.

4. John Thomas to Hannah Thomas, June 3, 1775, John Thomas Papers, Ms. N-1663, 171.1.10.30, MHS; "Journal of James Stevens," 47; "Diary of Samuel Bixby," 286.

5. Diary of Samuel Haws, 58.

6. John Thomas to Hannah Thomas, June 1, 1775, John Thomas Papers, Ms. N-1663, 171.1.10.26, MHS.

7. "The Journals of Lieut.-Col. Stephen Kemble," 43.

8. Entry for June 14, 1775, John Jenks diary, Pickering family papers, Ms. N-39, MHS; Lincoln, *Journals of Each Provincial Congress*, June 13, 1775, 330; June 16, 1775, 343–47.

9. Lincoln, *Journals of Each Provincial Congress*, June 13, 1775, 565.

10. Orders for June 14, 1775, in "Extracts from an Orderly Book, supposed to be Capt. Chester's," *Proceedings of the Massachusetts Historical Society* 14 (1875–76), 90; French, *First Year*, 176.

11. Lincoln, *Journals of Each Provincial Congress*, May 12, 1775, 543.

12. Ibid., June 14, 1775, 332–34.

13. Ibid., June 15, 1775, 569.

14. Lothrop Withington, ed., *Caleb Haskell's Diary, May 5, 1775–May 30, 1776: A Revolutionary Soldier's Record Before Boston and with Arnold's Quebec Expedition* (Tarrytown, NY, 1922), 10; James Knowles to wife, June 16, 1775, James Knowles Papers, Ms. 730a, MHS.

15. Entry for June 17, 1775, Nathan Stow Orderly Book, in *Putnam's Monthly Historical Magazine* 2 (1893), 306.

16. Peter Brown's letter to his mother, dated June 28, 1775, is printed in many places, but the most accessible is Henry Steele Commager and Richard B. Morris, eds., *The Spirit of 'Seventy-Six: The Story of the American Revolution as Told by Its Participants* (New York, 1958), 123–24.

17. Most sources are vague on the time of the departure; James Knowles, a sergeant in Chester's company of Spencer's Connecticut Regiment, took careful note of the hours. James Knowles to his wife, June 17, 1775, James Knowles Papers, Ms. 730a, MHS.
18. "Sundries supplied from Ordnance Store, 1775," COMSA.
19. Samuel Swett, *History of Bunker Hill Battle* (2nd ed., Boston, 1826), 19–20.
20. "Amos Farnsworth's Diary," 83.
21. Samuel Gray to Mr. Dyer, July 12, 1775, in Richard Frothingham, *History of the Siege of Boston, and of the Battles of Lexington, Concord, and Bunker Hill* (Boston, 1903), 393–95.
22. "Amos Farnsworth's Diary," 83.
23. Lincoln, *Journals of Each Provincial Congress*, April 26, 1775, 157.
24. "Judge Prescott's Account of the Battle of Bunker Hill," *Proceedings of the Massachusetts Historical Society* 14 (1875–76), 69.
25. French, *First Year*, 209–10.
26. William Prescott to John Adams, August 25, 1775, in Commager and Morris, *The Spirit of 'Seventy-Six*, 125–26.
27. "Journal of His Majesty's Ship *Lively*, Captain Thomas Bishop, Commanding," in Clark, *Naval Documents of the American Revolution*, 700.

SEVEN: MASTERS OF THESE HEIGHTS

1. French, *First Year*, 222; Richard M. Ketchum, *Decisive Day: The Battle for Bunker Hill* (New York, 1999), 121.
2. Francis, Lord Rawdon, to Francis, tenth Earl of Huntingdon, January 13, 1776, in Historical Manuscripts Commission, *Report on the Manuscripts of the late Reginald Rawdon Hastings, Esq., of the Manor House, Ashby de la Zouch* (3 vols., London, 1928–34), 3:167.
3. Lord Percy to General Harvey, April 20, 1775, in Bolton, *Letters of Hugh Earl Percy*, 52–53.
4. Letter of an anonymous British officer, July 5, 1775, in Commager and Morris, *Spirit of 'Seventy-Six*, 135.
5. French, *First Year*, 221–22.
6. Ketchum, *Decisive Day*, 121.
7. French, *First Year*, 221.
8. "Narrative of Vice Admiral Samuel Graves," June 17, 1775, in Clark, *Naval Documents of the American Revolution*, 704.
9. Peter Brown to his mother, June 28, 1775, in Commager and Morris, *Spirit of 'Seventy-Six*, 123; John Pigeon Ledger-book, MHS.
10. Peter Brown to his mother, June 28, 1775, in Commager and Morris, *Spirit of 'Seventy-Six*, 123.
11. Thomas James to Francis Downman, June 23, 1775, in Whinyates, *Services of Lieut.-Colonel Francis Downman*, 23–24. James, a lieutenant colonel of artillery, commanded the gondolas during the battle.
12. Williams, *Discord and Civil Wars*, 17.
13. Swett, *History of Bunker Hill Battle*, 22.
14. David How, *Diary of David How, A Private in Colonel Paul Dudley Sargent's Regiment of the Massachusetts Line* (Morrisania, NY, 1865), x.

15. "Judge Prescott's Account," 69.

16. *A Particular Account of the Battle of Bunker, or Breed's Hill, on the 17th of June, 1775, by a Citizen of Boston* (Boston, 1825), 12–13.

17. Swett, *History of Bunker Hill Battle*, 24–25; French, *First Year*, 217–18.

18. French, *First Year*, 214.

19. Brumwell, *Redcoats*, 236–45.

20. Spring, *With Zeal and With Bayonets Only*, 212.

21. For example, Thomas Gage to Lord Dartmouth, June 12, 1775, in Carter, ed., *The Correspondence of General Thomas Gage*, 1:404.

22. General orders, June 17, 1775, in Benjamin Franklin Stevens, ed., *General Sir William Howe's Orderly Book at Charlestown, Boston and Halifax, June 17 1775 to 1776 26 May* (London, 1890), 1–2.

23. Harold Murdock, *Bunker Hill: Notes and Queries on a Famous Battle* (Boston, 1927), 15–17.

EIGHT: THE ENEMY'S ALL LANDED AT CHARLESTOWN!

1. "Colonel Bancroft's Narrative," in John B. Hill, *Bi-Centennial of Old Dunstable* (Nashua, NH, 1878), 59–60.

2. Peter Brown to his mother, June 28, 1775, in Commager and Morris, *Spirit of 'Seventy-Six*, 123.

3. Letter of Daniel Putnam, *Collections of the Connecticut Historical Society* 1 (1860), 240.

4. William Heath, *Heath's Memoirs of the American War* (New York, 1904), 28.

5. Martyn, *Life of Artemas Ward*, 130.

6. Frothingham, *Siege of Boston*, 132 n.1.

7. Ibid., 178.

8. Martyn, *Life of Artemas Ward*, 130 n. 2; Andrew H. Ward, *History of the Town of Shrewsbury, Massachusetts, From its Settlement in 1717 to 1829* (Boston, 1847), 55; Frothingham, *Siege of Boston*, 132.

9. "Diary of Lieut. Col. Exp. Storrs, of Mansfield, Cn.," in *Massachusetts Historical Society Proceedings* 14 (1875–76), 85–86.

10. Force, *American Archives*, 4/2:1662–65.

11. "Diary of Samuel Haws," 58.

12. "Reminiscence of General Warren," *The New-England Historical and Genealogical Register* 12 (1858), 230.

13. John Stark to Matthew Thornton, June 19, 1775, in Caleb Stark, *Memoir and Official Correspondence of Gen. John Stark* (Concord, NH, 1860), 112–13.

14. "Sundries supplied from Ordnance Store, 1775," COMSA; Henry Dearborn, "An Account of the Battle of Bunker Hill," *The Port Folio*, 4th Series, 5 (1818), 181–82.

15. William Prescott to John Adams, August 25, 1775, in Frothingham, *Siege of Boston*, 395.

16. John Chester to Joseph Fish, July 22, 1775, in Frothingham, *Siege of Boston*, 389–91.

17. Murdock, *Bunker Hill*, 21.

18. William Howe to Richard Lord Howe, June 22, 1775, in Historical Manuscripts

Commission, *Report on the Manuscripts of Mrs. Stopford-Sackville, Of Drayton House, Northhamptonshire* (2 vols., London, 1904–10), 2:3–4.

19. Ben Z. Rose, *John Stark: Maverick General* (Waverley, MA, 2007), 23–51; Howard Parker Moore, *A Life of General John Stark of New Hampshire* (New York, 1949), 51–144.

20. Rose, *John Stark*, 55–57.

21. Frothingham, *Siege of Boston*, 186–87.

22. Dearborn, "An Account of the Battle of Bunker Hill," 182.

23. Reed's New Hampshire Regiment was quartered very close to the action. Unable to find billets in Cambridge or in Medford, Reed was ordered to take possession of "the Houses near Charlestown Neck" only five days before. Isaac W. Hammond, ed., *The State of New Hampshire: Rolls of the Soldiers in the Revolutionary War, 1775, to May, 1777* (Concord, NH, 1885), 37–39.

24. Dearborn, "An Account of the Battle of Bunker Hill," 183.

25. Louis Effingham De Forest, ed., *The Journals and Papers of Seth Pomeroy, Sometime General in the Colonial Service* (New York, 1926), 164–65.

26. "Reminiscence of General Warren," 230; Letter of Daniel Putnam, 247; "Judge Prescott's Account," 77.

27. Force, *American Archives*, 4/2:1094; Murdock, *Bunker Hill*, 121.

28. Force, *American Archives*, 4/2:1094.

29. Ibid.

30. Williams, *Discord and Civil Wars*, 21–22.

NINE: GRASS BEFORE THE SCYTHE

1. Letter of an anonymous British officer, July 5, 1775, in Commager and Morris, *Spirit of 'Seventy-Six*, 135; French, *First Year*, 749; William Howe to Richard, Lord Howe, June 22, 1775, *Report on the Manuscripts of Mrs. Stopford-Sackville*, 1:4.

2. Urban, *Fusiliers*, 1–17, 34–38.

3. Spring, *With Zeal and With Bayonets Only*, 140.

4. French, *First Year*, 239.

5. Dearborn, "An Account of the Battle of Bunker Hill," 179.

6. Urban, *Fusiliers*, 39, 328.

7. Frothingham, *Siege of Boston*, 195.

8. Rose, *John Stark*, 33.

9. Moore, *Life of General John Stark*, 157.

10. William Howe to Adjutant-General Harvey, June 22 and 24, 1775, in Commager and Morris, *Spirit of 'Seventy-Six*, 132.

11. Murdock, *Bunker Hill*, 87.

12. Abigail Adams to John Adams, June 18, 1775, in *Familiar Letters*, 169.

13. Drake, *Town of Roxbury*, 274.

14. "Diary of Samuel Bixby," 286–87; "Revolutionary War Journal, Kept by Phineas Ingalls," 84; "Diary of Samuel Haws," 58–59; Drake, *Town of Roxbury*, 273–76.

15. Lord Percy to the Duke of Northumberland, June 19, 1775, in *Letters of Hugh Earl Percy*, 56–57; *Heath's Memoirs of the American War*, 29; Drake, *Town of Roxbury*, 274.

16. French, *First Year*, 243; Force, *American Archives*, 4/2:1095; Murdock, *Bunker Hill*, 119–22.

17. Herbert T. Wade and Robert A. Lively, eds., *This Glorious Cause: The Adventures of Two Company Officers in Washington's Army* (Princeton, NJ, 1958), 22.

18. Force, *American Archives*, 4/2:1438.

19. John Chester to Joseph Fish, July 22, 1775, in Frothingham, *Siege of Boston*, 391.

20. Francis, Lord Rawdon, to Francis, Earl of Huntingdon, July 22, 1775, in Historical Manuscripts Commission, *Report on the Manuscripts of the late Reginald Rawdon Hastings*, 3:154–55.

21. Wade and Lively, *This Glorious Cause*, 20.

22. "Account of the Battle in Rivington's Gazette," August 3, 1775, in Frothingham, *Siege of Boston*, 398.

23. Petition of John Ewer, Doolittle's Regiment, May 29, 1776, Revolution Petitions Series 181:48, COMSA.

24. "Account of Adjutant Waller, Royal Marines," in Samuel Adams Drake, ed., *Bunker Hill: The Story Told in Letters from the Battle Field, By British Officers Engaged* (Boston, 1875), 29–30.

25. Samuel Webb to Joseph Webb, June 19, 1775, in Frothingham, *Siege of Boston*, 415–16.

26. Lushington, *Life and Services of General Lord Harris*, 41–42.

27. Sir Martin Hunter, *The Journal of Sir Martin Hunter* (Edinburgh, 1894), 10–12; Francis, Lord Rawdon to Francis, Earl of Huntingdon, June 20 and August 3, 1775, in Historical Manuscripts Commission, *Report on the Manuscripts of the late Reginald Rawdon Hastings*, 3:154–55, 156–58.

28. J. H. Temple, *History of Framingham, Massachusetts* (Framingham, MA, 1887), 291.

29. "Account of Adjutant Waller," 28.

30. Peter Brown to his mother, June 28, 1775, in Commager and Morris, *Spirit of 'Seventy-Six*, 124; "Amos Farnsworth's Diary," 83–84.

31. Memoir of Abel Parker, Joel Parker Papers, Ms. N-659, Box 1, MHS.

32. Ibid.

33. Isaac J. Greenwood, ed., *The Revolutionary Services of John Greenwood of Boston and New York* (New York, 1922), 12–13.

34. "Diary of Lieutenant-Colonel Exp. Storrs," 86.

35. Dearborn, "Account of the Battle of Bunker Hill," 177–78.

TEN: A GREAT THO DEAR BOUGHT VICTORY

1. "Judge Prescott's Account," 73.

2. Sir Martin Hunter, *Journal of Sir Martin Hunter, G.C.M.G., G.C.H., and Some Letters of His Wife, Lady Hunter* (Edinburgh, 1894), 12; "The Journals of Lieut.-Col. Stephen Kemble," 45.

3. James Knowles to wife, June 19, 1775, James Knowles Papers, Ms. S-730a, MHS.

4. John Clarke, "An Authentic and Impartial Narrative of the Battle Fought on the 17th of June, 1775, &c.," in Drake, *Bunker Hill*, 49; French, *First Year*, 256.

5. Letter of Ann Hulton, June 20, 1775, in Commager and Morris, *Spirit of 'Seventy-Six*, 137.

6. Clarke, "An Authentic and Impartial Narrative," 49.

7. Letter of Dr. Grant, *The Historical Magazine*, 2nd Series, 3 (1868), 361; "Account of Adjutant Waller," 29.

8. Thomas Gage to Dartmouth, June 25, 1775, and to Barrington, June 26, 1775, in Carter, *Correspondence of General Thomas Gage*, 1:405–406, 2:686–87.

9. Force, *American Archives*, 4/2:1094; William Howe to Adjutant-General Harvey, June 22 and 24, 1775, in Commager and Morris, *Spirit of 'Seventy-Six*, 132.

10. Whinyates, *The Services of Lieut.-Colonel Francis Downman*, 23.

11. Abigail Adams to John Adams, June 25, 1775, *Familiar Letters*, 71.

12. Letter of an anonymous British officer, July 5, 1775, in Commager and Morris, *Spirit of 'Seventy-Six*, 135–36.

13. Thomas Gage to Barrington, June 26, 1775, in Carter, *Correspondence of General Thomas Gage*, 687; French, *First Year*, 259 n. 7.

14. Spring, *With Zeal and With Bayonets Only*, 217; Francis, Lord Rawdon to Francis, Earl of Huntingdon, August 3, 1775, in Historical Manuscripts Commission, *Report on the Manuscripts of the late Reginald Rawdon Hastings*, 3:157.

15. Burgoyne to Lord Rochfort, 1775, in De Fonblanque, *Political and Military Episodes*, 147; French, *First Year*, 251.

16. Burgoyne to Lord Rochfort, 1775, in De Fonblanque, *Political and Military Episodes*, 147.

17. Petition of David Kemp, Prescott's Regiment, 1776, Revolution Petitions Series, 181:226, COMSA.

18. Frothingham, *Siege of Boston*, 176–80.

19. James Warren to John Adams, June 20, 1775, in *Warren-Adams Letters*, 1:63; Abel Parker memoir, Joel Parker Papers, Ms. N-659, Box 1 (1685–1848), MHS; entry for June 17, 1775, John Warren diary, John Collins Warren Papers, Ms. N-1731, Box 1a, MHS; Ketchum, *Decisive Day*, 195.

20. Lincoln, *Journals of Each Provincial Congress*, June 19, 1775, 357, and June 20, 1775, 363.

21. James Warren to John Adams, June 20, 1775, in *Warren-Adams Letters*, 1:63; James Warren to Samuel Adams, June 21, 1775, *Massachusetts Historical Society Proceedings*, 14 (1875–76), 81.

22. Samuel Adams to James Warren, June 28, 1775, *Warren-Adams Letters*, 1:69; James Knowles to wife, June 18, 1775, James Knowles Papers, Ms. S-730a, MHS.

23. Force, *American Archives*, 4/2:1662–65; petition of Colonel James Scammon, November 14, 1776, Revolution Petitions Series, 181:331, COMSA.

24. Report of the Committee of Safety, June 25, 1775, in Frothingham, *Siege of Boston*, 382; James Warren to John Adams, June 20, 1775, in *Warren-Adams Letters*, 63.

25. James Knowles to wife, June 18, 1775, James Knowles Papers, Ms. S-730a, MHS; John Stark to Matthew Thornton, June 19, 1775, in Nathaniel Bouton, ed., *Provincial Papers: Documents and Records Relating to the Province of New Hampshire from 1764 to 1776* (7 vols., Concord, NH, 1867–73), 7:523; Nathanael Greene to Jacob Greene, June 28, 1775, in *Papers of General Nathanael Greene*, 1:92.

26. Petition for Salem Poor, December 5, 1775, Revolution Petitions Series, 180:241, COMSA; Quintal, *Patriots of Color*, 21.

27. "Diary of Samuel Bixby," 287.

28. Note for June 20, 1775, "Sundries Supplied from Ordnance Store, 1775," COMSA.

29. Artemas Ward to the Committee of Supplies, June 24, 1775, Massachusetts Archives, Revolution Letters Series, 193:399, COMSA.

30. Force, *American Archives*, 4/2:1028, 1424–25, 1443, 1447, 1471; French, *First Year*, 272.

31. Lincoln, *Journals of Each Provincial Congress*, June 17–18, 1775, 571, June 28, 1775, 582; Force, *American Archives*, 4/2:1080–81, 1091, 1361, 1442, 1457–58, 1648.

32. French, *First Year*, 268–71.

33. Ibid., 259–60; Williams, *Discord and Civil Wars*, 20–21.

ELEVEN: NEW LORDS, NEW LAWS

1. Drake, *Town of Roxbury*, 80.

2. Ibid., 274.

3. John Hancock to Joseph Warren, June 18, 1775, in Smith, *Letters of Delegates*, 1:508–509. Warren, of course, never received the letter, having been killed the day before Hancock wrote it.

4. Lincoln, *Journals of Each Provincial Congress*, July 1, 1775, 438–39.

5. Ibid., 440.

6. Orders for June 30, 1775, Artemas Ward Orderly Book, Ward Family Papers, Ms. N-1724, MHS.

7. Samuel Adams Drake, *Historic Fields and Mansions of Middlesex* (Boston, 1874), 262.

8. "Revolutionary Journal of James Stevens," 49–50; "Revolutionary War Journal, Kept by Phineas Ingalls," 85.

9. Roger Sherman to David Wooster, June 23, 1775, in Edmund C. Burnett, ed., *Letters of Members of the Continental Congress* (8 vols., Gloucester, MA, 1963), 1:142; Force, *American Archives*, 4/2:1585–86; George Washington to Jonathan Trumbull, Sr., July 18, 1775, in W. W. Abbot et al., eds., *The Papers of George Washington, Revolutionary War Series* (19 vols., Charlottesville, VA, 1985–present), 1:132; Force, *American Archives*, 4/2:1658; French, *First Year*, 305.

10. James Warren to John Adams, June 27, 1775, *Warren-Adams Letters*, 1:68; George Washington to John Thomas, July 23, 1775, in Abbot, *Papers of George Washington, Revolutionary War Series*, 1:159–62; Charles Lee to John Thomas, July 23, 1775, John Thomas Papers, Ms. N-1663, 171.1.7.51, MHS.

11. John Thomas to Hannah Thomas, July 4 and July 27, 1775, John Thomas Papers, Ms. N-1663, 171.1.10.28 and 171.1.10.30, MHS.

12. John Stark to "Committee at Roxbury in charge of settling ranks, etc.," August 23, 1775, John Thomas Papers, Ms. N-1663, 171.1.7.55, MHS; Edmund Randolph to John Thomas, September 16, 1775, John Thomas Papers, Ms. N-1663, 171.1.7.57.

13. George Washington's address to the Massachusetts Provincial Congress, July 1, 1775, in Lincoln, *Journals of Each Provincial Congress*, 439; George Washington to John Augustine Washington, July 27, 1775, in Abbot, *Papers of George Washington, Revolutionary War Series*, 1:183; George Washington to Philip Schuyler, July 28, 1775, in Abbot, *Papers of George Washington, Revolutionary War Series*, 1:188–89.

14. Freeman, *Washington*, 486–87; Charles Lee to Benjamin Rush, July 20, 1775, in

Collections of the New-York Historical Society for the Year 1871: The Lee Papers (2 vols., New York, 1871), 1:196–97.

15. Force, *American Archives*, 4/2:1589.

16. General Orders for July 7, 1775, in Abbot, *Papers of George Washington, Revolutionary War Series*, 1:71.

17. General Orders for July 14 and July 23, 1775, in Abbot, *Papers of George Washington, Revolutionary War Series*, 1:114–15, 158–59.

18. George Washington to [Congress?], July 10, 1775, in Abbot, *Papers of George Washington, Revolutionary War Series*, 1:85–92; George Washington to Lund Washington, August 20, 1775, in Abbot, *Papers of George Washington, Revolutionary War Series*, 1:335–36; George Washington to Richard Henry Lee, August 29, 1775, in Abbot, *Papers of George Washington, Revolutionary War Series*, 1:372; Nathanael Greene to Samuel Ward, Sr., December 18, 1775, *Papers of General Nathanael Greene*, 1:163–64.

19. Joseph Reed to Thomas Bradford, August 24, 1775, in William B. Reed, *The Life and Correspondence of Joseph Reed* (2 vols., Philadelphia, 1847), 1:119; John Sullivan to the New Hampshire Committee of Safety, August 5, 1775, in Bouton, ed., *Provincial Papers*, 7:572; French, *First Year*, 487.

20. French, *First Year*, 301.

21. Abigail Adams to John Adams, July 16, 1775, in *Familiar Letters*, 79.

22. Force, *American Archives*, 4/2:1671, 1687.

23. Samuel Graves to Philip Stephens, July 24, 1775, in Clark, *Naval Documents of the American Revolution*, 1:961–62.

24. "Circular to the General Officers," September 8, 1775, in Abbot, *Papers of George Washington, Revolutionary War Series*, 1:432–34; "Council of War," September 11, 1775, in Abbot, *Papers of George Washington, Revolutionary War Series*, 1:450–51.

25. Abigail Adams to John Adams, December 10, 1775, in *Familiar Letters*, 128–29.

26. Allen French, *General Gage's Informers* (Ann Arbor, MI, 1932), 147–201.

27. George Washington to Joseph Reed, November 8, 1775, in Abbot, *Papers of George Washington, Revolutionary War Series*, 2:335; French, *First Year*, 503–512.

28. Jonathan Trumbull, Sr., to George Washington, December 7, 1775, in Abbot, *Papers of George Washington, Revolutionary War Series*, 2:511–12.

29. Force, *American Archives*, 4/3:1666–67.

30. "Diary of Simeon Lyman," *Connecticut Historical Society Collections* 7 (1899), 128–30.

31. Nathanael Greene to Samuel Ward, Sr., December 10, 1775, in Showman, *Papers of General Nathanael Greene*, 1:160–61.

32. John Pigeon ledger-book, folio 57, MHS.

33. George Washington to Joseph Reed, November 28, 1775, and January 14, 1776, in Abbot, *Papers of George Washington, Revolutionary War Series*, 2:449, 3:89.

34. George Washington to Philip Schuyler, December 24, 1775, in Abbot, *Papers of George Washington, Revolutionary War Series*, 2:599–600.

EPILOGUE

1. James Wilkinson, "A Rapid Sketch of the Battle of Breed's Hill," in Charles Coffin, ed., *History of the Battle of Breed's Hill* (Portland, ME, 1835), 12.

2. Justin Winsor, *The Memorial History of Boston* (4 vols., Boston, 1886), 3:83.
3. John Thomas to Hannah Thomas, July 27, 1775, John Thomas Papers, Ms. N-1663, 171.1.10.28 and 171.1.10.30, MHS.
4. Artemas Ward to John Adams, October 30, 1775, in Frothingham, *Siege of Boston*, 396–97.
5. Murdock, *Bunker Hill*, 123–34.
6. Reed, *Life and Correspondence of Joseph Reed*, 120.

Index

✳   ✳   ✳